THE WORLD OF KANJI

Alex Adler

THE WORLD OF KANJI

Learn 2136 Japanese characters
through real etymologies

by

Alex Adler

ISBN: 978-82-09-00421-8

Written, Designed & Published by Alex Adler

alex-adler.com

CONTENTS

FOREWORD

Chinese characters—or kanji—looks mysterious and exotic at first glance, and this is why it is fascinating for many: they arouse curiosity. This fascinating mystery is also a tool used daily by millions of people, and anyone who aspires to be able to communicate with it will have to decipher the mystery inescapably. The method of decipherment chosen, however, will undoubtedly influence the learning experience of the student for better or worse, so one has to be serious about the way to approach the characters.

This book is written with the intention to be one of the helpful and favorable approaches. The World of Kanji is conceived as a tool for deciphering the mystery of Chinese characters by trying to keep in the student that initial fascination summoned by curiosity throughout the entire learning process, for kanji may be more captivating as one sips deeper into its unexpected coherence and symbolism that is pointed out throughout the book.

I see kanji as a fascinating writing system because, in a figurative way, it represents an almost poetic world that serves as a conceptual link between words and ideas, something that, in turn, can be used with great effectiveness by the student to learn the characters himself.

The symbolic and associative power of kanji, however, is hidden in contemporary glyphs behind a linearization and a graphical simplification of the primitive pictograms and ideograms. The aim of the present book is, thus, to help the student decipher the original intended meanings to better understand the direct graphical relationships between Chinese characters and the world of ideas they represent, a world that I have tried to reveal and analyze for you:

The World of Kanji

ACKNOWLEDGEMENTS

The conception of this book has only been possible thanks to all the people from all over the world who supported this project with all their generosity and warmth in the funding campaign of summer 2017 and reprint campaign of winter 2019.

My most sincere thanks to all those people and the Kickstarter team for making this possible.

Special mention to:

A. En
Aaron Chuang
Abner Isaac M. Alvarado
Abram Bachtiar
Adam Andrzej Jaworski
Aidan Laurence McDonagh
Alex and Naomi
Alex Doroshenko
Alex Glatt
Alex Tucker
Alexander Alderete
Alexey Kazantsev
Alison Kidd
Alonso Schaich
Alonso Schaich
Alphonso N. Dandridge
Andre Chartier, MD
Andreas Bauer
Andreas Looser
Andrew Hamblen
Andrew Hovanec
Andrew Smith
Anthony Barker
Aretsuya
Bastiaan Thomas Burger
Berto Castelo
Brad Hansen
Brent Atkinson
Carl Söderberg
Carlos A. Monrroy-Tinoco
Casandra
Chris O'Mara
Christopher Hagon
Christopher Hall
Christopher Prusinski
Craig Sider
Cris P. Advincula, Jr.
Dale Thoms
Daniel Senf
Daniel Walker
Daniels Dekters
David A. Blake
David Poulten
Dean Szonyi
Denis Teo H. S.
Dimitri van Dijk
Dodjie Villamayor
Dodzidenu Dzakuma
Dodzidenu Dzakuma
Douglas, Kiyan, and Barrie Lew
Dr. Jim Laughton
Dr. Valentin Precup
Dr. Y
Dread Lioness
Duckiedale
Ebrahim Al-Bishri
Emmanuel Miranda
Emmanuel Miranda
Eric Wells
Eunbyol Choi
Fabian "throtran" Otte
Fabrissou
Fiikragg
Franklin E. Powers, Jr.
Georgina Toland
Ghashghai Atabak
Giacomo Boccardo
Gian Piero Santini
Giao Lan Tran
Gina North Curbo
Grant Pan
Gregory Bevens
Heidi Kathrin Harnisch
Henning Colsman-Freyberger
Isaac

Iskandar Azani
Jakob Inooraq Johannesen
Jakob Mœller
James Watson
James Welch
James Zwiers
Jared Trezise
Jarrett S.K. Jenny
Jdjfusion
Jenny Reed and Vicky Staubly
John M Berry, EIT, CTS, CTS-D
Jonathan Vauhkonen
Josh Smith
Joshua A. Torres
Joshua Buchanan
Justin Sison (triple_lei)
Jörg Sonnenberger
Jørgen André Karlsen
Karli Ann Bailey
KoapaSC - Marian Zsemlye
Lester F. Callif
level1imp
Lisa Ingrid Zech
Luis B. Mora
Luke Bennett
Marc Tischhauser
Martin Grant
María Teresa Arroyo
Mateo Gomez
Matt Edmiston
Matthew Ruhl
Menny Castro
Michael A. Desbrow
Michael Holger Keppler
Michael Holm
Michael M. McFall
Michael Negron
Michael Tucker
Mike Williams
Mitchell Smith
Mohammad Alzamel
Natan Akira Bussers
Neasa O'Sullivan
Nicholas James Schlavensky
Nicky Bramley
Olaf Schuchardt
Oscar Veldman
Otto Hubacher
Paul Anguiano
Pavlo Shtohryn
Psychopathwolfy
Randolph Kent Wilson III
Richie Bartlett, Jr.
Rik Smale
Robert D. Moser
Robin Touitou
Rodney Camba
Ross Williams
Rudolf Alexander Spoerer
Ryan Wallace
Samantha Walker
Sami El Khalifa
Sarah Beamish
Savannah Barber
Saz Wells
Sean Pelkey
Shifu Jennifer StJohn
Shinyuu
Stefan Pilger
Sterling Lau
Steven Dove
Steven Nakamura
Sus and Barrie
Susumu Binford
Suwijak Thanawiboon
Søren Larsen
Tariq Azeez Hasanradja
Thomas Shaw
Tida
Timm Knape
Timothy L Bialecki Jr.
Tobias Hultman
Tracey Booth and Olivier Van Acker
Tyler Romeo
Van Daatselaar Family
Veleath Yea
Vesko Gavrilov
Wanda Aasen
William J. Hartley
Xenon Ventures
Xeon Xai
Yoshiaki Obara
Zeital

PREFACE

The Difficulties of Kanji

Every student of Japanese knows how difficult and overwhelming learning *kanji*[1] can be. Every time you learn a new word in Japanese you have to learn not only how that word is pronounced, but also how to write the specific character (kanji) used to represent that word. In addition, it turns out that the same character can be pronounced in different ways depending on which word it is found in, while the number of characters that the Japanese Ministry of Education prescribes as necessary to be considered proficient in reading Japanese reaches 2136 units.

Learning 2136 different characters, with their different ways of reading, is not an easy task at any rate, and it becomes even more challenging if you want to memorize them as you encounter them in your everyday life, without an apparent logical order. Unfortunately for almost every first-time student of Japanese, that will be the first obstacle he will have to face in his attempt to understand what all those jumbled symbols that appear in a Japanese text mean: the lack of logic and structure in the learning and understanding of kanji.

In most teaching programs, kanji is introduced as you learn new vocabulary, perhaps with some advice on how to remember such and such character, but, in truth, this method is based on engraving the characters in your memory using brute force. This, basically, has been the method always used in the countries where this writing system is practiced (China, Japan, Taiwan and, until recently, Korea). In these countries, children obviously end up learning what they have to learn and, when they are adults, they are able to read any text in their native language full of Chinese characters. This "brute force" method is ultimately effective in these countries because: 1. A young child may not need so much a logical and coherent system to acquire new knowledge because his brain is still permeable and all new knowledge is impregnated with more vehemence from the beginning; 2. They have teachers around who force them to memorize each character, so not memoirizing the characters does not exist as an easy escape route option for them; 3. The native language of these students is full of words originating directly from Chinese characters (kanji) and they will be exposed to them every day, over many hours, all throughout the learning process; and 4. This learning process expands over years and years, from the time the individual is a young child until he or she reaches the age of college, i.e. over the entire period of time covered by compulsory schooling.

The great difficulty comes when an adult student who is not brought up in the countries where kanji is used in a natural way tries to follow the study method used in those countries. Trying to do so would be a great disadvantage for the adventurous student for the following reasons: 1. A trained adult holds in his mind a whole cognitive structure that will directly clash with the lack of logic and supposed arbitrariness—most adults not only want to learn but also want to

Kanji (漢字): Logographic characters of Chinese origin used in Japanese writing.

understand; 2. An adult's life is not usually about learning, learning rather becomes a complement to their everyday complexities. In other words, an adult is not usually "forced" to memorize a whole series of "meaningless" characters, but usually does so as a direct choice of his own or as an indirect result of his own choice; 3. To a student of Kanji in whose language these graphic elements have no presence, the sinitic characters will present a whole new paradigm about which everything is obscure and mysterious at first, since he will not feel any relation to it whatsoever (even though the common adult man already has much knowledge, little or none of it will help him with kanji). The lack of past and present reference —unless the student lives in Japan—is an obstacle that makes brute memorization even more difficult; 4. An adult who wants to learn Japanese does not have over ten years of schooling at his disposal anymore to learn how to read or write the language.

As we can see, following the system used by the Chinese or the Japanese can be regarded as a truly ineffective method. It will be much more convenient for the adult learner to use a system that best suits his or her circumstances. It is true that the circumstances of each individual may vary greatly, but the target reader of this book who wants to use it as a method of learning will most likely share these two characteristics: 1. He is not a child in primary school; 2. He has not been raised in Chinese or Japanese.

The individual who meets the above two characteristics will need a method for learning kanji that allows him to learn these characters as quickly and efficiently as possible. An efficient method of learning will have to solve the problems addressed in the preceding paragraphs: it will have to give logic and meaning to the seemingly chaotic set of kanji; it will have to enthuse, motivate and instill curiosity in the student in an organic and natural way; it will have to be entertaining enough so that the student does not quickly or easily consider the option of abandoning his commitment. The method used will also have to be able to provide a new paradigmatic model to underpin gradual learning; and finally, it will have to be efficient in the sense that it allows the student to learn kanji in the shortest time possible.

The main objective of this book is, therefore, no less than to serve as a solution to the problem of traditional kanji learning in keeping with the characteristics described above.

The Solution to the Difficulties of Kanji

Compiling a method for learning kanji in the form of a book, that is able to reveal the logic and meaning of Chinese characters, is entertaining and encouraging, provides a foundation for gradual study, and provides a saving in time invested, is not an easy task.

There have been some attempts to provide a methodology with the above mentioned objectives through the use memorization techniques based on mental associations invented by the different authors[2]. The downside of those pioneering methods is that in the end that system which, in principle, was intended to provide a rationale, eventually ends up losing cohesion, and the student ultimately has to resort to using memorization through brute force or even to wasting more time and effort inventing his or her own associative histories for each character.

The clear solution to this problem of lack of logic and cohesion is to look at the true composition of Chinese characters by examining their real etymology, that is, their compositional origin, since these logograms were not created randomly, but following a very cohesive conceptual logic. Learning the composition of kanji in an orderly manner makes its memorization happen naturally and progressively without the need of an extra effort, be it on the creative process of mnemonic associations or on the illogical and incoherent memorization by means of mere repetition. The most basic logograms or characters are symbolic representations of images that can be easily associated with everyday life concepts. The rest of the characters are mixtures or compositions made between two or more basic logograms. Essentially, this means that the vast majority of kanji or Chinese characters are related to each other and are much easier to study them if the student is able to see these relationships in a clear and orderly way from the start.

In the Eastern academic world there are several publications[3] that deal with this fact of the logical and coherent composition of Chinese characters in a quite reliable way through etymological studies, but it is evident that they are not addressed to new students of Chinese characters, but to people who use them on a daily basis. In the West there are also some publications on this subject, such as Cecilia Lindqvist's *Empire of Living Symbols* (2007), in which a fairly revealing and concise etymological analysis is made. That book, however, is not addressed to the student of Japanese kanji and does not cover all the characters needed to be able to read and write this language.

It is apparent, then, that a book was needed to provide the new student of kanji with a system that takes advantage of the etymological composition of Chinese characters in a way that is fully adapted to the learning of the Japanese language as a whole, so that this learning becomes fluid, organic and also faster and more efficient than "traditional" systems. The unsuccessful pursuit of such a method during my student years and the acknowledgement of its absence is what ultimately led me to compose the present book.

By writing *The World of Kanji* my intention was to offer a learning instrument that, encompassing the 2136 kanji of the official list for literacy provided by the Japanese ministry of education, gives the student a cohesive and gradual course of study using the actual etymologies of characters and their compositional logic. The student, with the help of this book, will progressively learn the basic components that make up the set of characters and the related characters that combine those elements, so that everything starts to assume such a powerful logic

---

[2] E.g. *Remember the Kanji* (James Heisig, 1985); kanjidamage.com

[3] E.g. 漢字樹 (廖文豪, 2011); 漢字の世界 (白川 静, 2001); 漢字百話 (白川 静, 1977)

that the student will even be able to interpret the approximate meaning of new characters on his own. In parallel, thanks to the etymological explanations and structured arrangement of the kanji, once the student learns a new character, he will not be able to forget it. *The World of Kanji* is thus intended to be an innovative and integrated system useful for irreversibly memorizing the kanji that are essential for reading and writing Japanese in a fast and efficient way.

Characteristics of This Book

As I have stated so far, the purpose of this book is, in short, to minimize the difficulty of the already complicated learning process of kanji. To this end, special emphasis is placed on memorizing the meaning of each character, while at the same time I intend to facilitate the identification of patterns of phonetic parity. Such memorization is guided through the use of an ordered structure based on a thematic categorization derived from the real etymologies of each character.

The World of Kanji, then, unlike other books, offers etymology—explained in an accessible and straightforward manner—as a fundamental help for memorization. This book also offers a gradual arrangement of primitive characters and subsequent compounds, with a thematic background so the learning process can maintain a solid cohesion that will facilitate the association between components. Finally, *The World of Kanji* has also the goal of facilitating the reading and writing of the Japanese language, which is why it covers the 2136 characters needed for enabling this task.

Although the main target reader of this book is the student of Japanese, it is worth mentioning that it can also be quite appealing for the curious one who has a little interest in the etymology of Chinese characters, and also for the person who already knows kanji, but simply needs a reference book to reinforce his knowledge (the book has several indexes at the end to fulfill such a function).

As a final note, I will say that to get the most out of the learning system presented here, it is recommended, before embarking on the study of characters, to acquire some fundamental notions of how they were formed and how they are graphically structured. The reader will be able to inquire into these specifications in the following introductory section.

I hope this book is to your liking and that you can make the most of it.

Alex Adler

January 2018

INTRODUCTION TO KANJI

Japanese And Kanji

One of the unique features of Japanese compared to other languages is its writing system.

The Japanese language does not use an alphabet to represent every word and sound, rather there are two syllabaries (*hiragana* and *katakana*) and at least 2136 logographic characters of Chinese origin called kanji. Hiragana is used for some of the words of purely Japanese origin and various lexemes with grammatical functions. On the other hand, katakana is used for words of foreign origin, onomatopoeia or emphasized words. Finally, kanji is used for the roots of a large number of common words and for almost all the words composed of affixes of Chinese origin taken in Japanese in the same way that Indo-European languages adopt prefixes and suffixes of Greco-Latin origin.

This complication places a burden on students of Japanese who are not familiar with Chinese characters, since they have to learn not only two different syllabaries, but also a large number of new symbols that seem arbitrary at first.

This book seeks to break with this arbitrariness by offering students of Japanese a logical system based on the original etymology of kanji and the orderly attainment of its learning that endows each character with meaning and renders them with a rational understanding.

What Is Kanji?

Kanji is the group of logograms originated in Chinese writing—*sinograms*—adapted to the Japanese language. A logogram is a graphic character that indicates a meaning and, in most cases, also a sound or phoneme associated with it.

A kanji is, more concisely, a graphical representation of a semantic concept (*meaning*) that in turn is represented by a certain pronunciation (*sound*) interpreted according to the phonetic patterns of the Japanese language.

The semantic correspondence of kanji with the original sinograms and, consequently, with the characters used in China today, is in most cases maintained to this date. That is why, for example, the character 人 means 'person' in both Chinese and Japanese. However, while Chinese always treats the phonetic correspondence of characters in the same way (it gives each character only one reading), in Japanese the same character can be read in different ways.

In Chinese, 人 will always be read as *rén*, but in Japanese its reading will vary depending on whether the character appears as a single word or as an affix forming part of a compound word. The logogram 人, in the case of functioning as a standalone character, representing a monolexemic word, will be read in Japanese as *hito*, while if it acts as an affix, it will adopt a pronunciation of

Chinese origin, as in the word 人生 (*jinsei*), 'human life', where 人 is read *jin*—or the word 人間 (*ningen*), 'human', where 人 is pronounced *nin*.

Using the example above, we see that a kanji adopts a different reading depending on whether it appears on its own or as a component of a word. In the former case, the reading—usually representing a word of purely Japanese origin—is called *kunyomi* or 'semantic reading', while in the latter case, the reading—representing a phoneme adapted from Middle Chinese pronunciation—is called *onyomi* or 'phonetic reading'. This is a widely applied rule that, however, can sometimes be broken, as the Japanese language learner will see throughout his learning process.

Be that as it may, in most cases, each kanji has a corresponding *kunyomi* and *onyomi* reading—or sometimes just an *onyomi* reading. Nevertheless, in the most common characters it can be also the case that a variety of different *kunyomi* readings have been adopted due to the semantic versatility of such character. In addition, there also can be a variation of *onyomi* readings due to the different phonetic adaptations that have been made through time. Although there is a certain consistency in the case of *onyomi* or phonetic readings and their graphical representation in each kanji, the student of Japanese will have no choice but to learn these variations independently of the graphical form of the character through both focus and exposure to kanji and its use within the context of the Japanese written language.

The Importance and Uniqueness of Kanji

The reader may wonder or have wondered why kanji has been continually used by the Japanese, when they could have adopted a phonetic alphabet like the Latin, or even make an exclusive use of their already available *hiragana* and *katakana* syllabaries.

This issue has also been raised on numerous occasions by the Japanese themselves, but despite the introduction of certain restrictions and standardizations, in the end it has always been decided to preserve the use of kanji.

In order to understand the reasons for the conservation of kanji, customary considerations aside, it is required first to understand the intrinsic functionalities of Chinese characters as individual elements and also as elements integrated within a systematic set.

As I will explain more in detail later on, each kanji is, or is composed of, an essential component that represents a concrete idea. That is, each character refers to a particular concept or a sum of concepts that together generate a new concept. A concept, basically, is a mental representation that is associated with a material or abstract meaning (idea). Such representation is usually made by means of a symbol, so to say, an element which, by convention or association, is considered to be representative of an identity. In the case of languages with an alphabetical writing system, the symbols used are merely phonetic. The letters symbolize sounds that together form the pronunciation of a word with a certain meaning. In contrast, sinitic symbols as kanji do not only have ex post phonetic associations, but are visual symbols themselves. In other words, each kanji or component is in origin associated not with a sound but with an image. Nevertheless, these representative images are not arbitrary, they are pictographic elements, strokes that deliberately seek a visual similarity with the object or concept to be represented. This type of symbolism can be addressed with the term *icon*, since an 'icon' is a sign that holds a certain degree of resemblance with the represented object. Kanji are not mere symbols, but *icons* in their own right, so they assume a meaningful identity of their own.

To exemplify what has been noted, I will discuss the kanji 手 and 足. The kanji 手, originally , is the graphic representation of an open hand. This kanji is clearly referring to the idea of 'hand'. Conversely, the kanji 足 is the graphic evolution of the icon , which represents a leg attached to a foot, thus symbolizing the concepts of 'leg and foot'. With a single pictographic symbol, the reader will be able to visually summon the concept of 'hand' or 'foot' accordingly. On the contrary, if the reader sees the words *hand* or *foot* written, he will mentally read the words and then associate the reproduced phonemes with the concepts to which they refer. The essential difference when encountering a visual icon instead of phonetic symbols is the immediacy of the associative progression. Although in reality this difference is of milliseconds, when this symbolic construction evolves into an interconnected system, that difference becomes more apparent and affects in a distinct way the mental processes and the relationship that the reader maintains with his written language. The immediate visual association provided by kanji allows the reader, for example, to examine the subject matter of a text more quickly by locating several key icons, as the connection between symbol and concept is made faster by visual association than by phonetics. That is why, on signage and placards that intend to convey a direct and forceful message, graphic symbols are often used instead of written words.

A further incentive of primordial sinitic characters or logograms of Chinese origin is that, as I mentioned before, they not only can act as individual icons of their own, but also as constituent elements of new icons, both in the formation of words and new characters. Taking the examples used above, we can see how 手 (*hand*) and 足 (*foot*), besides being independent icons, they act as components of a new kanji and a new word. If we combine 手 and 足 to form a new character, we get the kanji 捉[4], which symbolizes the image of a hand bumping into a foot and represents the meaning of 'to capture'. Besides, the element 足, pronounced with its *onyomi* reading as *soku*, is also used here as a phonetic guide, because 捉 adopts the same phoneme *soku* for its reading. We see that kanji composition can be made not only through logical elements, but also through logical and phonetic elements, turning the new characters formed in this way into logographic hieroglyphics. On the other hand, if we take the same elements but place them next to each other this time as individual kanjis, we get the word 手足, *hand* and *foot*, which, indeed, means 'hand and foot' or 'hands and feet'.

[4] The element 手, when used as a component, gets its original form simplified to 扌.

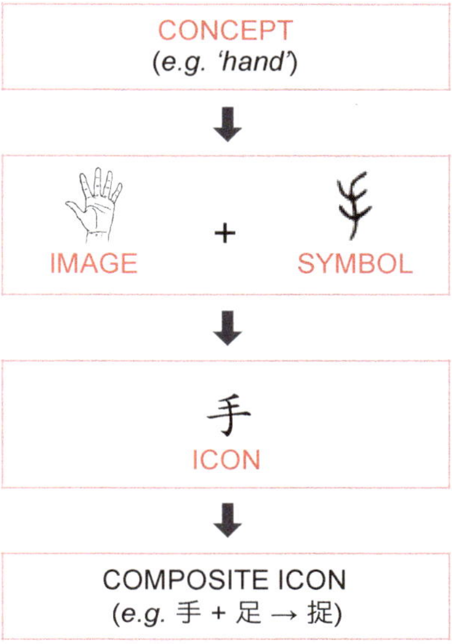

As we see, each essential logogram acts as a formative link, thus providing an intuitive cohesion to the whole set of writing systems based on Chinese characters, since the whole frame of complex kanji and words formed by them is based on these compositional principles that are also, in many cases, self-explanatory.

When we talk about kanji we are talking, in short, about a writing system that directly reinforces visual thought, something that purely phonetic systems cannot claim.

To conclude with the argument about the importance of using Chinese characters, I will refer to the more obvious practical reasons against not using them in Japanese. Japanese, known for its simple phonetic system of only five vowels and lack of consonant clusters, is characterized by the use of particularly long words and grammatical constructions and by the presence of a remarkable amount of homophones. In such circumstances, kanji efficiently solves the two main problems that can arise from writing such a language: the problem of space and the problem of semantic ambiguity. Kanji, if read with their *kunyomi* readings, allows to abridge in a single character a word that would require several phonetic symbols if written in a phonetic system, thus considerably reducing the space required to write that particular word. This is how, for example, the word *ashi* ('foot') goes from two to one character if we convert it from kana to kanji (あし → 足). As for the problem of semantic ambiguity, it is evident how a visual icon with its own meaning is able to define the meaning of a word independently of its sound. Thus, for example, the word *fusoku*, which can mean three different things[5], goes from being completely ambiguous out of context if written phonetically, to being able to be interpreted at a glance if written in kanji.

We can say that, specifically in Japanese, the complete abandonment of the use of kanji could ultimately prove to be more detrimental than helpful, and after

[5]ふそく (*fusoku*): 不足 'insufficient' ; 附則 'additional rules' ; 不測 'unexpected'

all, this unique writing system is one of the elements that draws many students' attention towards the language, not to mention that, once a considerable number of characters have been learned, the student will be able to guess the meaning of new words not only in Japanese but also in the Chinese written language.

Formation and Composition of Kanji

When a newcomer sees a kanji for the first time he may think it is an amalgam of meaningless strokes, but to think that would be totally misleading. The origin of Chinese characters is clearly pictographic—that is, each character, in its original form, represents a particular concept in a relatively reliable visual form, so that the strokes forming that character or symbol makes possible to summon the represented concept on their own.

The original forms of Chinese characters, from which the current characters ultimately derive, are called *oracle bone script* and *bronze-ware script*. The first one owes its name to the fact that it has been attested mostly in skeletal remains whereupon ancient oracles used to make divinations. The second type of writing, on the other hand, is called as such because it is most often found as inscriptions made on various bronze items dating back to the first millennium BC.

Both among oracle bone script and bronzeware script, there are a vast number of characters that represent tangible concepts as well as characters that, although not entirely pictographic, show ideas in a symbolic way with a representative approximation of intangible but descriptive concepts, usually formed by association between other compositional elements. The first type of characters is known as *pictograms* and the second type of characters is known as *ideograms*.

A combination of pictograms and ideograms are shown in the above sample of characters of the bronzeware script. The first five characters are pictographic representations of the concepts of 'person', 'child', 'eye', 'outstretched hand', and 'tree'. The last four characters are ideograms formed by association that represent the concepts 'to protect' (person + child), 'to look' (eye + person), 'to reach' (outstretched hand + person), and 'to rest' (person + tree).

Ideograms make up the vast majority of the compositional ground of Chinese characters, although these ideograms, as I have just pointed out, usually use pictograms for their formation. The pictograms used in the formation of other characters are called **Primitive Components**, and each kanji or sinogram is one of them or derives from at least one of them. There are also other graphs acting as phonetic or semantic components that are in turn formed by two or more primitive components.

Most of the ideograms, in compositional terms, can also be classified as

Semantic Compounds, since they have been formed by two or more primitive components based on their semantic value.

Each component has a meaning assigned to it and, usually, also a sound that, in origin, would be equivalent to a phoneme used to designate the corresponding meaning in ancient Chinese.

Given that the formation of new characters by a purely semantic association of components would be an arduous task requiring a high degree of imagination, a method known as *rebus* was quickly applied in order to greatly facilitate this formative process.

The rebus method involves the use of a component to which a particular phoneme has been assigned together with another component only for its semantic dimension. In this manner, the sound of a component is borrowed in order to be associated with the meaning of another component. This type of characters are called **Phonosemantic Compounds** and they make up the vast majority of Chinese characters used today.

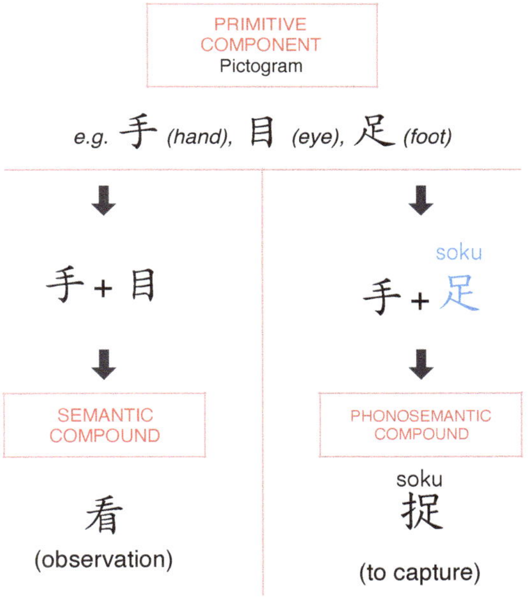

Many scholars conclude, perhaps due to a lack of rigorous etymological analysis, that in most of the phonosemantic characters the phonetic component has lost its semantic value, or in other words, that the phonetic component is used exclusively for its phonetic value while its semantic value is ignored. However, the people who, over the years, developed and standardized the Chinese writing system, took great care in choosing the components with a phonetic value so that their meaning was not only not lost, but also could emphasize more, if possible, the meaning of new graphic compositions. The learning system presented in *The World of Kanji* has been developed based on the principle, etymologically proven recently, that phonosemantic compounds also retain a semantic value in their phonetic component.

It can be summarized that component graphs, whether primitive or derived, are the essential core indispensable for the categorization, comprehension and, in the end, learning of kanji, for they shape and in them is based the totality of the sinitic logographic writing system, since the majority of Chinese characters have been formed by means of semantic or phonosemantic combinations of these components.

In the next section I will elaborate on the characteristics of components and how they can be used to their maximum potential when learning to read and write kanji.

Categorization of Kanji

As we have seen in the previous section, one can notice that the whole set of Chinese characters can be easily organized and structured in relation to their formative nature as it is shown below:

- **Primitive Components**: Primordial characters of mainly pictographic origin that are used to form compound characters.

- **Secondary Components**: Characters that are used as components for other characters, but which in turn derive from a particular primitive component or are formed by an association between several of them.

- **Semantic Compounds**: Characters that do not act as components and are formed by the association between two or more primitive and/or secondary characters.

- **Phonosemantic Compounds**: Characters formed of two or more components whereof one of them provides a phonetic value. This type of characters make up about 78% of the entire sinographic corpus.

Lastly, there are two additional categories that appear in far less extent:

- **Derived components**: A category consisting of pictographic characters derived directly from primitive components. They are also primitive components with some additions or modifications.

- **Independent Characters**: Characters that do not act as components nor are composed of other characters but have been formed either by an independent pictographic construction or by the derivation of an existing pictogram.

The structural scheme that has been just described can be illustrated through the bronzeware script example shown in the previous section:

Once transformed into the current script:

人 子 目 又 木 保 見 及 休

They can be categorized in the following way:

- 人, 子, 目, 又 and 木 are **Primitive Components** with the semantic value of 'person', 'child', 'eye', 'outstretched hand' and 'tree'.

- 保, 見, 及 and 休 are **Semantic Compounds** formed by the combination of the character 人 with the rest of the previous components.

If we select out the character for "outstretched hand" (又) we can see how the structural system continues to develop:

又 has a pictographic derivation in the graph 支 (*shi*) which represents a hand grasping some kind of branch or stick and adopts the meaning of 'to sustain'. 支 is thus a derived component that can give a phonosemantic value to new characters. From the character 支 derive, among others, the phonosemantic compounds 伎 (*ki*, person + to sustain = 'skill'), 技 (*gi*, hand + to sustain = 'ability') and 枝 (*shi*, tree + to sustain = 'branch'), which they all adopt a sound similar to the root sound of the component 支 (*shi*).

又 → 支 → 伎、技、枝 …

As we have been saying until now, components are essential to facilitate the understanding of Chinese characters. Components are not only useful to understand the etymology and the semantic and phonetic relationships between each character, but also to sort the characters in the indexes of reference books such as dictionaries or, as we shall see later, this very book.

The World View of the Creators of Chinese Characters

During the second millennium BC, in the Yellow River Valley, north of present-day

China, a culture emerged that would forever mark the destiny of East Asia: the culture of the Shang dynasty. In that cultural environment, the characters that would later evolve into the current sinographs and kanji developed in a decisive way, becoming one of the writing systems that have been used for the longest time in human history.

The people of the Shang dynasty lived within a social order that held together, at least symbolically, the common people with royalty, and royalty with the divine. The stabilizing base of the Shang dynasty was thus a trinity of people, king and god, under which order and continuity were maintained. But to maintain that order, it was necessary to legitimize the beliefs in such religious and social system. During the Shang dynasty, these beliefs were legitimized by establishing a complicated but well-defined ritual system.

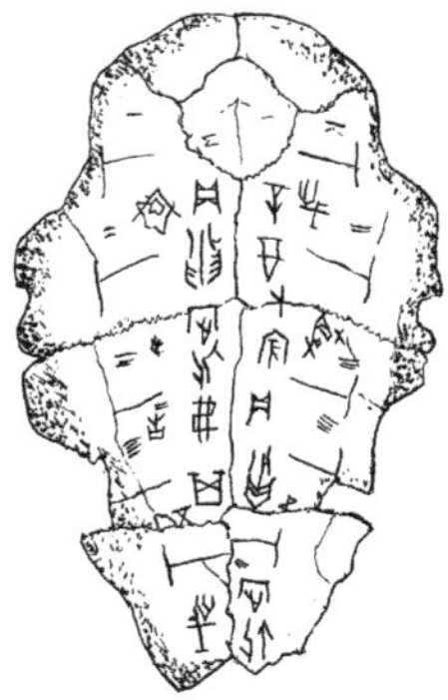

Turtle plastron with divinatory inscriptions.

The core of the rites of the Shang were a series of divinatory ceremonies through which advice was obtained for future tasks in a sort of communication with the numinous whose undertaking was reserved to the noble class, since its members were the only ones with the privilege of being able to exercise as priests.

The divinatory rites were performed using the bones of animals—especially ox scapulas or turtle shells (more specifically the shell bone, called plastron). A question was inscribed on these surfaces and then heat was applied to the bone until there appeared some providential cracks upon which an interpretation was written down. At first, the symbols engraved on the bone surfaces were probably mere representative indications, but gradually they evolved into a cohesive pictographic system known as *oracle bone script*.

The divinatory rites were subsequently followed by a cult to the ancestors and corresponding veneration rites, for which a series of bronze ritual vessels were used, and was on the surface of those vessels where eventually solemn inscriptions would be engraved, thus giving shape to the so-called *bronzeware script*.

Sample of bronze ritual vessels on which inscriptions were made.

The sum of ritual writings in bronzeware and oracle bone scripts would form a communicative system thanks to which the Chinese culture emerged and developed and, later on, also the Japanese one. These ancient ritual scriptures, which shaped a proper communicative system, were constituted taking into account and reflecting the world view of the society that developed them. It is obvious that the society of the Shang dynasty, that lasted throughout the second millennium BC, was quite different from our modern society, but we will see that its perception of the world, human at the end of the day, will not be so strange to us.

The people of the Shang dynasty managed to describe the immediate physical plane with a determined set of pictographic symbols; and with the combination of these primitive symbols with each other, they ended up developing a complete semantic writing system capable of satisfying all human communicative needs. A not very high number of primitive characters gave rise to a complex system that accounts its logographs in the thousands. It is quite interesting to find out how all those thousands of characters can be reduced to a few hundred interconnected primitive components.

The set of primitive characters which, as I said, reliably represents the physical plane, can be divided into four thematic sections: The Human Realm, the Natural Realm, the Material Realm and, finally, the Territorial Realm. These four divisions of the world suffice to categorize the enormous and complex conceptual frame represented by Chinese characters. Each essential component used to form any type of kanji belongs, semantically, to one of the aforementioned "realms". In turn, each of these realms can be further divided into three relevant categories. The Human Realm is composed of *People*, the *Human Body* and *Limbs*. The Natural Realm is composed of *Elements*, *Plants* and *Animals*. The Material Realm is made up of *Everyday Objects*, *Tools* and *Vessels*, and, finally, the Territorial Realm is made up of *Weapons*, *Spaces* and *Constructions*.

The progression of the learning system of *The World of Kanji* derives directly from this "world" arrangement inspired by the world view of the creators of the characters. The author of the present book believes that in order to learn kanji as naturally and logically as possible, it is necessary to have a cohesive and progressive system that is faithful to the formation and constitution of the sinograms, since in it lies the key to the rapid comprehension and consistent memorization of the characters.

GUIDELINES FOR READING KANJI

Overview

The complexity of Japanese writing lies not only in the existence of two different syllabaries plus kanji, but also in the possible readings of the latter. This is because, first, there are two basic ways to read a Chinese character: 1. Through an adaptation to Japanese phonetics of the original Chinese phoneme represented by the character; 2. Through a Japanese native word that alludes to the meaning represented by the character. As noted previously in the introduction, the first type of reading is called *onyomi* (phonetic reading) and the second type is called *kunyomi* (semantic reading).

The realization of one reading or the other depends on the context in which the kanji appears, but it is safe to assume that, in most occasions, the sinitic vocabulary that is pronounced with the *onyomi* reading is mostly written by a combination of two or more kanji, and that the written words with a single kanji will be native words pronounced with the *kunyomi* reading.

- **Onyomi Reading**: Phonetic reading of sinitic origin. Usually performed on words composed of two or more kanji.
- **Kunyomi Reading**: Vernacular semantic reading. Usually performed when single kanjis appear alone or followed by syllables written in hiragana.

There are some characters that have more than one *onyomi* reading or more than one *kunyomi* reading. There are also some rare composite words in which one of the kanji has a *kunyomi* reading and the other kanji has an *onyomi* reading. Finally, there are also words with special readings (*gikun*) that are used only in one word. These exceptional cases can only be learned by memorizing the corresponding vocabulary.

Onyomi Readings

Onyomi readings are typically used in sinoxenic words (words of Chinese origin), which generally can be easily distinguished by being composed of two or more kanji. These types of composite words are called *jukugo*. In cases where a character has several *on* readings, it will only be possible to determine which of them should be used by learning the pertinent vocabulary, but it has to be said that most kanji have only a single *onyomi* reading, and those with several of them are usually fairly common characters, whereas one of the possible readings is used far more often than the rest.

A particular *onyomi* reading can be modified if the pronunciation of the following kanji ends in the phoneme *tsu* (つ), which gets assimilated through reduplication into the first sound of the pronunciation of the following kanji. This is how, for example, the word 接戦 (*setsu* + *sen*) is not pronounced **setsusen* but *sessen*, or the word 借金 (*shaku* + *kin*) is not pronounced **shakukin* but *shakkin*.

Kunyomi Readings

Kunyomi readings are generally used when kanji is followed by syllables written in hiragana or when it represents a single noun on its own, although there are also certain *jukugo* with *kun* readings, as it can be seen in compounds used in many proper nouns and surnames.

The syllables that are written in hiragana and follow a kanji read in *kunyomi* are called *okurigana*. This *okurigana* may be inflected, making it variable, but the *kunyomi* reading will act as an invariable fixed lexeme.

Paradigm

By using the character 生 (*to live*) as an example, I am going to demonstrate how a single kanji can be read in different ways depending on how it appears within a text. I chose this character in particular because it is a character with an exceptionally high number of possible readings.

Word	Reading	Meaning
❶ 生	nama	raw
❷ 生きる	i.kiru	to live
❸ 生まれる	u.mareru	to be born
❹ 生活	sē-katsu	livelihood
❺ 人生	jin-sē	human life

❶ Kunyomi 1 [***nama***]: As a single character word without inflections, a native noun.

❷ Kunyomi 2 [***i-***]: As a kanji lexeme with an inflectional termination written in hiragana, a native verb.

❸ Kunyomi 3 [***u-***]: As another kanji lexeme with an inflectional termination written in hiragana, another native verb.

❹ & ❺ Onyomi 1 [*sē*]: As a sinoxenic lexeme used in composite words (*jukugo*).

GUIDELINES FOR WRITING KANJI

Overview

Knowing how to correctly write kanji is useful in three ways: 1. To make handwriting comprehensible and aesthetically appealing; 2. To know the first stroke and the number of strokes a character has when you want to look for it in dictionaries—or in one of the indices of this book[6]—; and 3. To recognize and understand other people's handwritten calligraphy. Moreover, the learning of kanji can always be more enriching if it is done according to aesthetic rules that will integrate the student into the compendium of the sinitic calligraphic tradition.

The calligraphic tradition of Chinese characters establishes three key points or *laws*:

1. **Law of strokes**: Each character is composed of a specific number of strokes. A stroke is every brush movement that is made without lifting the pen from the paper.

2. **Law of sequence**: The strokes of each character must be written in an established order following a given sequence and direction.

3. **Law of proportion:** Each character has to be approximately of the same size, regardless of the number of strokes and/or components it is composed of. All characters also have to be able to be written within the boundaries inferred by an equilateral square.

Each kanji, therefore, is made up of a few strokes that must be written in a particular order so that they occupy more or less the size of a square. The existence of these rules (as opposed to the Latin script, which does not specify any stroke order) is mainly due to one reason: to bring some clarity and comprehensibility upon the large number of existing characters and to allow an accurate distinction between them. If writing is done slowly, the resulting characters are likely to be intelligible despite the differences in stroke order, but as soon as writing is streamlined and strokes begin to come together or mingle due to the speed of the brush, it is imperative to follow a standard sequence that allows the reader to discern what path the writing utensil has followed while tracing the character.

Let us prove this fact setting an example with the character 文 (*writing*). First, let us see common serif and sans serif printed fonts:

---

[6] 2136 Character Index

文 文

In both graphemes four distinct strokes can be distinguished (丶一丿㇏), so reading and understanding these characters would not present a major problem. Likewise, from handwriting in a slow and regular style you will get a similar result, as printed fonts that are based on slow regular writing show:

文

The turning point is when the movement of the brush becomes faster and the strokes in cursive style begin to merge:

Here we see how the upper strokes (丶一) have merged and the lower strokes have been somewhat flattened. In spite of this phenomenon, the calligrapher or experienced reader will be able to see that this character is 文 thanks to the evident sequential (丶一丿㇏) and directional (↓→↙↘) order of strokes, without which another different and most probably unintelligible result would have come out. The existence of a definite number of strokes and an accepted order when writing kanji is due to the need to make them understandable when written fast. This is more evident the more cursive the writing is:

If it were not for the existence of an order of strokes and established direction it would be impossible to decipher that the character above is 文 fused into a single stroke.

In order for the student to achieve a correct writing and, perhaps most importantly, to be able to discern at first glance the order and the number of strokes of a given character, he or she will have to acknowledge and apply the three aforementioned rules, which I will explain one at a time in more detail hereafter.

Law of Strokes

The *Law of Strokes* states that each character has a certain number of strokes. Within the whole set of Chinese characters there is a series of repeating strokes and these can be easily sorted out. Let us see, then, what are the strokes used in the sinitic writing:

1. **Line**: Horizontal and straight line, going from left to right: 一. This stroke is

by itself also an independent character 一 (*one*). Exceptionally, the line can appear sharply inclined to the left, forming an oblique line (㇀), as in the character 七 (*seven*).

2. **Column**: Vertical and straight line written from top to bottom: 丨. The column can curve at the bottom forming a bent column: ㇓; or end in a hook, forming a column with a hook: 亅.

3. **Slash**: Starts to be written from an upper position and then goes down to the left: ㇒.

4. **Dot**: Stroke of short length that extends slightly from an upper position and then points down to the right: 丶. In many characters the path of the dot can be extended further downwards forming an extended dot: ㇏. This drop, like the column, can also end in a hook, forming a dot with a hook: ㇂.

In addition to these four common strokes and their variants there is also a series of compound strokes. These strokes are technically the combination of two common stroke shapes, but united by a single brush stroke:

5. **Upper Corner**: It consists of a line followed by a column: ㇕. This compound stroke has different variants, such as the shortened upper corner: ㇇; the extended upper corner: ㇍; the upper corner with an inward hook: ㇆ or the upper corner with an outward hook: ㇈.

6. **Lower Corner**: Combination of a column with a line: ㇗. This stroke usually appears slightly inclined: ㇛, ㇜. There are also the variants of the shortened lower corner: ㇙, or the lower corner with a hook ㇟.

7. **Zigzag**: Uncommon stroke that is formed by the combination of a line and a lower corner: ㇠. This stroke can have the exceptional variant ㇅ (as in the characters 凹 and 凸) or ㇌ (as in the component 乃).

8. **Reverse Zigzag**: Combination of a lower corner with an upper corner: ㇞, which have also the bent variant: ㇉.

Below there is a table summarizing the different types of strokes:

	Main Stroke	Variants	Direction
Line	一	㇀	→
Column	丨	亅	↓

Slash	㇒	㇓	↙
Dot	丶	㇏ ㇄	↘
Upper Corner	㇕	㇀ ㇂ ㇆ ㇈	→ ↓
Lower Corner	㇄	㇀ ㇄	↓ →
Zigzag	乙	㇅ ㇋	→ ↓ →
Reverse Zigzag	㇉	㇉	↓ → ↓

Once you learn these eight strokes and variants he will be able to determine in which direction they are written and how many of them a character is composed of.

Law of Sequence

The next aspect to take into account when writing kanji is the order in which the strokes of each character are written, that is, the *Law of Sequence*, which follows the principle that the writing of characters has to be economical: that is, so that it enables the hand to make the fewest movements while writing a certain number of strokes. This principle, applied to nearly every sinogram, has allowed the stroke sequence to remain virtually unchanged over the years.

The precepts stipulated in the Law of Sequence can be applied to most characters so that, with few exceptions, the student will know in which order of strokes to write a certain character without having to consult it in a dictionary. Let us now go on to describe these sequential precepts, or in other words, the general notions applicable when establishing the order of strokes of a character:

① From left to right & from top to bottom

川 (丿 丨 丨) 三 (一 一 一)

✤ *Leftmost column is written first:*

門 (丨 ㇕ 一 一 丨 ㇆ 一 一)

② Lines before columns

十 (一 丨) 上 (一 丨 一)

✤ *But if there is a cross (十, 丅) and a line below, the cross is written first:*

土 (一 丨 一) 王 (一 丨 一 一) 馬 (丨 一 丨 一 一 ㇆ ㇒ 丶 丶 丶)

③ Central columns before symmetrical sides

木 (一丨丿㇏) 水 (亅㇇丿㇏) 山 (丨𠃊丨)

④ Slashes before dots

父 (丿丶丿㇏)

⑤ Upper corners before slashes

刀 (𠃌丿) 力 (𠃌丿)

✤ *Except the graph* 九 (丿㇈)

⑥ Upper corners before lower corners

民 (𠃍一𠄌一㇂) 艮 (𠃍一一𠄌丿㇏)

⑦ Lines that cross several strokes are written at the end

女 (㇛丿一) 母 (㇛𠃌丶丶一)

⑧ Columns that cross several strokes are written at the end

聿 (𠃍一一一一丨)

⑨ Single dots are written at the end

玉 (王丶)

✤ *Unless the dot is at the top of the character:*

主 (丶王)

⑩ The component 辶 is written at the end

近 (斤辶)

⑪ The component 𠂇 is inconsistent

一丿: 左, 友, 在, 存

丿一: 右, 布, 有

In addition to these basic sequential precepts, there are two components whose graphic development is not easily distinguishable to the naked eye, so that it is not possible to guess, by looking at a printed typography, which are the separate strokes of such a component. Those ambiguous components are the following:

Ambiguous compositions

Graph	*Strokes*	*Stroke order*	*Direction*
口 口	*column / upper corner / line*	丨 ㇕ 一	↓ ┐ →
氵	*dot / dot / oblique line*	丶 丶 ㇀	↘ ↘ ↗

It is good to know this list of precepts before beginning the study of kanji, but it can be also practical to review and verify the list in parallel with that study.

Law of Proportion

At last I will talk about the proportions to follow when writing a character, or the *Law of Proportion*, a basic element, together with the laws of strokes and sequence, for the correct writing of kanji. The Law of Proportion dictates that any character, regardless of its number of strokes or components, must be written within the space delimited by an equilateral square:

漢 字

It is because of this quadrilateral proportion that some components have to change their size in order to match it. Compound characters, thus, follow predetermined compositional structures with regard to the location of their components. Let us see, then, what structures exist within compound characters:

- **Vertical Compounds**: Characters in which components are placed vertically side by side. They are the most common compounds. There are vertical characters with components that look narrower on the left (e.g. 地), others narrower on the right (e.g. 列), or others that appear in similar proportions (e.g. 秋). There are also compounds formed of three vertical components (e.g. 徹). Vertical components are written from left to right, that is, the first component to be written as a whole is the one on the left and the last the one on the right.

- **Horizontal Compounds**: Characters in which components are placed horizontally, one on top of the other. There are components that appear more squashed at the top (e.g. 宇, 宙), others more squashed at the bottom (e.g. 盈), or others in equal proportion (e.g. 雲). There are also horizontal compounds made up of three components (e.g. 尋). This type of compound is written from top to bottom, that is, the component on top is written first and the component below is written last.

- **Roofed Compounds**: Characters made up of a component that wraps the other component or components on the top and both sides (e.g. 問). This type of compound is written from top to bottom, that is, the envelope or "roof" is written first and the "wrapped" components inside later.

- **Boxed Compounds**: Compounds partially surrounded or wrapped by another component, either to the left (e.g. 区), or underneath (e.g. 凶). This type of compound is one of the least frequent. In the left wrappings the stroke order is as follows: top *line, content, lower corner*. In the lower wrappings the order is: *content, lower corner, column*.

- **Cornered Compounds**: Compounds that has a component that wraps another component around only in one corner (two sides). The wrapping corner can be at the top left (e.g. 灰), the top right (e.g. 気) or the bottom left (e.g. 道). In these compounds the wrapping is written first and the contents later, except in the characters with the wrapping component 辶, which is always written at the end.

- **Encircled Compounds**: Those compounds in which a component encircles another component or components by all sides (e.g. 国). The writing order of this type of compound is as follows: *left column, upper corner, content, bottom line*.

As you may have already inferred, the writing order of components follows precepts similar to the stroke order of primitive characters, so that each component is subject to its own stroke order, and the writing order of each component also follows the *Law of Sequence*. Compound characters should therefore be written as follows: *Component 1* (with its stroke order), *Component 2* (with its stroke order); while *Component 1* and *Component 2* are treated as different entities following the *Law of Sequence* within the stroke order of the whole character.

SYLLABARIES

Hiragana

PRIMARY PHONEMES

	∅	K	S	T	N	H	M	Y	R	W
A	あ a	か ka	さ sa	た ta	な na	は ha	ま ma	や ya	ら ra	わ wa
I	い i	き ki	し shi	ち chi	に ni	ひ hi	み mi		り ri	
U	う u	く ku	す su	つ tsu	ぬ nu	ふ fu	む mu	ゆ yu	る ru	
E	え e	け ke	せ se	て te	ね ne	へ he	め me		れ re	
O	お o	こ ko	そ so	と to	の no	ほ ho	も mo	よ yo	ろ ro	を o
N	ん n									

VOWEL LENGTHENING & CONSONANT DOUBLING

- Sounds ending in 'o' get lengthened to 'ō' by adding う
- Sounds ending in 'e' get lengthened to 'ē' by adding い
- Consonants double by having a preceding っ (a dwarfed つ)

DERIVED PHONEMES

	G	Z	D	B	P
A	が ga	ざ za	だ da	ば ba	ぱ pa
I	ぎ gi	じ ji	ぢ dji	び bi	ぴ pi
U	ぐ gu	ず zu	づ dzu	ぶ bu	ぷ pu
E	げ ge	ぜ ze	で de	べ be	ぺ pe
O	ご go	ぞ zo	ど do	ぼ bo	ぽ po

DIPTHONGS

	KI	GI	SHI	CHI	NI	HI	BI	PI	MI
A	きゃ kya	ぎゃ gya	しゃ sha	ちゃ cha	にゃ nya	ひゃ hya	びゃ bya	ピャ pya	みゃ mya
U	きゅ kyu	ぎゅ gyu	じゅ ju	ちゅ chu	にゅ nyu	ひゅ hyu	びゅ byu	ぴゅ pyu	みゅ myu
O	きょ kyo	ぎょ gyo	しょ jo	ちょ cho	にょ nyo	ひょ hyo	びょ byo	ぴょ pyo	みょ myo

Katakana

PRIMARY PHONEMES

	∅	K	S	T	N	H	M	Y	R	W
A	ア a	カ ka	サ sa	タ ta	ナ na	ハ ha	マ ma	ヤ ya	ラ ra	ワ wa
I	イ i	キ ki	シ shi	チ chi	ニ ni	ヒ hi	ミ mi		リ ri	
U	ウ u	ク ku	ス su	ツ tsu	ヌ nu	フ fu	ム mu	ユ yu	ル ru	
E	エ e	ケ ke	セ se	テ te	ネ ne	ヘ he	メ me		レ re	
O	オ o	コ ko	ソ so	ト to	ノ no	ホ ho	モ mo	ヨ yo	ロ ro	ヲ wo
N	ン n									

VOWEL LENGTHENING & CONSONANT DOUBLING

- Vowels get lengthened by adding ー
- Consonants double by having a preceding ッ (a dwarfed ツ)

DERIVED PHONEMES

	G	Z	D	B	P
A	ガ ga	ザ za	ダ da	バ ba	パ pa
I	ギ gi	ジ ji	チ dji	ビ bi	ピ pi
U	グ gu	ズ zu	ヅ dzu	ブ bu	プ pu
E	ゲ ge	ゼ ze	デ de	ベ be	ペ pe
O	ゴ go	ゾ zo	ド do	ボ bo	ポ po

DIPTHONGS

	KI	GI	SHI	CHI	NI	HI	BI	PI	MI
A	キャ kya	ギャ gya	シャ sha	チャ cha	ニャ nya	ヒャ hya	ビャ bya	ピャ pya	ミャ mya
U	キュ kyu	ギュ gyu	ジュ ju	チュ chu	ニュ nyu	ヒュ hyu	ビュ byu	ピュ pyu	ミュ myu
O	キョ kyo	ギョ gyo	ショ jo	チョ cho	ニョ nyo	ヒョ hyo	ビョ byo	ピョ pyo	ミョ myo

HOW TO USE THIS BOOK

Journey Through the World of Kanji

The system of *The World of Kanji* is based on the pictographic principle of Chinese character formation. When the ancient Chinese people began to develop their writing system they did so by looking at the world around them and by representing the concepts expressed by the language with a limited series of pictographic symbols—also called primitive characters—which were given a sound and a meaning. These symbols would later start to get combined with each other to form the large amount of Chinese characters that exist today (2136 of which are considered indispensable in Japanese).

The World of Kanji takes the premise that the student of kanji will be able to advance much faster in his learning if he has a notion of what these primitive pictorial symbols are and how they work. These symbols are divided into four "realms" or themes that are in accordance with the represented concepts. They are the **Human Realm**, the **Natural Realm**, the **Material Realm** and the **Territorial Realm**. The Human Realm concerns *people* and their social functions, the parts of the *human body*, and the actions performed by the *limbs*. The Natural Realm concerns the natural *elements*, *plants* and their applications, and *animals*. The Material Realm concerns *everyday objects*, work *tools* and *vessels*. Finally, the Territorial Realm encompasses *weapons* used in warfare for territorial gain, physical *spaces* and *constructions*.

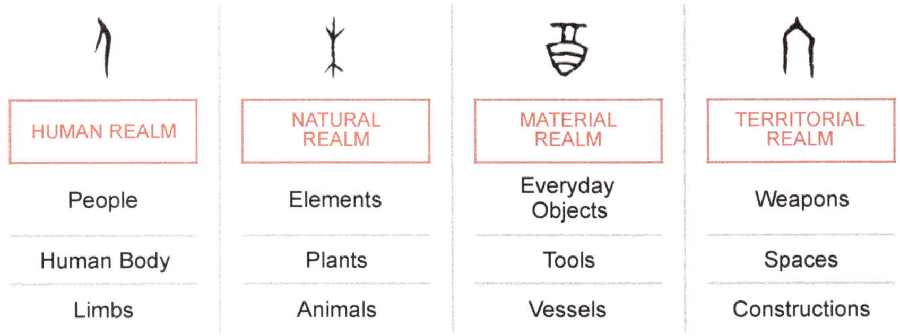

The thematic division of the book provides a cohesive view of the whole system and, therefore, enables a natural and logical understanding of the constituent elements. In addition, you will learn each character in a not only associative but also gradual way. The first characters you encounter in the beginning of a new section are primitive components, and the following compound characters appearing throughout the book will be always formed by components that have been already shown before.

Thanks to this book you will be able to acquire a new representative and a symbolic consciousness of the world around him, and he will be able to see in every new Chinese character he founds a scene that speaks directly to his mind.

Once you finish the book, he will have acquired a new world view of his own—related to the characters—, and he will be able to maintain an unimagined conceptual dialogue with the wonderful logographic system used in Japanese writing. Having completed the journey through each "realm" of interesting graphic icons reminiscent of scenes from a distant time and culture, but at the same time exceptionally familiar and self-explanatory, the reader will have obtained a profound and permanent vision and understanding of the scope of the visual code applied to the Japanese written language. Once you accomplish the adventure of *The World of Kanji*, Chinese characters will have gone from being a threat or obstacle to being the most intimate ally.

Study Process

To make good use of the book so you can learn the meanings of all the characters, I recommend that, following the order of the book, you pause at each entry, carefully read the explanations and finally concentrate on the composition and meaning of each kanji or component in order to retain the kanji meaning's in his memory.

I also suggest that during this memorization process, you write down each character several times as you try to learn them while focusing in their descriptions. At the end of each Realm's section there is a list called *Review on* [*name of the realm's section*] which contains all the characters that appear in the corresponding chapter grouped by components and compounds. When you have finished studying those groups of characters you can go to that list and try to recall each meaning so you can revisit them again if there is any character that you don't remember.

The memorization of the readings of each kanji is not the main objective of this book, since they are very varied and it is advisable to learn them together with some vocabulary, but these readings are indicated in each entry in hiragana (*kunyomi readings*) and katakana (*onyomi readings*) for informative purposes. If you don't know how to read the syllabaries (hiragana and katakana), you can refer to the section called *Syllabaries* which can be found just a few pages back. There are also several appendices dedicated to readings at the end of the book that you can consult and use at your convenience.

Appendices & Indices

At the end of the book there are a series of appendices and indexes that I will proceed to explain:

- **Semantic Components**: A list of semantic componentes sorted in order of appearance. It can be used as a reference or reinforcement once the student is already familiar with the book.
- **Phonosemantic Components**: A list of phonosemantic components sorted in

order of appearance. It can be used as a reference or reinforcement once the student is already familiar with the book.

- **Same Graph Components**: Small table showing those components whose variants are graphically identical to those of other components.

- **English Definitions**: A list of all characters arranged alphabetic by their meaning in English. This list can be used to look for a particular character when one remembers its meaning but cannot remember the exact way it looks or how it is read in Japanese.

- **Strong Phonetic Components**: A list sorted by Latin alphabetical order with sounds that share two or more characters with the same component. Although phono-semantic components also indicate similar phonemes, only characters with an identical phoneme appear in this list. This list may be used by the student as a guide to learn *onyomi* readings of several characters at the same time.

- **Onyomi Readings**: List of transcribed *onyomi* readings and their corresponding characters, arranged alphabetically.

- **Kunyomi Readings**: List of transcribed *kunyomi* readings and their corresponding characters, arranged alphabetically.

- **Radicals' Main Meanings**: Comprehensive list of the *radicals* used in this book's last index and their tentative meanings. Radicals are each component that is shared at least once by two characters within the whole set of Chinese characters. Radicals are also usually the most frequently occurring components. The list of radicals is composed of 139 semantic components and 8 graphic elements that act as radicals, forming a group of 147 elements in total.

- **Radicals Index**: List of radicals arranged by number of strokes, and within each number of strokes, arranged by stroke type as follows: ㇀ *(line)*; ㇑ *(column)*; ㇒ *(diagonal)*; ㇏ *(dot)* ㇕ *(upper corner)*; ㇄ *(lower corner)*.

- **2136 Characters Index**: List of all the 2136 official characters appearing in the book, arranged by radicals (sorted in turn by number and type of stroke). Within a group, the characters that share the same radical are grouped by total number of strokes. To consult a character in this list, you should identify first its radical (when there are two apparent radicals, the leftmost or uppermost shall be chosen). Once the radical has been identified, you should count the total number of strokes of the character, so you can find it in the list corresponding to its number of strokes within its radical group.

EXPLANATION OF ENTRIES

Overview

Within each realm there is a series of character entries semantically related to that realm. Within these characters, a division can be made between *primitive* characters, characters acting as *components* and characters composed of these components, that is, *compounds*. Each of these type of character is rendered a little bit differently.

Primitives and Components

The entries for this type of characters show the primitive characters and composite primitives that act as main components for other characters. In these entries the following information appears:

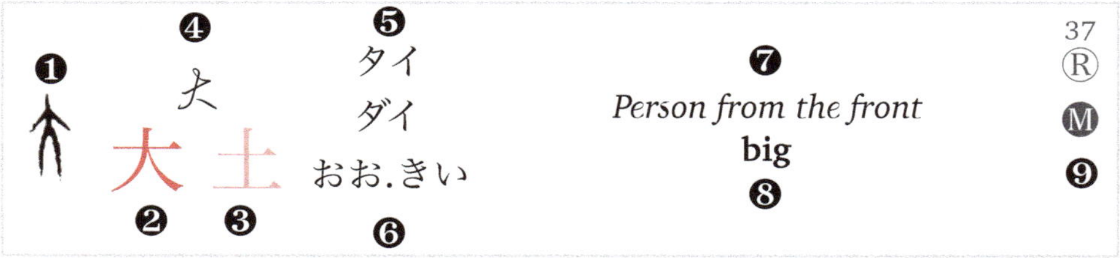

❶ The original pictogram in oracle bone or bronzeware script.

❷ The current standard version form of the character.

❸ Other variants used as components.

❹ Handwritten calligraphic version.

❺ *Onyomi* reading[7], written in katakana.

❻ *Kunyomi* reading[8], written in hiragana.

❼ Original meaning of the pictogram.

❽ Current most frequent meaning(s) of the character.

❾ Character's number and symbols indicating its typology.

After the informative stripe there appears an in-depth explanation of the character's etymology and its formative process. In this explanations the original

[7] Only the *onyomi* readings recognized by the Japanese Ministry of Education are included.

[8] Only the *kunyomi* readings recognized by the Japanese Ministry of Education are included, shown along their most frequent *okurigana*.

meaning appears again underlined when that meaning is used as a semantic aid in compounds, and the current meaning appears in **bold**.

If the component is only of a semantic nature, the main glyph is depicted in a strong red color and has the symbol Ⓜ for *meaning*, whereas the variants used only as a components are colored in a light red color, as shown in the previous example.

If the component also adopts a phonetic value, the color of the glyph is depicted in a strong blue color and it takes the symbol Ⓢ for *sound*, whereas the variants only used as components appear in a light blue color as shown in the following example:

並 並 幷

① ヘイ
① な.み
② なら.ぶ

Several people standing side by side

① **row**

② **to line up**

42
Ⓢ

It should be noted that there are components that are not separate standalone characters or are not part of the *jōyō kanji* list. In this case, the characters appear only in light color and their meaning and reading—if they have one—appear in gray color. In some cases, these characters, although not part of the *jōyō* list, are used in Japan for some personal names. These kind of characters, called *jinmēyō kanji*[9] in Japanese, appear with the symbol ㊔[10] below the number. In these cases, when the definition coincides with the meaning that the character takes as a component, the definition appears in black instead of gray.

辰 辰

シン

Person holding an agrarian tool

dragon sign (Chinese zodiac)

13
㊔
Ⓢ

Compounds

Compounds are formed by components and therefore, in most cases, they will not need a detailed etymological explanation, since the components themselves act as guides for understanding. The meaning of the components used in the compounds can be either the pictograph's original meaning or the character's current meaning. Entries for the compounds, in any case, are somewhat simpler. This type of entries appear as follows:

[9] Kanji intended for use in personal names.

[10] Character with the meaning of 'name'.

❷ 併 ❸ ヘイ ❺ 43 ❽

併 あわ.せる *Person* 亻 *along a row of people* 並 (ヘイ) ❻

❶ ❹ **to get together** ❼

❶ Current standard version form of the character.
❷ Handwritten calligraphic variant.
❸ *Onyomi* reading.
❹ *Kunyomi* reading.
❺ Compositional definition showing the components.
❻ Component acting as a phonetic guide and its sound.
❼ Most frequent current meaning(s) of the character.
❽ Character number.

Additional Information

Some characters require extra information, as they have some infrequent or special readings or need additional key explanations. Extra information may be represented in the following way:

- Reading in dark blue: Among several readings, this is the phoneme that compounds use. It also can indicate an occasional phonosemantic use of a character that normally acts just as a semantic component.
- Reading in light blue: This phoneme is only used in compounds where the character is acting as a phonosemantic component, and never as a reading of the character as a standalone.
- Reading in light red: Infrequent reading.
- Reading in light gray: Phoneme of a component that does not appear as a separate *jōyō* kanji but that forms part of phonosemantic compounds.

SPECIAL READING The reading after this note is unique to the combination shown within.

PLACE NAME USAGE The character with this label is used almost exclusively in place names.

NOTE Compound characters bearing this label require an additional etymological explanation.

Abbreviations, Symbols and Notes

Below there is a summarizing list of all the symbols and abbreviations used throughout the book entries:

Ⓡ Component also used as a radical.

㊔ Component also used as a character for names (*jinmēyō kanji*).

Ⓜ Component with semantic functions.

Ⓢ Component with phonosemantic functions.

[*fig.*] Concept used in a figurative or metaphorical way.

→ Evolution from a graphical form to another.

← Shows that the graphical form used is a more primitive version of the most common form.

×N Component appearing N times.

≈X A glyph that originally was different but that in current times is for practical purposes equivalent to the modern component X.

Notes on Etymology

Research on etymologies has been rigorous and well documented for this book[11], however, there are some characters whose etymology is ambiguous or varied. In such cases, the author has chosen the etymology that most closely is related to the current form of the character and/or the one that most helps to understand that character within the semantic framework proposed here.

[11] For reference, go to the '*Resources*' section at the end of the book.

THE HUMAN REALM

THE HUMAN REALM

The journey through The World of Kanji begins with an introspection towards ourselves. To understand the outside world, it is necessary first to know the inner world. The ego, the person, and people's personal relationships are the existential elements at which human beings firstly and most frequently aim their consciousness.

It is not surprising, then, that among the first artistic expressions made by prehistoric peoples there are, in fact, direct representations of themselves: the human being. It is notorious that these peoples established themselves as one of the primordial centers of their cosmographies. The creators of Chinese characters were no exception to that. Taking into account that the ritual inscriptions of the Shang people were developed within an activity with social functionality, it is also no coincidence that the representations of people and their actions play a key role within the whole corpus of primitive pictograms.

The human being is, therefore, one of the main subjects of Chinese characters. Graphemes grouped within the Human Realm are divided into the three following groups: Characters used to represent *people* or human figures in their own right, characters used to represent different parts of the *human body* and their functions, and, lastly, characters that place special emphasis on the different actions performed by the *limbs*.

PEOPLE	HUMAN BODY	LIMBS
1. The Upright Man	1. Bones	1. Hands
2. The Different Postures	2. Heart	2. Arms
3. Women and Gestation	3. Eyes	3. Feet
4. The Individual and Society	4. Nose, Ears and Hair	
5. Human Measures	5. Mouth	

THE HUMAN REALM AT A GLANCE

PEOPLE	HUMAN BODY	LIMBS

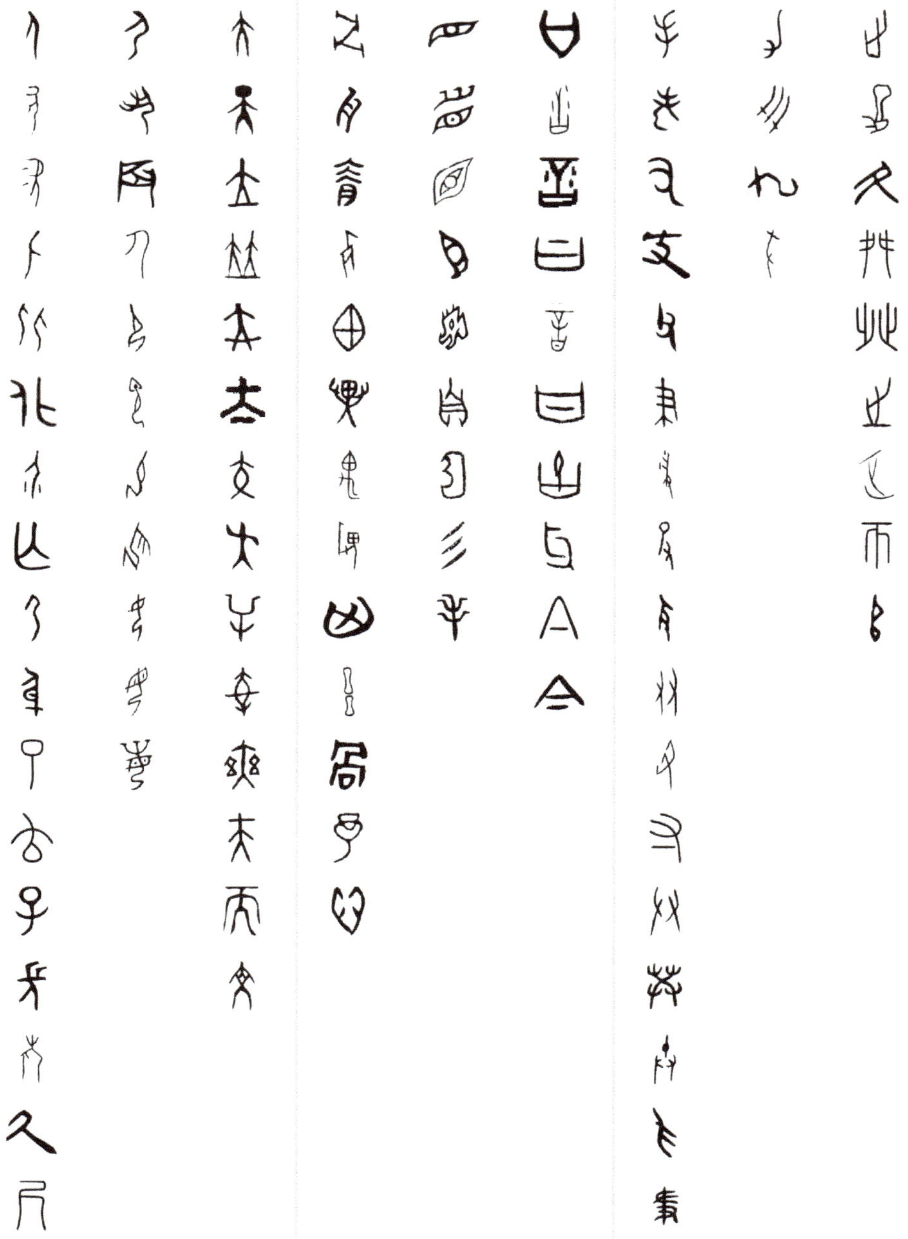

PEOPLE

1. THE UPRIGHT MAN

The most basic representation of 'man' is a depiction of a person in a standing position, a stance that differs clearly from the standard four-legged postures of animals. A man standing upright, seen from the side, drawn with two schematic strokes, 人 symbolizes the meaning of 'person', and from that pictograph others can be derived. For instance, if that person opens his mouth 欠 it represents someone 'exhaling air'. Just by changing the orientation of that simple iconographic image, other primordial grapheme was created: 匕, which represents a person turned to the opposite side or a 'person on his back'.

人 人 亻 儿 — ジン ニン ひと — **person** — 1 Ⓡ Ⓜ

The person, the human being. It is the most basic character and component because it is used to represent concepts related to humankind and the activities we do as people. The current character is the outlining of a pictograph showing a standing **person**, seen from the side, slightly curved to the left. The left stroke (丿) depicts the arms and head, and the right stroke (㇏), the trunk and legs.

c

欠 欠 — ケツ か.ける — *Person with an open mouth exhaling air* **to lack** — 2 Ⓡ Ⓜ

A *person* (人) with his <u>mouth open</u> (𠂊), <u>exhaling</u> air. As a standalone character it takes on the meaning of **to lack**, in reference to the lack of air when one has just breathed it out.

次 次 — ジ シ つぎ — *Breathing person* **subsequent** — 3 Ⓢ

A *person with an open mouth* (欠) who is inhaling the air that he had previously exhaled (冫), a person who is <u>breathing</u>. The action of inhaling air after having exhaled it suggests the **subsequent** breathing steps on which this glyph takes its meaning when it acts as a standalone character.

匕
匕

Person on his back

4
Ⓡ
Ⓜ

Mirror form of the character 人 (*person*). A person seen from the side, looking to the right, suggesting the idea of a person turning his back away. In the modern outlining, the stroke ⺃ stands for the head, trunk, and legs, while ⼃ represents the arms.

比
比

ヒ
くら.べる

Person next to another person
Several people
to compare

5
Ⓢ

A *person on his back* (匕 → 𠂤) placed next to another *person on his back* (匕), suggesting the idea of two or more people being **compare**d among each other.

化
化

カ
ケ
ば.ける

Person turning his back
to be transformed

6
Ⓢ

A standing *person* (人 → 亻) that has *turned his back* (匕) away, a person whose stance has been **transform**ed.

北
北

ホク
きた

Two people with their backs turned away
north

7
Ⓜ

A *person turning his back* (匕) to another person who also has *turned his back* (匕 → 丬): two people back to back, going toward opposite directions. The current meaning of the character was taken on making a relation to the movement of the sun, as it heads south at noon (in the Northern Hemisphere): going **north**wards understood as giving the back to the sun.

介
介

カイ

Person between two flanks
jam

8
Ⓢ

A *person* (人 → 𠆢) **jam**med between two flanks (丿丨).

亡 亡 ボウ モウ な.い

Buried person

perishing

9 Ⓢ

Originally 亾, a *person* (人 → 亠) buried in a hole underground (乚), a person who has **perish**ed.

2. THE DIFFERENT POSTURES

The next logical step in human representation, beyond the depiction of a mere standing man, is that very man in other postures that are better suited for suggesting specific situations, activities or states of mind. Among the different postures there is a ‘sitting person’ 尸, that further develops into a ‘person working with his hands’ 丮. We also have a ‘leaning person’ 勹, a ‘person on his knees’ 卩, or even a ‘huddling person’ 巳.

尸 尸

Sitting person

10 Ⓡ Ⓜ

A sitting person. This glyph originally was 𠃜, where ㇕ indicated the arms and trunk, and 厂 the legs resting on an implicit stool. Over time, the graph evolved from 𠃜 to 尸 as a result of writing becoming more fluid.

尼 尼 ニ あま

Person carrying another person on her back

nun

11 Ⓢ

A *person sitting* (尸) on the *back of another person* (匕). A person carrying another person on her back, taking care of him or her, as a **nun** would do.

丸 丮 丸

Person working with his hands

12 Ⓜ

A *sitting person* (尸 → ⺄) working with his two big hands (扌) while crafting something.

This component appears with the simplified form 丸, whose left part has been reduced to two strokes that now pierce the upper horizontal line.

辰

辰

シン

Person holding an agrarian tool

dragon sign (Chinese zodiac)

13 ㊔ Ⓢ

A man holding an agrarian tool with which he works the land. It may designate both the action of working as well as that of holding something. This component originally had the form 厎, in which you can perceive a structure similar to that of the right side of the component 丮 (*person working with his hands*), where the person is depicted by the stroke ⺄. The strokes on the left representing the agricultural tool eventually merged with the strokes on the right representing the person, thus making the form of the current character.

勹

勹

Leaning person

14 Ⓡ Ⓜ

A bending or leaning person, looking to the left, seen from the side. The stroke ノ depicts the head and arms, and the stroke ㇆ shows the trunk and legs.

匂

匂

にお.う

Person leaning over another person

to smell good

15 Ⓜ

A *person leaning* (勹) over another *person's back* (匕) because he or she **smells good**.

卩

卩 儿

Kneeling person

16 Ⓡ Ⓜ

A person sitting on his knees, or kneeling, looking to the left. ㇆ stands for the back and the head, and the vertical line 丨 depicts the union of the bent legs with the arms resting on them.

In some compounds the form 卩 gets transformed into one of the variant forms of the "person" component (儿), probably due to a semantic analogy.

卬

卬

Person kneeling before another person

17 Ⓜ

A *person kneeling* (卩) before a *person on his back* (匕 → ⺁).

仰 ギョウ 18

仰 コウ

あお.ぐ

Person 亻 *in front of a person kneeling before another* 卬

to look up (at)

 免 メン 19 Ⓢ

免 まぬ.かれる

Hiding person

to avoid

A *kneeling person* (卩 → 儿) covering himself with a big hat or cap (⺈冂) in order to **avoid** being spotted.

 㔾 ハン 20 Ⓢ

巳

Huddling person

Person kneeling and leaning to the right (乚), huddling, with his hands on his thighs (㇆), suggesting a distressing situation or feeling.

 巴 ハ 21 ㊔ Ⓢ

巴

Person with big hands

circular design

A kneeling person looking to the right (乚) with big hands and fingers (罒), suggesting a great endowment of skill on them.

 色 シキ 22 Ⓜ

色 ショク

いろ

Person on top of another person

color

A *person* (人 → ⺈) on top of a *huddling person* (巳 → 巴), suggesting the act of copulation and the glowing **color** of the skin derived from such an act.

3. WOMEN AND GESTATION

From the posture of a kneeling person seen in the previous section a new pictogram is developed: The figure of a 'woman' clasping her hands to the front, perhaps suggesting submission or pleading:  女. Women play a key role in the sinitic logical graphical representations for their own sake, and its icon diverts to a large number of secondary components and compound characters.

The concept of 'woman' also derives into the concept of 'mother' and other ideas related to gestation, such as childbirth or parenting. We can see how representing said concept of motherhood is done by enhancing the nipples of the icon for 'woman': 母, or how the concept of 'body' is suggested by the depiction of a pregnant woman about to give birth, with the body of a baby visibly inside her belly: 身. The pregnant woman, in turn, produces a 'fetus' 了 that, once its gestation is 'completed', becomes a newborn baby 𠫓, and then a full grown 'child' 子.

女 女

ジョ
ニョ
ニョウ
おんな
め

woman

23 Ⓡ Ⓜ

A **woman** sitting on her knees, with her hands clasped, possibly suggesting an attitude of submission. In the modern form, a visibly schematized glyph, the stroke く, points out the arms, the clasped hands, and the head, where the strokes 一 and ノ (フ) stand for the legs, trunk, and shoulders.

妄 妄

モウ
ボウ

Perishing 亡 (モウ) *woman* 女

delusion

24

娠 娠

シン

Woman 女 *holding something* 辰 (シン) *inside*

pregnancy

25

姿 姿

シ
すがた

Breathing 次 (ツ) *woman* 女

figure

26

母 母 毋

ボ
はは

Woman with exposed nipples

mother

27 Ⓜ

SPECIAL READING お母さん [おかあさん]: *mother*

A kneeling woman with her breasts and nipples exposed, evoking the image of a **mother** breastfeeding her offspring. The modern form of the character can be easily traced from the original character for "woman" (女), whose strokes have been elongated in order to make space for the two dots (丶丶) depicting the nipples.

When acting as a component, this character adopts a simplified form: 毋, in which the two dots have been united in a vertical line.

毎
毎
マイ

Scruffy woman
every

28 Ⓢ

Originally 毐, and later 毎, a *mother* (母 → 毋) with her hair disheveled (屮 → 𠂉), a mother with her external appearance unkempt as that of a scruffy woman, thought to be the common looks of each and **every** new mother who feels distressed in her new busy lifestyle.

侮
侮
ブ
あなど.る

Person 亻 *besides a scruffy woman* 毎 (マイ)
to disdain

29 Ⓢ

乃
乃
ナイ

Newly pregnant woman
from

30 ㊔ Ⓜ

A body seen from the side in which the belly looks slightly bulky, the body of a newly pregnant woman. The stroke to the left 丿 depicts the arms, whereas the sinuous stroke to the right ㇋ indicates the curved belly and the legs.

身
身
シン
み

Woman in full gestation
body [*fig.*]

31 Ⓜ

The body of a pregnant woman in full gestation, touching her belly, seen from the side. The meaning of **body** is thus doubly reinforced here with the figure of both the pregnant woman and that of the baby (a new body) within her. It can be seen that the strokes of this character are quite evolved: The stroke on top ㇒ shows the head, the oblique stroke in the middle 丿 points out the arms, the form resembling 目 on top of the latter suggests the pregnant belly with the baby inside and finally, the vertical line that arises from these last strokes, 亅, indicates, finally, the legs.

了
了
リョウ

Baby about to be born
realization

32

A baby who is fully formed but cannot yet outstretch his arms out, a baby that is about to be born since his physical formation process has been finally **realized**. The stroke ㇖ represents the child's head and the stroke 亅 the body.

 𠫓

Newborn baby

33 Ⓜ

A baby coming out headlong from the mother's belly, finally able to outstretch his arms, a baby that has just been born, a newborn baby. The stroke on top 丶 depicts the baby's legs, 厶 evokes the trunk and the head, and the horizontal line 一 indicates the outstretched arms.

 充 充

①② ジュウ

② あて.る

Baby becoming a full grown child

① **fill**

② to set aside

34 Ⓢ

A *newborn baby* (𠫓) that progressively becomes a *person* (人 → 儿), a **full** grown child who has seen his growth process fulfilled. As an additional meaning, this character has that of to **set aside**, figuratively taken from the idea of a grown up child that is set aside from the younger children in order to start a new life.

 子 子

シ

ス

こ

child

rat sign (Chinese zodiac)

35 Ⓡ Ⓜ

A **child** with a characteristic large head (乛), an upright trunk (亅) and outstretched arms (一). It is worth to notice that this character is the reversed form of the glyph 𠫓 (*newborn baby*). While that component evokes the image of a child upside down coming out of the mother's womb, this character shows us the image of that same child in an upright position, already active and aware of his surroundings.

好 好

コウ

この.む

す.き

Woman 女 and child 子

to like

36

4. THE INDIVIDUAL AND SOCIETY

By changing the point of view of the man from the side to the front, and by stretching his arms to the sides, the pictograph 大 大 appears. The creators of Chinese characters saw fit to give that depiction of a man a more contextual relevance in society, turning the meaning of 'person' into that of 'big' once it is shown from the front. Even greater than the physical dimensions of man is, however, the transcendence obtained by his spiritual endeavors. That is why the depiction of an already "big man" who has seen his head enlarged through mystical gnosis or heavenly connection, 天, receives the meaning of 'heaven'.

Position-wise, the man seen from the front can be also placed in relation to the ground: There is a person on top of the ground 立, representing a person who is 'standing', a person with his feet under the ground 亢, or even a person levitating over the ground 太, which represents something that is considered 'great'. Other possible postures are that of a person with his legs crossed 交, which represents an 'interchange', a 'wiggling person' 夭, or a person turned upside down 屰.

A big man who in old Chinese society reached the time when he could be considered 'adult' began to wear a distinctive hair attire made of a bun tied together with a hair-stick 夫. If the person grew older he used to let his hair particularly 'long' 長, graphically emphasizing the passage of time and experience.

One last pictogram referring to men and their function within society is 文, which represents a tattooed man or a person with some patterns drawn in his body that indicated some kind of societal role, an image that is now utilized to represent the concept of 'writing'.

大 | 大 土 | タイ ダイ おお.きい | *Person from the front* **big** | 37 Ⓡ Ⓜ

SPECIAL READING 大人 [おとな]: *adult*

A person seen from the front, with his arms and legs extended to the sides, suggesting a **big** figure. The central part 人 stands here for the full body and two legs, while the crossing line 一 represents the outstretched arms.

When acting as a component, the form 大 may sometimes be contracted to 土.

夾 | 夹 | キョウ | *Person in the middle of two other people* | 38 Ⓢ

Originally 夾, a *person seen from the front* (大) trapped in the middle of two *people* (人×2 → 丷).

天 天

テン
あま-
あめ

Enlightened person

heaven

39
Ⓜ

Originally 𠀘, a *person seen from the front* (大) with his head enlarged (口 → 一), indicating that he has attained <u>enlightenment</u> or gnosis towards the divine. A man who is aware of **heaven**. In many of the characters in which there was originally a thick line or a stain, there is now a thin horizontal line, due to the simplification attained while using brushes as a means of writing. From such process it turns out that the original character 𠀘, where 口 depicts an oversized head, has evolved into its current form: 天.

立 立

リツ
リュウ
た.つ

Standing person

to stand (up)

40
Ⓡ
Ⓜ

Originally 𡗓, a *person from the front* 大 to which a line underneath (一) has been added to indicate the situation of being **standing** on the ground. The original form 𡗓 of this glyph transformed over time into the current character: 立, where the legs have changed their orientation outwards (八) to inwards (丷).

位 位

イ
くらい

Person 亻 *standing* 立 *somewhere*

position

41

並 並 并

① ヘイ
① な.み
② なら.ぶ

Several people standing side by side

① **row**

② **to line up**

42
Ⓢ

Originally 竝, two *people standing* on the ground (立×2 → 竝 → 並), <u>side by side</u>, forming a **row**. Over time the strokes of both components were combined forming the current glyph 並, where the interior oblique strokes representing the legs of the original components became vertical lines, and the upper and lower horizontal lines got united into single lines.

As a component, this character usually takes a further simplified form: 并, in which the exterior oblique strokes 丷 have transformed into a single straight line and the other line depicting the ground has disappeared.

併 併

ヘイ
あわ.せる

Person 亻 *along a row of people* 并 (ヘイ)

to get together

43

亢
亢　コウ

Person with his feet under the ground

44 Ⓢ

A person with his feet <u>under the ground</u>, stuck in it. The upper strokes 亠 stand for the head and arms, the horizontal line crossing them 一 represents the ground, and the strokes 儿 depict the legs beneath.

太
太

① タ
① タイ
② ふと.い

Person over the ground
① **great**
② **to be plump**

45 Ⓢ

A *person seen from the front* (大) placed over ground (一 → 丶), with his feet being untouched by it, as if they were levitating. This character contrasts with the character 立 (*standing person*), in which the person directly "touches" the ground line—or the character 亢 (*person with his feet under the ground*), in which the feet "crosses" that line. The composition of the glyph suggests, therefore, the highness or superiority of those who are "above" everybody else. Eventually the character adopted the broad meanings of **great**, 'bigger than big', and, in a more mundane and perhaps unintended approach, also that of to **be plump**.

交
交

①② コウ
① まじ.える
② か.わす

Person with crossed legs
① **to mingle**
② **to interchange**

46 Ⓢ

A *person seen from the front* (大 → 六) with his legs crossed (乂). The notion of 'crossing one leg with the other' has resulted in a semantic association to the broader meanings of **mingling** and **interchanging**.

夭
夭

Wiggling person

47 Ⓜ

A person <u>wiggling</u> or swaggering while moving his hands and head. Originally 夭, the slanted stroke (丿) on top of the element 大 (*person seen from the front*) suggests that leaning movement.

妖
妖

ヨウ
あや.しい

Woman 女(ジョ) *who wiggles* 夭
bewitching

48

NOTE It is likely that the image evoked by this character is referring to the shamanistic role that women took in the ancient Chinese folk tradition (that role is still maintained to some degree in Korea and Japan), in which they acted as spiritual guides while moving sinuously and mysteriously, presumably possessed by the spirits. The meaning of **bewitching** is most probably derived from such a scene.

 𢆉 𢆉 屰 — *Person turned upside down* — 49 Ⓜ

A person turned upside down. This glyph is simply the character 大 (*person seen from the front*) reversed, where the strokes 䒑 stand for the prone legs, and the two crossing strokes 十 depict the trunk and the outstretched arms.

This component can also take the form 屰, where the central vertical stroke has been curved and the central horizontal stroke has been bent.

 幸 幸 — コウ / さいわ.い / しあわ.せ / さち — *Person standing upright and person turned upside down* — **fortune** — 50 Ⓡ Ⓜ

Originally 㚔, a *person seen from the front* (大 → 土), standing upright, and a *person turned upside down* (𢆉). This character suggests, therefore, the unpredictability of the fate or one's **fortune**, since sometimes one can turn out to be face-up, and other times face-down.

 執 執 — シツ / シュウ / と.る — *Person working out the fortune* — **to take command** — 51 Ⓜ

Originally 執, a *person working* (丮 → 丸) with a conceptualized *fortune* (㚔 → 幸), a person who decides his own destiny or that of the others, someone who becomes aware of his actions and takes **command** upon them.

 爽 爽 — ソウ / さわ.やか — *Person holding two heavy objets* — **invigorating** — 52

A *person seen from the front* (大) lifting two heavy objects (爻×2)—probably representing some kind of full vessels—, boasting his strength and **vigor**.

夫 夫 フ フウ おっと

Person with his hair tied in a topknot

Adult person

husband

53 Ⓢ

A *person seen from the front* (大) with a hair attire (一), most probably a bun tied with a hair-stick, that was used by grown up married men. The topknot worn by men is indeed extensively documented as a common and outspread hairstyle in ancient China, where it was known as *ji* (髻). This character, as a component, takes on the original meaning of 'grown up man' or adult person, but when acting as a standalone, it adopts the meaning of 'married person' or **husband.**

Man wearing a topknot

長 長 チョウ なが.い

Person with long hair

long

54 Ⓢ

Originally 镸, a *person* (人 → 儿 → 乂) with loose, **long** hair (镸).

老 老 耂 ① ロウ ① お.い ② ふ.ける

Person with long hair leaning on a walking stick

Old man

① old age

② to grow old

55 Ⓡ Ⓜ

A man with long hair leaning on a cane, the figure of an old man, also suggesting the meaning of **old age.** This character has suffered a steep transformation process. The upper part represents a *person with a long hair* (長 → 镸 → 土), hairstyle typically worn by old sages of ancient China that didn't feel it was necessary anymore to tie their hair in a bun—like the ones married men used to wear, as indicated by the character 夫 (*adult person*). The central stroke ノ depicts an arm holding a cane, and the element 匕 stands for the cane itself (乚) and a very simplified version of the man's body (ノ).

This glyph, when used as a component, omits the lower part 匕, appearing just as 耂, and it is placed on top in the compounds.

 孝 孝 コウ

Old man over a child

filial piety

56 Ⓢ

An *old man* (老 → 耂) above a *child* (子), or the latter below the former, a graphical representation of one of the key concepts of the Ancient China's Confucian morals, termed as **filial piety**, which refers to the subordination that in nuclear families children owe to their parents and, extrapolated to society in general, the subordination that people owe to those above their age.

 而 而 ジ

Person wearing a raincoat

and

57 ㊔ Ⓜ

A *person* (人 → | |) wearing a kind of hat (一) and a cloak or raincoat (冂) to protect himself from the rain.

 文 文 ブン モン ふみ

Tattooed person

writings

58 Ⓡ Ⓜ

A person seen from the front with a kind of design on his highlighted chest, probably some sort of symbolic tattoo. The strokes 亠 represent the head and arms, and the strokes 乂 represent the legs and trunk, given a space for the tattoo pattern. In the modern form of the character, however, only the outline remains, and the design of the tattoo itself has disappeared from the graph. Over time, due to the communicative nature of tribal tattoos or patterns, this glyph's meaning came to be that of 'message', 'letters' and, ultimately, anything related to **writing**.

5. HUMAN MEASURES

One of the last conceptual derivations that we can draw from the human figure is the proportion and measures obtained from it. It is notorious that prior to the international standardization of measures of length, most human groups used the human body as a reference. Chinese characters reflect this fact in two primitive characters. One stands for the span that goes from the head to the feet of a person in an upright position  久, and the other represents the 'length' of the calf of a sitting person  尺.

久

久

キュウ

ク

ひさ.しい

Upright person being measured

long time

59 Ⓜ

Originally 久, the span (丿) covering the distance that goes from the head to the feet of an upright *person* (人 → 入), the longest length within the human body scale. Over time this character expanded the meaning related to the spatial length to indicate also long temporal distances, being this meaning of **long time**, the only one that this character keeps today.

尺

尺

シャク

Calf of a person being measured

Measure

unit of length [~*30 cm*]

60 Ⓡ Ⓢ

The span (㇏) of the lower part of the bent leg of a *sitting person* (尸): the **length** of a calf. When this character acts as a component it may take on the meaning of <u>measure</u> or 'being measured'.

REVIEW ON PEOPLE

1 人欠次匕比化北介亡

2 尸尼丮辰勹包卩卬免巳
巴色

仰

3 女母每乃身了𠫓充子

妄娠姿侮好

4 大夹天立並亢太交夭屰幸執爽夫長
老孝而文

位併妖

5 久尺

HUMAN BODY

1. BONES

In the previous chapter we have seen how the concept of 'people' forms an essential part of the semantic and graphic set of sinitic components and characters. We have seen how people can be divided by age, sex, activity or social position.

Another thing in regard to people that has to be taken into account is their material nature, for a person is inconceivable without his physical body. The physical body can be analyzed from different levels, but it is reasonable to begin with what sustains it upright, the core structure without which the rest of the body would not stand up and could not be articulated: 'bones' 冎, which are of various types, such as the ribs 肉—representing 'meat' or body parts in general—the 'skull' 田, or the 'backbones' 呂.

冎

冎 另

Pile of bones 61 Ⓜ

A <u>pile of bones</u> on top of each other (冂×3).

In some compound this glyph may adopt the simplified form 另.

肉

肉 ニク

月 月

meat 62 Ⓡ 肉 Ⓜ

Body part

A slice of **meat**, probably the ribs of an animal, where 冂 represents the outline and 仌 the visible bones.

As a component, the glyph evolved from 肉 into 月, and ultimately into 月 or 月. When forming part of other characters, this graph expands the meaning of 'meat' into that of <u>body part</u>. Most of the characters that use 肉 (月) as a component usually have, then, a meaning related to the body.

背

背

① ハイ

① せ

② せい

③ そむ.く

Body part 月 *shown by two people that turn their backs away* 北 63

① **back**

② **stature**

③ to turn one's back

肥 肥 ヒ こ.える — *Meat 月 that fits in a big hand 巴* — **to get fat** — 64

 育 育 イク そだ.てる はぐく.む — *Body part becoming a newborn baby* — **to bring up** — 65 Ⓜ

A *body part* (肉 → 月) becoming a *newborn baby* (𠫓). The body part component symbolizes the woman's pregnant belly that generates a new being, a newborn baby who has to be raised and **brought up** henceforth.

 脊 脊 セキ — **spine** — 66

Body part (肉 → 月) made up of a set of bones that pile up one on top of another in an ascending manner (𡗗), the **spine**.

 骨 骨 コツ ほね — *Skeleton* — **bone** — 67 Ⓡ Ⓜ

Body part (肉 → 月) that constitute a *pile of bones* (冎), the skeleton, the **bones** *per se*.

 歹 歹 — *Bone remains* — 68 Ⓡ Ⓜ

Originally 歺, bone remains (⺊ → 一) that have been left on top of a piece of decaying *meat* (肉 → 月 → 夕).

 死 死 シ し.ぬ — *Remnant bones of a person* — **to die** — 69 Ⓜ

The *bone remains* (歹) of a person lying down with is *back* (匕) visible, the body of a person decomposed by the passage of time, the image of **death**. The top line of the component 歹 (*bone remains*) has been extended to cover also the component 匕 (*person on his back*).

囟
囟 田

Skull

70
Ⓜ

The upper part of the <u>skull</u>, seen from above (囗), with visible separations (メ → 十) between the frontal and parietal bones.

This component may appear in the simplified form 田.

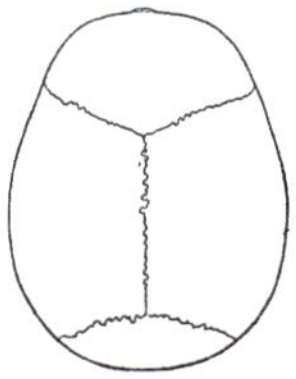

A human skull seen from top

異
異

イ
こと

Person putting on a skull mask
difference

71
Ⓡ
Ⓜ

Originally 異, a *person seen from the front* (大 → 六) putting on, with two raised hands (艸 → 艹), a mask with the appearance of a *skull* (囟 → 田), which makes him look like a **different** being from the ordinary man.

Jade masks from the Neolithic Liangzhu (良渚) culture

禺
禺

グ

Masked dancer

72
Ⓢ

A person who wears a mask with the appearance of a skull and wiggles his trunk and arms, a <u>masked dancer</u> with a strange and peculiar appearance. The upper part of the component, 田, shows the *skull* mask (囟 → 田), whereas the lower part 禸 shows the open arms (冂) and the body making a serpentine movement (厶).

偶 偶 グウ — *Person* 亻 *encountering a masked dancer* 禺 (グ) 73

unexpected

 畏 畏 イ おそ.れる — *Person wearing a skull mask and holding a stick* 74

to fear

A *person* (人 → 儿 → 𧘇) wearing a mask with the appearance of a *skull* (囟 → 田) and holding a club (一) while making threatening gestures causing **fear**. In a similar fashion to the character 辰 (*person holding a tool*), the strokes standing for the stick and the strokes representing the arms and legs of the person have merged into the form 𧘇.

 凶 凶 キョウ — *Open skull* 75 Ⓢ

calamity

A *skull* lacking its upper cover (囟 → 凶), a broken and <u>open skull</u>, a **calamity**.

胸 胸 キョウ むね むな- — *Body part* 月 *leaning* 勹 *towards the organs that otherwise would be unprotected as an open skull* 凶 (キョウ) 76

chest

 呂 呂 ロ — **backbones** [*fig.*] 77 Ⓢ

Two linked vertebrae (口 / 口), a graphical simplification of the **backbones**. The meaning of this character is mostly used in a figurative sense, in contrast to the character 脊 (*spine*), which withholds a literal sense.

侶 侶 リョ — *Person* 亻 *connected to other person like linked backbones* 呂 (ロ) 78

companion

 咼 咼 カ — *Pile of bones and backbones* 79 Ⓢ

A *pile of bones* (冎 → 冎) next to a single *backbone* (呂 → 口).

予 (small: 予) ヨ

Joined vertebrae

beforehand

80 Ⓢ

Two vertebrae graphically joined by a line. The composition of this character is very similar to that of 呂 (*backbones*), but that and this character have evolved differently, perhaps as a result of a need to distinguish both character's different assigned meanings. In the present glyph, the graphic elements depicting the vertebrae (口×2), have been simplified into the glyphs ㄗ and ㇖, and the link between them has been more accentuated with a long stroke 亅. As a standalone character and component, this graph takes on the meaning of **beforehand** or <u>before</u>, perhaps due to a phonetic loan. Nevertheless, this meaning may be associated with the concept of the beforehand need for the existence of a marrow and a connected spinal column in order to make the movement of vertebrate animals possible.

2. HEART

Protected by the thoracic bones, there is one of the most allegorically meaningful organs, the 'heart'  心, which conceptually is almost universally associated with 'feelings', and in the particular case of East Asia, and therefore in the context of Chinese characters, also with the mind.

心 (small: 心) 忄 ⺗

シン

こころ

heart

mind

Feelings

81 Ⓡ Ⓜ

Schematic representation of a heart, with its outline shown by the stroke ㇄ and the aortas, extending outwards, by the strokes ㇒, ㇔ and ㇔. The notion of heart also refers in Chinese and Japanese to the connotation of mind. This character therefore represents both thought and <u>feelings</u>: **heart**-and-**mind**.

When placed on the left of a compound, the glyph gets simplified into 忄 or, occasionally, into ⺗.

忘 (small: 忘) ボウ わす.れる

Perishing 亡 (ボウ) *heart-mind* 心

to forget

82

忙 (small: 忙) ボウ いそが.しい

Heart-mind 忄 *perishing* 亡 (ボウ)

busy

83

84
恣
恣 シ
Subsequent <ruby>次<rt>シ</rt></ruby> *feelings* 心
arbitrary

85
悔
悔 カイ
く.いる
くや.しい
Heart-mind 忄 *of a scruffy woman* <ruby>毎<rt>マイ</rt></ruby>
regretful

86
愚
愚 グ
おろ.か
Masked dancer's <ruby>禺<rt>グ</rt></ruby> *apparent heart-mind* 心
foolish

87 Ⓜ

思
思 シ
おも.う
Skull and heart
to think

Originally 恖 [囟心], the action achieved by the connection established between the mental power of the head—**thinking**—, represented by the *skull* (囟 → 田), and the consciousness, expressed through the feelings and perceptions symbolized by the *heart-mind* (心).

3. EYES

Another fundamental organ of the human body, needed for engaging in the visual nature of kanji, is the 'eye'  目. Eyes are also the focal point around which individual faces arise, for the 'face' is what surrounds the eyes  面. If the face gets a wider contour on which hair can rest, then we can infer the concept of 'head'  首.

88 Ⓡ Ⓜ

目
罒 目
モク
ボク
め
ま-
eye

An **eye**, with its pupil in the center, turned vertically (罒 → 目).

As a component it may sometimes appear in its horizontal, original form: 罒.

89
盲
盲 モウ
Perished <ruby>亡<rt>モウ</rt></ruby> *eye* 目
blind

 見 見 ケン み.る *Person with an open eye* **to see** **to look** 90 Ⓡ Ⓜ

A *kneeling person* (卩 → 儿) with a big *eye* (目) that allows him to **look** around and **see** things.

規 規 キ *Adult person夫 who is looking 見* **norm** 91

 艮 艮 コン *Looking person* *Still person* 92 Ⓢ

The original form of this glyph was 𥃩, the reverse form of 見 (*to look*). It represents a *person turning his back* (匕 → 𠤎) and looking with his *eyes* (目 → 日) at something, suggesting the meaning of a person who is <u>still</u> (while looking at something), not moving.

恨 恨 コン うら.む *Heart-mind 忄 kept still 艮(コン)* **to resent** 93

眼 眼 ガン ゲン まなこ *Part of the eye 目 that seems to stay still 艮(コン)* **eyeball** 94

 眉 眉 ミ ビ まゆ **eyebrow** 95

Bushy **eyebrows** (尸) over an *eye* (目).

 面 面 メン おもて おも- つら **face** [*fig.*] **mask** 96 Ⓢ

The contour (𠀅) surrounding the *eyes* (目), the **face**. The upper part of the contour (丆) appears to be the remainder of a variant of the pictogram where hair could be seen (). The upper and lower strokes of the eye (目, 二) overlap with the adjacent strokes of the contour. The meaning of this character and component is usually taken figuratively, in most cases it refers to surfaces, contours or actions such as facing something. When the character appears alone as a single word, it can also take on the meaning of **mask**.

臣 シン ジン *Eye looking down* 97 Ⓜ

An eye looking downwards. This graph is a derivation of the character 目 (*eye*), now leaning down and slightly deformed. The people who lower their eyes in front of other people are understood here as **vassals** or subjects of other people.

姫 ひめ *Woman 女 looking down 臣* 98

young lady

NOTE A woman looking down as a sign of submission, an image characteristic of a traditional society like that of ancient China in which women and young people had a lower social status than men and older people.

臥 *Person looking down* 99 Ⓜ

Originally 臥, a *person* (人 → 𠂉) *looking downwards with his eye* (臣).

首 ① シュ ② くび ① **head** [*fig.*] ② **neck** 100 Ⓜ

This character originally was the pictographic representation of a detailed head shown in profile. Over time, the shape of the glyph was reduced to an *eye* (目) crowned by a schematic representation of hair (䒑). This sinogram originally had the exclusive meaning of a physical **head**, however, at the present time, such meaning is mostly used figuratively. On the other hand, when the character appears alone as a word, it gets the derived meaning of **neck**.

頁 ケツ *Head* leaf 101 Ⓡ ㊔ Ⓜ

Originally 頁, the body of a *kneeling person* (卩 → 儿 → ハ) on which a big *head*

(首 → 𦣻) is resting. This component emerges as a semantic substitute for 首 (*head*). Both 首 and 頁 take on the meaning of **head**, but the former does it in figurative way and the latter in a literal, physical way. In any case, it is important to note that the present graph never acts as a standalone character with that meaning, but only as a primitive component for compound characters.

頃
頃 ころ — *What is on the back 匕 of the head 頁* — **around** 102

傾
傾 ケイ かたむ.く — *Transformed 化 (カ) head 頁* — **to lean** 103

頬
頬 ほお — *That in the middle of which 夹 is the head 頁* — **cheeks** 104

預
預 ヨ あず.ける — *What is before 予 (ヨ) the head 頁* — **to entrust** 105

4. NOSE, EARS AND HAIR

Besides the eyes, other facial organs related to the senses, such as the 'nose'  自 or the 'ear'  耳, appear within the compositional frame of sinitic characters. In addition, there is the outer element that covers the head, namely the 'hair'  彡, or, in the case of animals, the element that covers the whole body: 'fur'  毛.

自
自 シ ジ みずか.ら — *Nose* — **oneself** 106 Ⓜ

Originally 𦣹, a large <u>nose</u> and its nostrils (𦣹 → 自). This character only takes the meaning of 'nose' when acting as a component. As a standalone character it has the meaning of **self**, probably as an allusion to the characteristic gesture of touching the nose people from East Asian cultural environments make when they point to themselves.

息 107
息
ソク
いき

Nose's 自 feeling 心

breath

SPECIAL READING 息子 [むすこ]: *son*

 108 Ⓡ Ⓜ
耳
耳
ジ
みみ

ear

An **ear** seen from the side, with the outline represented by the encircling strokes 耳, and the inner folds by the straight strokes 二.

恥 109
恥
① チ
① はじ
② は.ずかしい

Ear 耳 listening to the heart-mind 心

① **shame**

② **ashamed**

 110 Ⓡ Ⓜ
彡

Hair

A simple depiction of a bush of hair represented by three slanted lines (㇒×3).

須 111
須
ス

Hair 彡 over the head 頁

required

 112 Ⓢ
毛
毛
モウ
け

fur

Abundant *hair* (彡) or **fur** coming out from what it appears to be the tail of an animal (乚).

尾 113
尾
ビ
お

Fur 毛 coming out from the behinds of a sitting animal 尸

tail

 114 Ⓢ
㐱
㐱
チン

Person with abundant long hair

Aged person

A *person* (人 → 𠆢) with long and abundant *hair* (彡), making an allusion to the idea of an aged person, since, as seen in the character for "old man" (老), long loose hair was associated in ancient China with the elderly.

5. MOUTH

Throughout this chapter we have so far reviewed the bones, heart, eyes, nose, ears and hair, but to finish, we still have to talk about a facial organ of utmost importance in relation to language (and by extension, to thought): the 'mouth' 口, an element that within the sinitic compounds set alludes directly to the notion of 'words'. We will see, then, that in kanji, the element for "mouth" is more closely related to the meaning of "speech" than that of "eating".

Everything related to speech, a primordial element of human social life, can be seen through many analytical spectra, therefore, sometimes, different connotational specifications are required. For example, "word" as a general concept (represented by the 'mouth' just shown) are not the same as specific words pronounced by a moving 'tongue' 舌. Chinese characters can get even more specific and, to express that someone 'says' something, it will be either shown as words coming out of a moving tongue: 言; or as words 'speaking' within the mouth itself: 曰. Finally, when the meanings of certain kanji are supposed to specify that something is 'told' or being addressed to someone in particular, it is done by turning upside down the mouth and the words coming out of it: 亼.

口 — ク / コウ / くち — **mouth** / *Words* — 115 Ⓡ Ⓜ

A big open **mouth**. As a component, this character very often takes on the meaning of things related to speech or words.

吹 — スイ / ふ.く — *Mouth 口 open and exhaling 欠* — **to blow** — 116

唇 — シン / くちびる — *What holds 辰 the mouth 口 together* — **lips** — 117

如 — ジョ / ニョ — *Women 女 and words 口* — **likeness** — 118

司 司 シ *Person depositing words* **ruler** 119 Ⓢ

A *person* (人 → ㇆) who puts *words* (口) down on the rest of the people, a **ruler**.

伺 伺 シ うかが.う *Person* 亻 *below a ruler* 司(シ) **to implore** 120

后 后 コウ *Person depositing words from the other side* **empress** 121

Akin to the character 司 (*ruler*), this glyph depicts a person depositing *words* (口) or rules on people. In this case, the person appears seen *from the back* (匕 → 𠂆), placed in reverse to the aforementioned character, seen from another side. This glyph refers, hence, to an ally of the ruler, as a first lady or **empress** can be.

兄 兄 キョウ ケイ あに *Person pronouncing words* **big brother** 122 Ⓢ

SPECIAL READING お兄さん [おにいさん]: *big brother*

A *person* (人 → 儿) with his *mouth* (口) visibly open, pronouncing some words. A person with the authority to speak with transcendence, someone with the powers to take care of family matters: the firstborn, the **big brother**. When this character acts as a component, the concept of 'big brother' can be understood more broadly as referring to those people who have some authority over others or have a high social position.

呪 呪 ジュ のろ.う *Words* 口 *spoken by big brothers* 兄(キョウ) **to cast a spell** 123

呉 呉 ゴ *Person subjugated to words* Wu [*place name*] 124 Ⓢ

A person bowing his head (𡗗) before *words* (口) pronounced by a leader or ruler. This character thus refers to a subjugated and obedient people and a stable kingdom. This glyph is mainly used to designate different kingdoms that have existed in the central zone of the Chinese coast, in particular the Wu State of the

Spring and Autumn period and the Eastern Wu State of the Three Kingdoms period within Chinese history. This graphically resounding character is also currently used in various Japanese and Chinese place names.

娯 娯 ゴ — 125

Woman 女 subjugated to one's words 呉 (ゴ)

amusement

 舌 舌 ゼツ した — 126 Ⓡ Ⓜ

Tongue moving outside the mouth

tongue

A **tongue** (千) coming out of a *mouth* (口). The tongue looks forked as that of a snake and has two dots in the middle (evolved later into a single straight, crossing line), just to evoke the idea of the movement that the tongue makes while talking.

憩 憩 ケイ いこ.い — 127

Tongue 舌 tasting and nose breathing 息

relaxation

 言 言 訁 — 128 Ⓡ Ⓜ

①② ゲン
①② ゴン
①② い.う
③ こと

Words coming out of a moving tongue

① **to say**
② **to tell**
③ **speech**

This character, in origin, is an evolution of the character 舌 (*tongue*), to which a line at the top was added to suggest words coming out from it. Over time, the strokes representing the moving tongue (千) and the stroke representing the pronounced words (一) merged into four horizontal lines: 三. The meaning of this character encompasses what has to do with **speech**: **saying** and **telling**.

In most compounds, this component appears at the left with the abridged form 訁.

信 信 シン — 129

Person 亻 believing a speech 言

faith

訳 訳 ヤク わけ — 130

Speech 訁 being measured 尺 (シャク)

translation

診
診 シン み.る
Speech 訁 *made to an aged person* 㐱(チン) 131
to diagnose

諮
諮 シ はか.る
Speech 訁 *and subsequent* 次 *words* 口 132
to consult with

詞
詞 シ
Speech's 訁 *ruler* 司(シ) 133
words

誤
誤 ゴ あやま.る
Speech 訁 *of a subjugated person* 呉(ゴ) 134
to make a mistake

話
話 ワ はな.す
Speech 訁 *of the tongue* 舌 135
to speak

曰
曰
Spoken words 136 Ⓜ

An open *mouth* (口) with spoken words inside (一). This glyph has an ideogrammatic composition similar to the character 言 (*to say*), but the words appear here retained inside the mouth instead of coming out of it, for the present character focuses more on the act of the pronunciation of words rather than on the speech that emerges from them.

旨
旨 シ むね
Person over spoken words 137 Ⓢ
principle

A *person on his back* (匕) standing upright over his *spoken words* (曰), reaffirming them. Someone consistent with his **principle**s.

脂
脂 シ あぶら
Meat's 月 *core principle* 旨(シ) 138
fat

詣 ケイ *Religious speech's* 訁 *principles* 旨 139
詣 もう.でる **to make a pilgrimage**

NOTE Originally this character had the connotation of 'accomplishment', in the sense of a *speech* (言 → 訁) whose *principles* (旨) have been demonstrated by action. Over time, however, this general meaning started to be concretized in that of 'religious accomplishment', and more specifically, in Japan, in the accomplishment of a **pilgrimage**, an important religious endeavor within the Japanese shintoist rite.

曷 曷 曷 カツ *Spoken words leaning over a person* 140 Ⓢ
Threatening words

Spoken words (日) *leaning* (勹) over somebody who is threatened to be *buried* (亾 ← 亡).

This glyph appears in an alternative version in some compounds, where the lower part 匃 is replaced by the component 匂 (*person leaning over another person*).

喝 *Words* 口 *that are threatening* 曷カツ 141
喝 カツ **exclamation**

謁 *Speech* 訁 *that is threatening* 曷カツ 142
謁 エツ **audience** (with a superior)

替 替 タイ か.える *Two adults speaking to each other* 143 Ⓜ
to exchange

Two *adults* (夫×2 → 扶) **exchanging** *spoken words* (日).

音 音 オン イン おと ね *Sound emerging from the words that come out of a moving tongue* 144 Ⓡ Ⓜ
sound

This character is a derivation of the character 言 (*speech*), to which a line has been added on top of the "words coming out" (三 + 一 → 立) to emphasize the **sound** that comes from *spoken words* (日).

惷 意 イ オク

Sound of the heart-mind 145 Ⓢ

idea

This character shows a very clear metaphorical description of the represented concept, the *sound* (音) of the *heart-mind* (心), that what is told by the heart (or mind, for that matter): an **idea**.

億 億 オク

One person's 亻 *ideas* 意(オク) 146

hundred million

臆 臆 オク

Bare body part 月 *conceptualized as an idea* 意(オク) 147

timidity

憶 憶 オク

Heart-mind's 忄 *ideas* 意(オク) 148

recollection

甘 甘 日 カン あま.い

Mouth tasting a piece of food 149 Ⓢ

sweet

A *mouth* (廿 ← 口) with a piece of food inside (一) which has an intense or **sweet** flavor. This glyph, of an appearance quite similar to the character 曰 (*spoken words*), keeps its outlining more faithful to the original pictogram (廿 instead of 口) in order be differentiated from said character. In some compounds, nevertheless, the simpler form 曰 is also currently used to represent the meaning of 甘 (*mouth tasting a piece of food*). The stroke in the middle (一) here always represents, in any case, a piece of food rather than words being spoken.

由 由 ユ ユウ ユイ よし

Piece of food entering into the mouth 150 Ⓢ

cause

Originally 由, a piece of food (十 ← ◇) entering the *mouth* (凵 ← 口). Food, nourishment, is represented here ideographically as the source of vital energy, the **cause** of our actions, because without food life and action would not be conceivable.

届
届 とど.ける
Sitting person 尸 bringing food to the mouth 由
to deliver
151

牙
牙 ゲ / ガ / きば
fangs
152 Ⓢ

Schematic representation of two large, crisscrossed **fangs** (匚, 丿亅).

亼
亼
Mouth talking down to someone
153 Ⓡ Ⓜ

An open mouth looking downwards, as the reverse version of the primitive form of the character for "mouth" (𠙵 → 冃 → 亼). A reversed mouth represents somebody talking down to someone, somebody who speaks to another person from a higher position, denoting a sense of power or control.

令
令 レイ
Mouth talking to a kneeling person
command
154 Ⓢ

A *mouth talking down* (亼) to a *kneeling person* (卩 → 卩). Put it another way, **commands** being told to a subject that is in a position of submission.

領
領 リョウ
Commands 令 (レイ) made by the head 頁
dominion
155

命
命 ①② メイ / ② ミョウ / ② いのち
Words 口 that imply commands 令 (レイ)
① **orders**
② **fate**
156

合
合 カツ / ガツ / ゴウ / あ.う
Two open mouths talking to each other
to come together
157 Ⓢ

A *mouth talking* (亼) to another *mouth* (口), two mouths speaking in unison, two people speaking with one voice, people **coming together**.

今 今 コン キン いま

158 Ⓢ

Retained words

now

This character is an ideographic derivation of the component 亼 (*mouth talking*), in which the words represented with a line (一) have got another line added below, which in turn represents a blockade (一 → フ): words <u>retained</u> in an instant, **now**. The ideographic form of this glyph can be thought as a reverse version of the component 曰 (*spoken words*).

吟 吟 ギン

159

Words 口 that become retained 今 (キン)

recital

含 含 ガン ふく.む

160

Words retained 今 (コン) *in the mouth 口*

to contain

念 念 ネン

161 Ⓢ

Retained feelings

sense

Feelings *retained* (今) in the *heart* (心): **sense**s or sentiments.

㑒 㑒 ケン

162 Ⓢ

Mouth talking to people pronouncing words

Authority

Originally 僉, a *mouth talking down* (亼) to *big brothers* (兄×2 → 兄兄 → 吅从 → 央), an ideograph that evokes a sense of an <u>authority</u> greater than the rest.

倹 倹 ケン

163

Person 亻 with authority 㑒 (ケン)

thrifty

REVIEW ON HUMAN BODY

---

1 冎肉育脊骨歹死囟異禺畏凶呂咼予

背肥偶胸脳侶

---

2 心思

忘忙恣悔愚悩

---

3 目見艮眉面臣臣𠂉首頁

盲規恨眼姫頃傾頻預

---

4 自耳彡毛㐱

息恥須尾

---

5 口司后兄呉舌言曰旨曷替音意甘由

牙亼令合今念㑒

吹唇如伺呪娯憩信訳診諮詞誤話脂詣喝謁

億臆憶届領命吟含倹

LIMBS

1. HANDS

So far we have seen how different parts of the body are useful to describe a broad range of human activities. Nevertheless, we still have to analyze a primordial element of the human being, without which it could not perform most of the daily activities. That is the 'hand' 手.

So often is the concept of hand used within Chinese characters compounds that different types of hand positions have also become primordial components on their own. Among these types of hands there is, for example, the outstretched hand 又, which appears 'again' and again holding several kinds of objects, such as a simple stick 丈—which symbolizes an extra 'length' of the reach of a hand —; a stone 父—which symbolizes the craftsmanship of the 'father' of a family —; a writing brush 聿; several tools/weapons such as a 'club' 殳, a 'mace' 殳, or a 'mattock' 攵. Other variations to the pictograph of the hand are, for example, the hand grasping something tightly 丑 or the hand grabbing something 爪, that evokes the shape of claws or 'nails'.

手

手 扌

シュ
て
た-

hand

164
Ⓡ
Ⓜ

The palm of the **hand** with outstretched fingers. The vertical stroke 亅 represents the wrist and the palm proper. The horizontal strokes 三 are a very schematic depiction of five extended fingers.

When this character acts as a component it usually gets simplified to the form 扌 and is placed to the left.

批
批

ヒ

Hand 扌 *comparing* 比 (ヒ) *things*

criticism

165

振
振

シン
ふ.る

Hand 扌 *working with an agrarian tool* 辰 (シン)

to wield

166

抑 **抑**	ヨク おさ.える	*Hand 扌 forcing a person to kneel before another person* 卬 **to suppress**	167
把 **把**	ハ	*Hand 扌 becoming big* 巴 (ハ) **grasp**	168
挟 **挟**	キョウ はさ.む	*Hand 扌 putting something in the middle of other things* 夾 (キョウ) **to insert**	169
拉 **拉**	ラ	*Hand 扌 helping a person to stand up* 立 (リュウ) **abduction**	170

NOTE This character originally had the connotation of someone stretching his or her hand in order to help someone—probably a child—to stand and walk. In Japanese the meaning of this character later came to refer to 'attraction' (the outstretched hand that attracts the child), and afterwards it derived to the negative sense of 'forced attraction' or **abduction**, which is the only meaning of the character that is currently used in contemporary Japanese.

抗 **抗**	コウ	*Hand 扌 reacting as it moves towards the ground* 亢 (コウ) **counteraction**	171
摯 **摯**	シ	*Hand 手 taking command* 執 **earnest**	172
扶 **扶**	フ	*Hand 扌 of an adult person* 夫 (フ) **aid**	173
択 **択**	タク	*Hand 扌 measuring* 尺 (シャク) *something* **selection**	174
拐 **拐**	カイ	*Hand 扌 taking a pile of bones* 另 → 另 **kidnapping**	175

看 看 カン 176

Hand 手 → 龵 over the eye

watching

括 括 カツ 177

Hand 扌 on the tongue 舌(ゼツ)

constriction

指 指 ①②シ ①ゆび ②さ.す 178

Hand's 扌 functional principle 旨(シ)

① **finger**
② **to point**

掲 掲 ケイ かか.げる 179

Hand 扌 that is threatening 曷カツ

to put up a notice

NOTE Originally it referred to warnings or announcements made with hand gestures. Later, due to the semantic derivation, this character started to refer to warnings or **notices** that are hung in posters.

抽 抽 チュウ 180

Hand 扌 taking out food from the mouth 由(ユウ)

extraction

拾 拾 シュウ ジュウ ひろ.う 181

Hands 扌 coming together 合

to pick up

捻 捻 ネン 182

Hand's 扌 senses 念(ネン) *intensified*

wrench

 失 失 シツ うしな.う 183 Ⓢ

Hand dropping something

to lose something

Originally [illegible], a hand (手 → 龵 → 夫) dropping an object (乙 → ノ) that ends up being **lost**.

又 又 𠂇 彐

また

Outstretched hand

again

184 Ⓡ Ⓜ

An <u>outstretched hand</u> with open fingers in position to grasp, touch or manipulate something. This schematic character, whose strokes represent an upwardly inclined hand with three simplified fingers, gets sometimes even more schematic when acting as a component, adopting the form 𠂇 which is placed at the top of the compounds. Additionally, in a few other compounds, the original tilted form 又 becomes horizontal: 彐. This glyph appears most frequently acting as a component with the meaning of 'outstretched hand', however, it also takes a place in the list of *jōyō* kanji as a standalone character with the meaning of **again**. This latter meaning may be related to the figurative idea of an added aiding outstretched hand that can be used again and again.

右 右

ウ
ユウ
みぎ

Hand outstretched to the mouth

right hand side

185 Ⓜ

An *outstretched hand* (又 → 𠂇) reaching the *mouth* (口), indicating the action of taking food to the mouth while eating, an action that most people perform with their **right hand**.

及 彶 及

キュウ
およ.ぶ

Outstretched hand touching a person

to reach out

186 Ⓢ

An *outstretched hand* (又) **reaching** a *person* (人 → ⺈). The original form of this character, still used occasionally as a component, is 彶, in which the outstretched hand is shown horizontally (彐 → 彐). When the character acts as a standalone, however, it takes the form 及, in which the hand is shown tilted (又).

急 急

ギュウ
いそ.ぐ

Person reaching out 彶 (チュウ) *his heart-mind* 心

to urge

187

吸 吸

キュウ
す.う

Mouth 口 *reaching out* 及 (キュウ) *to something*

to suck

188

扱 扱 あつか.う 189

Hand 扌 reaching a person 及

to deal with

 𠬝 190 Ⓜ

Kneeling person held by an outstretched hand

A *kneeling person* (卩) being captured and <u>held</u> by an *outstretched hand* (又).

報 報 ① ホウ ② むく.いる 191

Announced fortune 幸 of a held person 𠬝

① **to report**
② **to recompense**

服 服 フク 192

Body parts 月 held by an outstretched hand 𠬝

subjugation
clothing

NOTE **Clothing** understood as an object that touches the body and is held by it.

 奴 奴 ド 197 Ⓢ

Woman held by an outstretched hand

servant

A *woman* (女) being controlled by an *outstretched hand* (又), referring to a maid or female **servant**.

怒 怒 ド いか.る おこ.る 194

Servant's 奴 (ド) feelings 心

to get angry

 妻 妻 サイ つま 195 Ⓢ

Woman controlled by an outstretched hand

wife

Graphic composition that represents, literally, a *woman* (女) held by her hair (十) with an *outstretched hand* (彐 ≈ 又), in a figurative representation of a woman under control, a **wife** of the old times. The conceptual graphic composition of this character is similar to that of the character 毎 (*scruffy woman*).

有 **有**

ユウ
ウ
あ.る

196 Ⓜ

Outstretched hand holding a piece of meat

to have

An *outstretched hand* (又 → ナ) holding tight a piece of *meat* (肉 → 月 → 月), taking possession of it, **having** it.

臤 **臤**

ケン

197 Ⓢ

Eye touched by an outstretched hand

Delicate

An *eye looking down* (臣) that is being touched by an *outstretched hand* (又). This ideogram suggests the idea of something very <u>delicate</u> or fragile.

腎 **腎**

ジン

198

Delicate 臤 (ケン) *body part* 月

kidney

取 **取**

シュ
と.る

199 Ⓢ

Ear held by an outstretched hand

to take

An *outstretched hand* (又) grabbing an *ear* (耳), evoking the idea of a child being **taken** by the ear while being scolded.

丈 **丈**

ジョウ
たけ

200 Ⓜ

Outstretched hand holding a stick

length

An *outstretched hand* (又 → メ) holding a <u>stick</u> (一) that extends the **length** of the reach of said hand.

吏 **吏**

リ

201 Ⓜ

Words and sticks acting together

government official

A person that symbolically holds with his outstretched hand a *stick* (丈) and *words* (口), a person with the power of speech—represented by the mouth—and the power of coercion—represented by the stick. A person with great power, like a government official.

202

使 使 シ つか.う

Person 亻 acting as a government official 吏

to utilize

---

203 Ⓢ

君 君 ① クン ①② きみ

Guiding with words and a stick

① **mister**

② **you**

A hand holding a *stick* ((彐 + ノ) → 尹 ≈ 丈)) and a mouth pronouncing *words* (口). Being an ideogram with a graphical formation similar to the character 吏 (*government official*), this glyph also suggests the idea of a man or **mister** who leads with the power of speech—represented by the mouth—and the power of coercion—represented by the stick. The meaning of **you** is a semantic derivation as the word for 'mister' was used formally to call other people. Nowadays, however, this personal pronoun is used rather in a casual way in Japanese.

204

史 史 シ

Outstretched words

history

An *outstretched hand* (又 → メ) holding *words* (口), or put it another way, words that are chosen to be spread or outstretched: official chronicles, **history**.

---

205 Ⓢ

父 父 フ ちち

Hand holding a stone

father

SPECIAL READING お父さん [おとおさん]: *father*

An *outstretched hand* (又 → 乂) holding a stone used as a tool (丿), a representation of the hand of a man with responsibilities like the **father** of a family.

---

206 Ⓜ

聿 聿

Hand holding a brush

An *outstretched hand* (彐) holding a brush in vertical position, depicted by its handle (丨) and its bristles (二).

書 書 ショ か.く — *Hand holding a brush 聿 → 聿 that generates spoken words 曰* — 207

to write

 事 事 ジ ズ こと — 208

What can be written and told

affair

Something worthy of being written by a hand holding a *brush* (聿 → 事 → 事) or told through *words* (口): a particular event or an **affair**. The graphical composition of this character is very similar to that of the character 吏 (*government official*), but in this case, the hand, instead of holding a stick that reaches out longer distances, holds a writing brush. This subtle difference can be distinguished in the original script by a small stroke added in the upper part symbolizing the brush, analogous to the strokes of the component 聿 (*a hand holding a brush*), but turned upside down (聿 → 事). In the modern version of the character, such difference disappears (because the two bristles of the brush have merged into one), but two different compositional glyphs are kept for the hand element (⺕, 又) in order to differentiate the meanings.

 𠬶 シン — *Hands holding a club* — 209 Ⓢ

This pictogram originally depicts an *outstretched hand* (又) grabbing a kind of <u>club</u> with several spikes (⺕) by its handle (冖). The element ⺕, however, is very similar to the component for "outstretched hand" (⺕), hence letting the character being interpreted as the image of two hands (⺕, 又) holding a club (冖). Be it as it may, the concept represented by this character is that of a weapon used in attack.

侵 侵 シン おか.す — *Person 亻 using a club 𠬶 (シン)* — 210

to raid

 殳 殳 — 211 Ⓡ Ⓜ

Hand holding a mace

Strike

Originally 𠘧, an *outstretched hand* (又) gripping a <u>mace</u> (口 → 几) that can be used to <u>strike</u> something.

This component is always placed to the right in the compounds.

股 コ *Body part 月 that used to be struck 殳 in petty punishments.* 212

股 また **thigh**

設 セツ *Speech 訁 and maces 殳* 213

設 もう.ける **to establish**

NOTE It originally referred to the **establish**ment of military camps or new settlements, planned through a *speech* (言 → 訁) and defended with weapons such as *maces* (殳).

投 トウ *Hand 扌 throwing a mace 殳* 214

投 な.げる **to throw**

 攵 *Hand holding a mattock* 215 Ⓡ

攵 *Hit* Ⓜ

Originally 攴, an *outstretched hand* (又) holding a rudimentary <u>mattock</u> (⺊ → ノ) used to <u>hit</u> something. This glyph eventually became simplified into 攵 as its upper strokes merged. This component's structure and semantic scope is clearly analogous to that of 殳 (*hand holding a mace*).

This component always appears in the right side of the compounds.

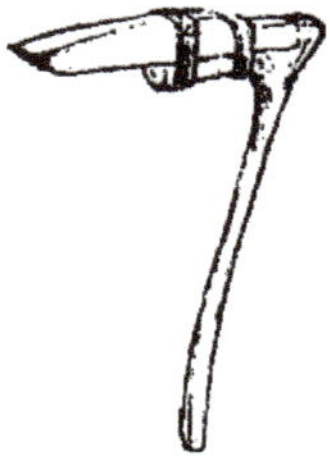

An ancient mattock, called ben (錛) *in Chinese*

教 ①② キョウ *Hits 攵 used to pass knowledge from elder men to children 孝(コウ)* 216

教 ① おし.える ② おそ.わる

① **to teach**

② **to be taught**

---

217 Ⓜ

敏 敏 ビン

Scruffy woman being hit

sensibility

A hand *hitting* (攵) a *scruffy woman* (毎), wounding her **sensibility**.

---

218 Ⓢ

𢿱 テツ

Child brought up by hitting

A child that is being *brought up* (育) by *hitting* (攵).

219

撤 撤 テツ

Hand 扌 *that takes a child off from being brought up by hitting* 𢿱テツ

withdrawal

220

双 双 ソウ ふた

Two outstretched hands

pair

A **pair** of *outstretched hands* (又×2) showcasing their similarity.

---

221 Ⓢ

友 友 ユウ とも

Two hands acting together

friend

Two *outstretched hands* ((又 → ナ), 又)) that act in the same way, two cooperating hands: **friend**ly hands. The pictographic composition of this character is actually the same as the character 双 (*pair*), but the current form of the present character developed in order to differentiate its meaning.

222

髪 髪 ハツ かみ

Long 長 → 镸 *hair* 彡 *stroked by two hands* 友ハツ

hair (of the head)

223

抜 抜 バツ ぬ.く

Hand 扌 *held by two other hands* 友ハツ

to pull out

224

摂 摂 セツ

Hand placed behind the ear to capture the sound

vicarious

Originally 攝, a *hand* (手 → 扌) placed behind the *ear* (耳) in order to capture the sound of a conversation that is **vicariously** listened to. The action of capturing the sound is reinforced by the addition of a simplified version of the component for a "pair of hands" (双 → 㐅).

丑 丑 チュウ

Hand gripping something tightly

ox sign (Chinese zodiac)

225 ㊔ Ⓢ

An *outstretched hand* (彐) with its fingers slightly bent, pointing downwards (丨), exerting an additional force on an object that is implicitly gripped.

寸 寸 スン

Wrist

Work

unit of length [~ *3 cm*]

226 Ⓡ Ⓜ

An *outstretched hand* (𠂇 → 寸) with its wrist visibly pointed out by a dot (丶). When this character works as a component, its meaning gets amplified to the scope of actions that imply hand movements made by the wrist, so to speak, any kind of manual work. On the other hand, when acting as a standalone it adopts the connotation of a unit of **length** (3 cm) that approximately matches the average length of a human wrist.

辱 辱	ジョク はずかし.める	*Work* 寸 *with an agrarian tool* 辰 **to disgrace**	227
耐 耐	タイ た.える	*Person with a raincoat* 而 *working* 寸 *under the rain* **to withstand**	228
対 対	タイ ツイ	*Writing* 文 *versus manual work* 寸 **opposite**	229
肘 肘	ひじ	*Body part* 月 *enabling work* 寸 **elbow**	230
討 討	トウ う.つ	*Speech* 訁 *over work* 寸 **to subdue**	231

付 付 フ つ.く

Person and his work

to be attached

232 Ⓢ

An ordinary *person* (人 → 亻) **attached** to his *work* (寸) in order to earn a living.

射 射 シャ い.る

Gestation of work

to emit

233 Ⓢ

An ideographic character that metaphorically represents the idea of *gestation* (身) produced by *work* (寸), i.e., the product of work, something that is launched or **emit**ted into the market.

謝 謝 シャ あやま.る

Speech 言 *being formally emitted* 射 (シャ)

to apologize

234

NOTE Originally referring to the issuance of some kind of official note of gratitude or **apology**.

廾 廾 ハ 臼

Two hands

235 Ⓡ 廾 Ⓜ

Originally 収, both a left outstretched hand (ㄗ) and a right *outstretched hand* (又) looking upwards. Two raised hands, as in the stance of holding or raising something. Over time, the strokes of this component got simplified and adopted the form 廾 in most compounds. This simplification can go even further into just two strokes with the form ハ that is found in several characters. This component also has a primitive variant with the hands placed in a horizontal position analogue to the form ヨ of the component 又 (*outstretched hand*). This form is 臼, which is attested in the original versions of many characters but does not remain with the same strokes in most contemporary compounds.

廾 虫

Two hands holding a person

236 Ⓜ

Originally 臾, *two hands* (廾 ≈ 臼 → 口) holding a *person* (人 → 丄).

共
共 共
キョウ
とも

Four hands acting together

together

237 Ⓢ

Originally 𦧵, four intertwined and *outstretched hands* (又 ≈ 屮×4 → 艸×2 → 卄 + ハ) acting **together**.

If this component appears in the upper part of a compound, it takes the compressed form 共.

供
供

① キョウ
② ク
① とも
② そな.える

Person 亻 acting together 共 (キョウ)

① **follower**
② **to provide**

238

恭
恭

キョウ
うやうや.しい

*Heart-mind ⺗ shared together 共*キョウ

respectful

239

关
关

Two hands grabbing a knob
Opening

240 Ⓜ

A schematic depiction of *two hands* (廾 → 大) grasping the knob (丷) of a door. The meanings related to this component usually suggest some kind of opening or new start.

咲
咲

さ.く

Words 口 describing a new opening 关

to bloom

241

保
保

ホ
たも.つ

Person carrying a child

to protect

242 Ⓢ

A *person* (人 → 亻) holding a *child* (呆 ← 子) with *two hands* (廾 → ハ), **protecting** him.

承
承

ショウ
うけたまわ.る

Two hands rising a baby

to accept

243

Two hands ((廾 ≈ 収) → フ二〈) raising a baby *child* (子), showing the **acceptance** of his birth.

爪 爪 爫 つめ つま- *Grabbing hand* **nail** 244 Ⓡ Ⓜ

A hand with three stylized stretched fingers pointing downwards, suggesting the action of grabbing something. As a standalone this character takes on the meaning of **nail**. The idea of grabbing something, thanks to the form the fingers take, can be easily associated to an animal's claw or, by extension, the nails.

As a component this character usually gets simplified into 爫.

妥 妥 ダ *Hand grabbing 爫 a woman 女* **gentle** 245

孚 孚 *Hand grabbing a child* 246 Ⓜ

Pictograph of a hand *grabbing* (爪 → 爫) a small *child* (子).

爰 爰 エン *Two hands caressing a person* 247 Ⓢ

A hand *grabbing* (爪 → 爫) a person who is being *enlightened* (天 → 𠂇) by the caresses of another *outstretched hand* (又).

媛 媛 エン *Woman 女 being caressed 爰(エン)* (a) beauty 248

PLACE NAME USAGE 愛媛県 [えひめけん]: *Ehime Prefecture*

援 援 エン *Hand 扌 that caresses 爰(エン)* **assistance** 249

奚 ケイ *Hand grabbing an adult man* 250 Ⓢ

A hand *grabbing* (爪 → 爫) an *adult person* (夫).

㥯	オン		*Heart held by two hands*	251 Ⓢ

Two *outstretched hands grabbing* ((爪 → ⺤) + (又 ≈ ⺕ → 彐) → 爫彐) a *heart* (心), probably figuratively referring to a state of restlessness or fear that makes the individual intuitively take his <u>hands to the heart and hold it</u>, as if it were to prevent it to come out of the chest.

	印 印	イン しるし	*Hand grabbing a kneeling person* **mark**	252

A hand *grabbing* (爪 → ⺕) a subservient *kneeling person* (卩) in order to leave a **mark** on him.

	爭 争	ソウ あらそ.う	*Two hands fighting over a stick* **to fight**	253 Ⓡ Ⓢ

Originally 爭, two hands *grabbing* (爪 → ⺤ → ⺈) + ⺕ ≈ 又) a rope or stick (亅), **fighting** over it, like in a contending game of thug of war.

2. ARMS

A complementary element to the hands is their prolongation, the arms, that can appear both in a bent position 力—which highlights muscular 'strength'; or in an outstretched position 九, which highlights its reach.

	力 力	リキ リョク ちから	*Arm* **strength**	254 Ⓡ Ⓜ

A bent <u>arm</u> with an outstretched hand at its end. The left part of the character is visibly a deformation of the "outstretched hand" component (又 → ナ → ナ), while the right part shows a slightly bent arm (𠃌). This arm posture seems to evoke the image of a biceps increasing its volume as the arm bents, making an allusion to physical **strength**.

勉 勉 ベン 255

Avoided 免 (メン) physical strength 力

studious

努 努 ド つと.める 256

Strength 力 of a servant 奴 (ド)

to strive

効 効 コウ き.く 257

Interchanging 交 (コウ) strengths 力

to be effective

加 加 カ くわ.える 258 Ⓢ

Strength and words

to add

The physical *strength* (力), complemented by the power of *words* (口), the **addition** of two different but complementary forces.

劦 劦 キョウ 259 Ⓢ

Several arms

Several *arms* (力×3) working together.

脅 脅 キョウ おど.す おびや.かす 260

Several arms 劦 (キョウ) over meat 月

to threaten

脇 脇 わき 261

Body part 月 placed next to the arms 劦

beside
armpit

九 九 キュウ ク ここの.つ 262 Ⓢ

Outstretched arm

nine

In this character, which is the counterpart of the character 力 (*arm*), the arm gets unbent (𠃌 → ㇈) while the muscle force gets weakened, indicating its extension and outstretching. As a standalone character the meaning of **nine** is taken, most probably due to a phonetic borrowing. It's not hard to imagine, however, the outstretched arm as a metaphor to represent the odd number that is "about to reach" the "round" number that is ten.

263

尻

尻 しり

Sitting person's 尸 bottom pointed out by an outstretched arm 九

buttocks

SPECIAL READING 尻尾 [しっぽ]: *tail*

264

喪

喪 ソウ も

Words caught by a buried person's outstretched hand

mourning

Several **mourning** *words* (口×2) reached by the *outstretched arm* (九 → 十) of a buried person (亡 ← 亾 → 𠄌).

---

265 Ⓡ ㊔ Ⓜ

尤

尤 ユウ

Person raising his arm

plausible

A *person* (人 → 儿) rising his arm and hand (ナ).

3. FEET

Feet, as expected, complete the section dedicated to the limbs, and they appear in several forms and shapes. A foot stepping over the ground 止 tells us about the idea of making a 'footstep', implying also the idea of 'stopping' on something. If the stepping 'foot is turned upside down' 夂, it reinforces the notion of immobility. Conversely, movement is represented by two feet acting together, be it as 'two moving feet' ' 舛, 'two feet going upwards' 癶, and also by a 'foot coming out and going forward' 㞢 and a 'foot going backward' 帀.

---

266 Ⓡ Ⓜ

止

止 ⻊ シ と.まる

Footstep

to stop

Stylized image of the print of a footstep on the ground. The lower stroke 一 represents the mark of the sole of the foot, whereas the upper strokes 丨 and ト represent the mark of the toes. The current standalone meaning of **to stop** is directly related to the concept of footstep: a step that stops still on the ground for a moment.

As a component this glyph can take the simplified form ⻊.

企 キ 267
企 くわだ.てる
Person 人 → 𠆢 making footsteps 止
to undertake

肯 268
肯 コウ
Footsteps 止 over meat 月
assertion

此 シ 269 ㊔ Ⓢ
此
Footsteps left behind
this

Footsteps (止) left behind by a person who walks away *turning his back* (匕).

先 セン 270 Ⓢ
先 さき
Person walking on another one's footsteps
previous

A *person* (人 → 儿) walking in the *footsteps* (止 → 𠂉) **previous**ly left by another person.

走 ソウ 271 Ⓡ Ⓜ
走 はし.る
Person wiggling over his feet
to run

Originally 𧺆, a person *wiggling* (夭 → 土) over his own *footsteps* (止 → 龰) as he **runs**.

趣 シュ 272
趣 おもむき
Running 走 after something in order to take it 取 (シュ)
preference

足 ①② ソク 273 Ⓡ Ⓜ
足 𧾷 ① あし
② た.す
① **foot and leg**
② **to add up**

A *foot* (龰 ← 止) and a leg extending upwards to the knee, which is stylized as 口. This character means both **foot and leg**, as so does the Japanese word あし. The additional meaning of **to add up** comes from the image of the leg 'added' to the foot.

When this component is placed on the left, it takes the following narrowed form: 𧾷.

促
促 ソク うなが.す

Person's 亻 foot and leg 足 (ソク)

to press [*fig.*]

274

捉
捉 ソク と.らえる

Hand 扌 grabbing an ankle placed between the foot and the leg 足 (ソク)

to capture

275

夊
夊

Foot turned upside down

Still foot

276 Ⓡ Ⓜ

A foot looking downwards. This is the character 止 (*footstep*) turned upside down, suggesting immobility in contrast to the movement evoked by the footprint of the foot looking upwards. This component is used to evoke the image of standing, still feet.

夏
夏 カ ゲ なつ

Head 頁 → 百 kept still 夊 due to the heat

summer

277

舛
舛

Two moving feet

278 Ⓡ Ⓜ

A right *foot turned upside down* (夊 → 夕) and a left foot pointed to the opposite direction (㐄 → 㐄), suggesting the idea of two moving feet.

癶
癶

Two feet going upwards

279 Ⓡ Ⓜ

The left and right feet ((㞢 + 止) → 址 → 癶) looking upwards: two feet moving in an upward direction.

㞢
㞢
士 之

シ

Foot coming out and moving forward

of

280 ㊔ 之 Ⓢ

A *footstep* (㞢 ≈ 止) coming out from the ground (一) in order to start a path forward.

The original form 㞢 gets simplified in the compounds into 士 or further into

之.

---

281 Ⓢ

志 **志** シ こころざ.す

Heart-mind moving forward

to intend

Originally 㞢, *heart-mind* (心)—feelings and thought—that come out and moves *forward* (㞢 → 士) when having an **intention.**

282

誌 **誌** シ

Speech's 言 *recorded intentions* 志

document

---

283 Ⓢ

寺 **寺** ジ てら

Work moving forward

temple

A place where *work* (寸) is carried out in a constant and *forward* (㞢 → 土 → 士) manner. In origin this character probably was making reference to some kind of administrative institution or working field, but over time it was taken to designate religious temples—more concretely Buddhist **temples**—where, in any case, manual work is constantly required.

284

侍 **侍** ジ さむらい

Person 亻 *of a temple* 寺

warrior
samurai

285

詩 **詩** シ

Speech 言 *made in temples* 寺

poem

286

持 **持** ジ も.つ

Hand 扌 *working in a temple* 寺

to hold

287

乏 **乏** ボウ とぼ.しい

Blocked foot

limited

An obstacle (㇒) that **limits** the movement of a foot wanting to move *forward* (㞢 → 之).

帀 帀 帀 | *Foot moving backward* | 288 Ⓜ

A foot moving forward turned upside down (㞢 → 帀), suggesting a returning or backward movement.

 𠂤 スイ | *Footprint* *Traces* | 289 Ⓡ 𠂤 Ⓢ

Schematic representation of a footprint or traces left on the ground, where only the more prominent parts of the foot's plant (𠂤) and toes (‐) remain visible.

師 師 シ | *Traces* 𠂤 (スイ) *to which one goes back* 帀 | 290

teacher

REVIEW ON LIMBS

手失又右及𠬝奴妻有臤取丈吏君史
父聿事𠬶殳攵敏散双友摂丑寸付射
1 廾虫共关保承爪孚爰奚急印争

批振抑把挟拉抗摯扶択拐看括指掲抽拾捻
急吸扱報服怒腎使書侵股設投教撤髪抜辱
耐対肘討謝供恭咲妥媛援

力加劦九喪尤
2
勉努効脅脇尻

止此先走足夂舛癶屮志寺乏帀白
3
企肯趣促捉夏誌侍詩持師

THE NATURAL REALM

THE NATURAL REALM

Once we have dealt with the *self*, people and the human body, it makes sense to look at the surroundings, the most immediate thing encompassing the life of man: Nature.

Ancient people divided nature into the intangible and the tangible. The intangible is essential to maintain the spiritual and divine order and the tangible is essential to maintain the material and economic order. Both aspects were considered indispensable for keeping social stability.

Within the intangible aspect there are not only gods and divine power, but also time, meteorology, astronomy and what is related to divination, a fundamental part of life at the time when Chinese characters were created, and something to which Chinese characters themselves owe their development.

The tangible aspect includes everything related to plants and animals, elements that are paramount for the survival of any society.

Elements of nature—earth, water, fire, air (or energy)—stars, plants and trees, oviparous animals and mammals, all of them are extensively present within the Chinese characters corpus. All these glyphs are grouped, within the Natural Realm, into the following three groups: Characters used to represent the active *elements* of nature, characters used to represent *plants* and trees, and lastly, characters used to represent *animals* and some of their by-products.

ELEMENTS	PLANTS	ANIMALS
1. Energy	1. Small Plants	1. Oviparous
2. Stars	2. Trees	2. Mammals
3. Water	3. Grains	3. Animal Manipulation
4. Fire		4. Silk Production
5. Earth		
6. Heaven		

THE NATURAL REALM AT A GLANCE

ELEMENTS	PLANTS	ANIMALS

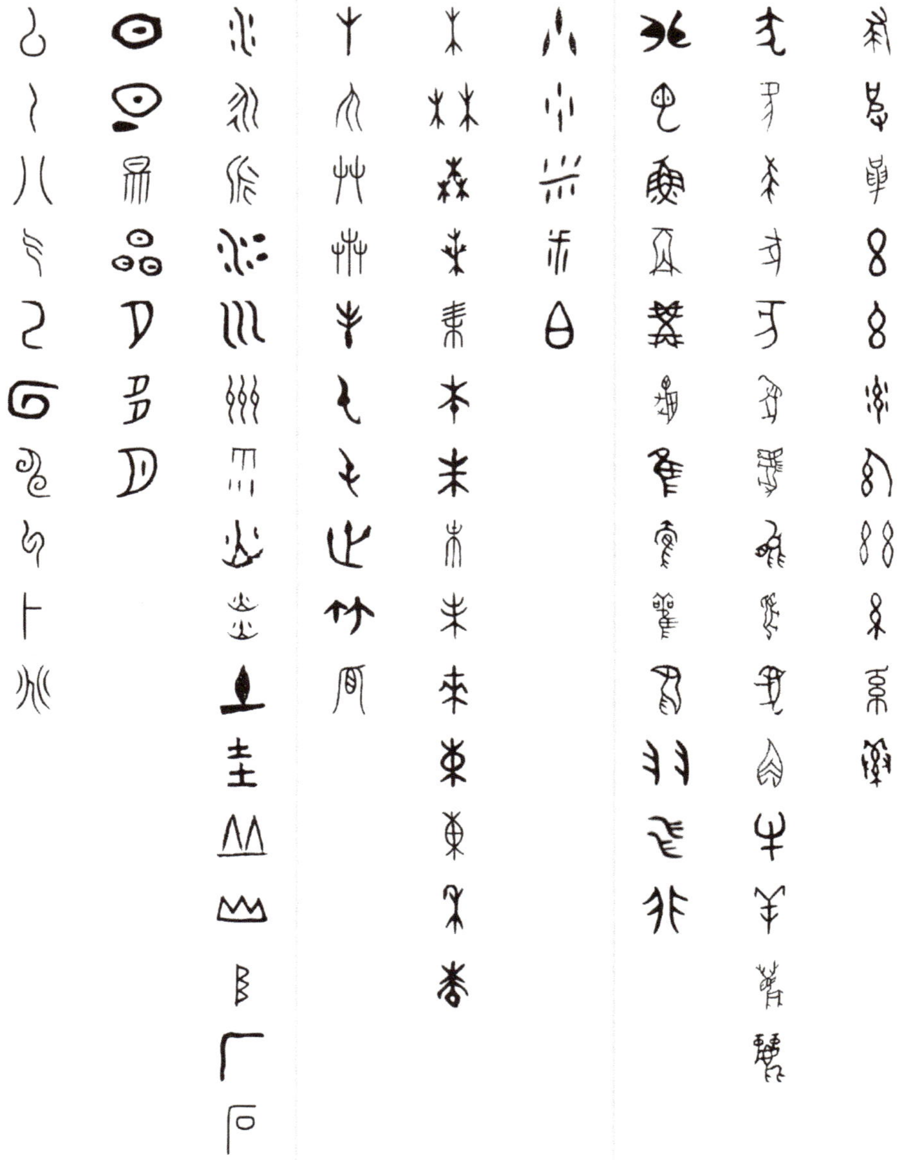

ELEMENTS OF NATURE

1. ENERGY

Energy was understood by ancient people, at least by the ancient people that created the Chinese characters, as the essential intangible element endowing cognitive beings and natural phenomena with spiritual substance and physical force. Energy, therefore, can be understood as a conceptualization of the spirit or *anima*, a spirit that is invisible and intangible but also very meaningful. But how can one represent what cannot be seen nor touched? Chinese characters give an answer by representing energy as a flow of movement, depicted by abstract lines.

The movement of energy is thus represented by continuous lines of different paths, and different types of energy movements are used to represent different ideas. Among those movements there is the 'flowing energy' 厶, or the primeval energy; 'energy being unfolded' 乚, alluding to something that can be easily reached; energy spread into two different directions 八, which represents the something that is 'distributed'; ' energy circulating on a fixed path 己, which represents the conscious 'self'; energy making a rotation 回, which depicts a 'revolving' movement; or even 'intertwined energies' 丩, which represents confluence.

 厶 厶 — *Flowing energy* — 291 Ⓜ

Symbolic representation of energy <u>flowing</u> freely while revolving around itself.

仏 **仏** ブツ ほとけ — *Person 亻 filled with flowing energy 厶* — **Buddha** — 292

勾 **勾** コウ — *Leaning person's 勹 flowing energy 厶* — **slanted** — 293

払 **払** フツ はら.う — *Hand 扌 flowing 厶* — **to clear away** — 294

弁 **弁** ベン

Flowing energy 厶 *of hands* 廾

delivery

295

 以 **以** イ

Flowing energy linked to a person

by means of

296 Ⓢ

Flowing energy (厶 → 𠃊) next to a *person* (人 → 人), implying that the former revolves through the latter. This character makes reference, therefore, to the intangible energy that makes people move and act. The representation of energy along a man is thus used here to indicate the meaning of 'means' or **by means of.**

似 **似** ジ に.る

Person's 亻 *energy linked to another person* 以(イ)

to resemble

297

 鬼 **鬼** キ おに

Bare skull and flowing energy

ghost

298 Ⓡ Ⓜ

Flowing energy (厶) of a *person* (人 → 儿) whose *skull* (囟 → 甶) is visibly exposed. The bare skull implies a deceased person. A deceased person who still has energy flowing through, that is, a **ghost**.

 台 **台** タイ ダイ

Energy in the mouth

Contained energy

podium

299 Ⓢ

Flowing energy (厶) <u>contained</u> within the *mouth* (口), possibly referring in origin to breath: the physical representation of numinous energy. This graph, when used as a standalone character, is taken by its phonetic value for the meaning of **podium**, which, however, can easily be associated with the original representational meaning by thinking of podiums as places that enhance, thanks to their elevated place, the voice—which can be understood in turn as energy contained in the mouth.

始 **始** シ はじ.まる

Woman 女 *containing something* 台(タイ) *inside*

to start

300

NOTE In clear reference to pregnancy and the **start** of new life.

胎 **胎** タイ — *Body part 月 containing energy 台* 301

womb

怠 **怠** タイ / おこた.る / なま.ける — *Contained 台 heart-mind 心* 302

to neglect

乙 乚 乙 オツ — *Unfolded energy* 303 Ⓡ Ⓜ

second (2nd)

Current of energy that appears in an unfolded form: 乚; in contrast to the representation of primeval flowing energy that appears revolving on itself: 厶. The original grapheme 乚 is transformed into the more complex form 乙 when the character acts as a standalone, perhaps to make it more aesthetically and proportionally fit to other characters. The meaning of the character when it appears as a standalone is that of **second** in rank, meaning that originates from the Sinitic ordinal system known as Heavenly Stems (天干), in which ten concrete primitive characters are used to designate different ordinal positions, among which 乙 takes the second one, after 甲 (コウ) and before 丙 (ヘイ). The adoption of this graph to mean 'second' may be due to the fact that unfolded energy can be understood as the second step of creation after the energy revolving on itself (厶).

孔 **孔** コウ — *Child 子 unfolding energy 乚* 304

Confucius

乱 **乱** ラン / みだ.す — *Tongue 舌 unfolding energy 乚* 305

to disarrange

NOTE Ideographically pointing to the fact that careless speech can disturb any situation.

乳 **乳** ニュウ / ちち / ち — *Hand grabbing a child 孚 in order to unfold energy 乚 to him* 306

milk

breast

也 也 チ — *Mouth unfolding energy* 307 ㊔ Ⓢ

Extended energy

to be

Originally 㔾, a *mouth* ((廿 ← 口) → 㔾) *unfolding energy* (乚) that extends through continuous breath.

他 他 タ ほか — 308

A person's 亻 social extension 也

other(s)

 八 ハチ や.つ よう — 309 Ⓡ Ⓜ

Distributed energy

eight

Two streams of energy spreading into diverging paths (丿, ㇏), being distributed into different parts. This sinogram, when used as standalone, takes on the meaning of **eight**, probably due to a phonetic loan. The number eight, nevertheless, can be easily associated with the notion of distribution thanks to its high divisibility.

When this character acts as a component, it is usually simplified in ハ or ソ, which is just a reduction in length of the strokes of the original graph.

 亦 亦 エキ — 310 ㊔ Ⓜ

Person's distributed energy

also

Originally 亦, a *person seen from the front* (大 → 亣) consciously or unconsciously *distributing energy* (八 → ハ).

恋 恋 レン こい — 311

Person distributing 亦 *his feelings* 心

endearment

跡 跡 セキ あと — 312

Feet's 𧾷 *energy distributed by a person* 亦

tracks

変 変 ヘン か.える — 313

Man's distributed energy 亦 *becoming still* 夂

to change

 兑 兑 エツ — 314 Ⓢ

Energy distributed through words pronounced by a person

Exposure

Energy distributed (八 → ﾉ) by *big brothers* (兄), indicating that something becomes exposed as big brothers or people with a high social position or authority speak to society.

315
脱 脱 ② ダツ ① ぬ.ぐ

Body parts 月 *being exposed* 兑(エツ)

① to undress
② to get rid of

316
悦 悦 エツ

Heart-mind 忄 *that is exposed* 兑(エツ)

joy

317
説 説 セツ ゼイ と.く

Speech 言 *being exposed* 兑(エツ)

to explain

---

318 Ⓜ
 夋 夋

Energy distributed on the feet

Flowing energy (厶) that is *distributed* (八 → 儿) into *still feet* (夂) in order to make them move.

319
俊 俊 シュン

Person's 亻 *moving with feet filled with energy* 夋

swift

320
唆 唆 サ そそのか.す

Words 口 *that make feet move* 夋

to instigate

---

321 Ⓢ
 公 公 コウ おおやけ

Portion of distributed energy

public

Distributed energy (八 → ハ) that becomes a new portion of *flowing energy* (厶). This character suggests the notion of a part extracted from the whole, which translates into the meaning of **public**, since something public can be understood as something that belongs to all—the whole—but that at the same time can be enjoyed by the parts.

322

訟 訟 ショウ

Speech 言 *becoming public* 公 (コウ)

litigation

---

323 Ⓢ

忩 忩 (コウ) ソウ

Public heart-mind

Public (公) *heart-mind* (心), referring to the public sphere and common ground of a society.

---

324 Ⓢ

气 气 キ

Floating energy

Several streams of energy moving upward, evoking the image of a kind of ether floating in the air. Over time, what used to be three representative lines of *unfolded energy* currents (乚×3) slightly inclined upward, became stylized into three distinct graphical parts (𠂉, 一, ⺄).

---

325 Ⓜ

乞 乞 こ.う

Unfolded floating energy

to beg

A part of *floating energy* (气 → 𠂉) that is meant to be *unfolded* (乙) again, something obtained from the air, something that has to be **begged** or asked for.

---

326 Ⓢ

己 己 コ キ おのれ

Circulating energy

self

sixth

A stream of unfolded energy that turns back and revolves around itself to later unfold again, thus creating a continuous cycle of energetic movement or circulating energy. This circular conception of energy expressed by this glyph lets this character, when acting as a standalone, take on the meaning of **self**, referring to the fact that energy, even after being unfolded, ultimately returns to its original state, to itself as it is.

327

妃 妃 ヒ

Woman 女 *making energy circulate* 己 (キ)

princess

忌 キ *Circulating* 己 *heart-mind* 心 328
忌 い.む **to refrain** (from)

NOTE A clear allusion to the control of one's own impulses to which many religions and disciplines are committed.

記 キ *Speech* 言 *that circulates* 己 329
記 しる.す **to write down**

改 カイ *Circulating* 己 *hits* 攵 330
改 あらた.める **to reform**

起 キ *Running* 走 *circulating energy* 己 331
起 お.きる **to get up**

包 ホウ *Person leaning over something and encircling it* 332
包 つつ.む **to wrap** Ⓢ

A person or some other entity that *leans* (勹) over some object and encircles it, like *circulating energy* (己), in order to **wrap** it.

胞 *Body part* 月 *that wraps* 包 333
胞 ホウ **placenta**

抱 ① ホウ *Hand* 扌 *wrapping* 包 *something or someone* 334
抱 ① いだ.く ① **to embrace**
① だ.く ② **to hold in the arms**
② かか.える

回 カイ *Revolving energy* 335
回 エ **to revolve** Ⓜ
まわ.る times

Originally 囘, a stream of flowing energy that makes a further revolution around itself, forming a sort of spiral of moving energy, graphically emphasizing the notion of rotation or **revolution**. This character that was originally represented with a continuous line, over time began to be depicted with a square inside another square in order to make its writing faster and easier. The meaning of 'revolving' also derives into the notion of 'times', as in the number of times an action is repeated, through an analogy to the repetitive nature of rotations.

---

336 Ⓢ

申 电 申 シン もう.す

Expanded energy

to expound

monkey sign (Chinese zodiac)

A stream of circulating energy that starts revolving at its ends in order to expand itself as it moves towards new directions. The current graphical depiction of the character is the result of a convergence between the connotatively similar components of *unfolded energy* (乚) and *revolving energy* (回 → 回 → 日). In some compounds and as a standalone character this component gets simplified to the form 申. As a standalone character the meaning of **expounding** is expressed as a more concretized semantic derivation of the concept of 'expansion'.

337

伸 伸 シン の.ばす

Person 亻 *expanding energy* 申 (シン)

to expand

338

俺 俺 おれ

Person 亻 *expanded* 电 *into a bigger person* 大

me

---

339 Ⓢ

丩 丩 キュウ

Intertwined energies

Two streams of *unfolded energy* ((乚 → 𠄌) + (㇆ → 丨)) intertwining with each other.

340

叫 叫 キョウ さけ.ぶ

Mouth 口 *exhaling intertwined energies* 丩 (キュウ)

to shout

341

収 収 シュウ おさ.める

Intertwined energies 丩 (キュウ) *given by an outstretched hand* 又

to yield

---

342 Ⓢ

句 句 ク

Intertwined words

sentence

A series of *words* (口) being *intertwined* (丩 キュウ → 勹), referring to constructed **sentences**.

343

局
局　キャク

Sitting person 尸 *intertwining words* 句 ク → 司

bureau

344

拘
拘　コウ

Hand 扌 *among intertwined words* 句 ク

arrest

2. STARS

After invisible and untouchable energies, the natural elements following the rank of metaphysical importance under the world view of the ancients were those things that cannot be touched, but yet can be seen, that is, the elements of the sky. The elements of the sky govern the passing of time, the days and nights, the hours and the months. The most important star in the sky is undoubtedly the luminous 'sun' 日, ruler of the day. At night it is the moon who governs, and it can appear in a dim light as a 'crescent moon' 夕 or with a notorious 'moonlight' 月 that brightens the night sky.

---

345 Ⓡ Ⓜ

日 日 日

① ② ニチ
② ジツ
① ② ひ
② -か

Sunlight

① **sun**

② **day**

SPECIAL READINGS 今日 [きょう]: *today*

A solar halo with a spot in its center depicting the sunlight. This character was originally written with circular strokes, but later on, as in many other characters, the strokes became straightened, turning the solar circle into a square (囗) and the central luminous spot into a horizontal line (一). The meanings of this character, apart from 'sunlight' are those of **sun** and **day**.

As a component, this character takes the squashed form 日—identical to the component for "spoken words" (曰)—when is placed at the top or bottom of the compounds.

晩 晩 バン — *Sunlight 日 being avoided 免*（メン） **dusk** 346

唱 唱 ショウ となえる — *Mouth 口 beaming sunlight 日 while speaking 曰* **to chant** 347

暗 暗 アン くら.い — *Sunlight 日 indistinguishable as a loud sound 音*（オン） **dark** 348

暖 暖 ダン あたた.かい — *Sunlight 日 as warm as a caress 爰*（エン） **warm** 349

時 時 ジ とき — *Sun 日 movements measured in a temple 寺*（ジ） **time** 350

昆 昆 コン — *Several people under the sun* **swarm** 354 Ⓢ

Sunlight (日 → 曰) shining over *several people* (比), referring to a large group of people being out in the open. Over time, by analogy, this character went on to designate a large number not only of people in the open, but also a large number of animals and, ultimately, a large number of insects or a **swarm**, which is the current main meaning of the character when it appears as a standalone.

普 普 フ — *Lined up days* **regular** 355 Ⓢ

A *row* (並) of *days* (日 → 曰) that follow each other on a **regular** basis.

譜 譜 フ — *Speech 言 becoming regular 普*（フ） **notation** 353

旧 旧 キュウ — *The span of the sun* **old times** 354

An abstract mark (丨) that encompasses the whole span of the *sun* (日),

understood here as an entity that conditions time since very long ago, since the **old times.**

 旦 日 タン ダン *Sun rising over the ground* **daybreak** 358 Ⓢ

The *sun* (日) rising above the horizon (一) at dawn or **daybreak.**

但 但 ただ.し *Person 亻 along the sun rising over the ground 旦* **but** 356

昼 昼 チュウ ひる *Measurable 尺 span of time during which the sun is over the ground 旦* **daytime** 357

胆 胆 タン *Body part 月 making people rise over the ground 旦 (タン)* **gallbladder** **guts** 358

NOTE In countries within the Chinese sphere of cultural influence the **gallbladder** is associated with courage, as **guts** are in English speaking countries.

担 担 タン かつ.ぐ にな.う *Hand 扌 making something rise over the ground 旦 (タン)* **to carry on one's shoulder** 359

 昜 昜 ヨウ *Rising sun emitting rays of light* *Sun rays* 360 Ⓢ

The *sun rising above the ground* (旦) and emitting its rays of light (勿) over it.

腸 腸 チョウ *Body part 月 spreading like sun rays 昜 (ヨウ)* **intestines** 361

揚 揚 ヨウ あ.げる *Hand 扌 rising high like the sun rays 昜 (ヨウ)* **to raise** 362

旬 旬 シュン ジュン *Encircled days* **ten-day period** 363 Ⓢ

Days (日) surrounded by an encircling arm (勹), ideographically evoking the idea of a cycle of a number of days that gets concretized in ten: a **ten-day period**. The component representing the surrounding arm (勹) is a derivation of the primitive component 力 (*arm*), in which the size of the hand has been reduced. It is, therefore, unrelated to the graphically identical component 勹 with the meaning of "leaning person".

殉 殉 ジュン *Bone remains* 歹 *exposed during ten days* 旬(ジュン) **martyr** 364

晶 晶 ショウ *Several stars* **crystal** 365 Ⓜ

Several luminous *suns* (日×3) or stars radiating light, allegorically suggesting great brightness and, consequently, clarity. Over time, the meaning of 'clarity' went on to refer more specifically to **crystal**, by means of association between clarity and the translucency provided by a crystal, as exemplified by the English expression "crystal clear".

参 参 ① サン ① ② まい.る *Aged person looking at the stars* ① **to participate** ② **to be nonplussed** 366 Ⓢ

Originally 曑 [晶㐱], an *aged person* (㐱(チン))—suggesting a person of great knowledge—looking, astonished, at a constellation of *several luminous stars* (晶 → 厶). Two meanings derive from this ideogram: The first is **to participate**, drawn from the idea of an old man explaining constellations to a group of pupils participating in a lesson. The second meaning is that of **being nonplussed**, which is derived from the idea of astonishment produced by the sight of luminous stars in the sky.

惨 惨 サン ザン まじ.め *Heart-mind* 忄 *that is nonplussing* 参(サン) **wretched** 367

夕 夕	セキ ゆう	*Crescent moon* **evening**	368 Ⓡ Ⓜ

A crescent moon that also represents the moment of the day in which it appears: the **evening**.

多 多	タ おお.い	*Several evenings* **many**	369 Ⓜ

Several consecutive *evenings* (夕×2), ideogram chosen to represent the idea of '(too) much' or **many**, probably due to the implication of weariness that is suggested by the idea of spending several evenings in a row without sleep.

夗 夗	エン	*Person huddling in the evening*	370 Ⓢ

A person *huddling* (㔾 ハン) under the moon in the *evening* (夕).

怨 怨	オン エン	*Feelings 心 of a person huddling in the evening 夗 (エン)* **grudge**	371

名 名	ミョウ メイ な	*Words pronounced in the evening* **name**	372 Ⓢ

Words (口) pronounced to catch the attention of someone whose **name** is called out because he cannot be seen in the darkness of the *evening* (夕).

夜 夜	ヤ よ よる	*Person alongside the moon* **night**	373 Ⓜ

Originally ⿺亦夕 (亦 + 夕), a *person's distributed energy* (亦) in the *evening* (夕), an allegorical image alluding to an anthropomorphised divinity that makes the **night** fall. This glyph has undergone a great graphical transformation over time, as we can see how the strokes of the components 亦 and 夕 have merged to form a new composition that blurs the original elements.

月 月

①②ゲツ
②ガツ
①②つき

Moonlight
① **moon**
② **month**

374 Ⓡ Ⓜ

A *crescent moon* (夕) with a spot inside (一) indicating light—moonlight—in a similar way to the character for "sunlight" (日). This character means both **moon** and **month**, in reference to the lunar cycles on which the months are based.

朔 朔

ソ

Moon turned upside down
New moon
first day of the month

375 ㊔ Ⓢ

Ideogram representing a *moon* (月) that is *turned upside down* (屰), a metaphorical representation of the start of a new lunar cycle, a new moon.

明 明

①②③ ミョウ
①②③ メイ
① あか.るい
② あき.らか
③ あ.かり

Sun and moon
① **bright**
② **clear**
③ **illumination**

376 Ⓢ

SPECIAL READING 明日 [あした]: *tomorrow*

Sunlight (日) and *moonlight* (月), indicating a great **brightness**, **clarity** and **illumination**.

3. WATER

The first of the visible and touchable natural elements to be addressed is water, an element without which human life would not be possible. The main way of representing 'water' within the kanji corpus is by means of its movement or flow through the bed of a river: 水. If the water of the river freezes it could break away in fragments of 'ice': 氷. If the flow of that 'river' speeds up it will turn out to be a fast moving stream of water: 川. Rivers are very important to obtain potable water, but so is the water of the 'rain' that falls from clouds: 雨; graph that will also be useful for designating and understanding various types of atmospheric phenomena.

水 **水** 氵氺	スイ みず	*Flowing water* *Fluid* **water**	377 Ⓡ Ⓜ

A stream of **water** flowing through what appears to be the bed of a river. The central stroke 亅 represents the riverbed, while フ and 〈 depict the running water. The meaning of 'water' can be expanded to that of any kind of <u>fluid</u> in some compounds.

As a component, it mostly appears in the simplified form 氵, which is placed to the left in the compounds, and occasionally as 氺, which is placed at the bottom.

尿 **尿**	ニョウ	*Sitting person* 尸 *excreting fluids* 水 **urine**	378
泥 **泥**	デイ どろ	*Fluid* 氵 *on a nun* 尼(ニ) (wet) **dirt**	379
氾 **氾**	ハン	*Water* 氵 *over a huddling person* 㔾(ハン) **inundation**	380
海 **海**	カイ うみ	*Water* 氵 *that is scruffy* 毎(マイ) **sea**	381
泣 **泣**	キュウ な.く	*Water* 氵 *"standing"* 立 *vertically on the face* **to cry**	382
汰 **汰**	タ	*Water* 氵 *that is great* 太(タ) **cleanse**	383
沢 **沢**	タク さわ	*Water* 氵 *whose length can be measured* 尺(シャク) **brook**	384

385

滑 **滑**

① ② カツ
① コツ
① すべ.る
② なめ.らか

Water 氵 *sliding down on a bone* 骨(コツ)

① to slide
② smooth

386

渦 **渦**

カ
うず

Water 氵 *turning someone into piles of bones and backbones* 咼(カ)

whirlpool

387

況 **況**

キョウ

Water 氵 *discussed by big brothers* 兄(キョウ)

situation

NOTE This character is probably referring to some **situation** of agricultural dispute, regarding irrigation or distribution of *waters* (水 → 氵), over which the local *big brothers* (兄) discus.

388

活 **活**

カツ

Water 氵 *tasted by the tongue* 舌(ゼツ)

living

389

渇 **渇**

カツ
かわ.く

Water's 氵 *threat* 曷(カツ)

to be thirsty

390

潜 **潜**

セン
ひそ.む
もぐ.る

Water 氵 *exchange* 替

to be submerged

391

混 **混**

コン
こ.む
ま.ざる

Water 氵 *around swarms* 昆(コン)

to be mixed

392

油 **油**

ユ
あぶら

Fluid 氵 *that can enter into the mouth as a piece of food* 由(ユ)

oil

393

津 **津**

シン
つ

Water 氵 *washed brush* 聿

watery

浸 浸 シン ひた.す

Water 氵 in which a club is 𠬶(シン) inserted 394

to immerse

没 没 ボツ

Water 氵 striking 殳 395

sinking

洪 洪 コウ

Water 氵 acting together 共(キョウ) 396

flood

港 港 コウ みなと

Water 氵 where people act together 共キョウ and energy circulates 己(コ) 397

harbor

SPECIAL READING 香港 [ホンコン]: *Hong Kong*

浮 浮 フ う.く

Water 氵 from which a child can be drawn out by a hand 孚 398

to float

渓 渓 ケイ

Water 氵 from which an adult man can be drawn out by a hand 奚ケイ 399

creek

浄 浄 ジョウ

Water 氵 after a fight 争(ソウ) 400

clean

洗 洗 セン あら.う

Water 氵 poured previously 先(セン) 401

to wash

踏 踏 トウ ふ.む

Feet 𧾷 crossing over water 水 about which spoken words 曰 can tell a tale 402

to step on

403

治 治

① ② ジ
① ② チ
① なお.す
② おさ.める

Water 氵 *contained* 台 (タイ)

① **to heal**

② **to govern**

NOTE This character alludes to a religious act of purification with sacred water, referring to the sacred *water* (水 → 氵) that has been stored or *contained* (台) for some time so it can be used to **heal** others. From this sense of healing the second meaning of the character derives, that of **govern**ing, for in the time of ancient China, those who enjoyed a healing religious power also enjoyed a political power, since the priests or shamans were the elite of that society. The sense of 'governing' can also be understood in a more pragmatic way by making a semantic association between the idea of governing and that of healing people by solving their problems.

404

池 池

チ
いけ

Water 氵 *that is extended* 也 (チ)

pond

405

汽 汽

キ

Water 氵 *floating in the air* 气 (キ)

vapor

406

泡 泡

ホウ
あわ

Water 氵 *that wraps* 包 (ホウ)

bubbles

407

湯 湯

トウ
ゆ

Water 氵 *below sun rays* 昜 (ヨウ)

hot water

408

液 液

エキ

Fluid 氵 *seen at night* 夜

liquid

NOTE This composition most probably referred originally to alcohol, because it is a **liquid** that looks similar to water and is usually drunk at night.

---

409 Ⓜ

次 次

Spitting person

A *person with an open mouth* (欠) spitting out a watery *fluid* (水 → 氵).

 沃 沃 ヨク

Water flowing wiggly
fertile

410 Ⓜ

Abundant *water* (水 → 氵) that flows rapidly and *wiggly* (夭) making the land **fertile.**

添 添 テン そ.える

Fertile 沃 heart-mind 小
to satisfy

411

渋 渋 ジュウ しぶ.い

Water stopping its flow
astringent

412

Water (水 → 氵) that *stops* (止) flowing, making the moisture of its surroundings disappear so the environment becomes **astringent**. The original glyph of this character was 澁, with three "footsteps" (止×3 → 歮) enhancing the idea of "stopping". Later on the lower part of the component (歮) was simplified into the graph ⺍, that can be thought as a mark alluding to the disappearance of the water.

 永 永 エイ なが.い

Person going along the flowing water
perpetual

413 Ⓢ

A person going along the <u>flow</u> of water, being carried away by the current, figuratively following the course of **perpetuity**. The modern graphic composition of this character has been made by associating the component of "water" (水) with that of "person" (人 → 亻), which flows within the former. The central stroke of "water" (亅) has merged with the vertical stroke of "person" (丨), while the upper stroke of the latter component appears as a dot (丶) at the top of the compound.

詠 詠 エイ よ.む

Speech's 言 flow along which a person goes エイ 永
to recite

414

泳 泳 エイ およ.ぐ

Water's 氵 flow along which a person goes エイ 永
to swim

415

 𠂢 *Person going against the flow* 416 Ⓜ

This is the reverse version of the character 永 (*person going along the flowing water*), evoking the idea of a person going against the current, in the opposite direction of the flow of water. The modern version of this character has undergone a great evolution, but it is still possible to point out the reversed "water" component at the bottom (水 → 氺 → 𠂢) and the reversed and simplified form of the "person" component at the top (丶 → ㇀).

脈 **脈** ミャク — *Body part 月 transporting fluids up and down without a fixed current 𠂢* — **vein** 417

派 **派** ハ — *Person breaking off a current of water 氵 in order to go against it 𠂢* — **dispatch**, **faction** 418

 攸 攸 ユウ *Person being purged with water* 419 Ⓢ

Originally 攸, a person (人 → 亻) who is being metaphorically *hit* (攵) with *water* (氵 → 丨) in order to be purged from evil.

悠 **悠** ユウ — *Purged 攸(ユウ) heart-mind 心* — **composure** 420

修 **修** シュウ, シュ, おさ.める — *Person purging himself 攸(ユウ) as he becomes older 参 → 彡* — **to master** 421

 氷 氷 冫 ヒョウ こおり ひ *Solidified water* **ice** 422 Ⓡ Ⓜ

Originally 冰, *water* (水) from which fragments of solid matter (冫 → 丶) are breaking away, so to speak, fragmented solid water: **ice**.

As a component this character most usually appears in the original incomplete form 冫, which is always placed to the right of the compounds.

尽 **尽** ジン つ.くす — 423

Measured 尺 *ice* 冫 → ⺀

to run out

冷 **冷** ① レイ ① つめ.たい ① ひ.える ② さ.める — 424

Ice 冫 *forming through a command from heaven* 令

① **cool**
② **to cool down**

凄 **凄** セイ — 425

Ice cold 冫 *wife* 妻 (サイ)

terrific

冶 **冶** ヤ — 426

Ice 冫 *that is contained* 台

melting

冬 **冬** トウ ふゆ — 427 Ⓢ

Still foot over ice

winter

Still foot (夂) on top of *ice* (氷 → 冫 → ⺀), an image characteristic of **winter** time, being also an analogy to the stillness of ice during said season.

川 **川** 巛 川L セン かわ — 428 Ⓜ

Stream of water

river

This glyph has a composition similar to that of the character 水 (*water*), but unlike that one, this shows its continuous lines of water following towards the same direction, suggesting an uninterrupted and fast movement like that of a stream or **river** flowing down a mountain.

As a component, it appears sometimes in the variant 巛. When the component is placed at the bottom, it takes the form 川L.

順 **順** ジュン — 429

Stream 川 *of thoughts in the head* 頁

order

訓 訓 クン 430

Speech 訁 *flowing as a stream* 川

instruction

semantic reading

拶 拶 サツ 431

Hand 扌 *near a stream of water* 巛 *and pieces of meat* 月 → 夕 → 夕

approach

 㐬 㐬 リュウ *Newborn baby pushed out by a stream of amniotic fluid* 432 Ⓢ

Originally 㐬, a *newborn baby* (𠫓) pushed out by a *stream* (川 → 巛 → ⺄) of the amniotic fluid of a mother giving birth.

流 流 リュウ ル なが.れる 433

Water 氵 *that pushes a newborn baby out* 㐬 リュウ *in its birth*

to flow

 𡿺 ノウ *Stream inside the skull* 434 Ⓢ

Originally 𡿺 [巛囟], a *skull* seen from above (囟 → 凶) through which a *stream* (巛 → ⺍) flows, highlighting the stream of thought and thus what is inside the skull. The modern version of the character, which depicts an *open skull* (凶) also reinforces the concept of what is 'inside the skull' by showing it through an open skull instead of a closed one.

脳 脳 ノウ 435

Body part 月 *located inside the skull* 𡿺 ノウ

brain

悩 悩 ノウ なや.む 436

Feelings 忄 *inside the skull* 𡿺 ノウ

to be worried

 州 州 シュウ す 437 Ⓢ

Pieces of land surrounded by rivers

province

Pieces of land (丶×3) surrounded by *rivers* (川), a suitable territory for establishing a governmental **province**.

 昔 **昔** シャク セキ むかし — *The days of the flooding streams of water* — **older times** 438 Ⓢ

Originally 㳻 [㷌日], an allegorical allusion to the ancient *days* (日 → 日) in which great *streams of water* (川 → 巛 → 㷌 → 龷) flooded the earth, in reference to a legendary deluge that supposedly took place in **older times**. The myth of a flood occurring in a very ancient time, which is well known within Christianity, is interestingly shared by many other cultures, including the Chinese, where the legend is known as the flood of Gun-Yu (鯀禹治水).

借 **借** シャク か.りる — *Person* 亻 *from older times* 昔 (シャク) — **to borrow** 439

NOTE This character refers to the scholarly practice of **borrow**ing knowledge from people of older times in order to apply it to their studies and dissertations.

惜 **惜** セキ お.しい — *Heart-mind* 忄 *of older times* 昔 (セキ) — **pitiful** 440

措 **措** ソ — *Hand* 扌 *of older times* 昔 (シャク) — **means** 441

 雨 **雨** ⻗ ウ あめ あま- — *Water drops falling from clouds* — **rain** 442 Ⓡ Ⓜ

Raindrops (丶×4) falling from clouds in the sky (冂).

As a component this sinogram is placed in the upper part of the compounds compressed in the following graph: ⻗.

震 **震** シン ふる.える — *Rain* ⻗ *over a person holding an agrarian tool* 辰 (シン) — **to shake** 443

霊 **霊** レイ リョウ たま — *Rain* ⻗ *invoked by several people standing side by side* 並 (ヘイ) → 亚 — **soul** 444

NOTE The meaning of **soul** is derived from an allusion to the spirits that shamans invoked through collective rituals made to ask for rain.

零
零 レイ
Rain ⻗ *falling like a command from heaven* 令 (レイ)
zero
445

NOTE The original meaning of this character alluded to the act of falling down, but, over time, such a concept of physical falling derived into that of a fall or drop in quantity, and finally it started denoting the concept of 'nothing' or **zero**.

雪
雪 セツ ゆき
Rain ⻗ *that can be held by an outstretched hand* ⺕ → 彐
snow
446

SPECIAL READING 吹雪 [ふぶき]: *blizzard*

電
電 デン
Expanded energy 电 *seen under the rain* ⻗
electricity
447

漏
漏 ロウ も.れる
Fluid 氵 *coming out of the buttocks of a sitting person* 尸 *like rain* 雨
to leak out
448

 需
需 ジュ
Person wearing a coat under the rain
demand
449 Ⓢ

Person wearing a *raincoat* (而) when it *rains* (雨 → ⻗), alluding to the high **demand** of raincoats on rainy days.

儒
儒 ジュ
Person 亻 *in demand* 需 (ジュ)
Confucian
450

4. FIRE

In contrast to water there is 'fire', with its flaring flames  火, an essential natural element for humans, because it can be used for lighting, heating and cooking and so becoming a representative element of home and families.

火 火 灬 カ ひ ほ-

Fire flames

fire

451 Ⓡ Ⓜ

A flame of **fire** (人) and its surrounding sparks (⺀×2).

When this glyph acts as a component usually adopts a simplified version 灬 which is located at the bottom of compounds.

炊 炊 スイ た.く

Fire 火 leaving one's mouth open 欠

to cook

452

煩 煩 ハン ボン わずら.う

Fire 火 in the head 頁

to worry (about)

453

災 災 サイ わざわ.い

Flood of water streams 巛 and fire 火

disaster

454

炎 炎 エン ほのお

Several fire flames

flames

455 Ⓢ

Several *fire flames* (火×2) and their surrounding sparks.

談 談 ダン

Speech 言 spreading like flames 炎 (エン)

discussion

456

淡 淡 タン あわ.い

Water 氵 extinguishing flames 炎 (エン)

diluted

457

灰 灰 カイ はい

Fire grasped by a hand

ash

458 Ⓜ

Originally 炙, and later 灰, *fire* (火) that can be touched by an *outstretched hand* (又 → ナ → 厂), something that comes from fire but does not burn: **ash**.

黒 黒 コク くろ.い *Person with a mask painted with the ashes of a fire* **black** 459 Ⓢ

Originally 黑, a *person seen from the front* (大 → 土) wearing a *skull* mask (囟 → 罒 → 田) that has been painted **black** with ashes coming from a fire (火 → 灬).

光 光 コウ ひかり *Person with fire* **light** 460 Ⓡ Ⓜ

Originally 灮, a *kneeling person* (卩 → 儿) with a flame of *fire* (火 → ⺌) with which he **lights** things up.

赤 赤 セキ シャク あか.い *Person burnt in a fire* **red** 461 Ⓜ

Originally 烾, and later 𤆍, a *person seen from the front* (大 → 土) on top of *fire flames* (火 → 丿小丶), evoking the **red** color of burns on the skin.

嚇 嚇 カク *Words 口 putting several people on fire 赤×2* **menacing** 462

赦 赦 シャ *Person burnt 赤 and hit 攵* **pardon** 463

叟 叟 ソウ *Outstretched hand grabbing a torch* 464 Ⓢ

Originally 叜 [𦥔又], an *outstretched hand* (又) carrying a <u>torch</u> (𦥔 → 申), in which the stroke 丨 represents the torch handle and the element 臼 depicts the flames of a flaring fire. The current element 申 might have been developed as an analogy to the character 申 (*expanded energy*), since fire can be understood as a visibly expanding energy.

捜 捜 ソウ さが.す *Hand 扌 holding a torch 叟ソウ in the dark* **to seek** (for) 465

5. EARTH

After water and fire, we have to analyze the most representative element of the material and tangible natural world: ‘earth’; represented in Chinese characters by the depiction of clay being molded on top of a potter's wheel 土, since clay is a material taken directly from the ground. But earth should not be understood just as a means of obtaining construction material, but also as the soil and ground on top of which people live. The ground may be flat, or elevated in the form of small ‘hills’ 丘. If the hills are taller and bigger they may form ‘mountain’ ranges 山. Mountains can also appear in the shape of a ‘cliff’ 厂, from where pieces of ‘stone’ 石 can break off, whereas stone, closing the cycle, becomes a construction material itself, harder than clay.

土 土 ト ド つち *Potter's wheel* **earth** **soil** 466 Ⓡ Ⓜ

A potter's wheel (一) with a piece of clay (◆ → 十) being molded on top. This character, which originally meant what it pictographically represents, a potter's wheel, soon came to denote, instead, the element which clay comes from: **earth**-and-**soil**.

Two hands working on a potter's wheel

塀 塀 ヘイ *Earth-soil 土 on which there is sitting 尸 a row of people 并 (ヘイ)* **fence** 467

坑 坑 コウ *Earth-soil 土 that has been pushed down below the ground 亢 (コウ)* **pit** 468

塑 **塑** ソ — 469

New 朔 (ソ) earth-soil 土

moldable

堅 **堅** ケン かた.い — 470

Delicate 臤 (ケン) earth-soil 土

tough

吐 **吐** ト は.く — 471

Mouth 口 with earth 土 (ト) inside

to vomit

塊 **塊** カイ かたまり — 472

Earth 土 filling the ghosts 鬼 (キ)

mass

地 **地** ジ チ — 473

Earth-soil 土 that is extended 也 (チ)

ground

場 **場** ジョウ ば — 474

Earth-soil 土 that can be lit by sun rays 昜 (ヨウ)

site

均 **均** キン — 475

Earth-soil 土 being leveled (二) by a leaning person 勹

leveling

墨 **墨** ボク すみ — 476

Black 黒 (コク) earth 土

black ink

圭 圭 圭 ケイ — 477 ㊔ Ⓜ

Earth over earth

Mound

jade tablet

Several <u>mounds</u> of *earth* (土×2), one on top of each other.

佳 **佳** カ — 478

Person 亻 elevated on a mound 圭

excellent

封 封 | フウ ホウ | *Mound 圭 on which work 寸 is done* | 479
enclosure

 坐 坐 | ザ | *Several people working on a potter's wheel* | 480 ㊔ Ⓢ
to squat

Several *people* (人×2) **squatting** while working on a piece of clay that is spinning on a *potter's wheel* (土).

挫 挫 | ザ | *A hand 扌 that looks like it is suatting* 坐 (ザ) | 481
sprain

 尭 尭 | ギョウ | *Person carrying several pieces of clay* | 482 ㊔ Ⓢ
lofty

A *kneeling person* (卩 → 儿) carrying several pieces of clay (土×3 → 垚 → 垚) over his head.

暁 暁 | ギョウ あかつき | *Sun 日 shining over pieces of clay* 尭 (ギョウ) | 483
(at) **dawn**

焼 焼 | ショウ や.く | *Fire 火 over pieces of clay* 尭 (ギョウ) | 484
to heat

 圣 圣 | ケイ | *Outstretched hand working on a potter's wheel* | 485 Ⓢ

An *outstretched hand* (又) working on a piece of clay on top of a *potter's wheel* (土).

怪 怪 | カイ あや.しい | *Feelings 忄 produced by an unfinished object that is being made on a potter's wheel* 圣 (ケイ) | 486
weird

丘 丘 业 キュウ おか *Two hillocks* **hill** 487 Ⓜ

Originally 丠, two adjacent hillocks (丨厂 → 斤) rising above the ground (一), forming a group of **hills**.

As a component, this glyph can take the form 业, which is a simplification of the original glyph 丠.

山 山 サン やま *Three hillocks* **mountain** 488 Ⓡ Ⓜ

Several hillocks (丨×3) rising above the ground (一), forming a **mountain**.

仙 仙 セン *Person 亻 in a mountain* 山(サン) **hermit** 489

峡 峡 キョウ *A mountain's* 山 *middle space* 夹(キョウ) **gorge** 490

炭 炭 タン すみ *Mountain* 山(サン) *ash* 灰 **coal** 491

岳 岳 ガク たけ *Hill* 丘 *on top of a mountain* 山 **peak** 492

阜 阜 阝 フ mountain range *Mountains* 493 Ⓡ Ⓜ

PLACE NAME USAGE 岐阜県 [ぎふけん]: *Gifu Prefecture*

Originally 𠂤, and later 𠂤, a mountain range turned vertically to highlight the verticality of the mountains. The contemporary form of the character (阜) is an evolution of the variant 𨸏 (𠂤 + 山), in which the component 山 (*mountain*) was added to the original primitive component 𠂤 to differentiate it from the primitive glyph with the meaning of "footprint", that has exactly the same graphical appearance (𠂤).

When this character acts as a component it always does it with the simplified version 阝 that is placed, without exception, on the left side of the compounds.

隅 隅 | グウ すみ | *Part of mountains 阝 where masked dancers 禺(グ) act* | 494

nook
corner

限 限 | ゲン かぎ.る | *Mountains 阝 making a person stay still 艮(コン)* | 495

to limit

険 険 | ケン けわ.しい | *Mountains 阝 that assert authority 㑒(ケン)* | 496

precipitous

附 附 | フ | *Mountains 阝 that are attached 付(フ)* | 497

affixed

隠 隠 | イン かく.す | *Mountains 阝 where someone is holding his heart with two hands 㥯(オン)* | 498

to hide

陽 陽 | ヨウ | *Mountains 阝 on which sun rays 昜(ヨウ) are reflected* | 499

sunshine
yang (positive principle)

陛 陛 | ヘイ | *Mountains 阝 compared 比(ヒ) to the earth-soil 土* | 500

highness

降 降 | ①② コウ ① お.りる ② ふ.る | *Two feet descending mountains* | 501

① **to descend**
② **to precipitate**

Mountains (阜 → 阝) through which two feet pointing downwards (夂+(㐄 → 㐄) → 夅) descend.

Cliff | 502 Ⓡ Ⓜ

A steep cliff, with its wall (丿) and its top (一).

503

压
圧　アツ

Cliff 厂 over the earth-soil 土

pressure

504

丸
丸　ガン
まる

Person rolling down a cliff

round

Originally 丮, a *person* (人 → 𠆢 → ㄨ) rolling down a *cliff* (厂 → ㇏ → ⺄). Over time the notion of 'rolling' derived into the sense of **round** in general. This character should not be confused with the simplified version of the component 丮 (丮 → 丸) (*person working with hands*), since they have a totally different etymology.

---

505 Ⓜ

厄
厄　ヤク

Person huddling under a cliff

misfortune

A *person huddling* (㔾) under a *cliff* (厂), either because he has fallen from the top or because he has come across it with the inability to continue his way. In either case the scene undoubtedly represents a sign of **misfortune**.

506

危
危　キ
あぶ.ない
あや.うい

Person leaning 勹 → ⺈ over the edge of a cliff 厂 while he looks at a person who is huddling 㔾 below

dangerous

---

507 Ⓜ

产
产

Writings on a cliff

Visible

Originally 产, a *writing* (文 → 立) engraved on the wall of a *cliff* (厂), indicating high visibility.

508

顔
顔　ガン
かお

Visible 产 part of the head 頁 surrounded by hair 彡

face

---

509 Ⓢ

反
反　② ハン
② タン
② ホン
① そ.る

Outstretched hand against the wall of a cliff

① **to arch**

② **reverse**

An *outstretched hand* (又) arching to grab the ledges of a *cliff* (厂), a scene representing both the bending movement of the fingers of the **arch**ed hand and the position of a hand against the cliff wall, almost **reverse**d to its normal stance.

仮 仮 | カ ケ かり | *Person* 亻 *acting in reverse* 反 | 510

provisional
sham

坂 坂 | ハン さか | *Earth-soil* 土 *that is arched* 反 (ハン) | 511

slope

阪 阪 | ハン さか | *Mountains'* 阝 *arched parts* 反 (ハン) | 512

hillside

PLACE NAME USAGE 大阪府 [おおさかふ]: *Osaka Prefecture*

厓 厓 厓 | ガイ | *Cliff formed by mounds of earth* | 513 Ⓢ

Crag

A *cliff* (厂) formed by *mounds of earth* (圭), a crag.

涯 涯 | ガイ | *Water* 氵 *reaching mountain crags* 厓 (ガイ) | 514

shore
horizon [*fig.*]

NOTE From the meaning of shore, that is, the limits of water on a coast, derives the figurative meaning of **horizon** to which this character refers, since the limit marked by the line of the water is one of the most common representations of the horizon.

崖 崖 | ガイ がけ | *Mountain* 山 *over a crag* 厓 (ガイ) | 515

precipice

 段 叚 段 | ダン | *Hand breaking the rocks of a cliff with a mace* | 516 Ⓢ

steps

Originally 㡌 [厂叚], a *hand striking with a mace* (⺕ ≈ 殳), step by step, the wall of a *cliff* (厂) until several rocks break off from it (㠯). The notion conveyed by this character is always that of gradual **steps** done in a given action and never that of literal steps done with the feet. The current form of the character gets rid of the "cliff" component (⺁) and stylizes the strokes of the rest of the compound (𠃊 → ⺕). As a component this character sometimes preserves the primitive variant 叚.

暇 | 暇 | カ, ひま, いとま | *Part of the day 日 in which action steps 叚 can be taken* | **spare time** | 517

石 | 石 | シャク, セキ, コク, いし | *Rock detached from a cliff* | **stone** | 518 Ⓡ Ⓜ

A piece of rock (口) detached from a *cliff* (⺁ → ア): a falling **stone**.

妬 | 妬 | ト, ねた.む | *Woman's 女 seeing a precious stone 石* | **jealous** | 519

硫 | 硫 | リュウ | *Stone 石 coming out from the soil abruptly like a baby being born* 㐬 (リュウ) | **sulphur** | 520

拓 | 拓 | タク | *Hand 扌 clearing out stones 石* | **cleared land** | 521

砲 | 砲 | ホウ | *Object with a stone 石 wrapped* 包 (ホウ) *inside* | **cannon** | 522

岩 | 岩 | ガン, いわ | *Mountain 山 stone 石* | **rock** | 523

声 | 声 | セイ, ショウ, こえ, こわ- | *Hand striking a stone musical instrument* | **voice** | 524

Originally 殸 [声殳], a hand *striking* (殳) a primitive percussion instrument made of stones, or lithophone—called in Chinese *bianqing* (編磬)—made of hanging stone chimes (声), to which the component for *foot coming out and going forward* (㞢 → 土) has been added in order to highlight the notion of sound coming from the stone. The meaning of this character is therefore focused on the sound produced by the percussive strike rather than the instrument itself, and that connotation of sound derived later into the concept of **voice**.

The modern version of the character is a simplification made by the removal of the "striking mace" component (殳).

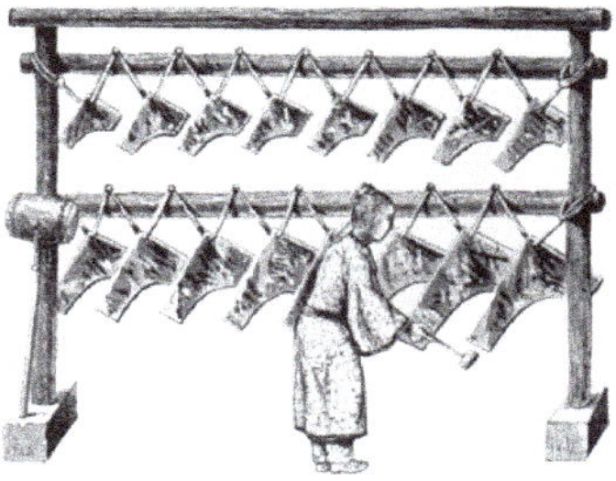

Person hitting the chimes of a 'bianqing'

6. HEAVEN

After exploring the earthly elements, we are going to study that casuistry that derives from heavenly providence, something that marked the daily lives of the people of the ancient world. Heavenly Designs were communicated through omens and prophecies which, in the case of ancient China, were interpreted through of 'providential' cracks made on turtle shells 卜 卜.

卜 卜

Providential crack formed in oracle bones 525
Providence (名)
divination (S)

Two adjacent cracks on the surface of a turtle's bone appearing after having applied heat onto it. In ancient China divinatory rituals were an essential part of the spiritual and political life, and in order to perform such rituals turtle shell bones or scapulae of other animals were heated to make appear cracks that were to be interpreted so <u>providential</u> divinations could be made upon them. Over time such divinations began to be written on the surface of the bones besides the formed cracks, leaving for posterity the first examples of writing in Chinese characters.

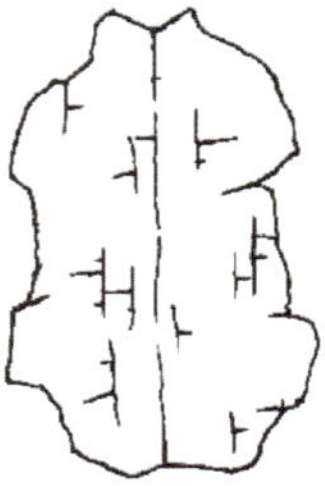

Turtle shell with cracks

訃 **訃** フ — 526

Speech 言 *marked by providence* 卜 (フ)

obituary

赴 **赴** フ / おもむ.く — 527

Running 走 *providence* 卜 (フ)

to proceed

外 **外** ① ガイ / ① ゲ / ① そと / ① ほか / ② はず.す — 528

Providence 卜 *interpreted by the help of the moon* 夕

① **outside**
② **to take off**

掛 **掛** か.かる — 529

Hand 扌 *taking a mound* 圭 *of bones with providential cracks* 卜

to take (time or money)
to hang

NOTE This character depicts the scene of a person who takes the reins of his destiny, an idea represented by a *hand* (手 → 扌) **taking** a *mound* (圭) of bones with *providential cracks* (卜) on it. The second meaning of **to hang** comes from the fact that the word denoting 'to take' and the word denoting 'to hang' are homonyms in Japanese: かかる.

占 **占** ① ② セン / ① うらな.う / ② し.める — 530 Ⓢ

Words interpreting providence

① **to divine**
② **to take up**

Words (口) pronounced while interpreting *providential cracks* (卜 → ⺊) through a

divination ritual. To **take up** is an additional meaning that this character takes from the notion of accepting divine providence.

点
点 テン

Taken up 占(セン) *fire spark* 灬 531

spot

兆
兆 ① ② チョウ ① きざ.し

Several providential cracks 532 Ⓢ

① **omen**

② trillion

A large number of providential cracks (冫く, 儿) appearing on the bone of a turtle shell, indicating an important **omen**.

眺
眺 チョウ ながめる

Eye 目 *looking at an omen* 兆(チョウ) 533

to gaze

挑
挑 チョウ いど.む

Hand 扌 *acting over an omen* 兆(チョウ) 534

to challenge

跳
跳 チョウ と.ぶ は.ねる

Feet ⻊ *over an omen* 兆(チョウ) 535

to jump

万
万 マン バン

Symbol of eternity 536 Ⓜ

ten thousand

A late simplification of the Buddhist symbol 卍, which represents the cycle of life and expands to the notion of eternity or infinity. This symbol is used within Chinese characters to figuratively designate, at first, a large, indefinite quantity. Over time the connotation of large quantity became concretized in the number **ten thousand**.

A Buddha with the symbol of the cycle of life on his chest

厉 537
厉 Ⓜ

Cliff rock rolling as the cycle of life

This component denotes a rotatory movement, represented figuratively by the symbol of the *cycle of life* (卍 → 万) rolling as if it was falling down a *cliff* (厂).

励 538
励 レイ
はげ.む

Arm 力 making a rock fall down a cliff 厉

to endeavor

REVIEW ON ELEMENTS

1

厶以鬼台乙也八亦兑夋公㕕气乞己
包回申丩句

仏勾払弁似始胎怠孔乱乳他恋跡変脱悦説
俊唆訟妃忌記改起胞抱伸俺叫収局拘

2

日昆普旧旦昜旬晶参夕多夗名夜月
朔明

晩唱暗暖時譜但昼胆担腸揚殉惨怨

3

水次沃渋永𠂢攸氷冬川㐬凶州昔雨
需

尿泥氾海泣汰沢滑渦況活渇潜混油津浸没
洪港浮渓浄洗踏治池汽泡湯液添詠泳脈派
悠修尽冷凄冶順訓捞流脳悩借惜措震霊零
雪電漏儒

4

火炎灰黒光赤叟

炊煩災談淡嚇赦捜

土圭坐尭圣丘山阜降厂丸厄产反厓
段石声

5 塀坑塑堅吐塊地場均墨佳封挫暁焼怪仙峡
炭岳隅限険附隠陽陛圧危顔仮坂阪涯崖暇
妬硫拓砲岩

卜占兆万历

6
訃赴外掛点眺挑跳励

PLANTS

1. SMALL PLANTS

Within the things encompassed by the domain of nature, perhaps the most relevant to our world view is the existence of life, because it is thanks to life that the universe—nature—can be understood, for without life there is no apparent consciousness. Be it as it may, one of the most basic visible forms of life are 'small plants' 屮, which are an indispensable source of oxygen and food, so it is better if they appear in great numbers 艹, or with 'lush' leaves 丰. The germination process of plants is also represented. In such process a 'sprout' 乇 appears first, then a bud with leaves 屯—which represents 'growth'—and, finally, several buds with leaves 世—which represent a whole 'generation' of plants.

The world of kanji also takes in particular consideration the 'bamboo' plant 竹, since in ancient Chinese cultures that plant was used to make a great variety of objects.

屮

屮 十

Small plant

539

Ⓜ

A <u>small plant</u> with its stem standing straight and leaves coming out of it.

This graph is usually represented under simplified strokes such as 十 or other variants.

端

端

タン

はし

は

Plant growing while absorbing rain water

edge

540

Originally 耑, this glyph is an ideogram representing a *small plant* (屮 → 山) absorbing rain as a *raincoat* (而), probably referring to the germination of plants made possible thanks to rain water. The original meaning of the character was that of 'germination' or 'start', and eventually it started to denote the notion of an extreme or **edge**—in the sense that a beginning is related to an end. The component 立 (*to stand*) was added later to reinforce the idea of the upright position of the plant, that is, to clarify that the plant has grown and that the germination has been indeed produced.

余 余 ヨ あま.る *Talking growing and distributed* **to remain** 541 Ⓢ

Mouth talking (亼) words that grow like *small plants* (屮 → 十 → 亍) and are distributed (八 → ハ) among the people: Words that spread among people and penetrate, words that **remain**.

敘 叙 ジョ *Remains 余 (ヨ) taken by an outstretched hand 又* **assessment** 542

塗 塗 ト ぬ.る *Water 氵 remaining 余 on earth 土 (ト)* **to smear** 543

除 除 ジョ ジ のぞ.く *Mountains' 阝 remains 余 (ヨ)* **to remove** 544

早 早 ソウ サッ はや.い *Plant lit by the rising sun* **early** fast 545 Ⓢ

The *sun* (日 → 曰) rising above *small plants* (屮 → 十), indicating the first light of the morning, the **early** hours.

𠦝 カン *Person waking up along the early sun* *Sunrise* 546 Ⓡ Ⓢ

Originally 𠦝, this component is a modification of the character 早 (*early*), to which the component for *person on his back* (匕 → 十) was added at the top in order to highlight the idea of human activity at the time of dawn, reinforcing the connotation of sunrise.

乾 乾 カン かわ.く *Sunrise 𠦝 (カン) making people beg 乞* **to get dry** 547

朝
朝 ①②チョウ ①あさ 548 Ⓢ

Sun rising and moon hiding

① **morning**

② dynasty

SPECIAL READING 今朝 [けさ]: *this morning*

Time when the *sun rises* (𠦝) and the *moon* (月) hides behind it, scene that indicates the beginning of a new **morning**.

嘲
嘲 チョウ あざけ.る 549

Words 口 *heard in the morning* 朝 (チョウ)

to sneer

NOTE This character originally referred to the morning song of birds. That characteristic chirping sound would later be associated with the humorous, sharp tone that is commonly used when **sneer**ing at someone.

潮
潮 チョウ しお 550

Water 氵 *of the morning* 朝 (チョウ)

tide

NOTE Originally this character referred to morning tides, while the now obsolete character 汐 [*water+moon*] referred to night tides. Over time the present character became a reference to both morning and night **tide**s.

生
生 551 Ⓢ

①②③ショウ
①②③セイ
① う.まれる
② い.きる
③ は.える
③ お.う
④ なま
④ き

Plant coming out of the earth-soil

① **to be born**

② **to live**

③ **to grow** (something)

④ **raw**

Originally 㞢, a *small plant* (屮 → 𠂉) born from the *earth-soil* (土). This image suggests, initially, the idea of **birth**—the main meaning of the character—, but it also extends to what birth entails: **life**. Within a broader semantic field, there is also found in this character the more literary notions of **growing** something—giving birth to a plant—and **raw**—something taken or presented as it was born.

姓 ショウ セイ

姓 — *Woman 女 giving birth 生* (ショウ) — **family name** — 552

性 ①②セイ ①ショウ

性 — *Heart-mind 忄 of a living 生 (ショウ) being* — ① **disposition** ② **gender** — 553

隆 リュウ

隆 — *Mountains 阝 kept still 夂 while plants grow 生* — **burgeoning** — 554

産 サン う.まれる うぶ-

産 — *Plants visibly 产 cultivated 生* — **to be produced** — 555

SPECIAL READING 土産 [みやげ]: *gift*

吿 告 コク つ.げる

Words being born — **to announce** — 556 Ⓢ

Originally 吿, *words* (口) that are *born* (⾥ → 生 → 㞢) to communicate or **announce** something.

星 星 セイ ショウ ほし

Living sun — **star** — 557 Ⓢ

A celestial body that *lives* (生 ショウ) in the sky as the *sun* (日 → 日): a **star**.

不 不 フ ブ

Plant turned upside down — **no** — 558 Ⓢ

A small plant turned upside down (屮 → 不 → 不), life becoming non-life: a symbol of **negation**.

否 ヒ いな

否 — *Mouth 口 saying no 不* (フ) — **denial** — 559

艸	艹 / 艹	*Several plants* *Plant*	560 Ⓡ Ⓜ

Several *plants* together (屮×2 → 艸 → 艹). This component symbolizes the overall concept of all types of plants rather than the notion of multiple plants.

花 花	カ はな	*Plant 艹 that has been transformed* 化 (カ) **flower**	561
茨 茨	いばら	*Plant 艹 that makes people exhale* 次 briar	562

PLACE NAME USAGE 茨城県 [いばらきけん]: *Ibaraki Prefecture*

芯 芯	シン	*Plant's 艹 heart* 心 (シン) **pith**	563
葛 葛	カツ くず	*Plant 艹 that threatens* 曷 (カツ) **kudzu** (*Pueraria lobata*)	564

NOTE **Kudzu** is a perennial plant very common in East Asia that is characterized by its invasive nature. Since it grows very fast, spreading in all directions, it can end up being threatening to the environment.

芽 芽	ガ め	*Plant 艹 incipient like a tusk* 牙 (ガ) **bud**	565
葬 葬	ソウ ほうむ.る	*Plants 艹 covering the remnant bones of a person 死 by the help of two hands* 廾 **to bury**	566
芝 芝	しば	*Plant 艹 on which feet move forward* 之 **lawn**	567

莖 茎 ケイ くき *Part of a plant 艹 that is malleable like clay molded on a potter's wheel 圣(ケイ)* 568

stalk

艸 草 ソウ くさ *Plants 艹 in an early 早(ソウ) stage of growth* 569

grass

荼 茶 チャ サ *Plant 艹 remains 余 → 汆* 570

tea

 荅 荅 トウ *Several plants put together* 571 Ⓢ

Provisions

Several *plants* (艹) assembled in one place, *coming together* (合(ゴウ)) in order to be used as food provisions in the future.

搭 搭 トウ *Hand 扌 with provisions 荅(トウ)* 572

freight

塔 塔 トウ *Earth-soil 土 elevation with provisions 荅(トウ) inside* 573

tower

 若 若 ジャク ニャク わか.い *Hand feeding plants to a mouth* 574 Ⓢ

young

An *outstretched hand* (又 → ナ) taking a handful of edible *plants* (艹) to the *mouth* (口), showing an acquisition of vigor and energy through food. The notion of vigorousness later was associated with the connotation of **youth**. The lower part of this sinogram is graphically identical to the component for "right hand" (右).

諾 諾 ダク *Speech 訁 of the young 若(ジャク)* 575

accordance

NOTE It refers to the Confucian mentality in which juniors are supposed to respect and be in **accordance** with seniors.

 荒 荒 コウ あら.す *Plants perishing in a stream of water* **to devastate** 576 Ⓢ

Plants (艹) *perishing* (亡) and being **devastate**d by a strong *stream of water* (川 → 川).

慌 慌 コウ あわ.てる *Heart-mind* 忄 *being devastated* 荒(コウ) **disconcerted** 577

 蒸 蒸 ジョウ む.す *Plants being heated* **to steam** 578

A *kneeling person* (卩 → 了) grabbed by *two hands* (廾 ≈ 収 → フく), put inside a pot (一) over *fire* (火 → 灬), representing the action of burning a person as a death penalty. Over time, this depiction of capital punishment became metaphorical and started to allude to the burning of food and **steaming**. From that point on the component for *plants* (艹) was added to the character in order to reinforce these latter connotations.

 卉 卉 *Abundant plants* 579 Ⓜ

Originally 芔, a lot of *plants* (屮×3 → 芔 → 卉) growing together.

 奔 奔 ホン *Person running through plants* **hustle** 580

Originally 奔 [夭卉], a person *wiggling* (夭 → 大) while running in a **hustle** through a field full of *plants* (卉).

 莫 莫 バク ボ *Sun behind the plants* *Hidden* not being 581 ㊔ Ⓢ

Originally 莫 [茻日], and then 莫, the *sun* (日 → 日) <u>hiding</u> behind a horizon full of *plants* (艹 ← 艸×2 → 茻 → 廾 → 夫).

膜 **膜** マク 582

Meat 月 that is hidden 莫 (バク)

membrane

慕 **慕** ボ したう 583

Hidden 莫 (ボ) feelings ⺗

to yearn (for)

暮 **暮** ボ く.れる 584

Hidden 莫 (ボ) sunlight 日

to get dark

募 **募** ボ つの.る 585

Hidden 莫 (ボ) strength 力

to become stronger

漠 **漠** バク 586

Water 氵 hidden 莫 (バク) below the surface

desert

墓 **墓** ボ はか 587

Hidden 莫 (ボ) in the arth 土

grave (tomb)

 丰 丰 龶 588 Ⓡ Ⓜ

Lush plant

Originally 𡴀, a *plant* (屮) taller and with more leaves than usual, a lush plant. The original form 𡴀 eventually got simplified into 丯, and later into its current form 丰.

When this component is placed on top of the compounds it adopts a flattened form 龶.

毒 **毒** ドク 589

Lush plant 龶 acting as the mother 毋 of other plants

poison

NOTE This character originally referred to some type of medicinal plant cultivated domestically, hence the occurrence of the component for "mother" (母 → 毋), which alludes to the maternal care usually linked to healing processes. Over time the meaning of 'medicinal plant' ended up drifting, ironically, into that of **poison**, possibly due to an association between the bitter taste and poisonous nature (taken in large quantities) of some medicinal plants.

 麦 麦 バク むぎ

Still foot standing by a lush plant 590 Ⓡ Ⓜ

barley

wheat

A *lush plant* (丰 → 龶) by which people stand *still* (夂) in order to cultivate them, a clear reference to cultivation fields and more specifically to **barley** or **wheat** fields.

麺 麺 メン

Wheat's 麦 visible face 面(メン) 591

noodles

 夆 夆 ホウ

Still foot on lush plants 592 Ⓢ

A *foot standing still* (夂) on top of a *lush plant* (丰). This component, conceptually similar to the character for "barley" (麦), differs from it because that one designates a passive action—a plant stumbling upon feet—whereas this one designates an active action: feet standing on top of the plant.

峰 峰 ホウ みね

Part of a mountain 山 *where there are lush plants that can be stepped on* 夆(ホウ) 593

summit

 勃 勃 ボツ

Lush plant growing like a child 594

erection

Originally 孛, a *lush plant* (丰 → 𠀆) growing up high quickly as a *child* (子). Over time the component 力 (*strength*) was added to the character to emphasize the idea of a sudden growth in size and, consequently, in strength: an **erection**.

 寿 寿 ジュ ことぶき

Lush plant gotten through work 595 Ⓢ

longevity

A *lush plant* (丰 → 𡗗) obtained through *work* (寸), implying the idea of a cultivation made over a time long enough for the plant to grow a thick, lush foliage. The long cultivation time happens to be symbolically associated, therefore, with **longevity**.

 拝 拜 ハイ おが.む 596

Hand holding a long lush plant

to pay homage

A *hand* (手 → 扌) grasping the lushest and leafiest of the plants (丰 → 手) to be delivered as a sign of **homage**.

 奉 奉 𡗗 ブ ホウ たてまつ.る 597 Ⓡ Ⓢ

Two hands giving a lush plant

to offer

Originally 𠦬 [丰収], *two hands* (収 ← 廾) **offer**ing a *lush plant* (丰) in a religious or state service. Over time this character underwent a visible graphical transformation. The "two hands" component got intermingled with the "lush plant" component, giving rise to the upper set of strokes 𡗗, which shows a part of the two hands next to the leaves of the lush plant; and the lower set of strokes 𠂒, which shows the stem of the lush plant also mixed with some strokes of the two hands.

When this character is placed as a component at the top of compounds it adopts the following reduced form: 𡗗.

俸 俸 ホウ 598

Person 亻 *with an offering* 奉(ホウ)

salary

奏 奏 ソウ かな.でる 599

An offering 𡗗 *to heaven* 天

to play music

NOTE This ideogram originally referred to religious offering ceremonies, that presumably were accompanied by **musical instrumentation**.

泰 泰 タイ 600

An offering 𡗗 *of water* 氺

peaceable

Thailand

 庚 庚 ⿸厂肀 コウ 601 ㊔ Ⓢ

Two hands holding a lush plant

seventh

Originally ⿸厂肀, *two hands* ((⺕ + ⺕) → (丿 + ⺕)) holding a *lush plant* (丰 → 𠂒 → (亠+人)). This character has suffered, visibly, a quite drastic graphic evolution, but ideographically it is very similar in origin to the character 奉 (*to offer*). The difference between both of them is that the present character represents the action of 'receiving', or holding, instead of the notion of 'offering'. Such a nuance can be clearly seen in the original ideogram, in which the hands laterally 'grab' (𠂇彐) the plant instead of lifting it up (収) as it is offered.

When this character is placed as a component at the top of compounds it adopts the following reduced form: 𢆉.

康 康 コウ — *Two hands holding a lush plant* 𢆉 *from which water* 氺 *falls* — 602

ease

 唐 唐 トウ — *Two hands feeding a lush plant to the mouth* — 603

Tang dynasty

Two hands holding a lush plant (庚 → 𢆉) that is fed to the *mouth* (口). The concrete meaning of this ideogram seems to allude to that of a generous ruler or a fertile land. This glyph of positive connotations was adopted in any case by the Chinese **Tang dynasty** royal family to refer to its clan.

 坴 坴 — *Lush plants distributed in the earth-soil* — 604 Ⓜ

Cultivation

Originally 坴, *lush plants* (丰 → 丰 → 土) *distributed* (八 → ハ → 儿) in the *earth-soil* (土) through extensive cultivation.

睦 睦 ボク — *Eye* 目 *looking closely at cultivations* 坴 — 605

harmonious

陸 陸 リク — *Mountains* 阝 *with cultivations* 坴 — 606

land

 埶 埶 — *Person cultivating lush plants* — 607 Ⓜ

Originally 執 [坴丮], a person *working with his hands* (丮 → 丸) in the *cultivation of lush plants* (坴 → 坴).

勢 セイ *Strength 力 of a person who cultivates lush plants 執* 608
勢 いきお.い **force**

熱 ネツ *Person putting cultivated lush plants 執 on fire 灬* 609
熱 あつ.い **hot** (thing)

陵 リョウ *Person placing lush plants on top of mountains* 610
陵 みささぎ (imperial) **grave mound**

A *kneeling person* (卩 → 儿) with his *still feet* (夂) on top of a *mountain* (阜 → 阝) where he deposits some *lush* plants (丰 → 龶 → 土) as an offering, the image of a funerary ritual made in an imperial **grave mound**. Tombs in East Asia were traditionally built by erecting mounds on the ground—also known as *tumuli*—under which the deceased were buried.

舞 ブ *Person moving with his feet while holding lush plants* 611 Ⓢ
無 舞 ま.う **to dance**

Originally 亦 [大卌], a *person seen from the front* (大) grasping with each hand some *lush plants* (丰×2 → 丰丰 → 卄卄). This character has an ideographic composition similar to the character 奏 (*to play music*), which depicts a person moving or **dancing** while holding some kind of lush plants that fulfill a decorative function. This character also shows the use of lush plants as a decorative element and refers to a kind of ceremonial dance, probably shamanistic. The notion of dance and movement was reinforced later with the addition of the component 舛 (*two moving feet*) that appears in the graph when it acts as a standalone character. The current form of the glyph is a visibly evolved version, and the strokes that formerly made apparent the different formative components in the original form 亦 have merged together forming the ambiguous set of strokes 無, wherein the upper part 𠂉 is a vestige of the head and arms of the man seen from the front (亠 → 𠂉); the bottom line 一 is the evolution of the lower part of that same component (ㅅ → 一); and the four vertical lines crossed by a horizontal line (卌) is a simplification of the old components that depicted the lush plants (丰×2 → 丰丰 → 卄卄 → 卌).

無 ブ *Person putting lush plants 無ブ on fire 灬* 612
無 ム **to not be**
な.い

乇
乇 タク

Sprout

613 Ⓢ

The budding germ of a plant, a <u>sprout</u>. The small stem of the incipient plant is indicated by the stroke L, while the nascent leaves are indicated by the upper stroke ノ. The central horizontal stroke 一 is the linearization of the thickness of the stem originally shown by an ink stain.

託
託 タク

Speech 言 *that sprouts* 乇 (タク)

commitment

614

屯
屯 トン

Sprout growing up

growth

military camp

615 Ⓢ

A sprout with **grown** leaves or flowers (乇 → 屯). The original meaning of 'growth' later became to be associated with 'accumulation' and 'gathering' and later on those nuances gave rise, probably due to a phonetic association, to the meaning of **military camp**, the "gathering of troops",

---

頓
頓 トン

Growth 屯 (トン) *of the head* 頁

determined

616

春
春 シュン
はる

Growth of lush plants under the sun

springtime

617

Originally 萅 [艹屯日], several *plants* (艹) *growing* (屯) under the *sun* (日), depicting a distinctive **spring**-like scene. Over time the top component 芚 got simplified into the form 夫, which is graphically identical to the reduced version of component 奉 (*two hands holding a lush plant*).

世
世 セ
セイ
よ

Several sprouts

generation

world

618 Ⓜ

Several consecutive plant <u>sprouts</u> of different sizes, figuratively showing germinations from the past, the present and the future, alluding thus to different **generations**. The meaning of 'generation' is also sometimes expanded to that of **world**, understood as a psychological rather than a physical place, a space that can house all generations. The stems of the sprouts are represented by the strokes ㄴ, ㄴ and 丨, while the thickness mark of the leaves have been joined in a horizontal line 一.

竹 竹 竹 ⺮ チク たけ **bamboo plant** (*Bambuseae*) 619 Ⓡ Ⓜ

Several **bamboo** plants with long stems (丨 亅) and their leaves (𠂉×2) hanging down.

As component this glyph appears with the flattened form ⺮, which is placed at the upper part of the compounds.

The semantics of this character, when acting as a component, besides commonly alluding to objects made of bamboo, occasionally points to the wobbly movement and elasticity shown by bamboo plants.

Hanging bamboo leaves

620

笑 笑 ①② ショウ ① わら.う ② え.む

Person wiggling 夭 like a bamboo plant ⺮

① **to laugh**
② **to smile**

NOTE This character is a metaphorical, almost poetic, association of the *wiggly* and graceful movement (夭) of *bamboo plants* (竹 → ⺮) with the idea of a **smile** shown on the face, which becomes flexible and light as bamboo. The metaphorical sense of this character is conveniently corroborated by the Japanese poetic term 山笑う (*yamawarau*), "smiling mountain", which refers to mountains in spring when they have all their trees in bloom.

621

笛 笛 テキ ふえ

Bamboo stem ⺮ (チク) entering the mouth 由

flute

答 答 トウ こた.える — *Shared talk between two mouths 合 (ゴウ) going back and forth like bamboo plants ⺮* 622

to answer

符 符 フ — *Bamboo ⺮ pieces that are attached 付 (フ)* 623

token

筆 筆 ヒツ ふで — *Bamboo ⺮ brush 聿* 624

(writing or painting) **brush**

筋 筋 キン すじ — *Body part 月 that is strong 力 and pliant like a bamboo plant ⺮* 625

sinew

等 等 トウ ひと.しい — *Bamboo tablets ⺮ arranged at temples 寺* 626

equivalent (to)

NOTE The etymological understanding of this character requires a bit of historical background, since it is necessary to know that in ancient China, primitive books or administrative writings were made of thin sliced bamboo slabs joined together in a vertical position by threads. Ancient religious temples and monasteries, as in the West, were distinguished as places where books and documents where elaborated and preserved, hence the relation of **equivalence** between books—or bamboo slats—and religious temples.

 算 算 サン — *Two hands handling an abacus made of bamboo* 627

calculation

Two hands (廾) handling a *bamboo* object (竹 → ⺮) with a rectangular shape with grilles (目), which represents a computational abacus or *suanpan* (算盤)—called *soraban* in Japanese—used to make **calculations.**

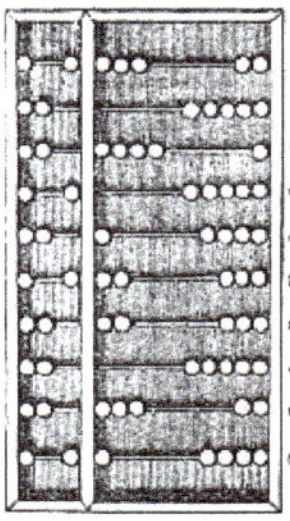

Common abacus or 'suanpan'

散 散 サン ち.らかす 628

Hand hitting plants under the moonlight

to scatter

A *hand with a mattock hitting* (攵) *bamboo plants* (竹 → 龷) away at night under the *moonlight* (月 → 月), alluding, plausibly, to a scene depicting a party of hunters or warriors **scatter**ing across.

瓜 瓜 コ 629 ㊔ Ⓢ

Gourd plant

gourd

A gourd, squash, melon or any other of the plants from the cucurbit family, which are characterized by having their fruits growing while hanging from the branches.

A hanging gourd

孤 孤 コ 630

Child 子 born in solitude like a gourd in a gourd plant 瓜

solitary

2. TREES

Large plants with sturdy trunks are known as 'trees' 木, and like the smaller plants that we have already seen, they take great prominence within the compositional elements of Chinese characters, since trees also serve to refer to wood and objects made of it. From the morphology of the tree some other concepts derive, such as that of 'root' 本, which denotes an origin or principle, or that of the top of a tree 末, which denotes an 'end'.

Thanks to the wood obtained from trees one can make a 'bundle' to transport things 束, and from this bundle a 'backpack' 東 can be also made. But trees are not only used to get wood and create objects with it, since they also bear fruit, and a tree with 'fruits' 禾 is distinctly used as a symbol of fruitfulness. There are even trees that bear fruits so heavy they they 'droop' off the branches 垂.

木 **木** ボク モク き こ- **tree** **wood** 631 Ⓡ Ⓜ

Originally 朩, a tree with a trunk (丨) from which branches appear extending upwards (凵 → 一) and roots extending downwards (八). As a component, this glyph gets the meaning not only of 'tree' but also of 'wood' (**tree**-and-**wood**).

休 **休** キュウ やす.む — *Person 亻 leaning on a tree-wood 木* — **to rest** 632

校 **校** コウ — *Tree-wood 木 being interchanged 交* (コウ) — **school** 633

NOTE Probably referring to a place where wooden counting rods where shared and interchanged in order to learn to count as one would do in a **school**.

梅 **梅** バイ うめ — *Tree 木 that looks scruffy 毎* (マイ) — **plum tree** (*Prunus mume*) **plum** 634

SPECIAL READING 梅雨 [つゆ]: *rainy season*

Prunus mume tree

根 根	コン ね	*Part of the tree 木 that stays still 艮*（コン） **root**	635
杉 杉	すぎ	*Tree 木 that looks like it had hair 彡 on its top* **redwood tree** (*Cryptomeria japonica*)	636

Redwood tree

検 検	ケン	*Tree-woods 木 under authority 僉*（ケン） **examination**	637
枚 枚	マイ	*Tree-wood 木 that has been hit 攵* **flat object**	638
村 村	ソン むら	*Tree-woods 木 along which work 寸*（スン）*is done* **village**	639
架 架	カ か.かる	*Addition 加*（カ）*of tree-woods 木* **to assemble**	640
条 条	ジョウ	*Still 夂 tree-wood 木* **prerequisite**	641
傑 傑	ケツ	*Person 亻 with two moving feet 舛 on top of a tree 木* **outstanding**	642

札 ① サツ *Tree-wood's 木 unfolded energy 乚* 643

札 ①② ふだ **① piece of paper** **② banknote**

NOTE In reference to the fact that **paper**—and therefore also **banknotes** —come from trees.

松 ショウ まつ *Evergreen tree 木 with leaves always shown to the public 公 (コウ)* 644

pine tree (*Pinus*)

pine

染 セン そ.める *Arm 九 pouring water 氵 mixed with tree 木 leaves* 645

to dye

板 ハン バン いた *Tree-wood 木 that is reversed 反 (ハン)* 646

board

朴 ボク *Tree 木 with providence 卜* 647

magnolia tree (*Magnolia obovata*)

NOTE The flowers of the **magnolia tree** were regarded in ancient China as a scarce and precious product, and for that reason it was associated with good fortune and providence.

桃 トウ もも *Tree 木 with good omen 兆 (チョウ)* 648

peach tree (*Prunus persica*)

peach

NOTE **Peach**es were considered in ancient China as a symbol of longevity—the result of a good omen—reflected in Chinese mythology through the Peaches of Immortality (仙桃), which was considered as food eaten by the immortals.

栃 とち *Tree 木 with fruits looking like a rolling rock 厉* 649

horse chestnut tree (*Aesculus turbinata*)

PLACE NAME USAGE 栃木県 [とちぎけん]: *Tochigi Prefecture*

A chestnut

650

杯
杯 ①② ハイ ② さかずき

Tree-wood 木 object that spills like a plant turned upside down 不(フ)

① **cup**
② **sake cup**

651

模
模 ボ モ

Tree-wood 木 that is hidden 莫(ボ)

mold

652

棒
棒 ボウ

Tree-wood 木 part of a lush-plant offering 奉(ホウ)

stick

653

葉
葉 ヨウ は

Plant-like 艹 sprouts 世 that come out of a tree 木

leaf

---

654 Ⓜ

林
林 リン はやし

Several trees

grove

Several *trees* (木×2) placed together forming a **grove**.

---

655 Ⓢ

厤 レキ

Wooded pass on the top of a cliff

Passage

A *grove* (林) above a *cliff* (厂), representing a mountain pass, a geographic feature figuratively adapted to reflect the passage of time.

656

歴
歴 レキ

Mountain pass 厤(レキ) *with footsteps 止 on its surface*

passage of time

暦 657

暦 レキ こよみ

Passage (of time) 厤 (レキ) *dictated by the sun* 日

calendar

森 658

森 シン もり

Many trees

forest

A big amount of *trees* (木×3) placed together, a **forest**.

乗 659 Ⓢ

乗 ジョウ の.る

Person on top of a tree

to ride

Originally 椉 [亠舛木], and then 乘, a *person seen from the front* (大 → 亠 → ノ) with both *moving feet* (舛 → 北) on top of a tree (木), a scene that shows a man climbing a tree or, literally, **riding** it. This character eventually underwent a further simplification process with the transformation of the glyph 乘 into 乗, where the central strokes got intertwined.

采 660 Ⓢ

采 サイ

Hand grabbing wood

baton

A hand *grabbing* (爪 → ⺥) a piece of *tree-wood* (木), namely a stick, cane or **baton**.

彩 661

彩 サイ いろど.る

Hand grabbing a piece of tree-wood 采 (サイ) *with hair* 彡 *at its tip*

to color

NOTE This is an ideogram making a clear reference to a painting brush with animal hair bristles at its tip.

採 662

採 サイ と.る

Hand 扌 *grabbing a piece of tree-wood* 采 (サイ)

to pick

菜 663

菜 サイ な

Plants 艹 *on pieces of tree-wood that can be grabbed* 采 (サイ)

vegetables

 相 相 — ①② ソウ / ①② ショウ / ② あい — 664 Ⓢ

Tree observed by an eye

① **appearance**

② **mutual**

Tree (木) being observed by an *eye* (目) examining its solid **appearance.** This character also takes the secondary meaning of 'mutual', alluding to the shared—**mutual**—space of both the observing entity and the observed object.

想 想 — ソウ / ソ — 665

Appearance 相 (ソウ) *of the heart-mind* 心

thought

霜 霜 — ソウ / しも — 666

Rain's ⻗ *solid appearance* 相 (ソウ)

frost

箱 箱 — はこ — 667

Bamboo ⺮ *with a solid appearance* 相

box

NOTE Probably it originally referred to ancient trunks made of bamboo wood.

 某 某 — ボウ — 668 Ⓢ

Sweet tree-wood

(a) **certain**

A *tree-wood* (木) with a **certain** *sweet taste* (甘), such as licorice or *gancao* (甘草)—*kanzō* in Japanese, that stands out.

媒 媒 — バイ — 669

Woman 女 *that is certain* 某 (ボウ)

matchmaker

謀 謀 — ボウ / ム / はか.る — 670

Speech 言 *that is certain* 某 (ボウ)

to scheme

 桼 桼 — 671 Ⓜ

Fluid coming out of a tree

Sap

Originally 桼 [木水], a *fluid* (水 → 氺) coming out of a *tree* (木) in the form of drops (ヘ): the sap from trees.

膝 膝 ひざ — *Body part* 月 *soft as sap* 桼 — **knee** 672

漆 漆 シツ うるし — *Fluid* 氵 *that covers surfaces as sap* 桼 — **lacquer** 673

 者 者 シャ もの — *Mouth eating cooked food* — **person doing an action** 674 Ⓢ

This glyph shows some branches of a tree emitting sparks of *fire* (朮 → 火 → 耂) and a *mouth with food inside* (甘 → 日) or, in other words, a mouth eating food that has been cooked on the embers, scene depicting one of the most basic **actions** that a human being can do: eating.

暑 暑 ショ あつ.い — *Sun* 日 *acting* 者(シャ) — **hot** (weather) 675

諸 諸 ショウ — *Speech* 言 *and actions* 者(シャ) — **various** 676

煮 煮 シャ に.る — *Acting* 者(シャ) *fire* 灬 — **to boil** 677

著 著 ①② チョ ① あらわ.す ② いちじる.しい — *Plants'* 艹 *action* 者(シャ) — ① **to author** ② **remarkable** 678

NOTE One of the original meanings of this character was 'to blossom' or 'to bear fruit'. That meaning eventually derived into the sense of 'producing' and finally into the current meaning of writing or **author**ing.

箸 箸 はし — *Bamboo sticks* ⺮ *acting* 者 — **chopsticks** 679

---

680 Ⓢ

尞 リョウ

Wood burnt on a fire over which people talk

Bonfire

Originally 尞 [夾火], branches of a tree emitting sparks (夾) of *fire* (火 → 小), a depiction of a <u>bonfire</u>. Later on the component 日 (*spoken words*) was added to reflect the idea of a bonfire around which people talk and converse.

681

僚 リョウ

Person 亻 *by a bonfire* 尞 (リョウ)

colleague

682

瞭 リョウ

Eye 目 *seeing things that are lit by the light of a bonfire* 尞 (リョウ)

clearness

683

桑 ソウ くわ

Tree with hanging bunches of mulberries

mulberry tree (*Morus*)

A *tree* (木) top from which several bunches of **mulberries** (叒) hang.

---

684 Ⓡ Ⓜ

耒

Heavily branched tree

A *tree* (木) with many lush <u>branches</u> (丰).

685

耗 モウ コウ

Tree's branches 耒 *becoming like fur* 毛 (モウ)

decrease

686

籍 セキ

Bamboo tablets ⺮ *on which there are written heavy branches* 耒 *of older times* 昔 (セキ)

register

---

687 Ⓜ

本 ①②③ ホン ① もと

Root of a tree

① **foundation**

② **book**

③ long object

The roots of a *tree* (木) represented by a line (一) in the lower part of the trunk.

The meaning of root derived from this character is interpreted figuratively, rendering 'root' as the origin or **foundation** of something. When the character appears as a single word, it also adopts the meaning of **book**, probably due to a phonetic loan, although books can be understood as the 'root' of knowledge.

688

体
体
タイ
テイ
からだ

A person's 亻 foundation 本

body

---

689 Ⓢ

朱
朱
シュ

Cut tree branches

scarlet

A *tree* (木) with branches (一) that have been cut (丿), leaving their inner part exposed, which usually has a reddish or scarlet color.

690

殊
殊
シュ
こと

Bone remains 歹 cut like tree branches 朱 (シュ)

peculiar

691

株
株
かぶ

Trees 木 turned into cut branches 朱

stock

---

692 Ⓢ

末
末
マツ
バツ
すえ

Top of a tree

ending

The top of a *tree* (木) pointed out by a long horizontal line (一) on the upper part of the component. The top of the tree figuratively marks the **end** of it.

693

抹
抹
マツ

Hand 扌 making an ending 末 (マツ)

erasure

---

694 Ⓢ

未
未
ミ

Leafy tree not yet fruitful

not yet

goat sign (Chinese zodiac)

A *tree* (木) with small leaves (一) but no fruit **yet**, a tree that is about to bloom.

妹 **妹** マイ いもうと *Woman 女 that has not grown up yet 未* **younger sister** 695

味 **味** ミ あじ *Food in the mouth 口 that has not been swallowed yet 未* **taste** 696

魅 **魅** ミ *Presence of a ghost 鬼 whose figure has yet 未 to appear* **fascination** 697

昧 **昧** マイ *Sunlight 日 that has not appeared yet 未* **unclear** 698

 来 **来** ライ く.る *Fruits sprouting from a tree* **to come** 699

Originally 來, a *tree* (木) with branches from which fruits in bloom (从 → 䒑) are hanging, a tree that attracts people and animals and makes them come for fruits. This glyph also suggests the idea of people who **come** home with fruits in their hands after having collected them.

 束 **束** ソク たば *Bundle of wood* *Tied* **bundle** 700 Ⓡ Ⓢ

A **bundle** of *wood* (木) tied together with a rope (口).

勅 **勅** チョク *Bundle 束 of strength 力* **imperial decree** 701

 頼 **頼** ライ たの.む たよ.る *Tied head* **to rely** (on) 702 Ⓜ

A *tied* (束) *head* (頁), a head attached to an external entity on which it depends and on which consequently needs to **rely**.

瀬 瀬 せ — 703

Water 氵 that can be relied on 頼

current (of water)

 東 東 トウ ひがし — 704 Ⓢ

Backpack

east

Originally 東, a *bundle* (束) with contents inside (丷 → 一), a bag or <u>backpack</u>. Although the meaning of **east** is taken from a phonetic association, this glyph metaphorically evokes the scene of a backpack stuck in the ground breaking the horizon, making a contrast point between the sky and the earth like a sun rising from the east at dawn.

凍 凍 トウ こお.る こご.える — 705

Ice 冫 on a backpack 東(トウ)

to freeze

陳 陳 チン — 706

Backpack 東 visible on the climbing of mountains 阝

exhibit

棟 棟 トウ むね むな- — 707

Tree-wood 木 part of a backpack 東(トウ)

ridgepole

NOTE Metaphorical ideogram in which the idea of a wooden branch holding a backpack standing upright is extrapolated to the idea a wooden beam holding the roof of a house.

 曹 曹 ソウ — 708 Ⓢ

Words spoken over soldiers carrying backpacks

sergeant

Originally 𣍘 [𣗥日], two full *backpacks* (東×2 → 𣗥 → 曲) and *spoken words* (日), ideogram that refers to the notion of a **sergeant** giving orders to backpack carrying soldiers.

槽 槽 ソウ — 709

Wooden object 木 shared by sergeants and soldiers 曹(ソウ)

tub

710 Ⓢ

重 **重**

① ジュウ
① チョウ
① おも.い
② かさ.ねる

Person carrying a backpack loaded with earth

① **heavy**
② **to pile up**

This is a highly evolved character that originally had very distinguishable parts, which are: a *person* (人 → ㇀) on top, a *backpack* (東) in the middle, and *earth* (土) at the bottom; forming the glyph 重 [㇀東土], which represents the idea of a bag being **piled up** with earth-like **heavy** contents carried by a person. Eventually the form 重 evolved into the current glyph 重 as the strokes in the middle (个) were absorbed by the lower component (土).

711

腫 **腫**

シュ
は.れる

Body part 月 becoming heavy 重 (ジュウ)

to swell

712

薫 **薫**

クン
かおる

Plants 艹 on a heavy 重 fire 灬

smoky scent

---

713 Ⓢ

動 **動**

ドウ
うご.く

Heavy strength

to move

Heavy (重) *strength* (力) that enables the body to **move**.

714

働 **働**

ドウ
はたら.く

Person 亻 moving 動 (ドウ)

to work

715

勲 **勲**

クン

Movement 動 like that of fire 灬

merit

NOTE This graph seems to allude to the **merit** derived from physical effort, represented by a vigorous movement that generates heat or a burn of energy similar to those produced by fire.

---

716 Ⓢ

量 **量**

② リョウ
① はか.る

Mouth speaking about heaviness

① **to weigh**
② **volume**

Mouth speaking (甘 → 日) about *heaviness* (重 → 重) while **weighing** something in order to know its **volume**.

禾
禾 カ

Tree bearing fruit
fruit [*fig.*]

717 Ⓡ ㊔ Ⓜ

A **fruit** (丿) hanging from the top of a *tree* (木).

718

季
季 キ

Arrival of fruit's 禾 *children* 子

season

719

和
和
①② ワ
① オ
① なご.む
① やわ.らぐ

Fruits 禾 *besides which there is a mouth* 口

① **peaceful**
② Japan

SPECIAL READING 大和 [やまと]: *Ancient Japan*

720

香
香
① コウ
② キョウ
① か
① かお.り

Fruits 禾 *taste in the mouth* 日

① **aroma**
② incense

721

秩
秩 チツ

Fruits 禾 *cut from trees* 失 (シツ)

regularity

722

穏
穏
オン
おだ.やか

Fruits 禾 *and feelings held by two hands* 㥯 (オン)

tranquil

723

稽
稽 ケイ

Principle 旨 *by which it is plausible to raise your arm* 尤 *and efficiently pick fruit* 禾

training

724

私
私
① シ
② わたくし
② わたし

Fruit's 禾 *energy flowing around itself* 厶

① **private**
② **I**

税 税 ゼイ *Fruits 禾 being exposed 兑* **tax** 725

移 移 イ うつ.る *Fruits 禾 of which there are many 多* **to relocate** 726

種 種 シュ たね *Fruits' 禾 heavy 重(ジュウ) part* **seed** (a) **kind** 727

委 委 イ ゆだ.ねる *Fruits of a woman* **to assign** (to) 728 Ⓢ

Fruits (禾) born by a *woman* (女), in reference to the fact of bearing children, a role traditionally **assign**ed to women in society.

萎 萎 イ な.える *What plants' 艹 destiny is assigned to 委(イ)* **to shrivel** 729

秀 秀 シュウ ひい.でる *Fruits of a pregnant woman* **to excel** 730 Ⓢ

The foreseeable *fruit* (禾) of a *pregnant woman* (乃), children, referring to an **excel**lent result within the parameters expected for a woman in traditional society.

誘 誘 ユウ さそ.う *Speech 言 that excels 秀(シュウ)* **to persuade** 731

兼 兼 ケン か.ねる *Hand holding two fruits* **to work simultaneously** 732 Ⓢ

An *outstretched hand* (彐 ≈ 又) grasping two *fruits* (禾×2): hands that **work simultaneously.**

嫌 嫌 ケン ゲン いや きら.う 733

Woman 女 *working simultaneously* 兼 (ケン)

to dislike

謙 謙 ケン 734

Speech 言 *and work done simultaneously* 兼 (ケン)

humble

 秋 秋 シュウ あき 735 Ⓢ

Fruit trees on fire

autumn

A tree whose *fruits* (禾) and leaves turn into the color of *fire* (火) during **autumn**. This ideogram could also refer, in origin, to the stubble burning that was traditionally done in fall in ancient agricultural societies.

愁 愁 シュウ うれ.い 736

Feeling 心 *arising while seeing fruit trees on fire* 秋 (シュウ)

to be distressed

 垂 垂 スイ た.れる 737 Ⓢ

Fruits hanging from a tree

to droop

Originally 𠂹, and then 𠂹, a *fruit tree* (禾 → 千 → 亻), from which many fruits (𠂹) hang. The sense of 'hanging' or **drooping** that emanates from the character was eventually reinforced with the addition of the "earth" component (土)—to highlight the downward direction, pointing to the ground, of hanging fruits—thus giving rise to the form 垂, which would then got simplified into the current glyph: 垂.

唾 唾 ダ つば 738

Something drooping 垂 *from the mouth* 口

saliva

睡 睡 スイ 739

Drooping 垂 (スイ) *eyes* 目

drowsiness

740

華
華
カ
ケ
はな

Exuberant lush plant
splendor

Originally 蕐 [艹 𠌶], a *plant* (艹) as **splendorous** as a *tree that bears many fruits* (𠌶 → 𠌶).

3. GRAINS

In addition to plants, there are some other vegetal elements held in high esteem because they are also a key source of food. Those elements are the 'small' grains 小 that can be obtained from some plants. Within the Asian diet the most important kind of grain is undoubtedly the one that comes off the 'rice plant' 米, from which 'white' rice grains 白 can be extracted.

741
Ⓢ

小
小 ⺌
ショウ
こ
お-
ちい.さい

Small cereal grains
small

Small grains of some kind of <u>cereal</u>.

This component also can take the simplified form ⺌ in some compounds.

742
Ⓢ

肖
肖
ショウ

Cereals and meat
similar

Cereals (小 → ⺌) and *meat* (月 → 月), two of the basic food types ingested by humans, two elements with a **similar** nutritional function.

743

消
消
① ② ショウ
① け.す
② き.える

Water 氵 *over cereals and meat* 肖 (ショウ)

① **to make disappear**
② **to disappear**

744

硝
硝
ショウ

Stone powder 石 *covering cereals and meat* 肖 (ショウ)

saltpeter

NOTE This character can be better understood if it is taken into account that

saltpeter was used as a preservation element in some traditional cuisines.

 当	トウ あ.てる	*Hand aiming at something* **to hit**	745

Originally 彐, an *outstretched hand* (彐 → ヨ) aiming at a *small* (小 → ⺌) object, in order to **hit** it precisely. The literal meaning of the character, 'to hit a target' oftentimes adopts more figurative nuances, such as that of facing or confronting something.

  隙	ゲキ すき	*Small sun rays penetrating through the mountains* **gap**	746

Small (小×2) *sun* (日 → 曰) rays penetrating through the **gaps** of *mountains* (阜 → 阝).

  少	ショウ すく.ない すこ.し	*Several small cereal grains* **little** **few**	747 Ⓢ

Extended form of the glyph 小 (*small cereal grains*), it shows a handful of small cereal grains, which, however, is not large enough to be considered as a meal, i.e. a small amount of cereals, **few** cereal grains. This character also represents the derived concept of **little**.

 妙	ミョウ	*Woman 女 that is little 少* (ショウ) **exquisite**	748
 省	① セイ ②③ ショウ ③ はぶ.く	*Little things 少* (ショウ) *scrutinized by an eye 目* ① **focus** ② **ministry** ③ **to leave out**	749
 抄	ショウ	*Hand 扌 picking a little thing 少* (ショウ) **excerpt**	750

751
劣 劣 レツ おと.る
Little 少 strength 力
to be inferior (to)

752
沙 沙 サ
Water 氵 next to small grains 少 (ショウ)
sand [*fig.*]

753
砂 砂 サ シャ すな
Stone's 石 small grains 少 (ショウ)
sand

754
秒 秒 ビョウ
Fruit's 禾 small grains 少 (ショウ)
second (time unit)

NOTE This glyph originally represented a few *small grain*-shaped elements (少) placed inside *tree fruits* (禾), that is, the seeds or pips of fruits. Over time, the character began to denote anything the size of a seed, or in other words, something tiny. This sense of 'smallness' was finally extrapolated to the more concrete meaning of **second** (as a time unit) to which the character refers today.

755 M
歩 歩 ①② ホ ③ フ ① ある.く ① あゆ.む
Few footsteps
① **to walk**
② **step**
③ pawn

A *few* (少) *footsteps* (止), enough to start **walking**, **step** by step.

756
頻 頻 ヒン
Thinking steps 歩 made by the head 頁
constantly

757
捗 捗 チョク
Hand 扌 making steps 歩
progress

758
渉 渉 ショウ
Water 氵 over which steps 歩 are made
ford

米	米	ベイ マイ こめ	*Rice plant* **rice**	759 Ⓡ Ⓜ

Several grains of **rice** coming off a rice plant's (一) ears (丷, 个).

A rice plant

粒	リュウ つぶ	*Rice plant's 米 part that make people stand upright* 立 (リュウ) **grain**	760
隣	リン とな.る	*Mountains 阝 toward one can go with his moving feet 舛 in order to get rice 米* **to neighbor**	761
粘	ネン ねば.る	*Rice grains 米 that can be easily taken up* 占 (セン) **sticky**	762
菊	キク	*Plant 艹 with leaning 勹 petals looking like rice grains 米* **chrysanthemum** (*Chrysanthemum morifolium*)	763

Diagram of a chrysanthemum flower

764

糖
糖 トウ

Rice grains 米 fed in the mouth 唐 (トウ)

sugar

NOTE The original meaning of this character alluded to a kind of sweet cake made with rice. After the sugar cane was introduced into East Asia the meaning of this character was changed to refer to the element extracted from it: **sugar**.

765

糧
糧 リョウ
ロウ
かて

Rice 米 in a big volume 量 (リョウ)

food

766

娄
娄

Woman picking rice Ⓜ

A *woman* (女) picking *rice* (米).

767

数
数 ①②スウ
①②ス
①かず
②かぞ.える

Woman picking rice 娄 while being hit 攵

① **number**
② **to count**

NOTE Reference to forced—through hits—agricultural labor that requires a **number**ed amount of production.

768

楼
楼 ロウ

Tree-wood 木 structure where picked rice 娄 is stored

high building

769

歯
歯 シ
は

Bones of the mouth used to chew rice Ⓡ Ⓜ

teeth

Originally 𠚕, this graph represented, pictographically, a *mouth* (凵) with its two rows of **teeth** inside (㸚). Over time the component 止 (シ) (*footstep*) was added to the pictogram as a phonetic element, giving rise to the form 齒. Finally the form 齒 was transformed into the current glyph 歯, where the pictographic component representing the teeth (㸚) has been replaced with the semantic component 米 (*rice*), giving rise to a new ideogrammatic reinterpretation of the character, which now shows the element of the mouth (口 → 凵) that stands *stopped* (止) inside and serves to chew *rice* (米) or other food.

齢 770

齢 レイ

Teeth 歯 *counting under command* 令 (レイ)

(one's) **age**

NOTE This character originally referred to the **age** of animals, which was usually determined under a careful inspection of the condition of their teeth.

---

771 Ⓢ

巻 巻 类

カン まく

Two hands rolling rice

to roll (up)

(a) scroll

Two hands manipulating grains of *rice* ((収 + 米) → 类) in order to turn them into **rolls** resembling the symbolic rolled form of *circulating energy* (己).

As a component this character can appear in the abbreviated form 类, in which the lower part of the composition has been taken away.

拳 772

拳 ケン こぶし

A hand 手 *that is rolled up* 类 (カン)

fist

---

773 Ⓢ

暴 暴

ボウ バク あばれる

Four hands fighting for the rice to be eaten

to act violently

Four hands (共 → 共) of people who fight over some *rice* (米 → 氺) that they want to put into their *mouths* (甘 → 日), a scene that is indicative of **violence**.

爆 774

爆 バク

Fire 火 *acting violently* 暴 (バク)

explosion

775

氣 気

キ ケ

Floating energy obtained from rice

air

mood

Originally 氣, the *energy that floats* (气) in the **air** arisen from the intake of food like *rice* (米 → メ). From the physical meaning of 'air' also derives the psychological meaning of **mood**.

釆
采

Isolated rice grain

776 Ⓜ

A particular grain (㇒) isolated from the rest of the grains obtained from a *rice plant* (米).

釈
釈 シャク

Measured 尺 *and isolated* 釆 *parts*

interpretation

777

朮
术 ジュツ

Hand separating a rice grain from the rest

778 Ⓢ

An *outstretched hand* (又 → 屮 → 十) *distributing* (八 → ハ) a grain of rice (丶), separating it from the rest, in reference to a sieve.

白
白

ハク
ビャク
しろ
しら-

White grain of rice

white

Clarity

779 Ⓡ Ⓢ

SPECIAL READING 白髪 [しらが]: *white hair*

A single grain of rice, chosen for its **white**ness and gleam. The angular strokes 口 represent the contour—once pictographical, now linearized—of a round grain of rice. The upper stroke ㇒ is a vestige of what was the depiction of the sharp tip of the grain, and the inner line 一 is an abstract mark that reinforces the idea of what is seen within the grain's contour: the color white. As a component, this glyph usually takes on the meaning of clarity or 'clear', as an evident derivation from the original meaning of 'white'.

Standard shape of a grain of rice

伯
伯 ハク

Person 亻 *with clarity* 白

chief

780

SPECIAL READING 伯父 [おじ]: *father*

拍 **拍** ハク ヒョウ — 781

Hand 扌 *making a clear* 白 (ハク) *sound*

clap

泊 **泊** ハク と.まる — 782

Water 氵 *that is clear* 白 (ハク) *and shallow*

to lodge at

NOTE The allusion to clear and shallow water indicates a suitable area for the anchorage of ships where it is possible to moor and spend the night at some nearby **lodging**.

皆 **皆** カイ みな — 783 Ⓢ

Several people collecting white grains of rice

everyone

Several people (比) collecting *white grains of rice* (白) in order to eat them, an allegorical scene highlighting white rice as the kind of food that **everyone** eats, since white rice is the staple food in ancient and contemporary China.

諧 **諧** カイ — 784

Speech 言 *made by everyone* 皆 (カイ)

consonance

階 **階** カイ — 785

Part of the mountains 阝 *where everyone collect white grains of rice* 皆 (カイ)

storey

楷 **楷** カイ — 786

Tree-wood 木 *used by everyone* 皆 (カイ)

regular style (in writing)

泉 **泉** セン いずみ — 787 Ⓢ

Clear water

fountain

Clear (白) *water* (水) coming out of a **fountain.** It is worth noting that the original form of this character was a pictogram directly showing the water flowing out of a cave, but the part that represented the cave was later replaced by the component 白 (*clarity*).

腺 788
腺 セン

Body part 月 *that secretes liquids like a fountain* 泉(セン)

gland

原 789 Ⓢ
原 ① ゲン ② はら

Fountain springing from a cliff

① **source**

② wilderness

Originally 厡, a *cliff* (厂) acting as the **source** of a fountain of *clear water* (泉 → 㴰).

願 790
願 ガン ねが.う

Source 原(ゲン) *of thought of the head* 頁

to desire

源 791
源 ゲン みなもと

Water's 氵 *source* 原(ゲン)

fountainhead

REVIEW ON PLANTS

1 中端余早𠦝朝生告星不艹荅若荒蒸
卉奔莫丰麦夆勃寿拝奉庚唐坴埶陵
舞乇屯春世竹算散瓜

叙塗除乾嘲潮姓性産隆否花茨芯葛芽葬芝
茎草茶搭塔諾慌膜慕暮募漠墓毒麺峰俸奏
泰康睦陸勢熱無託頓笑笛答符筆筋等孤

2 木林厤森乗采相某桼者尞桑耒本朱
末未来束頼東曹重動量禾委秀兼秋
垂華

休校梅根杉検枚村架条傑札松染板朴桃栃
杯模棒葉歴暦彩採菜想霜箱媒謀膝漆暑諸
煮著箸僚瞭耗籍体殊株抹妹味魅昧勅瀬凍
陳棟槽腫薫働勲季和香秩穏稽私税移種萎
誘嫌謙愁唾睡

3 小肖当隙少歩米娄歯巻暴気釆朮白
皆泉原

消硝妙省抄劣沙砂秒頻捗渉粒隣粘菊糖糧
数楼齢拳爆釈伯拍泊諧階楷腺願源

ANIMALS

1. OVIPAROUS

Animals are, along plants, another key natural element in any culture because they not only provide food but can also be used for many other functions such as transport or clothing.

Within the existing animals two major divisions can be made according to the way in which they are born: oviparous animals, which are born from 'eggs' 卵; and mammalian animals, which are born directly from their mother's womb. Within the oviparous group there are animals as diverse as 'insects' 虫, 'fish' 魚, 'turtles' 亀, or 'birds' 隹 and 'poultry' 鳥, characterized by their wings full of 'feathers' 羽.

792

卵

卵 ラン たまご

Spawn

egg

Several eggs (𠂎, 卩) from a spawn of fish, frogs, insects or any of the species that lay small eggs that stick together and have a black spot in their center. This pictogram currently refers to the broad concept of **egg**.

Eggs from a frog spawn

793 Ⓡ Ⓜ

虫

虫 チュウ むし

Serpent

insect

Cobra type snake, with an upright body, a notoriously large head (口) and a meandering tail (厶). Over time this character began to be associated with any kind of creature with a thin and elongated body, such as worms, and, eventually, any kind of **insect**.

Primitive version of the pictograph for 'snake'

蚕 **蚕** サン かいこ — *Wiggling 夭 → 天 insect 虫* — **silkworm** 794

蛮 **蛮** バン — *People whose distributed energy 亦 is like that of insects 虫* — **barbarian** 795

蚊 **蚊** か — *Insect 虫 that pierces the body like a tattoo 文* — **mosquito** 796

蜂 **蜂** ホウ はち — *Insect 虫 standing still on lush plants 夆 (ホウ)* — **bee** 797

 蜀 **蜀** — *Person picking insects* 798 Ⓜ

A *leaning person* (勹) looking with his *eyes* (罒 ← 目) over an *insect* (虫) in order to pick it up.

濁 **濁** ダク にご.る — *Water 氵 picking insects 蜀* — **to be polluted** 799

 属 **属** ゾク ショク — *Creature sitting on a person picking insects* — **to belong to** 800 Ⓢ

Originally 屬 [尸蜀], an ape-type animal, sitting with its *tail* (尾 → 尸) on top of a person who is *picking up insects* 蜀. This ideogram evokes the scene of a certain kind of animal in relation to another animal of another species, making reference to the interdependence that all living beings maintain, all **belonging** to the same nexus. The lower part of the character (丰 + 蜀) over time got simplified into the strokes 禹.

801

囑 嘱 ショク

Words 口 that make belong 属 (ショク)

entrustment

802 Ⓡ Ⓜ

魚 魚 ギョ うお さかな

fish

A **fish**, drawn vertically. The pointed head is represented by 𠂊 and the body with its scales is represented by 田. The lower strokes 灬 are a schematization of the moving tail of the fish while swimming in the water, a graph that is not semantically related to the simplified version of the component for "fire" (火 → 灬), although it is graphically identical to it.

Primitive version of the pictograph for 'fish'

803

漁 漁 ギョ リョウ

Water 氵 covering fish 魚 (ギョ) *that are going to be caught*

fishing

804 Ⓜ

再 再 サ サイ ふたた.び

Trapped fish

one more time

Fish trapped (冉) between the two ends of a fish trap (工). This character takes its meaning in reference to the fact that fish always fall into the fishing traps **one more time**.

805 Ⓢ

冓 冓 コウ

Fishing trap

A complex net of fishing traps in which several fish have been trapped. The lower part of the graph is the component for "trapped fish" (再), while the upper part is the same component turned upside down and simplified (井), alluding in this way to a multitude of fish trapped thanks to a complex trap or set of traps.

講 講 コウ

Speech 訁 *that captures as a trap* 冓(コウ) 806

lecture

溝 溝 コウ みぞ

Water's 氵 *trap* 冓(コウ) 807

gutter

構 構 コウ かま.える

Tree-wood 木 *turned into a trap* 冓(コウ) 808

to set up

亀 亀 キ かめ 809

turtle

A **turtle** depicted vertically, with the tip of the head represented by ⺈, the protruding head proper depicted by 田, and the body and tail by 电.

隹 隹 スイ

Bird 810 Ⓡ Ⓜ

A rampant <u>bird</u> with folded wings and a short tail, probably a falcon, seen from the side. The left part 亻 represents the bird's body profile (丨) and the head (ノ), while the right part 圭 represents the unfolded plumage.

携 携 ケイ たずさ.える

Hand 扌 *making birds* 隹 *pregnant* 乃 *in order to obtain eggs* 811

to take part in

唯 唯 ユイ イ

Solitary song produced by the mouth 口 *of a bird* 隹(スイ) *in the morning* 812

only

誰 誰 だれ

Sung speech 訁 *of a bird* 隹 *used for calling the attention of other birds* 813

who

someone

NOTE It refers to the question arisen from an unknown voice whose identity has to be ascertained.

雅 雅	ガ	*Fang-shaped* 牙 (ガ) *feathers on a bird* 隹 **elegance**	814
推 推	スイ お.す	*Hand* 扌 *holding a bird* 隹 (スイ) *before its flight* **to support**	815
隻 隻	セキ	*Bird* 隹 *held by an outstretched hand* 又 (a) **single** vessel (vehicle)	816
雌 雌	シ めす め-	*The sex that stays behind* 此 (シ) *during birds'* 隹 *copulation* **female**	817
准 准	ジュン	*Ice* 冫 *instead of water in bird's* 隹 *nourishment* **semi-**	818
堆 堆	タイ	*Earth-soil* 土 *on top of which birds* 隹 (スイ) *rest* **heap**	819

NOTE Originally this character meant 'hill' or 'sea rock', making use of an ideographic association analogous to the form 島[12] (*island*). Over time, however, this glyph began to designate any type of mound or **heap**.

催 催	サイ もよお.す	*Person* 亻 *seen high on a mountain* 山 *like a bird* 隹 (スイ) **to show signs** (of)	820
椎 椎	ツイ	*Tree* 木 *where birds* 隹 (スイ) *rest* **chinquapin tree** (Castanopsis)	821
稚 稚	チ	*Fruits* 禾 *only eaten by birds* 隹 (スイ) **immature**	822

[12] See character #840.

823

雄
雄

ユウ
お
おす

Energetic arm carrying a bird

male

The original glyph was 厷, which represents an *outstretched hand* (又 → ナ) filled with *flowing energy* (厶), highlighting the concept of energy or force evoked by the **male** sex. Later on, the component 隹 (*bird*) was most probably added through an analogy to the character for "female" (雌), which shares said component in reference to the position that the female bird takes in copulation. In contrast, this character can be associated with the active (energetic) role that male birds take in the reproductive act.f

---

824 Ⓢ

焦
焦

① ② ショウ
① こ.げる
② あせ.る

Bird burning in a fire

① to burn

② to fret

A *bird* (隹) that **frets** as it **burns** in a *fire* (火 → 灬).

825

礁
礁

ショウ

Submerged stone 石 that causes fret 焦 (ショウ)

shoal rock

reef

---

826 Ⓜ

集
集

シュウ
あつ.める
つど.う

Birds on a tree

to gather

Originally 雧 [雥木], several *birds* (隹×3 → 雥 → 隹) on top of a *tree* (木), showing the tree as a place where many birds congregate or **gather**, because it is in the tops of trees where a large number of birds can be seen together at rest.

---

827 Ⓜ

奞
奞

Bird unfolding wings

A *bird* (隹) becoming *bigger* (大) while unfolding its wings to take off on a flight.

828

奪
奪

ダツ
うば.う

Work 寸 applied upon a bird that unfurls its wings 奞 trying to escape

to snatch

 雈 カン *Bird with a crest and deep eyes* 829 Ⓢ

Big bird

Originally 雚, a *bird* (隹) with a noticeable crest (艹 → 𠂉) and deep eyes (吅 → 一), a big bird whose physiognomy can be seen in the distance.

歡 歓 カン *Big bird* 雈カン *leaving one's mouth open* 欠 830

delight

觀 観 カン *Big bird* 雈カン *in sight* 見 831

view

勸 勧 カン すす.める *Big bird* 雈カン *that is strong* 力 832

to recommend

權 権 ケン ゴン *Big bird* 雈カン *on top of a tree* 木 833

authority
rights

 蒦 蒦 カク *Outstretched hand grabbing a crested bird* 834 Ⓢ

Snare

An *outstretched hand* (又) snaring a crested bird (隹 + 艹 → 萑 → 雈) on the fly.

護 護 ゴ *Speech* 言 *snaring* 蒦カク *an argument* 835

defense

NOTE This character originally referred to an argumentative **defense** against an accusation. Over time, that connotation was extended to any type of defense or protection.

穫 穫 カク *Fruits* 禾 *snaring* 蒦カク 836

harvest

鳥 **鳥** チョウ とり — poultry **bird** — 837 Ⓡ Ⓜ

A fowl depicted in profile, with a body that is smaller and plumper than that of birds that fly at great heights. The upper part of the graph, 白, represents the beak (丿) and the head with its eyes (日). The middle part ㇉ shows the body and folded wings, and, finally, the bottom part 灬 is a representation of the feet of the bird. Over time, the character's meaning of 'fowl' or **poultry** was expanded to also cover any type of **bird**, while the original character designating such concept (隹) has been relegated to be used only as a component. The original meaning of this character, 'poultry', is mainly reserved in contemporary Japanese for the sense of 'chicken meat'.

Primitive version of the pictograph for 'poultry'

鳴 **鳴** メイ な.く — *Words 口 of a bird 鳥* — **to chirp** **to make sound** — 838

鶏 **鶏** ケイ にわとり — *Bird 鳥 that can be caught even as an adult 奚ケイ* — **chicken** — 839

島 **島** トウ しま — *Mountain 山 overflown by birds 鳥 → 鳥* — **island** — 840

羽 **羽** ウ は はね — *Wings* **feather** — 841 Ⓡ Ⓜ

Two <u>wings</u> (习×2) unfolded and showing their **feathers**.

翌 **翌** ヨク — *Wings 羽 making a bird that was previously standing 立 on the ground fly* — **the following** — 842

NOTE In reference to the succession of movement: The state of flying motion **following** the state of rest.

翼 翼 ヨク つばさ — *Feathers 羽 that are different 異* — **wing** 843

翁 翁 オウ — *Public 公(コウ) man wearing feathers 羽* — **venerable old man** 844

NOTE Referring to the image of a respectable shaman or warlord wrapped in a garment decorated with feathers like those of several tribes in Siberia and North America.

習 習 シュウ なら.う — *Wings 羽 flapping in a clear 白 movement* — **to learn from** 845

翟 翟 タク — *Bird with spread wings* 846 Ⓢ

Originally 翟 [羽隹], a *bird* (隹) with its two *wings* <u>spread</u> (羽 → ヨヨ).

躍 躍 ヤク おど.る — *Feet ⻊ spreading 翟(タク)* — **to leap** 847

曜 曜 ヨウ — *Days 日 spreading 翟 during the week* — **weekday** 848

濯 濯 タク — *Water 氵 spreading 翟(タク)* — **rinse** 849

飛 飛 ヒ と.ぶ — *Bird flapping wings* — **to fly** 850

Originally  two wings spread in full **flight** at high speed. Over time, the component 羽 (*wings*) was added to the original glyph to reinforce the meaning, forming the graph 羽飞, which would later become simplified into 飛 and finally into the current version: 飛. It should be noted that the graphic element 升 of the current version evolved like that due to an analogy with the character 昇[13] (*to rise*), which has the component 升 in it.

非 ヒ

Wings flapping against each other

negation

851 Ⓢ

Two wings spread in opposite directions, **negating** flight and subsequently any action.

俳 ハイ

Person 亻 negating 非 his own personality

actor

852

悲 ヒ かな.しい

Negative 非 feeling 心

sad

853

排 ハイ

Hand 扌 making gestures of negation 非

expulsion

854

2. MAMMALS

Mammalian animals are the ones that have the closest relationship with humans, as many of them have been domesticated. One of the most distinctive domesticated mammals is the 'dog' 犬, which not only helps with cattle or to act as a guardian but also serves as a companion. Another important mammal is the 'hog' 豕, which helps with dietary needs. There are also larger animals, such as the 'elephant' 象 or the 'horse' 馬. We have, as well, some mammals that are aggressive and indomitable, such as the 'capable' bear 能 or the 'tiger' 虎, or those characterized by their 'horns' 角, such as the oxen or 'cattle' 牛, the 'sheep' 羊 or the 'deer' 鹿.

犬 犭 ケン いぬ

Mammalian animal

dog

855 Ⓡ Ⓜ

[13] Character #1053

An animal standing on four legs, with a tail and pointed ears, depicted in a vertical position. This is a generic pictographic representation that suggests many types of mammalian animals, from which the concept of **dog** was taken for the base meaning of the character when working as a standalone. The horizontal line 一 represents at the same time the head and the front legs, the oblique line ノ also represents the head and the hind legs, while the drop 丶 represents the ears and the stroke ㇏ the body and an upright tail.

When the character acts as a component and is placed on the left of the compounds, it adopts the form 犭, which is more similar to the original pictograph.

Primitive version of the pictograph for 'dog'

伏 伏 フク ふ.す *Person 亻 adopting the pose of an animal 犬* 856
to bow down

犯 犯 ハン おか.す *Animal 犭 making a person huddle* ハン *㔾* 857
to violate

狭 狭 キョウ せま.い *Animal 犭 in the middle of people* キョウ *夹* 858
narrow

NOTE Referring to a **narrow** pass, in the middle of a forest or a mountain, where it is easy to come across animals.

独 独 ドク ひと.り *Animal 犭 waiting alone to hunt an insect 虫* 859
alone

獲 獲 カク え.る *Animal 犭 capturing a big bird* カク *蒦* 860
to obtain

獄 獄 ゴク *Place where speeches 言 are made among animals 犭犬* 861
prison

862

猟

猟 リョウ

Dog and furry animals

game-hunting

Originally 巤 [𡿺 [illegible]], a hairy head (𡿺 ← 囟) surrounded by more hair ([illegible]), a furry head, presumably the head of a fierce animal. Over time the component 巤 was simplified into the form [illegible] and the component for “dog” (犬 → 犭) was added, suggesting the scene of a dog helping with the hunting.

---

863 Ⓜ

臭

臭 臭 シュウ くさ.い にお.う

Nose of an dog

to smell

The *nose* (自) of a *dog* (犬), notorious for its great **smelling** power.

When this graph appears as a standalone character it takes, in Japanese, the graph 臭, which has omitted the stroke 丶 of the “dog” component (犬 → 大), making the lower part of the character graphically identical to the component 大 (*big*), which can evoke the idea of a big smelling nose.

864

嗅

嗅 キュウ か.ぐ

Action made by the mouth 口 *and the nose of a dog* 臭(シュウ)

to sniff

NOTE The original form of this character was 齅 [鼻臭], formed by the component 鼻 (*nose*) and the component 臭 (*to smell*). The component 鼻 was eventually replaced by 口 (*mouth*) to reduce the number of strokes and facilitate writing.

---

865 Ⓢ

然

然 ゼン ネン

Meat of an animal on fire

thus

Meat (肉 → 夕) of an *animal* (犬) cooked on *fire* (火 → 灬), referring to what is as it should be, what is duly, **thus**, in the expected manner, in that manner.

866

燃

燃 ネン も.える

More fire 火 *added to meat of an animal on fire* 然(ネン)

to get fired up

867

黙

黙 モク だま.る

Animal in the black night

to be silent

Originally 默 [黑犬], an *animal* (犬) **silent** in the *black* (黑 → 黒) darkness of the night.

類 類 ルイ たぐ.い — *Plant, animal and person* **type** — 868

Originally 類 [米犬頁], a *rice plant* (米), alluding to plants in general, an *animal* (犬 → 大), referring to animals in general, and a person with an enhanced *head* (頁), referring to the human being. Ideographic composition that encompasses the most synthesized **type**s of living beings: plants, animals and human beings.

豸 豸 — *Beast* — 869 Ⓡ Ⓜ

A four-legged mammal opening its mouth as a sign of ferocity and aggressiveness: a <u>beast</u>.

貌 貌 ボウ — *Beast 豸 and person 儿 clearly 白 told apart* — 870

NOTE **Aspect** regarded as the thing that distinguishes clearly animals from people.

貇 貇 コン — *Still beast* — 871 Ⓢ

A wild *beast* (豸) that stays is calm and *still* (艮).

懇 懇 コン ねんご.ろ — *Heart-mind 心 of a still beast 貇* **friendly** — 872

墾 墾 コン — *Earth-soil 土 where beasts stay still 貇* **farmland** — 873

求 求 キュウ もと.める — *Furry animal* **to pursue** 874 Ⓢ

A four-legged animal with particularly long fur: a <u>furry animal</u>. The current graph is presumed to be a derivation of the glyph 犬 (*animal*) with the addition of more strokes that represent the animal's long fur (丶 〈). The meaning of the standalone character alludes to the need to **pursue** furry animals in order to make clothes.

救 救 キュウ すく.う — *Furry animal* 求(キュウ) *dispersed with hits* 攵 **to save** 875

豕 豕 — *Hog* 876 Ⓜ

A pig, <u>hog</u> or the like, drawn vertically. The top line 一 represents the head and the lower part 豕, represents the body, the four legs and the curly tail.

豚 豚 トン ぶた — *Meat* 月 *of a hog* 豕 **pork** **pig** 877

㒸 㒸 — *Distributed hogs* 878 Ⓜ

Hogs (豕) *distributed* (八 → ソ) through the population.

隊 隊 タイ — *Hogs distributed in the mountains* **regiment** 879 Ⓢ

Hogs distributed (㒸) along *mountains* (阜 → 阝), referring to the need to distribute food and other commodities to **regiments** stationed in military camps located in the mountains.

墜 墜 ツイ — *A regiment* 隊(タイ) *passing through the earth-soil* 土 **crash** 880

 亥 亥 ガイ *Skeleton of a hog* *Framework* boar sign (Chinese zodiac) 881 ㊔ Ⓢ

The skeleton of a hog. An earlier version of the current graph was 豕, which clearly is 豕 (*pig*) with fewer strokes: a pig without the flesh. The meaning of 'skeleton of a hog' has then been extended to mean any type of supporting structure, so to say, a <u>framework</u>.

骸 骸 ガイ *Bones* 骨 *that make up a framework* 亥(ガイ) **skeleton** 882

該 該 ガイ *Speech* 言 *arranged in a framework* 亥(ガイ) **aforementioned** 883

劾 劾 ガイ *Framework* 亥(ガイ) *with strength* 力 **denunciation** 884

核 核 カク *Tree-wood's* 木 *framework* 亥(ガイ) **kernel** 885

 象 象 ① ゾウ ② ショウ ① **elephant** ② **image** 886 Ⓢ

An **elephant** depicted vertically. The upper strokes ⺈ represent the curved trunk, the central strokes 罒 represent the head and the lower part 豕 represents the four legs, the body and the tail, as the lower strokes in 豕 (*hog*). The second meaning of **image** probably derives from the fact that elephants were not common in ancient China—nor in contemporary China—so the sight of such an animal was only possible for most people through mental or artistic imagination.

Primitive version of the pictograph for 'elephant'

像 像 ゾウ — *Person 亻 making a mental image 象 (ゾウ)* — **depiction** 887

 為 為 イ — *Hand grabbing an image* — **deed** 888 Ⓢ

SPECIAL READING 為替 [かわせ]: *money order*

Originally 爲 (爪爲), a hand *grabbing* (爪 → ⺥ → 丶) an image (象 → 爲 → 為), sense figuratively understood as the fixation on a thought or mental image in order to consequently perform a **deed**.

偽 偽 ギ いつわ.る にせ — *Person 亻 grabbing an image 為 (イ)* — **to fake** 889

 馬 馬 バ うま ま- — **horse** 890 Ⓡ Ⓜ

A **horse** depicted vertically. The head practically has been reduced to an eye (目) and the mane (三), while the four legs have become four dots (灬) and the tail a hook on the right (𠃌).

駄 駄 ダ — *Horse 馬 that is plump 太 (タ)* — **packhorse** 891

駅 駅 エキ — *Horse 馬 travels measuring 尺 (シャク) place* — **station** 892

駒 駒 こま — *Horse 馬 whereupon sentences 句 are made* — **board game piece** 893

験 験 ケン ゲン — *Horse 馬 examined by an authority 㑒 (ケン)* — **verification** 894

篤 篤 トク — 895

Bamboo チク⺮ *spears over horses* 馬

serious

騒 騒 ソウ さわ.ぐ — 896

Horse 馬 *on which an outstretched hand* 又 *places insects* 虫

to make noise

能 能 ノウ — 897 Ⓜ

Bear

capability

An animal with large jaws (⺼), a small tail (厶) and legs that end in sharp claws (⺒): a bear. The original meaning of <u>bear</u> has been displaced by that of **capability**, a meaning which, although probably due to a phonetic loan, can be understood as an association to the extraordinary capabilities bears have compared to other mammals, such as the ability to hibernate for a long time or the ability to climb trees despite their heavy weight and large size.

態 態 タイ — 898

Capability 能 *of the heart-mind* 心

condition

熊 熊 くま — 899

Bear 能 *that can be cooked with fire* 灬

bear

虎 虍 虎 コ とら — 900 Ⓡ Ⓜ

tiger

A **tiger**, drawn vertically. The head and the mouth with its fangs are depicted by ⺊ and 乛, the body and the tail are represented by the stroke 丿 and the legs by 七.

When acting as standalone character this glyph gets the component for "person" (人 → 儿) added below, ideographically referring to the threat posed by tigers to man.

Primitive version of the pictograph for 'tiger'

虞 **虞** おそれ — *Tiger 虍 subjugating a person 呉* 901

anxiety

慮 **慮** リョ — *Menacing tiger 虍 making a person think 思* 902

consideration

 虚 **虛** キョ コ — *Hill with tigers* 903 Ⓜ

void

A *hill* (丘 → 业) inhabited by *tigers* (虍). The sense of **void** understood initially, deducing by the ideograph, as 'void of people' because of the menace of the tigers.

 虐 **虐** ギャク しいた.げる — *Tiger crushing a person* 904

to harass

Originally 虐, a *tiger* (虍) pouncing on a *person who is facing away* from him (匕 → 彐).

 兔 **兔 兎** ト — rabbit 905 ㊔ 兎 Ⓜ

A **rabbit** drawn vertically. The tip of the head is represented by ⺈, the prominent ears by the strokes 罒, the body and legs by 儿 and the tail by the stroke 丶.

When the character appears as a standalone (forming part of some names) it does so with the variant 兎.

 角 **角** ①② カク ① つの ③ かど — ① **horn** ② **angle** ③ **corner** 906 Ⓡ Ⓜ

A sharp pointed and scaled **horn** of an animal. The tip of the horn is represented by the strokes ⺈, which are used identically to represent a sharped tip in other characters referring to animals such as 魚 (*fish*), 亀 (*turtle*) or 兔 (*rabbit*). The body of the horn proper is depicted by 用. The derived meanings of **angle** and **corner** come from the allegorical interpretation made about the angular shape of horns. It should be noted as well that the word 'corner' itself comes from the Latin word *cornu*, which, indeed, means 'horn'.

触 **触** ショク さわ.る ふ.れる

Horn-like 角 antennas providing the sense of touch to insects 虫

to touch 907

 牛 牛 牛 ギュウ うし

Animal head with horns

cattle

cow 908 Ⓡ Ⓜ

The head of a horned bovid seen from the front. The strokes ⺧ represent the horns, the head proper is depicted by the vertical stroke 丨 and the ears by the horizontal line 一. This character can be used to designate any kind of **cattle**, but in modern Japanese it most commonly refers to **cow**.

Primitive version of the pictograph for 'cattle'

件 **件** ケン

Person 亻 dealing with cattle 牛

case 909

牧 **牧** ボク まき

Cattle 牛 dispersed with hits 攵

shepherd 910

特 **特** トク

Cattle 牛 in a temple 寺

special 911

牲 **牲** セイ

Cattle 牛 that is alive 生 (セイ) offered in religious services

sacrificial animal 912

 半 半 ハン なか.ば

Distributed cattle

half 913 Ⓢ

Distributed (八 → ソ) *cattle* (牛 → 十), pieces of beef that are distributed among the people by previously cutting the animal in two **halves**.

伴 伴 ハン バン ともな.う 914

Person 亻 going along his other half 半 (ハン)

to accompany

羊 羊 羊 ⺷ 𦍌 ヨウ ひつじ 915 Ⓡ Ⓜ

sheep

Auspicious

A **sheep**'s head seen from the front. The upper part, 䒑, is a schematization of the curved horns (originally most sheep had horns). The horizontal stroke in the middle, 一, represents the ears. The lower horizontal stroke 一 represents the snout and the vertical stroke 丨 represents the thickness of the face of the sheep. The sheep is considered within the compendium of Chinese characters as an <u>auspicious</u> symbol. It seems that sheep were one of the preferred animals in ancient China (Shang Dynasty) for the sacrifice to the gods in prospects of good crops and fortune.

When this graph appears as a component it can do so in the variant ⺶ or, more commonly, in the reduced version 𦍌.

Primitive version of the pictograph for 'sheep'

美 美 ビ うつく.しい 916

Auspicious sheep 𦍌 *that is big* 大

beautiful

着 着 ① ② チャク ① き.る ② つ.く 917

Sheepskin ⺶ *over the head and eyes* 目

① **to wear**

② **to reach**

NOTE With regard to the second definition, **to reach**, it can be interpreted as an auspicious prediction that is fulfilled and appearing before the eyes, reaching the material world.

詳 詳 ショウ くわ.しい — *Speech 訁 that is auspicious 羊 (ヨウ)* — **accurate** 918

群 群 グン むら — *Mouth and a stick 君 (クン) guiding the sheep 羊* — **flock** 919

羞 羞 シュウ — *Sheep 羊 being tightly gripped 丑 (チュウ)* — **embarrassment** 920

洋 洋 ヨウ — *Water 氵 that is auspicious 羊 (ヨウ)* — **ocean** / **western** 921

羨 羨 セン うらや.む — *Person spitting 次 to another person's auspicious 𦍌 endeavors* — **to envy** 922

様 様 ヨウ さま — *Tree-wood 木 used to allow sheep 𦍌 (ヨウ) to cross the water 氺* — **manner** / **Mr.** 923

鮮 鮮 セン あざ.やか — *Meal of fish 魚 and sheep 羊* — **fresh** 924

善 善 ゼン よ.い — *Auspicious words* — **goodness** 925 Ⓢ

Originally 譱 [羊誩], several *sayings* (言×2 → 誩 → 𠮛) that become *auspicious* (羊), something unequivocally **good**.

膳 膳 ゼン — *Served meat 月 that is good 善 (セン)* — **dining tray** 926

927 Ⓢ

敬

敬

ケイ
うやま.う

Hand hitting a barbarian

Menacing

to show respect

Originally 敬 [苟攴], a *hand hitting with a mattock* (攴 → 攵), threatening or menacing a *leaning person* (勹) who is related to *sheep* (羊 ≈ 芊 → 艹) and pledges clemency with his *mouth* (口). Such a scene represents both an act of <u>menace</u> by that coercing hand and also an act of inferred **respect** that has to be shown by the victim. The person related to the sheep makes a reference to the Qiang (羌), an ethnic group that was the barbarian archenemy of the peoples of the Shang Dynasty and they were said to be sheep breeders. The character used to designate the Qiang is, in fact, 羌, which represents a person (人 → 儿) under a sheep (羊 → ⺶).

928

警

警

ケイ

Menacing 敬 (ケイ) *speech* 言

admonition

929

驚

驚

キョウ
おどろ.かす

Menacing 敬 (ケイ) *horse* 馬

to surprise

930 Ⓡ Ⓜ

鹿

鹿

しか
か

deer

A **deer** seen from the side. The antlers on the top have been reduced to 亠. The head has been shrunk into the "eye" component (目 → 罒 → 丗), the left part of the body has become 丿, and the four legs are represented by 比.

931

麓

麓

ロク
ふもと

Place with groves 林 *where deer* 鹿 *live*

foot of a mountain

932

麗

麗

レイ
うるわしい

Deer with exuberant horns

magnificent

A *deer* (鹿) with particularly large and tall antlers (丽), symbol of elegance and **magnificence**.

933

薦 薦 セン すす.める

Deer among plants

to encourage

A *deer* running (鹿 → 廌) among *plants* (艹), a game upon which hunt can be **encouraged.** The component for "deer" (鹿) changes in this character the original strokes depicting the legs (比) for the element 灬, which better evokes the rapid movement of the animal's legs by means of an analogy to the lower element of the character for "horse" (馬).

934

慶 慶 ケイ

Deer standing still

jubilation

A *deer* that, after running (鹿 → 廌 → 严), remains at rest with its *feet still* (夂), rejoicing at the **jubilation** caused by the state of calmness, enhanced by the component for "heart" or "feeling" (心).

3. ANIMAL MANIPULATION

Another very important function that animals provide is the supply of fur. Ancient people, in order to keep themselves warm in winter, needed to 'catch' an animal  隶, remove its 'skin'  皮 and modify it with two hands  革 to use it in the form of 'leather' clothes or other elements.

935 Ⓡ Ⓜ

隶 隶

Hand holding the tail of an animal

Catch

An *outstretched hand* (彐 ≈ 又) <u>catching</u> an animal by its *tail* (毛 → 氺 → 氺).

936 Ⓢ

皮 皮 ヒ かわ

Hand removing the skin of an animal

skin

An *outstretched hand* (又) tearing off the **skin** (|) of an elongated animal (厂), probably a snake.

937

披 披 ヒ

Hand 扌 *holding the removed skin of an animal* 皮

exposure

破 破 ハ やぶ.る

Stone 石 used to tear off the skin of an animal 皮(ヒ) 938

to rip

 波 波 ハ なみ

Skin of water 939 Ⓢ

wave

The *skin* (皮(ヒ)) of *water* (水 → 氵), in reference to the surface of the water and the phenomena, such as **waves**, that occur on it.

婆 婆 バ

Waves 波(ハ) *carrying a woman 女 away* 940

old woman

 革 革 カク かわ

Two hands removing the skin of an animal 941 Ⓡ Ⓜ

leather

modification

Originally 革 [廿臼], *two hands* ((臼 ≈ 廾) → 囗) stretching the skin of an animal—**leather**—to **modify** it. The animal is schematically depicted by the element 廿, which shows the head (廿), the body (丨) and legs (一).

靴 靴 カ くつ

Leather 革 that gets transformed 化(カ) 942

shoes

4. SILK PRODUCTION

A very interesting aspect of animal manipulation is the production of silk by the use of silkworms, and silk had a very important role in ancient Chinese culture and trade. Through the components related to silk it is possible to observe its entire production process, for there are characters used to depict the selection of small silkworm 'cocoons'  幺, the extraction of their very 'dim' fibers  玄, and the elaboration of silk 'threads'  糸.

 幺 幺

Silk cocoon 943 Ⓡ Ⓜ

A pair of hanging silk cocoons.

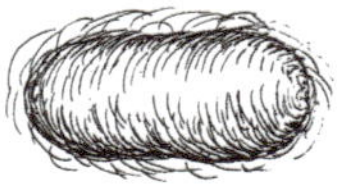

A silk cocoon

944

幼 幼 ヨウ おさな.い

Cocoon 幺 becoming strong 力

infancy

---

945 Ⓢ

玄 玄 ゲン

Tiny thread of silk coming out of a cocoon

dim

A small thread starting to come out (亠) of a *silk cocoon* (幺), a hardly visible, somewhat **dim** element.

946

率 率 ① リツ ② ソツ ② ひき.いる

Silk threads being twisted

① **ratio**

② **to lead**

A *silk cocoon* (幺) from which separate threads (亠十) get twisted in an incessant movement (冫 冫) in order to form strong threads for the textile industry, suggesting the importance of taking into account the proportion or **ratio** of virgin yarn to be used. The movement of a small threat that later becomes a bigger thing also suggest the secondary meaning of **to lead**.

947

幻 幻 ゲン まぼろし

Thread hanging from a silk cocoon

illusion

A barely visible thin thread (𠃌) hanging from a *silk cocoon* (幺). The almost transparent color of the thread evokes the midpoint between the visible and the invisible, the real and the unreal, the world of **illusions**. This character has a morphosemantic structure similar to the character 玄 (*dim*).

---

948 Ⓜ

幺幺

Several silk cocoons

Several *silk cocoons* (幺×2) in a row.

幽
幽 ユウ — 949

Silk cocoons 幺幺 in the middle of a mountain 山

confinement

NOTE This ideogram evokes the idea of something small (*silk cocoons*) **confined** within something much larger (a *mountain*), suggesting the scene of an ancient sage spending long periods of seclusion and isolation in the mountains.

樂
楽 ① ガク ② ラク ② たの.しい — 950 Ⓢ

Instrument made of wood and threads that produce a clear sound

① **music**
② **enjoyable**

Originally 樂 [幺幺白木], a musical instrument made of *wood* (木) and strings coming out of several silk cocoons (幺幺 → ⺀) that emit a *clear* (白) and harmonious sound, an ideogram associated with **music** in general and, by extension, pleasure and **enjoyment**.

藥
薬 ヤク くすり — 951

Plants 艹 that are enjoyable 楽 (ガク)

medicine

茲
兹 ジ — 952 Ⓢ

Plant strands coming out of cocoons
Flourishing

Originally 茲 [艹幺幺], a metaphorical representation of the breaking of the chrysalis of silkworms that have emerged from their *cocoons* (幺幺) as if they were flourishing like plants (艹 → 丷).

慈
慈 ジ いつく.しむ — 953

Flourishing 兹 (ジ) heart-mind 心

to be affectionate (to)

滋
滋 ジ — 954

Water 氵 making plants flourish 兹 (ジ)

exuberant

磁
磁 ジ — 955

Stone 石 with a flourish 兹 (ジ)

porcelain
magnet

 糸 **糸** シ / いと — **thread** — *Tiny* 956 Ⓡ Ⓜ

Small (小) **threads** coming out of *silk cocoons* (幺).

As a component sometimes this graph may adopt the meaning of <u>tiny</u> by semantic association.

絶 **絶** ゼツ / た.える — *Tiny 糸 color 色* — **to die out** 957

統 **統** トウ / す.べる — *Tiny thing 糸 set aside 充* (ジュウ) — **to supervise** 958

絞 **絞** コウ / しぼ.る / し.める — *Threads 糸 being mingled 交* (コウ) — **to squeeze** 959

紋 **紋** モン — *Thread-made 糸 writing 文* (モン) — **coat of arms** 960

細 **細** サイ / ほそ.い / こま.かい — *Tiny 糸 skull 田* — **slender** 961

絹 **絹** ケン / きぬ — *Threads 糸 coming out of the mouth 口 of a meaty 月 insect* — **silk** 962

紺 **紺** コン — *Plant threads 糸 that are tasty to the mouth 甘* (カン) — **dark blue** 963

NOTE This character originally referred to woad plants, used to make tea, which give an intense color to the water. Such a color would be in a rather dark green tone, but it should be noted that in East Asia, traditionally, the same term (青) is used to denote both green and **dark blue** colors.

964

給 給 キュウ たま.う

Threads 糸 *coming together* 合 (ゴウ)

to bestow

NOTE Referring to the creation of social links through gift giving or **bestowing** as an engagement, a custom that is still maintained today in many Asian countries.

965

級 級 キュウ

A certain thread 糸 *that has been reached* 及 (キュウ)

rank

966

緊 緊 キン

Delicate 臤 (ケン) *thread* 糸

tense

967

繁 繁 ハン

Sensibility 敏 *used in the weaving of threads* 糸

luxuriant

968

緩 緩 カン ゆる.い

Thread 糸 *that caresses* 爰 (エン)

loose

969

紫 紫 シ むらさき

Threads 糸 *left behind* 此 (シ)

purple

NOTE Most probably referring to an unintentionally mixed dyeing color, the blend of red and blue—**purple**—, discarded and left behind because it was not the color originally intended.

970

総 総 ソウ

Thread 糸 *tying the public heart-mind* 忩 (ソウ)

overall

971

紀 紀 キ

Thread 糸 *tying what circulates* 己 (キ) *throughout time*

chronicle

972

紳 紳 シン

Linking threads 糸 *that get expounded* 申 (シン)

sir

NOTE Referring to the social network available to the noble gentry.

糾 糾 キュウ *Threads 糸 getting intertwined* キュウ 丩 973

twist

線 線 セン *Thread 糸 of clear water coming out of a fountain* セン 泉 974

line

終 終 シュウ お.わる *Plant threads 糸 in the winter* トウ 冬 975

to end

経 経 ① ケイ ② キュウ ① へ.る *Thread 糸 slit along the diameter of a piece of clay that is being worked on* ケイ 圣 976

① **to elapse**
② sutra [*Buddhism*]

NOTE Among the many ancient ceramic objects found throughout East Asia one can find several ornamental marks made by the pressure applied on it with different types of ropes or threads. It is this type of artisan object to which this character originally alluded and from which its current meaning of to **elapse** derives through the allegorical connection between a continuous diametral decorative line to the linear passage of time.

素 素 ソ ス *A lush plant's 龶 single thread 糸* 977

element

SPECIAL READING 素人 [しろうと]: *amateur*

純 純 ジュン *Thread 糸 that is still growing* トン 屯 978

sheer

緒 緒 ショ お *Thread 糸 on which an action is performed* シャ 者 979

twine

練 練 レン ねる
Threads 糸 of a bound backpack 東 980
to elaborate

繕 繕 ゼン つくろう
Thread 糸 tying something in a good way 善 (ゼン) 981
to mend

縄 縄 ジョウ なわ
Thread like a serpent 982
rope

Originally 黽 [乚臼], *two hands* (臼) holding a *serpent* (虫 → 乚) and manipulating it. The glyph later evolved into the form 黾 and then into 黾. The character alludes then to a long, serpentine and malleable shape. Finally the component 糸 (*thread*) was added to reinforce the more concrete meaning of **rope**.

維 維 イ
Bird tied with a thread 983 Ⓜ
maintenance

A *bird* (隹) that has its legs tied with a *thread* (糸) in order to be kept—**maintain**ed—as it is prevented from flying.

縁 縁 ① エン ② ふち
Outstretched hand ⺕ → ヨ tying a hog 豕 with a thread 糸 984
① **connection**
② verge

系 系 ケイ
Binding made out of threads 985 Ⓢ
link

A knot (丿) **linking** *threads* (糸) together.

係 係 ①② ケイ ② かかり
Person's 亻 links 系 (ケイ) 986
① **correlation**
② clerk

孫 孫 ①② ソン ② まご
Child that is linked 987 Ⓢ
① **descendants**
② **grandchild**

Child (子) or children to whom one is *linked* (系): one's **descendants**.

---

988 Ⓢ

県 縣 県 ケン

Head hanging from a thread

prefecture

A *head* turned upside down (首 → 県 → 県 → 県) hanging from a *knotted thread* (系), scene indicating the display of a person punished with the death penalty, a symbol of dominance by force and, by extension, the symbol of a controlled territory: a **prefecture**.

As a single character this glyph uses the abbreviated form 県, in which the right component has been removed.

989

懸 懸 ケン ケ

Hanging 縣 (ケン) *heart-mind* 心

suspension

990

索 索 サク

Two hands pulling off a thread

search

cord

Two hands (廾 → 冖) pulling threads (十小) from a *silk cocoon* (幺), either to **search** for its origin, or to form a **cord**.

---

991 Ⓜ

㬎 显

Threads of light

Originally 㬎 [日絲], several *threads* (糸×2 → 絲 → 业) of light coming from the sun (日 → 日).

992

顕 顕 ケン

Threads of light 显 *produced by the head* 頁

manifestation

993

湿 湿 シツ しめ.る

Water 氵 *impregnating something like threads of light* 显

wet

---

994 Ⓜ

由

Bound thoughts

Skull (囟 → 田) whose thoughts are bound and interrelated by a knot of a figurative cord (十).

專 専 セン *Bound thoughts* 叀 *applied to work* 寸 995

speciality
exclusive

 恵 恵 ケイ エ めぐ.む *Thoughts bound to the heart-mind* 996 Ⓜ

to bless

Thoughts bound (叀) to the *heart-mind* (心), or vice versa, indicating an optimal congruency and a sense of **bless**ing.

穗 穂 スイ ほ *Fruit's* 禾 *blessed* 恵 *part* 997

ear (of a plant)

REVIEW ON ANIMALS

卵虫蜀属魚再冓亀隹雄焦集奞雈蒦
鳥羽翟飛非

1 蚕蛮蚊蜂濁嘱漁講溝構携唯誰雅推隻雌准
堆催椎稚礁奪歓観勧権護穫鳴鶏島翌翼翁
習躍曜濯俳悲排

犬猟臭然黙類豸貇求豕㒸隊亥象為
馬能虎虚虐兎角牛半羊善敬鹿麗薦
慶

2

伏犯狭独獲獄嗅燃貌懇墾救豚墜骸該劾核
像偽駄駅駒験篤騒態熊虞慮触件牧特牲伴
美着詳群羞洋羨様鮮膳警驚麓

隶皮波革

3

披破婆靴

幺玄率幻𢆶楽兹糸縄維系孫県索显
由恵

4 幼幽薬慈滋磁絶統絞紋細絹紺給級緊繁緩
紫総紀紳糾線終経素純緒練繕縁係懸顕湿
専穂

THE MATERIAL REALM

THE MATERIAL REALM

If we understand culture as the manifestation of the collective intellectual achievements of a society, we can find among the objects manufactured by man, one of the first cultural manifestations, and that is the topic the material realm is about.

Artificial objects, made by men, vary greatly in form and complexity, and also in degree of appreciation and consideration. Such consideration is usually measured by the material in which the object in question is made. Objects made of wood or bamboo have a lesser consideration and are usually relegated to everyday use. On the other hand, metal objects—bronze in the period when Chinese characters were developed—were held in high esteem and were reserved for special uses. The consideration for the objects also depends on their functionality, since there are tools that are indispensable for the expansion of a domain or territory, such as counting tools, monetary tools and, above all, work tools. Also, vessels are especially important, since they were key in the various religious rituals of the Shang dynasty.

Different types of objects, tools and vessels take prominence within Chinese characters and can be grouped within the Material Realm, which is divided into the following groups: Characters used to represent *everyday objects*, characters used to represent *tools*, and lastly, characters used to represent *vessels*.

EVERYDAY OBJECTS	TOOLS	VESSELS
1. Wooden Objects	1. Counting Tools	1. Food and Drinking Vessels
2. Bamboo Objects	2. Monetary Tools	2. Bags and Boxes
3. Cloths	3. Work Tools	3. Plates and Trays
	4. Nets and Baskets	4. Boats

THE MATERIAL REALM AT A GLANCE

EVERYDAY OBJECTS

TOOLS

VESSELS

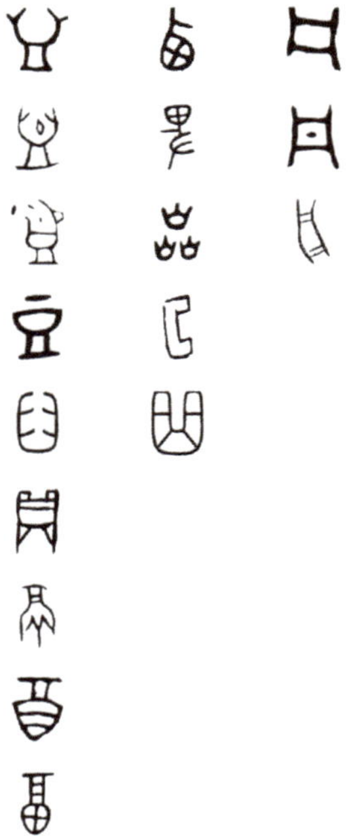

EVERYDAY OBJECTS

1. WOODEN OBJECTS

One of the most basic materials for the production of everyday objects is wood, which is malleable and easy to obtain. The most basic wooden object is certainly the 'stick' 丂, because a stick can simply be a branch ripped from a tree. However, in spite of their simplicity, sticks can be used to create very complex things, because if there is some 'talent' involved, with several upright sticks 才 even buildings can be erected. Common furniture such as 'stools' 几 or tables 片 are also just elaborated big 'pieces' of wood. With small pieces of wood, on the other hand, it is possible to make kitchen utensils such as 'ladles' 斗 and 'pestles' 午. Wood can, 'moreover', be elevated to the spiritual realm, because 'altars of sacrifice' 且 used in religious rituals were made with it.

丂 丂 — コウ — *Stick* — 998 Ⓡ Ⓢ

A slightly curved wooden stick. The upper stroke 一 represents the handle and the lower strokes ㄣ are a deformation of the stick as such.

号 号 — ゴウ — *Words* 口 *made by a stick* 丂 (コウ) — **sign** — 999

朽 朽 — キュウ / く.ちる — *Tree-wood's* 木 *fallen stick* 丂 (コウ) — **to decay** — 1000

考 考 — コウ / かんが.える — *Old man with a walking stick* — **to ponder** — 1001 Ⓢ

An *old man* (老 → 耂) leaning on a walking *stick* (丂 → 与), representing a stereotyped sage who devotes much of his time thinking and **ponder**ing. This graph is actually a cognate of the character 老 (*old man*), in which the walking stick is represented by the strokes 匕. The component 丂 (*stick*) was later added redundantly to the present character to differentiate it from the glyph previously mentioned.

拷 1002

拷 ゴウ

Hand 扌 *making people ponder* 考(コウ)

torture

 1003 Ⓢ

可

可 カ

Sticks and words

able

Words (口) and *sticks* (丂(コウ) → 丁) acting together, the power of speech and the power of weapons, a symbol of the **ability** or complete capacity to act.

歌 1004

歌 カ うた.う

Great ability 可(カ)×2 *of the open mouth* 欠

to sing

河 1005

河 カ かわ

Water 氵 *able to* 可(カ) *run free*

waterway

苛 1006

苛 カ

Plants 艹 *able to* 可(カ) *grow free*

torment

NOTE This character originally referred to weeds that grow uncontrollably, but later its meaning derived into that of anything uncontrollable that produces discomfort and **torment**.

 1007 Ⓢ

何

何 カ なに なん

Person carrying a stick on his shoulder

what

Originally 何, a *person* (人 → 亻) carrying a *stick* (丂(コウ) → 丁) on his shoulder, evoking the scene of someone who comes out, armed, behind the track of something or someone who has caught his attention and whose intention is to discover **what** is the thing that has aroused his interest. Over time the character turned its original pictographic component 丁 (*stick*) into the component 可(カ) (*able*) due to its graphic and phonetic correspondence, giving rise to a possible ideographic association with the scene of a *person* (人 → 亻) armed with a *stick* (丂 → 丁) asking with his *mouth* (口) what has caught his attention.

荷 **荷** カ に

Plants 艹 carried in a bundle tied to a stick 何 1008

load

 奇 **奇** キ

Person balancing on a stick 1009 Ⓢ

unusual

Originally 丂, a *person seen from the front* (大) balancing on a *stick* (丂 → 丁), a somewhat **unusual** sight for the ancient man. Over time, in a process similar to that of the character 何 (*what*), this glyph saw its component 丁 (*stick*) transformed into 可 (*able*) due to a phonetic and semantic association, since being 'able' to stay up on a stick is quite rare.

埼 **埼** さい

Earth-soil 土 that is unusual 奇 1010

promontory

PLACE NAME USAGE 埼玉県 [さいたまけん]: *Saitama Prefecture*

崎 **崎** さき

Mountain 山 that is unusual 奇 1011

headland

椅 **椅** イ

Tree-wood 木 object that is unusual 奇 1012

chair

NOTE **Chairs** were in fact a very rare object in ancient China and the rest of East Asia.

騎 **騎** キ

Person balancing 奇 on a horse 馬 1013

horseman

 才 **才** サイ

Lifted sticks 1014 Ⓢ

Upright

talent

Several wooden sticks (一ノ亅) placed vertically, upright on the ground, indicating the beginning of the construction of a building made of wood. The meaning of **talent**, if literally understood, refers to the much appreciated and needed ability to erect buildings. This meaning can also be analyzed in a more metaphorical way, in the sense of the 'talent' required to raise, start and maintain any kind of enterprise.

In some compounds, the glyph 才 becomes 𠂇.

存 **存** ソン ゾン — *Upright 𠂇 サイ child 子* — **existence** 1015

在 **在** ザン あ.る — *Standing upright 𠂇 サイ on the earth-soil 土* — **to be at** 1016

材 **材** ザイ — *Tree-wood's 木 lifted sticks 才 サイ* — **timber**, **material** 1017

 㫃 — *Flaming flag attached to a pole* 1018 Ⓡ Ⓜ

An *upright wooden stick* (才 → 方) to which a flag fluttering in the wind (𠂉) is attached.

施 **施** シ セ ほどこ.す — *Flags 㫃 that are extended 也 チ* — **to perform** 1019

NOTE It refers to flags displayed in military campaigns, implicitly indicating the **perform**ance of military activities and conquests.

 旅 **旅** リョ たび — *People carrying a flag* — **travel** 1020

Originally 㫃 [㫃从], several *people* (人×2 → 从 → 𠄌 → 𠂢) carrying a *flag* (㫃) on a military expedition **travel**.

 主 **主** ①② シュ ② ス ① おも ② ぬし — *Wooden beam* — ① **main** ② **lord** 1021 Ⓢ

A beam (亠) made of *wood* (木 → 土) supporting a roof. The meaning of this character comes from the structural function of beams, that of supporting the roofs under which people live. From this meaning derives both the notion of **main**—because beams are the main supporting element of roofs; and that of **lord**, referring to the owner of a house, since it is the owner who 'supports' the household.

住 住 ジュウ す.む *Person 亻 under beams 主* (シュ) 1022

to dwell

注 注 チュウ そそ.ぐ *Water 氵 seeping through beams 主* (シュ) 1023

to pour

柱 柱 チュウ はしら *Tree-wood 木 acting like a vertical beam 主* (シュ) 1024

pillar

駐 駐 チュウ *Horse 馬 under beams 主* (シュ) 1025

stop-over

几 几 キ *Stool* 1026 Ⓢ

A wooden stool in an upright position. The upper stroke 一 represents the seat and the lower strokes 儿 the legs.

肌 肌 はだ *Meat 月 on a stool 几* 1027

human skin

NOTE Originally this character stood for "flesh", a meaning that is still held in Chinese.

机 机 キ つくえ *Tree-wood 木 object similar to a stool 几* (キ) 1028

desk

処 処 ショ *Person sitting still on a stool* 1029 Ⓢ

location

A person sitting on a *stool* (几) and staying *still* (夂) on it, implicitly pointing out the constant position in a certain place: a **location**.

拠 1030
據 キョ コ

Hand 扌 placed on a certain location 処(ショ)

basis

殿 1031
殿 テン デン との どの

Person sitting on a throne with a mace

palace

Originally 殿 [𡱂殳], a *person sitting* (尸) on a stool of a height equivalent to two *stools* (几×2 → 丌 → 共)—a throne—and holding a *mace* (殳) or baton, making a clear reference to a ruler or a king. The meaning of 'king' subsequently became that of the 'residence of the king' or **palace**.

片 1032
片 ヘン かた Ⓡ Ⓜ

Table

piece

A <u>table</u> depicted vertically, made with several **piece**s of wood put together. The vertical stroke ノ represents the surface, and the strokes of the right, ⊥ and ㇕, represent the legs.

版 1033
版 ハン

Piece of wood 片 being pressed reversely 反(ハン) on paper

printing

丬 1034
丬 ショウ Ⓢ

Table

Pieces

Originally 爿, a <u>table</u> represented vertically, made with several pieces of wood. The vertical stroke 丨 depicts the surface, and the lateral strokes 冫 the legs. This component is simply a mirrored version of the glyph 片 (*table*), and as such its meaning can also refer to <u>pieces</u>. This inverted position of the graph serves to mark out a different phonetic value (ショウ).

状 1035
状 ジョウ

Table 丬(ショウ) on which an animal 犬 is being examined

state of things

将 **将** ショウ

Two hands grabbing pieces — 1036 Ⓢ

will

(a) general

Two hands *grabbing* (爪 → 爫) several *pieces* (丬 ショウ) of wood and *working* (寸) with them, representing the **will** to build something. The meaning related to entrepreneurship would later go on to mean also 'leadership' and, finally, 'leader' or **general**.

奨 **奨** ショウ

Will 将 (ショウ) *that is big* 大 — 1037

encouragement

疒 **疒**

Person lying on a bed — 1038 Ⓡ Ⓜ

Illness

A *table* (丬) with a *person on his back* (匕 → 𠂉) lying on it, representing convalescence and illness.

痕 **痕** コン あと

Illness 疒 *that remains still* 艮 (コン) — 1039

scar

疫 **疫** エキ ヤク

Illness 疒 *striking* 殳 — 1040

epidemic

痩 **痩** ソウ や.せる

Illness 疒 *burning a person like a torch* 叟 (ソウ) — 1041

to get thin

療 **療** リョウ

Illness 疒 *burnt in a bonfire* 尞 (リョウ) — 1042

cure

瘍 **瘍** ヨウ

Illness 疒 *that makes skin shine like sun rays* 昜 (ヨウ) — 1043

ulcer

疲 **疲** ヒ つか.れる

Illness 疒 *felt on the skin* 皮 (ヒ) — 1044

to get tired

斗 ト *Hand holding a ladle* 1045 Ⓡ Ⓜ

ladle

unit of volume [~*18 l*]

Originally 斗, a <u>ladle</u> (ㅋ → 乚) grasped by a hand (又 → ナ → ⼀). The originally meaning derives into a secondary meaning describing the equivalent approximate volume capacity of that ladle (around 18 liters).

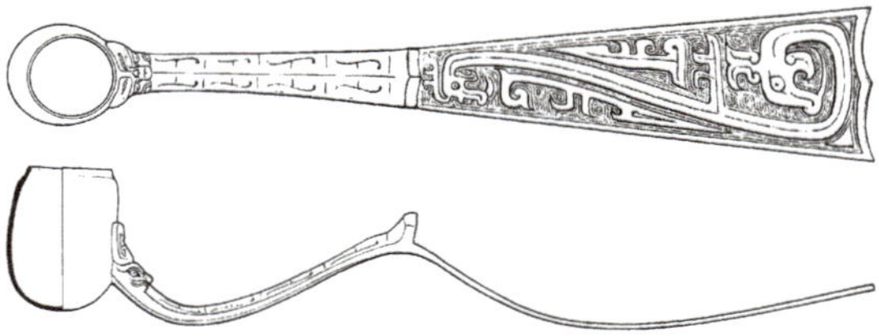

A bronze ladle from the Shang dynasty, called 'dui' (斗)

料 リョウ *Rice 米 in a ladle 斗* 1046

foodstuff

charge

科 カ *Fruits 禾 examined with a ladle 斗* 1047

science

斜 シャ なな.め *Remains 余 taken with a ladle 斗* 1048

slantwise

勺 シャク *Ladle with food inside* 1049 ㊔ Ⓢ

unit of volume [*18 mm*]

A ladle (ㅋ → 勹) with food (丶) inside.

的 テキ まと *White rice 白 to which a ladle 勺 (シャク) is directed* 1050

aim

約 1051

約 ヤク

Thread 糸 *tying a ladle with food inside* 勺 (シャク)

promise
approximately

NOTE In reference to the **promise**—binding—of food or salary in exchange for servitude or work.

 升 1052 Ⓢ

升 ショウ ます

Hand holding a ladle with food inside

unit of volume [~*1.8 l*]

A hand holding a ladle with food inside. This character has visibly suffered a major distortion of strokes. The strokes ㇀, ノ and 丨 (勺 → 丿丨) represent the ladle with contents inside and the horizontal line 一 represents the outstretched hand (ナ → 一). As a standalone character, this glyph, analogously to the character 斗 (*ladle*), refers to a unit of volume, in this case of 1.8 liters.

昇 1053

昇 ショウ のぼ.る

Hand taking a ladle with food inside 升 (ショウ) *up to the mouth* 日

to rise

 与 1054 Ⓢ

与 兴 ヨ あた.える

Two hands giving a ladle with food inside to two receiving hands

to give

Two hands delivering a ladle with food to two receiving hands, representing the action of **giving** and taking. This character suffered an abrupt process of simplification. The original form of the character was 舁 [臼与廾], which is made up of *two hands* (臼 ≈ 廾) holding a spoon with food inside turned upside down (勺 → 与) that is delivered to two other receiving hands (廾). As a solo character, the graph was simplified into the form 与, in which only the inverted spoon (与) and the two receiving hands (廾 → 一) are reflected. On the other hand, when the character acts as a component, it takes another simplification: 兴, in which the simplified giving hands can be seen in the form ⺍ (臼 → ⺍), the inverted spoon is turned into a horizontal line 一 (与 → 一) and the two receiving hands have become the strokes ハ (廾 → ハ).

誉 1055

誉 ヨ ほま.れ

Given 兴 (ヨ) *speech* 言

praise

挙 キョ *Hand* 手 *rising a giving* 兴 1056
挙 あ.げる **to elevate**

 串 くし **skewer** 1057 Ⓜ
串

A wooden **skewer** (丨) with several pieces of meat stuck in it (吕).

患 カン *Skewer* 串 *piercing the heart-mind* 心 1058
患 わずら.う **to suffer**

 午 ゴ *Pestle* 1059 Ⓢ
午 **noon**
horse sign (Chinese zodiac)

A primitive hammer-like big pestle made of wood, with the head represented by the strokes 𠂉 and the body by 丨, with the horizontal stroke 一 marking its thickness. The meaning of **noon** is given because since ancient times this character was taken to indicate the double hour that goes from 11 am to 1 pm. The selection of this character for the time period may be due to the relationship between noon time and cooking, for which the use of a mortar and pestle was often required.

Hammer-like pestle

許 キョ *Speech* 言 *accompanied by a strong pounding of a pestle* 午 1060
許 ゆる.す **to permit**

 缶 カン *Mortar and pestle* 1061 Ⓜ
缶 **tin can**

A *pestle* (午) on a mortar (凵). This pictogram, as a component, represents its original meaning of a <u>mortar and pestle</u>, but later, when acting as a standalone character, it started to designate any type of food container and, eventually, **tin cans**.

陶 陶 トウ *Leaning person 勹 making a tin 缶 out of clay from mountains 阝* 1062

pottery

䍃 䍃 ヨウ *Hand hitting a mortar with a pestle* 1063 Ⓢ

A hand *grabbing* (爪 → 爫) a *pestle* (午) used to pounder the mortar (凵).

謡 謡 ヨウ うたい *Speech 言 made along the rhythm of the pounding of a mortar and pestle 䍃* 1064

chanting

揺 揺 ヨウ ゆ.れる *Hand 扌 pounding a mortar with a pestle 䍃* 1065

to waver

御 卸 おろし *Kneeling person using a mortar and a pestle* 1066 Ⓜ

wholesale

Originally 御 [缶卩], a *kneeling person* (卩) grinding grain with a *mortar and pestle* (缶 → 缶) in order to sell it **wholesale**. It is very likely that the transformation of the component 缶 into 缶 is due to a deliberate addition of the component 止 (*to stop*), to specify or emphasize that the grain has stopped being ground and is therefore being sold.

且 且 ソ か.つ *Altar of sacrifice* 1067 Ⓢ

moreover

A small wooden altar (且) with several shelves inside (二) used to deposit various <u>sacrificial</u> items. The meaning of '**moreover**' derives from the fact that ancient Chinese religious practice always required, after consultations or requests to the gods, to perform, in addition ('moreover') to the rites and prayers, various sacrifices in order to please the gods and, thus, get good results.

助 助 ジョ たす.ける 1068

Sacrifices 且 providing strength 力

to assist

阻 阻 ソ はば.む 1069

Mountains 阝 in the middle of sacrifices 且

to hinder

査 査 サ 1070

Wood 木 of an altar of sacrifice 且

revision

NOTE It refers to the periodic review of the condition of the wood of sacrificial altars done in order to keep them always pristine for the gods.

租 租 ソ 1071

Fruits 禾 given as a sacrifice 且

tariff

粗 粗 ソ あら.い 1072

Rice 米 used in sacrifices 且

coarse

狙 狙 ソ ねら.う 1073

Animal 犭 used for sacrifices 且

to be after (something)

NOTE When the purpose of religious prayers was of considerable importance, the use of sacrificial animals was required.

組 組 ソ く.む 1074

Thread 糸 linking sacrifices 且

to unite

2. BAMBOO OBJECTS

Bamboo stems are used in East Asia as a resistant wood-like material. The most important bamboo objects of ancient China were undoubtedly 'books' 𠕋 冊, which were made of bamboo strips tied to each other. From the layout of these bamboo books derives the traditional way of writing Chinese characters from top to bottom and also their square proportion.

冊 冊 サツ サク — 1075 Ⓢ

Bamboo slips

volume of a book

Several <u>bamboo slips</u> tied together and placed in an upright position and tied together, on which Chinese characters were written: a primitive form of the **books** of ancient China. The vertical lines 冂 represent the edges of the bamboo strips and the horizontal line 一 the string that holds them together.

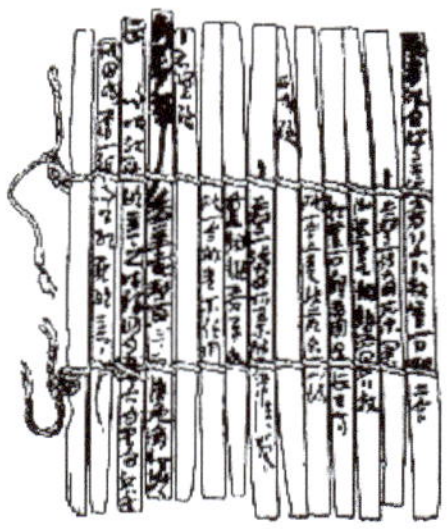

Book made of bamboo slips

嗣 嗣 ツ — 1076

Words 口 deposited by a ruler 司(シ) in a book 冊

heirdom

柵 柵 サク — 1077

Tree-woods 木 arranged like bamboo slips 冊(サク)

palisade

侖 侖 ロン — 1078 Ⓢ

Talking book

A *book* (冊) conveying messages as a *talking mouth* (亼).

倫 倫 リン — 1079

Person 亻 acting as a talking book 侖(ロン) says

ethics

論 論 ロン — 1080

Speech 言 based on what a talking book 侖(ロン) says

argument

1081

 典 典 テン

Two hands holding a book

code

Two hands (廾 → ハ) holding and lifting a *book* (冊 → 曲) to show what is written in it, meaning that it is a law or **code** that must be referred to.

1082

傘 傘 サン かさ

umbrella

An **umbrella** composed of a handle (十), bamboo stripes (仌) and a sunshade (ヘ).

A woman with a bamboo umbrella

3. CLOTHS

The textile industry is one of the backbones of every sedentary society, since clothing is an essential tool for survival in certain climatologies. The existence of a large-scale textile production system has a direct impact on the economy, development and expansion of any society. One of the first textile manufacturing tools to be found in ancient societies is the loom with which 'cloths' are made 巾 巾, and with it, other things such as 'garments' 衣 衣 or 'hats' 冃 冃 can also be produced.

1083 Ⓡ Ⓜ

 巾 巾 キン

Threads hanging from a loom

cloth

Threads (丨) coming out of a loom (冂), a part of the **cloth** production process.

Woman working with a thread hanging from a loom

帳 帳 チョウ *Cloth* 巾 *that is long* 長 (チョウ) 1084

notebook

NOTE Initially this character referred to a type of cloth that was hung in public places and had announcements or mandates written on it.

帥 帥 スイ *Person leaving footprints* 𠂤 (スイ) *and carrying a cloth* 巾 *flag* 1085

commander

幕 幕 バク マク *Cloth* 巾 *that hides* 莫 (バク) *things* 1086

curtain

 布 布 フ ぬの *Hand holding threads coming out of a loom* 1087 Ⓢ

fabric

An *outstretched hand* (又 → ナ) working with the threads that come out of a loom while creating *cloth* (巾) or **fabric**.

怖 怖 フ こわ.い *Heart-mind* 忄 *squeezed like fabric* 布 (フ) 1088

frightening

 希 希 キ *Fabric with visible interweaving* 1089

exceptional

A cross (乂) woven *fabric* (布), a fine and presumably high quality fabric, an **exceptional** one.

帛
帛

White cloth 1090 Ⓜ

A piece of *white* (白) *cloth* (巾).

綿
綿 メン わた

Threads 糸 of a white cloth 帛 1091

cotton

帚
帚

Hand holding a broom 1092 Ⓜ

A *cloth* (巾) attached to a handle (冖) that can be held by an *outstretched hand* ((⺕ → 彐) ≈ 又). A representation of a rudimentary broom.

婦
婦 フ

Woman 女 holding a broom 帚 1093

lady

掃
掃 ソウ は.く

Hand 扌 handling a broom 帚 1094

to sweep

敝
敝 ヘイ

Cloth hit with a mattock 1095 Ⓢ

Rags

Cloth (巾) drilled with holes (⺀⺀) since it has been *hit* (攵). Cloth that has turned into rags.

弊
弊 ヘイ

Rags 敝 made by two hands 廾 1096

breakage

蔽
蔽 ヘイ

Plants 艹 over rags 敝 1097

occultation

幣
幣 ヘイ

Ragged 敝 cloths 巾 1098

cash

shinto paper streamers

NOTE This character originally referred to any kind of worn-out or ragged cloth, then it started to implicitly denote cloths worn out by some type of writing made on it. After that, 'ragged cloths' started to be associated also with ragged paper and, finally, the sinogram adopted both the meaning of **cash** (as paper money), and that of **paper streamers** used specifically in the offerings of the Japanese Shinto religion.

Shinto streamer, called 'shide' (紙垂), folded in the traditional way

---

爾

爾 尔 ジ

Cloths being embroidered on a loom

thou

1099 ㊔ 爾 Ⓢ

Threads of *cloth hanging from a loom* (巾) with an advanced mechanism (丅) capable of *distributing* (八 → ハ) those threads and intertwining them (㸚) in different ways so that the new fabric shows different patterns and <u>embroidery</u>.

In some compounds this character adopts the simplified version 尔.

1100

称

称 ショウ

Fruits 禾 with embroidery 尔

reputation

appellation

NOTE This glyph was originally associated with the meaning of **reputation** or renown, something whose name is known by many people or, as the English expression goes, something that has its name in lights, in this case represented metaphorically by the image of the fruits of one's life adorned with embroidery thanks to one's name. This notion of reputation associated with name made the meaning of the ideogram finally derive into the more prosaic concept of 'naming' or **appellation**.

1101

繭

繭 ケン まゆ

Threads spun by insects among the plants from which cloths can be made

cocoon

A natural container made by *threads* (糸) formed with the saliva of an *insect* (虫) that is found among *plants* (艹) and from which the material to produce *cloths* (巾

→冂) can be extracted: the **cocoon** of a silkworm.

衣 **衣** 亠 𧘇 衤 イ ころも **garment** **clothes** 1102 Ⓡ Ⓜ

Originally 衣, a top **garment** or **clothes** with an open collar (亠), sleeves and a junction in the chest area (从 → 𧘇).

When this character acts as a component it can take, in addition to the standard form 衣, two additional forms: The simplification 衤 when the component is placed to the left, or the distortion 亠𧘇, which separates the parts 亠 and 𧘇 to leave a space in the center where a new component is placed.

Traditional Chinese garment

依 **依** イ エ *Person 亻 and his clothes 衣* (イ) **reliant** 1103

褒 **褒** ホウ ほ.める *Clothes 亠𧘇 used for protection 保* (ホ) **to exalt** 1104

褐 **褐** カツ *Clothes 衤 that look threatening 曷* (カツ) **brown** 1105

NOTE **Brown** clothes are here understood as dirty and worn-out clothes, clothes worn by someone who can be intimidating or threatening.

袖 **袖** ショウ そで *Part of clothes 衤 that often reaches the mouth 由* (ユウ) **sleeve** 1106

被 被 ①②ヒ ② こうむ.る — *Clothes 衤 on the skin 皮* (ヒ) — 1107

① overlay

② **to endure**

表 表 ②③ヒョウ ②おもて ①あらわ.す — *Fur on clothes* — 1108 Ⓢ

① **to reveal**

② **surface**

③ **chart**

Originally 裘 [亠毛 (モウ) 𧘇], the *fur* (毛 → 龶) that is left visible or **revealed** on fur *clothes* (衣 → 𧘇), the **surface** of it.

俵 俵 ヒョウ たわら — *Person 亻 looking like he was wearing a furry coat 表* (ヒョウ) — 1109

straw bag

NOTE It is the image of a man carrying a **straw bag** on his back, making him look like a hairy beast.

People carrying straw bags on their backs

褱 カイ — *Crying baby covered in clothes* — 1110 Ⓢ

Originally 褱 [亠 罒 𧘇], *clothes* (衣 → 亠𧘇 → 衣) covering a <u>baby crying</u> with *watery* (水 → 氺 → 丰 → 十) *eyes* (目 → 罒).

懷 懐 ①カイ ① なつ.かしい ②ふところ — *Feelings 忄 caused by a crying baby covered in clothes 褱* (カ) — 1111

(イ) *leaning on the bosom*

① **dear**

② **bosom**

壊 カイ *Earth-soil* 土 *left with babies crying* 褱カイ 1112

壞 こわ.す **to destroy**

衰 スイ *Clothes made of bamboo* 1113

衰 おとろ.える **to weaken**

Originally 衰 [⿱亠林], *clothes* (衣 → ⿱亠) made of *bamboo* (竹 ≈ 林 → 冄), in reference to a kind of raincoat made with bamboo strips (簑), which was characterized by its rapid deterioration and its **weaken**ing image.

Representation of the deity Saonetsuhiko wearing a bamboo raincoat

---

卒 ソツ *Garment tied with a belt* 1114 Ⓢ

卒 **finish**

SPECIAL READING 何卒 [なにとぞ]: *please*

A top *garment* (亠 ← 衣) tied at the bottom with a belt (十), making the garment finally worn and fit, indicating the end or **finish**ing of the dressing process.

When this character acts as a component it takes the simplified form 卆.

Traditional Chinese garment tied with a belt

砕 砕 サイ くだ.く — *Stone 石 being finished 卆* — **to smash** 1115

枠 枠 わく — *Tree-wood 木 structure that is finished 卆* — **frame** 1116

粋 粋 スイ いき — *Rice 米 whose elaboration process is finished 卆* — **refined** 1117

雜 雑 ザツ ゾウ — *Gathering of different clothes* — **miscellaneous** 1118

Originally 襍 [衤集], a *gathering* (集) of different *clothes* (衣 → 衤) combined, metaphorically representing the idea of a **miscellaneous** set of things. This character finally took, over time, the variant 雜 [𠆢木隹], in which the element for "clothing" (衤 = 衣) becomes 𠆢—as in the character 卒 (*finish*)—and the element for "collection" (集) is divided into two parts (木隹). Eventually, this form of the character was simplified into the current glyph 雑, where the element 𠆢 has became 九.

乍 乍 サ — *Folded clothes* 1119 Ⓢ

The pointed fold of the collar of a top garment, the place where the two wrapping parts meet. Although the contemporary form of the character diverges a lot from the original pictogram, in the strokes 𠂉 one can see the pointed edge of the collar, and in the strokes ⺊ its inner decorative lining.

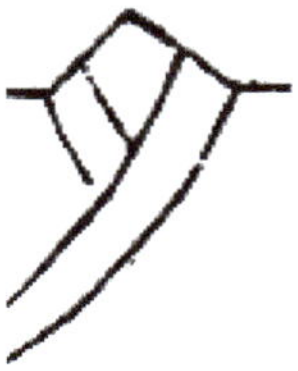

Collar of a traditional Chinese garment

1120

作 作　サ　サク　つく.る

Person 亻 folding clothes 乍 [サ] *that have been just made*

to make

1121

詐 詐　サ

Speech 言 made while covering the mouth with one's folded clothes 乍 [サ]

deception

1122

昨 昨　サク

Sun 日 covered with folded clothes 乍 [サ]

yesterday
preceding

SPECIAL READING 昨日 [きのう]: *yesterday*

1123 Ⓜ

冃 冃 冃 冃

Hat

A kind of traditional hat whose brim descends slightly towards the eyes. This character currently adopts the squashed form 冃 in the compounds and is placed on top of them.

1124 Ⓢ

冒 冒　ボウ　おか.す

Hat covering the eyes

to risk

The brim of a *hat* (冃 → 冃) completely covering the *eyes* (目), hindering visibility and putting the person at **risk**.

1125

帽 帽　ボウ

Cloth 巾 worn over the eyes 冒 [ボウ]

headgear

1126 Ⓢ

曼 曼　マン

Hand putting a cover over the eyes

An *outstretched hand* (又) covering the *eyes* (目) with a *hat* (冃 → 冃).

慢
慢 マン
Heart-mind 忄 *being covered* 曼 (マン) 1127
ridicule

漫
漫 マン
Uncontrolled fluids 氵 *being covered* 曼 (マン) 1128
unrestrained

最
最 サイ もっと.も
Hand taking off a hat 1129 Ⓢ
utmost

A hand *taking* (取 (シュ) → 取) a *hat* (冃 → 日) off the field of vision of the eyes, thus allowing the **utmost** clairvoyance.

撮
撮 サツ と.る
Hand 扌 *taking off a cover over the eyes* 最 (サイ) 1130
to take pictures

REVIEW ON EVERYDAY OBJECTS

丂考可何奇才扩旅主几処殿片丬将疒斗勺升与串午缶䍃卸且

1 号朽拷歌河苛荷埼崎椅騎存在材施住注柱駐肌机拁殿版状奨痕疫瘦療瘍疲料科斜的約昇誉挙患許陶謡揺助阻査租粗狙組

冊侖典傘

2 嗣柵倫論

巾布希帛帚敝爾繭衣表褱衰卒雑乍冃冒曼最

3 帳帥幕怖綿婦掃弊蔽幣称依褒褐袖被俵懐壊砕枠粋作詐昨帽慢漫撮

Tools

1. COUNTING TOOLS

The prosperity of a given society is directly determined by its technological development, for which a series of tools is vital. Among those tools there are abstract counting tools, which lay the foundations for any kind of calculation that would become indispensable to develop more advanced technologies. The first counting tools that appeared in the Yellow Valley were a kind of counting rods. If those rods were placed horizontally 一, they indicated the 'units', and if they were placed vertically 十, they indicated the 'tens'.

一 | イチ
イツ
ひと.つ | *Counting rod*
one | 1131 Ⓡ Ⓜ

SPECIAL READINGS ① 一人 [ひとり]: *one person* ／ ② 一日 [ついたち]: *first day of the month* ／ ③ 一昨日 [おととい]: *the day before yesterday*

A counting rod, such as those of the positional numeral system that was used for counting in ancient China, where each rod represented a unit or the number **one**.

百 | ヒャク | *Clearer counting rod*
hundred | 1132 Ⓜ

A *counting rod* (一) that has its positional value multiplied to represent a larger amount, an amount that, being larger, is more *clear* (白). That larger, 'clearer' amount was eventually set at one **hundred**.

二 | ニ
ふた.つ | *Two counting rods*
two | 1133 Ⓢ

SPECIAL READING 二人 [ふたり]: *two people*

Two *counting rods* (一×2) representing **two** units.

仁 ジン 1134

仁 ニ

Characteristic of a person 亻 *shared between two* 二 *people*

humanity

三 サン 1135

三 み.つ

Three counting rods

three

Three *counting rods* (一×3) representing **three** units.

十 ジッ 1136 Ⓡ Ⓜ

十 ジュウ

と

とお

Thick rod

ten

SPECIAL READING 二十日 [はつか]: *twentieth day of the month*

Originally ｜, a counting rod placed vertically and perpendicularly to the horizontal *counting rod* (一) representing the units, in order to show the end of the units' positional value and the beginning of the **tens**. In one of the rod numeral systems used in ancient Asia, the units were represented as follows: ＿ (1), ＝ (2), ≡ (3), ≣ (4), ䷀ (5), ⊥ (6), ⊥ (7), ≟ (8), ≣ (9); and the start of the tens was represented by the change of orientation of the counting rod: ｜ (10), ｜＿ (11), ｜＝ (12), etc. Over time the transcription of the vertical counting rod for the tens (｜), began to be written with greater thickness than the horizontal rod, probably to reinforce the new singularity of the tens and the concept of '**ten**' as an independent number or quantity rather than just a positional value. The thickness of the vertical line finally, as in many other characters, became linearized with the addition of a horizontal line (一). This concept of <u>thick rod</u> is adopted by some compounds in which this glyph appears as a component.

計 ケイ 1137

計 はか.る

Speech 言 *about results given by thick counting rods* 十

to reckon

SPECIAL READING 時計 [とけい]: *clock*

協 1138

協 キョウ

Ten 十 *arms acting together* 劦 (キョウ)

cooperation

汁 汁 ジュウ しる — *Fluid* 氵 *prepared with a thick rod* 十 (ジュウ) 1139

soup
juice

準 準 ジュン — *Water* 氵 *at a depth of a thick rod* 十 *in which a bird* 隹 *can touch the bottom* 1140

level

千 千 セン ち — *Ten people reproducing* 1141

thousand

A *person* (人 → 亻) crossed by a horizontal line that forms the character for "ten" (十). It is very likely that this glyph is a modification of the character 人 (*person*) adapted to mean **thousand** through a phonetic borrowing. In any case, it can be interpreted ideogrammatically by using the concept of multiplicity and associating it with that of reproduction, insofar as an initial group of ten people can end up becoming a clan or tribe of a thousand people.

年 年 ネン とし — *Fruits reproducing* 1142

year

Originally 秊 [禾十], a *thousand* (千) *fruits* (禾), or a large quantity of fruit being reproduced over time, in reference to the **year**ly harvest and planting cycles. This character has been considerably simplified over time and its original strokes blended together. First, the two upper strokes of the component 禾 became the element 𠂉 and then the lower oblique lines of 禾 became a straight, united line, thus giving rise to the form 秊. Later, that form was simplified into 秊—with the center line shortened—, and finally it developed into the current form 年, in which the central line has ended up in a vertical position to facilitate the fluidity of writing the strokes.

古 古 コ ふる.い — *Words passing through ten mouths* 1143 Ⓢ

old

Words that have gone through *ten* (十) *mouths* (口), words that have been repeated many times since olden times, words that speak of something **old**.

克 克 コク *Person 儿 that is old 古* 1144
overcoming

故 故 コ ゆえ *Old times 古 hitting 攵* 1145
happenstance

NOTE A reference to indirect causality, in the sense that past actions affect present events.

湖 湖 コ みずうみ *Water 氵 that is an old 古 body 月* 1146
lake

苦 苦 ク にが.い くる.しい *Plants 艹 that are old 古* 1147
bitter
painful

枯 枯 コ か.れる *Tree-wood 木 becoming old 古* 1148
to wither

居 居 キョ い.る *Person sitting on a place since an old time* 1149 Ⓜ
to stay

A *person sitting* (尸) in the same place since *old* times (古), a person who **stays** in a certain place.

据 据 す.える *Hand 扌 making something stay 居* 1150
to set

裾 裾 すそ *Part of the clothes 衤 that stays put 居* 1151
hem

支 支 シ ささ.える *Outstretched hand holding onto a thick rod* 1152 Ⓢ
to sustain

An *outstretched hand* (又) holding a *thick rod* (十) or stick, evoking the image of a hand holding onto the branch of a tree that **sustains** it.

伎 伎 キ 1153

Person 亻 sustaining 支 himself

skill

肢 肢 シ 1154

Body part 月 that sustains 支 itself onto the trunk as branches

limb

技 技 ギ わざ 1155

Hand 扌 sustaining 支 a person

ability

岐 岐 キ 1156

Mountain 山 with protruding thick rods on which a hand can be held 支

ramification

枝 枝 シ えだ 1157

Tree's 木 thick rods on which a hand can be held 支

branch

2. MONETARY TOOLS

An accumulation of all kinds of tools and everyday objects at the end of the day is subjected to trade and exchange between different members of society. When the volume of trade and commerce begins to be large, the implementation of a monetary system that facilitates transactions is necessary. One of the first coins used in ancient China was cowrie 'shells' 貝, as they were imitation proof and a scarce object and, therefore, valuable. Another type of valuable and sought-after objects were those made of jade, such as 'jade discs', that were kept together in strings 玉, and ended up becoming a symbol of economic power.

貝 貝 かい 1158

seashell Ⓡ

Money Ⓜ

A cowrie **seashell**. The upper contour 口 represents the exterior body of the shell, while the two central lines (二) and the two lower strokes (ハ) represent the inner marks of the shell. Cowrie shells were used in remote antiquity, at least among the elite, as currency, and it was customary to tie them together with a string to facilitate transactions. It is from this monetary use of cowrie shells that the meaning of <u>money</u>, used by this character when acting as a component, comes from.

Specimen of cowrie shell

資 資	シ	*Subsequent* ツ 次 *money* 貝 *earnings* **assets**	1159
貨 貨	カ	*Transformed* カ 化 *money* 貝 **goods**	1160
賛 賛	サン	*Two adults* 夫×2 *exchanging money* 貝 **approval**	1161
唄 唄	うた	*Words* 口 *turned into money* 貝 **ballad**	1162
貪 貪	ドン むさぼ.る	*Retained* 今 *money* 貝 **to covet**	1163
賄 賄	ワイ まかな.う	*Money* 貝 *and held meat* 有 **to supply**	1164
賢 賢	ケン かしこ.い	*Delicately* ケン 臤 *earned money* 貝 **intelligent**	1165
敗 敗	ハイ やぶ.れる	*Money* バイ 貝 *hit* 攵 *and destroyed* **to fail**	1166

賀 賀 ガ 1167

Added 加 *money* 貝

congratulations

貼 貼 チョウ は.る 1168

Money 貝 *that has been taken up* 占

to adhere

NOTE Metaphorical idea in reference to the attachment someone feels for newly obtained money.

販 販 ハン 1169

Money 貝 *going in reverse* 反 *directions*

sale

賭 賭 ト か.ける 1170

Money 貝 *acting* 者

to bet

購 購 コウ 1171

Money 貝 *that has been trapped* 冓

purchase

財 財 ザイ サイ 1172

Money 貝 *earned with talent* 才

wealth

櫻 桜 桜 オウ さくら 1173

Blooming feminine tree

cherry tree (*Prunus serrulata*)

Originally 櫻 [木賏女], a *tree* (木) whose fruits are feminine as *women* (女) and its bloom is plentiful as the riches of *money* (貝×2 → 賏 → ⺍), concepts that were allegory represented by the flowers of the cherry tree, also known internationally as ‘sakura’.

⿱臾貝 貴 貴 キ とうと.い たっと.い 1174 Ⓢ

Two hands holding a person with money

valuable

Originally ⿱臾貝 [臾貝], *two hands holding a person* (臾 → 虫) that has *money* (貝): An ideographic representation of **value** beheld by money.

潰 カイ *Water* 氵 *swallowing valuable things* 貴(キ) 1175
潰 つぶ.れる **to be crushed**

 負 フ *Person carrying money* 1176
負 お.う ① **to carry on one's back**
ま.ける ② **to lose**

A *leaning person* (勹 → ⺈) carrying a sum of *money* (貝) on his back as a burden, referring to debt money that has to be returned, so to say, money that is eventually **lost**.

 賁 1177
賁 フン *Abundant money*
Abundantly

Cowrie shells (貝) growing in plenty as <u>*abundant*</u> *plants* (卉 → 卉).

憤 フン *Feelings* 忄 *arousing abundantly* 賁(フン) 1178
憤 いきどお.る **to be enraged**

噴 フン *Words* 口 *arousing abundantly* 賁(フン) 1179
噴 ふ.く **to spout**

墳 フン *Earth-soil* 土 *accumulated abundantly* 賁(フン) 1180
墳 **tumulus**

 貫 カン *Thread going through a seashell* 1181 Ⓢ
貫 つらぬ.く **to go through**

A knot (十) made at the end of a rope that goes **through** holes (口) made on *cowrie shells* (貝) that are tied together in a string. Since ancient times it was common in East Asia to tie together several seashells in strings in order to facilitate monetary transactions requiring large amounts of shells. Later on, currency evolved from cowrie shells into coins made of copper or other metals that, however, maintained the faculty of being able to be bound in strings, since they were made with a hole in their middle in order to let pass a string through it.

String of Chinese coins

慣	カン	Feeling 忄 going through 貫 (カン)	1182
慣	な.れる	**to get used to**	

			String of jade disks	1183
	玉	① ② ギョク	① jade	Ⓡ
	玉 王	③ たま	② **jewel**	玉
			③ **sphere**	Ⓜ

A string of three jade discs (王) bound with a rope topped with a knot (丶). In ancient China jade was an element of luxury profusely used in various ritual objects. Some of the most important among those objects were a kind of flat discs called *bi* (璧), which had a hole in the middle and presumably symbolized heaven. This type of jade disc, the *bi*, eventually went on to designate 'jade' in general and, more recently, **jewel**s and precious stones. From the circular shape of the *bi* derives, in turn, the meaning of **sphere**.

When this character acts as a component and is placed to the left of the compounds, it takes the form 王, which drops the dot 丶.

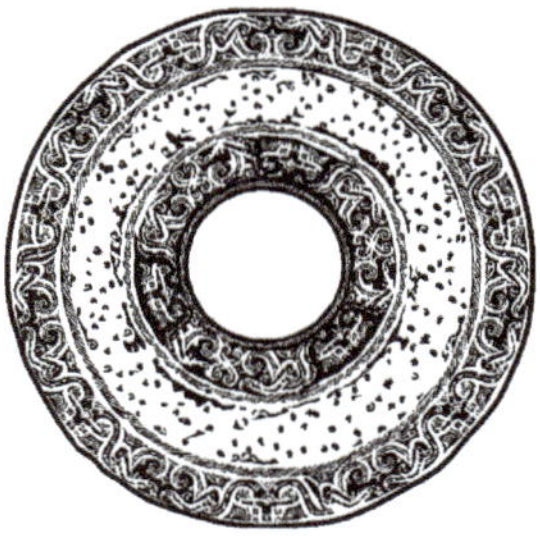

Ornamented jade disk, called 'bi' (璧)

珍	チン	Jewel 王 that is aged 㐱 (チン)	1184
珍	めずら.しい	**rare**	

現 ゲン *Jewel* 王 *that can be seen* 見(ケン) 1185

現 あらわ.れる **to be revealed**

珠 *Jewel* 王 *of a scarlet color* 朱(シュ) 1186

珠 シュ **gem**

球 キュウ *Jewel* 王 *being sought after* 求(キュウ) 1187

球 たま **ball**

NOTE A jewel with a round shape, evoking purity.

璽 *Embroidered* 爾(ジ) *jade* 玉 1188

璽 ジ **imperial seal**

NOTE It refers to the seals or sigils used by the emperor or other governmental agencies, whose handles were made of jade and had inscriptions and carvings that recall the embroidery on clothing.

The turtle-shaped handle of a seal

The seal proper

 玨 1189

玨 ハン *Several jewels* Ⓢ

Several jewels strings (玉×2 → 玨 → 玨 → 玨).

斑 *Several jewels* 玨(ハン) *full of writings* 文 1190

斑 ハン **mottled**

琴 1191

琴 キン こと

Jewels 𤤴 *that are retained* 今(キン)

Asian zither

NOTE Called *guqin* (古琴) in Chinese and *koto* in Japanese, a percussive string instrument whose sound, designed to accompany the words of poems, was supposed to be as delicate as jewels.

Woman playing the koto

全 1192 Ⓢ

全 全 ゼン すべ.て まった.く

String of jewels tied with a tight knot

completely

whole

A string of *jewels* (玉 → 王) tightly tied at its tip with a rope (へ), a string of jewelry **completely** sealed, making with the parts a **whole** entity. The dot 丶 of the component 玉 (*jewel*), which originally represented a small knot, disappears here because the strokes へ now represent a larger knot.

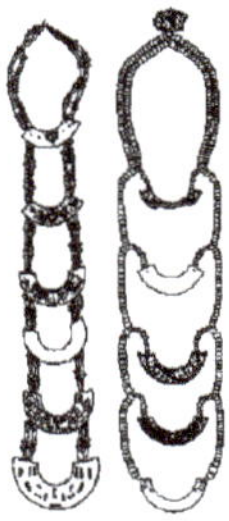

Strings of jade jewels from Shang dynasty China, called 'peiyu' (佩玉)

詮 1193

詮 セン

Speech 言 *analyzed as a whole* 全(ゼン)

inquiry

栓 栓 セン *Tree-wood 木 piece that covers the whole ゼン全* 1194

stopper

 朋 朋 ホウ *Several strings of jewelry tied together* 1195 ㊔ Ⓢ

pal

Several strings of jewels (玨) hanging from the same rope (冂), a pictographic representation of <u>jewelry</u> that gave rise to the graph 朋 and later to the current form 朋, whose compositional elements, in spite of their graphic similarity, have nothing to do etymologically with the components 月 (*moon*) or 肉 (*meat*).

崩 崩 ホウ くず.す *Jewelry ホウ朋 falling down from a mountain 山* 1196

to pull down

棚 棚 たな *Tree-wood 木 furniture made for storing jewelry 朋* 1197

shelf

3. WORK TOOLS

One of the characteristics of social expansion is the settlements of people, which are produced thanks to the development of the domestication of plants and animals or, in other words, livestock and agriculture. To carry out such development it is paramount to have a series of work tools for daily use, such as the 'hoe'  工, that tills the field, or the 'nails'  丁, that fixes building structures.

Once a great degree of domestication of certain animals has been achieved, they can be used to help with agricultural tasks, and for this purpose there are tools that facilitate the handling of those animals, such as the 'yoke' for a single head 丙, or that of 'two' heads 両. In an even more advanced state of technological development this element can also be used for transport, joining it to a cart pulled by wheels and thus forming a 'chariot' 車.

 エ 工 ク コウ *Hoe* 1198 Ⓢ

craft

A multi-purpose tool with a handle on top (一), a trunk (丨) and a metal blade (一) used to dig or strike: A <u>hoe</u>, indispensable for physical work activity, or **craft**.

Blade of a hoe from ancient China

項 1199

項 コウ

Craft 工(コウ) of the head 頁

item

攻 1200

攻 コウ せ.める

Craft 工(コウ) used in hitting 攵

to attack

功 1201

功 コウ ク

Craft 工(コウ) done with strength 力

success

巧 1202

巧 コウ たく.み

Hoe 工(コウ) and stick 丂(コウ)

craftsmanship

江 1203

江 コウ え

Water's 氵 craft 工(コウ)

inlet

虹 1204

虹 にじ

Serpent's 虫 craft 工

rainbow

NOTE It is very likely that the neolithic society of ancient China identified the **rainbow** with a mythological snake-like creature—the rainbow serpent—as many other cultures throughout the world do and have done.

差 1205

差 ① サ ② さ.す

Auspicious 𦍌 craft 工

① **distinction**

② **to be noticeable**

紅 紅 コウ ク くれない — *Thread 糸 used in crafting 工(コウ)* — **crimson** 1206

貢 貢 コウ ク みつ.ぐ — *Craft 工(コウ) paid with money 貝* — **to pay a tribute** 1207

巩 巩 — *Person working with a hoe* 1208 Ⓜ

A *person working with his hands* (丮 → 卂 → 凡) while using a *hoe* (工).

恐 恐 キョウ おそ.れる — *Feelings 心 caused by a person handling a hoe 巩* — **dreadful** 1209

築 築 チク きず.く — *Person working with a hoe 巩, bamboo ⺮ and wood 木* — **to construct** 1210

左 左 サ ひだり — *Hand helping with a hoe* — **left hand side** 1211 Ⓢ

An *outstretched hand* (又 → ナ) serving as an aid in the manipulation of a *hoe* (工). If the right hand serves as the main force while handling a hoe, the aiding hand has to be the **left hand**.

佐 佐 サ — *Person's 亻 hand helping with a hoe 左(サ)* — **assistant** 1212

惰 惰 ダ — *Feelings 忄 in a body 月 that has to help with a hoe 左(サ)* — **laziness** 1213

尋 尋 ジン たず.ねる — *Hands working and words pronounced* — **to inquire** 1214

Two hands *working* (寸 + ((⺕ ≈ 又) → 彐)) with a *hoe* (工) while *words* (口) are pronounced: **Inquiry** into a matter through questions and exhaustive work.

展 テン *Sitting person displaying hoes on top of some clothes* 1215

exhibition

Originally 展 [尸𡭔衣], a *sitting person* (尸) **exhibiting** a handful of *hoes* (工×4 → 𡭔 → 丗) on top of some *clothes* (衣 → 𧘇).

襄 ジョウ *Two hands extracting hoes from a bag* 1216 Ⓢ

Work in the field

Two hands (廾 → ハ) taking out a bunch of *hoes* (工×4 → 𡭔 → 𠀎) from some *clothes* (衣 → 𧘇) that act as a bag, in reference to the preparation for an agricultural activity or work in the field.

孃 ジョウ *Woman* 女 *helping in the field* 襄 (ジョウ) 1217

girl

讓 ジョウ ゆず.る *Speech* 言 *made while working in the field* 襄 (ジョウ) 1218

to allow

壤 ジョウ *Earth-soil* 土 *where field work* 襄 (ジョウ) *is done* 1219

land lot

壬 ニン *Thick and heavy hoe* 1220 ㊔ Ⓢ

ninth

Originally 壬, a *hoe* (工) with a thick trunk: a thick and heavy hoe. The thickness of the handle is shown in the contemporary graph, as in so many other characters, with a horizontal line (一). The upper stroke of the glyph, 一, was later tilted to differentiate this component from the character 王[14] (*king*).

妊 ニン *Woman* 女 *that has become thick and heavy* 壬 (ニン) 1221

pregnant

[14] Character #1649

淫 淫 イン みだ.ら — *Water-soaked 氵 hand grabbing 爫 a thick and heavy hoe 壬* (ニン) 1222

lewd

NOTE It seems that this character initially alluded to the abundant sweat caused by excessively hard work. Eventually the notion of 'sweat' would begin to be associated with sex and **lewd**ness.

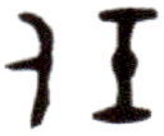 任 任 ニン まか.せる — *Person with a thick and heavy hoe* 1223 Ⓢ

to give responsibility

A *person* (人 → 亻) with a *thick and heavy hoe* (壬 (ニン)), with the **responsibility** to work with it in spite of himself.

賃 賃 チン — *Responsibility 任* (ニン) *concerning money 貝* 1224

fee

 巨 巨 キョ — *Person measuring something in the distance with a hoe* 1225 Ⓢ

huge

Originally , representation of a *person seen from the front* (大) holding with his *outstretched hand* ((⺕ ≈ 又) → コ) a *hoe* (工 (コウ) → 匚) that he uses to measure, in the distance and in a comparative way, an object or element that despite its **huge** original size seems equivalent to that of the hoe, as when a person makes the gesture of catching the moon with his fingers. Over time, the original component for "person" (大) disappeared and the glyph was left depicting just a hoe (工 → 匚) being held by a hand (⺕ → コ).

拒 拒 キョ こば.む — *Bare hand 扌 in comparison as a hand holding a hoe 巨* (キョ) *at the time of measuring something* 1226

to refuse

距 距 キョ — *Something that can be measured by feet ⻊ or by a hand holding a hoe 巨* (キョ) 1227

distance

丁
丁

チョウ
テイ

Nail
block
fourth

1228 Ⓢ

A stick (亅) with a thicker part on top (一), a tool that serves to fasten two or more elements: a <u>nail</u>. The meaning of **block** that this character takes when acting as a standalone is given by the functionality nails have to join together in block pieces that were previously separate.

頂
頂
チョウ
いただ.く

Nail's 丁(チョウ) *head* 頁
top
1229

訂
訂
テイ

Speech 言 *fastened with nails* 丁(テイ)
correction
1230

打
打
ダ
う.つ

Hand 扌 *hitting a nail* 丁(テイ)
to strike
1231

灯
灯
トウ
ひ

Fire 火 *that is nailed down* 丁(テイ)
lamp
1232

丙
丙

ヘイ

Single yoke
third

1233 Ⓢ

A <u>yoke</u> designed for a single animal, with its crossbar (一) and an undulation below it (内) that is adapted to the shape of the necks of the cattle. This character, when appearing as a standalone, takes on the meaning of **third** in rank, meaning that originates from the Sinitic ordinal system known as Heavenly Stems (天干), wherein ten concrete primitive characters are used to designate different ordinal positions, among which 丙 takes the third one, after 甲 (コウ) and 乙 (ヘイ). The adoption of this grapheme to denote 'third' may be due to the fact that a single yoke can be considered as bad or 'third' tier compared to the more common double yoke.

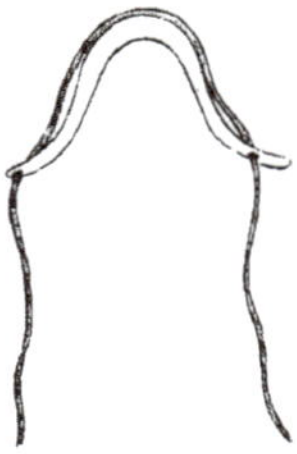

Yoke for a single head

柄
柄 ① ヘイ ① がら ② え — *Wood 木 with which a single yoke 丙 (ヘイ) is made* 1234

① **body build**
② **grip**

病
病 ①② ビョウ ①② ヘイ ① やまい ② や.む — *Illness 疒 weighing like a yoke 丙 (ヘイ)* 1235

① **sickness**
② **to fall sick**

更
更 ① コウ ② さら ③ ふ.ける — *Single yoke being fixed* 1236 Ⓢ

① **renewal**
② **even more**
③ to get late

Originally 㪅 [丙攴], a single head *yoke* (丙) being fixed and **renewed** by a *hand hitting with a mattock* (攴 ← 攵), implying that it can be used for **even more** time. The middle strokes of the original glyph (内＋卜), by means of a process of simplification, finally ended up merging into the form 申.

便
便 ①② ビン ① ベン ② たよ.り — *Person 亻 getting renewed 更* 1237

① **convenience**
② correspondence

硬
硬 コウ かた.い — *Stone 石 that is renewed 更 (コウ)* 1238

hard

梗
梗 コウ — *Tree-like 木 element that looks renewed 更 (コウ)* 1239

flower stalk

両 両 リョウ *Double yoke* **both** 1240 Ⓜ

Originally 兩, a <u>double yoke</u>, with room for two animal heads, **both** of them. In a process of simplification, the middle lines depicting the undulations (从) of the yoke ended up becoming the element 凵.

Yoke for two heads

満 満 ①②マン ① み.たす ② み.ちる *Water drunk by oxen held by a yoke* ① **to fulfill** ② **full** 1241

Two oxen held by a *double yoke* (兩 → 両) approaching their *mouths* ((廿 ≈ 口) → 卄) to a *water* source (水 → 氵) in order to satisfy their thirst and feel **fulfill**ed.

車 車 シャ くるま *Chariot* **car** 1242 Ⓡ Ⓜ

A <u>chariot</u> seen from above pulled by two cattle or horses. The upper line 一 represents the double yoke, which is linked to the transport box (田) through a wooden bar (丨) that ends up connected to a perpendicular axis (一) that holds the wheels. The meaning of 'chariot' was later adapted to the more modern meaning of **car**.

Two-wheeled carriage pulled by an ox

軟 軟	ナン やわら.かい	*Quality that chariots 車 lack 欠* **soft**	1243
較 較	カク	*Chariots 車 being interchanged* 交(コウ) **contrast**	1244
軸 軸	ジク	*Part of a chariot 車 that enters the mouth 由 of the wheels* **axle**	1245
撃 撃	ゲキ う.つ	*Hand 手 striking 殳 a chariot 車* **to beat**	1246
軌 軌	キ	*Chariot's 車 figurative arms* 九(ク) **rail**	1247
軽 軽	ケイ かる.い かろ.やか	*Chariot 車 that has been made on a potter's wheel* 圣(ケイ) **to be light**	1248
陣 陣	ジン	*Chariots 車 stationed along mountains 阝* **camp**	1249
範 範	ハン	*Chariot 車 made of bamboo ⺮ where a person can huddle* 㔾(ハン) **exemplary**	1250
輩 輩	ハイ	*Negation* 非(ヒ) *of a chariot 車 getaway* **comrade**	1251
輪 輪	リン わ	*Part of a chariot 車 with many bamboo strips like a talkative book* 侖(リン) **wheel** **hoop**	1252

井 井 井 ショウ セイ い **water well** *Pit* 1253 Ⓜ

The rectangular outline of the wooden structure of a **water well** seen from above. As a component this glyph takes on the derived meaning of pit.

Two women at a well

耕 耕 コウ たがや.す *Heavy branched trees 耒 made to grow in pits 井* **to till** 1254

丼 丼 丼 セイ どん どんぶり *Pit full of food* **bowl** 1255

A *pit* (井) full of food (丶), a **bowl** with a lot of space to store food in it.

录 录 录 ロク *Pulley drawing water from a well* 1256 Ⓢ

A pulley (彐) drawing a well's bucket (一) wherefrom *water* drips (水 → 氺).

緑 緑 リョク ロク みどり *Thread 糸 dyed with a color similar to that of water drops falling from a bucket drawn from a well 录* (ロク) **green** 1257

NOTE In the Sinosphere, the colors **green** and blue have historically been grouped together under the same concept (green-blue).

4. NETS AND BASKETS

Another essential tool for survival is the 'net' 冂, which in its most basic form can be used to catch fish. If a stick is added to a simple net it can become a 'simple' butterfly net 単, useful to catch bugs instead of fish. If nets are made of wood or bamboo instead of cloth, more sophisticated objects can be made, such as winnowing 'baskets' 甘, which are essential for sowing. We see therefore how the elaboration of nets and networks is an essential aspect of fishing, hunting and agriculture.

冈 罓 罒 *Net* 1258 Ⓜ

Originally 冈, a fishing net with its sticks (冂) and its intertwined ropes (メ), an objet that was adopted to represent any kind of <u>net</u>. This component got later simplified into the form 罓—with the inner strokes メ flattened into 䒑. On most compounds, however, a further simplified form is used: 罒, which is identical in appearance to the tilted version of the character for "eye" (目 → 罒).

Two people handling a fishing net

署 署 シヨ *Net* 罒 *of people performing actions* 者 (シャ) 1259

police station

罪 罪 ザイ つみ *Net* 罒 *used negatively* 非 1260

crime

罵 罵 バ ののし.る *Net* 罒 *blocking horses'* 馬 (バ) *movement* 1261

to curse at

罷 罷 ヒ — *Net 罒 blocking any capability 能* — **termination** 1262

網 網 モウ あみ — *Threads 糸 forming a net 冂 that make fish perish 亡* (モウ) — **network** 1263

羅 羅 ラ — *Net 罒 maintaining 維 things together* — **encompassing** 1264

買 買 バイ か.う — *Net 罒 of money 貝* (バイ) *used for purchasing* — **to buy** 1265

岡 岡 コウ おか — *Net of mountains* — ridge 1266 Ⓢ

PLACE NAME USAGE 岡山県 [おかやまけん]: *Okayama Prefecture*

A *net* (冂) of *mountains* (山) placed in a line: a mountain **ridge**.

綱 綱 コウ つな — *Thread 糸 thick as the line of a ridge 岡* (コウ) — **hawser** 1267

単 甲 単 タン — *Insect caught in a net* / *Butterfly net* — **simple** 1268 Ⓢ

Originally 單 [吅甲], an insect (吅) caught in a butterfly net (甲). The insect can be noticed in the elements protruding from the network, the antennas (吅 → 𭕄), and the butterfly net itself is depicted by its *net* (冂 ← 冈 → 田) and its thick handle (十). The way of capturing insects or other animals through a net is understood as a **simple** form of hunting that, however, is certainly effective.

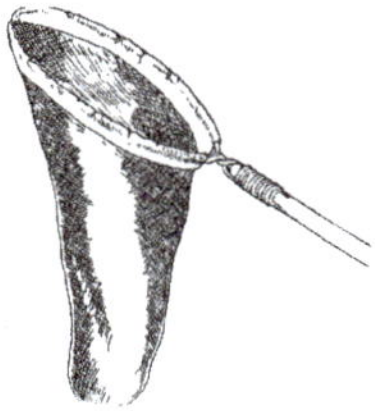

Butterfly net

 獸 獣 ジュウ けもの *Animal catching another animal* 1269

beast

Originally 獸 [嘼犬], an *animal* (犬) that catches another animal or insect with a metaphorical *butterfly net* (單 → 単), denoting the condition of bestiality—fierceness—shown in carnivorous animals. Over time the component 口 (*mouth*) was added to the character, forming the element 嘼 ((單 + 口) → 嘼 → 嘼), in order to reaffirm the notion of the alimentary function of preying and link it to fierce animals or **beasts**.

巢 巣 巣 ソウ す *Wooden network in a tree* 1270

nest

A *net* (冖 ← 网 → 田) of wooden sticks placed on top of a *tree* (木) containing several small birds (⺍) inside: a **nest**.

 卓 卓 タク *Person caught in a net* 1271 Ⓜ

impressive

table

Originally 䒞, and later 𠦝, a *person* (人 → 𠂉 → ⺊) caught with a *butterfly net* (畢 → 早), implying that such a scene is something extraordinary or **impressive**, because in the ancient world it was more precious to catch human capital—slaves—after battles than simple animals of prey. The derivation of the original glyph denoting the element for “butterfly net” (畢 ≈ 単) in the form 早 is most likely due to a graphic analogy with the component 早 (*early*) and 𠦝 (*sunrise*), even though their etymological meanings have nothing to do with each other. The meaning of **table** originates through a phonetic loan, although it is possible to associate the meaning of ‘impressive’ with something that is placed on top, and to think of a table as an object that holds objects in a high place.

悼 悼 トウ いた.む *Feelings 忄 of a person that has been caught 卓* 1272

to lament

 离 离 リ *Bird trapped in a net* 1273 Ⓢ

A butterfly net in which a bird is trapped. In this case the glyph shows a rather peculiar and complex graphic evolution. The logical form of the component after a linearization process of the original pictogram would have had to be like 罓 [㐫 罓], where it is possible to distinguish a bird with its head and wings (㐫) trying to fly away from the *butterfly net* (罓 ← 毕) in which it is trapped. This form, however, ended up being inverted, probably by analogy with other graphic compositions such as the component 禺 (*person dancing with a mask on*), and what should be the head and wings of the bird now resembles more a tail (内) coming out of the lower part of a butterfly net shown upside down (凶).

離 リ 1274
離 はな.れる

Bird 隹 escaping from the net it was trapped in 离

to leave

璃 1275
璃 リ

Jewel 王 that traps birds 离 inside

glass

1276 ㊔ 其 Ⓢ
其 キ

Winnowing basket

it

A winnowing basket, made with straw intertwined like a *net* (甘 ≈ 冈 → 冂).

In most compounds this glyph takes the form 其, which is a variant with the element for "two hands" added ((甘 + 廾) → 其 → 其). When this variant gets placed on top of the compounds it takes the flattened form 其.

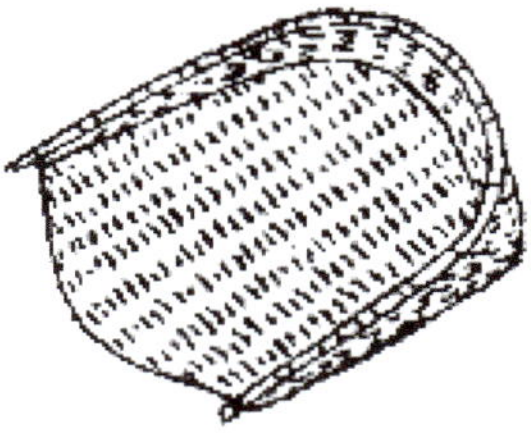

Winnowing basket

欺 ギ 1277
欺 あざむ.く

Basket 其 with lacking 欠 content

to deceive

期 期 キ ゴ — *Grain sieve made with a winnowing basket 其(キ) according to the moon cycles 月* — **period of time** 1278

基 基 キ もと もとい — *Earth-soil 土 where the content of a basket 其キ falls* — **base** 1279

碁 碁 ゴ — *Stone 石 pieces kept in a basket 其キ* — **go** (board game) 1280

NOTE ***Go*** (*'weiqi'* in Chinese) is an abstract strategy board game for two players whose aim is to surround more territory than the opponent. The pieces used in the game are shaped like small circular stones and they are kept in baskets before they are put into the board. One player plays with white stones and another with black stones.

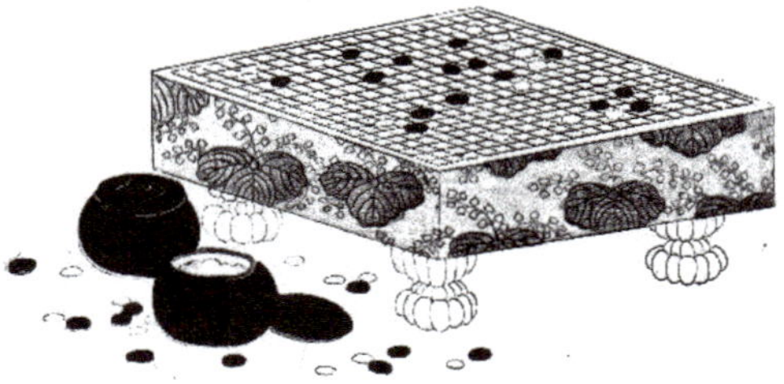

Go board and stones

棋 棋 キ — *Wood 木 piece kept in a basket 其(キ)* — **chess piece** 1281

旗 旗 キ はた — *Flaming flag 㫃 that can be kept in a basket 其(キ)* — **flag** 1282

鼻 鼻 ビ はな — *Nose smelling a basket held by two hands* — **nose** 1283

Two hands (廾) grasping a *basket* (甶 → 田) and taking it to the *nose* (自) to smell its contents, scene that was taken later to more concretely represent the **nose** rather than the act of smelling.

1284

棄

棄 キ

Newborn baby deposited in a wooden basket

abandonment

A *newborn child* (𠫓) placed inside a *basket* (𠀠 → 丗) made of *wood* (木).

1285 Ⓢ

敢

敢 カン

Hand shoving a furry animal into a basket

bravery

A hand *hitting* (攵) a *furry beast* (求 → 丁) in order to shove it into a *basket* (𠀠 → 甘 → 耳), an action showing **bravery**.

1286 Ⓢ

害

害 ガイ

Basket dropping the old

harm

Originally 周 [冃古], a *basket* turned upside down (𠀠 → 甘 → 耳 → 冃) dropping the *old* (古), a symbolic representation of the neglect of the old things, implying that forgetting ancestors and ancient traditions is **harm**ful. The shape 周 would eventually evolve in the composition 害, in which the traces depicting the basket facing down have been flattened (冃 → 宔).

1287

轄

轄 カツ

Chariot 車 *being dropped* 害

jurisdiction

NOTE Implying a controlled place where there is no need to use a chariot to move around, a territory upon which control can be made and hence the law is respected: a **jurisdiction**.

1288

憲

憲 ケン

Basket dropping an eye into the heart-mind

constitution

A *basket* turned upside down (𠀠 → 甘 → 耳 → 冃 → 宔) dropping a figurative *eye* (罒) into the *heart-mind* (心) of people in order to control them, writings inside a basket that legislatively controls the lives of people, a figurative image describing legal **constitutions** of states or kingdoms.

 良 良 良 リョウ よ.い *Sieve filtering grain* 1289 Ⓢ

good

A *person* (人 → 丶) sieving grain in a *winnowing basket* (𠀠 → 甘 → 日) to filter it from dust and dirt, which falls down (𡿨): A filter that expels the bad and keeps the **good**.

When this component is placed to the left of the compounds it is simplified into the following narrowed form: 良.

Woman filtering grain with a sieve

娘 娘 むすめ *Good 良 woman 女* 1290

daughter

朗 朗 ロウ ほが.らか *Good 良リョウ moon 月* 1291

brilliant

浪 浪 ロウ *Water 氵 that sieves 良リョウ* 1292

billow

REVIEW ON TOOLS

一百二三十千年古居支

1 仁計協汁準克故湖苦枯据裾伎肢技岐枝

貝桜貴負責貫玉玨全朋

2 資貨賛唄貪賄賢敗賀貼販賭購財潰憒噴墳
慣珍現珠球璽斑琴詮栓崩棚

工巩左尋展襄壬任巨丁丙更両満車
井丼录

3 項攻功巧江虹差紅貢恐築佐惰孃讓壊妊淫
賃拒距頂訂打灯柄病便硬梗軟較軸撃軌軽
陣範輩輪耕緑

冂罔単獣巣卓离凶鼻棄敢害憲良

4 署罪罵罷網羅買綱悼離璃欺期基碁棋旗轄
娘朗浪

VESSELS

1. FOOD AND DRINKING VESSELS

As we have already stated on several occasions, bronze made objects and, specifically, bronze vessels, were of utmost importance in the religious life of the China in which sinograms were invented. That is why a great variety of vessels make a presence in the repertoire of Chinese characters. Among all these vessels, the most basic are the bowls for food 皿. Although their original function is to house food as 'dishes', they were also frequently used for ritual ceremonies, in which they were used even to store 'blood' 血. But if the vessels are too full, then even in ritual ceremonies their contents can 'easily' spill 易. In order to prevent this form happening, it is possible to put a curved lid on them and thus create 'bean-shaped' bowls 豆. Another type of food vessels are the 'mortar' 臼, the simple 'cauldron' 鼎 or the 'three-legged cauldron' 鬲.

Vessels designed to store alcoholic beverages were also an indispensable complement in both facets of social life, culinary and religious, since 'wine jars' 酉 were used both to store alcohol for consumption and as containers used in religious libations. Such important objects were these types of vessels that they were even made in a larger size, as 'big alcohol vessels' 畐 that could store more quantity of wine.

皿

さら

Bowl with two handles

Food vessel

dish

1293 Ⓡ Ⓜ

Originally 皿, a vessel with a bowl (皿), two handles (ハ) and a foot (一). Over time, the inclined strokes representing the handles became vertical and were joined with the upper and lower horizontal lines, forming the current composition 皿. The original meaning of 'bowl', due to its frequent use as a food vessel, ultimately came to mean **dish**.

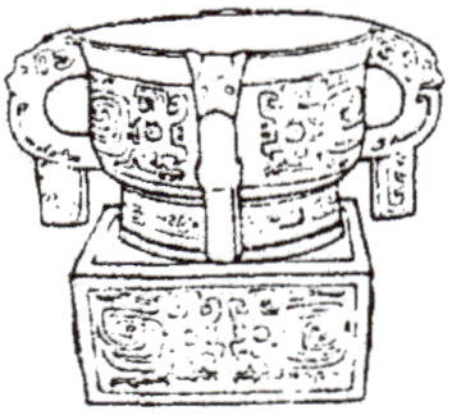

Ritual bronze vessel with handles, called 'gui' (簋)

盗 盗 トウ ぬす.む 1294

Person accumulating subsequent 次 → 次 food vessels 皿

to steal

盟 盟 メイ 1295

Bright 明 (メイ) food vessel 皿

alliance

NOTE A shining, good quality ritual vessel bestowed as a present in the enactment of an **alliance**.

温 温 オン あたた.かい 1296

Water 氵 in a food vessel 皿 heated by the sun 日

warm (thing)

塩 塩 エン しお 1297

Mineral from the earth-soil 土 eaten by a person's 人 → 𠂉 mouth 口 from a food vessel 皿

salt

猛 猛 モウ 1298

Animal 犭 putting a child 子 on a figurative food vessel 皿 in order to eat him

ferociousness

 益 益 エキ ヤク 1299

Water overflowing from a vessel

benefit

A stream of *water* placed horizontally (水 → 氺 → 䒑) contained in a *food vessel* (皿), a bowl full of water that is about to overflow, symbol of abundance and **benefit**.

 血 血 ケツ ち 1300 Ⓜ

Blood on a vessel

blood

A ritual *food vessel* (皿) with a drop of **blood** (丿) inside, most probably alluding to some kind of sacrificial ceremony.

衆 衆 シュウ シュ 1301

Several people sharing the same blood

populace

Originally 眾 [血㐺], several *people* (人×3 → 从 → 㐺 → 乑) united under the same *blood* (血): the **populace** of a nation.

監 監 カン ラン *Person looking at a vessel with blood on it* 1302 Ⓢ

to oversee

Originally 監 [臥血] , a *person looking down* (臥 → 臣𠂉) on a ritual vessel with *blood* inside (血 → (皿 + 一)), **overseeing** that the ritual ceremony is being performed correctly.

覧 覧 ラン *Overseeing* 監 (ラン) → 臣𠂉 *and looking* 見 1303

perusal

濫 濫 ラン *Water* 氵 *overseen by a person* 監 (ラン) 1304

overflow

藍 藍 ラン あい *Plant's* 艹 *dyeing process overseen by a person* 監 (ラン) 1305

indigo (color and plant)

易 易 イ エキ やさ.しい *Water spilling from a bowl* 1306 Ⓜ

easy

A bowl full of water, turned upside down and <u>spilling</u> that water. The element 日 represents the foot of the bowl and part of the water. The element 勹 represents the edges of the bowl, and the strokes ノノ represent the water spilling. This graph refers to the **ease** with which water can spill out of a bowl or glass that is full.

賜 賜 シ たまわ.る *Money* 貝 *that comes easily* 易 1307

to be granted

豆 豆 ズ トウ まめ *Bean-shaped bowl with a lid* 1308 Ⓢ

beans

Round vessel shaped like a **bean**, with a <u>lid</u> (一), a wide bowl (口) and a foot (䒑).

Ritual bronze vessel with a rounded shape and a lid, called 'duo' (豆)

頭 頭 ズ トウ ト あたま かしら 1309

Bean-shaped 豆(トウ) head 頁

head

痘 痘 トウ 1310

Illness 疒 that produces bean-shaped 豆(トウ) pimples

pox

 登 登 ト トウ のぼ.る 1311 Ⓢ

Ritual lidded bowl going up to an altar

to ascend

A ritual *lidded bowl* (豆(トウ)) that is *going upwards* (癶) towards an altar. This ideogram is a figurative resource suggesting that something spiritual **ascends**.

澄 澄 チョウ す.む 1312

Water 氵 inside a ritual bowl that is on top of an altar 登(トウ)

to become clear

 壴 壴 1313 Ⓜ

Bowl from which sound comes out

Percussion instrument

A *bowl* or pot (豆 ≈ 皿 ≈ 豆) from whose interior sound *comes out and moves forward* (㞢 → 士), a percussion instrument.

喜 喜 キ よろこ.ぶ 1314

Words 口 pronounced to the rhythm of a percussion instrument 壴

to rejoice

鼓 鼓 コ つづみ 1315

Percussion instrument 壴 hit by a thick rod held by a hand 支

drum

膨 (膨) ボウ ふくら.む 1316

Body part 月 *with hair* 彡 *pumping like a percussion instrument* 壴

to become inflated

樹 (樹) ジュ 1317

Tree-wood 木 *coming out of a bowl* 壴 *and being worked on* 寸

trees

NOTE Originally this character had the meaning of 'cultivating' or 'planting'—presumably in pots—but then the cultivated element, the plant and, later, the concept of **trees** in general, began to supplant the original meaning.

豊 (豐) ホウ ゆた.か 1318 Ⓡ Ⓜ

Pot from which several lush plants come out

bountiful

Originally 豐 [曲豆], several *lush plants* (丰×2 → 丰丰) *coming out from a pot* (豈 ≈ 壴)), a symbol of **bountiful**ness. Through a simplification process, the upper strokes of the element (曲) got reduced, forming the current composition: 曲.

艶 (艷) エン つや 1319

Bountiful 豊 *color* 色

luster

艮 1320 Ⓡ Ⓜ

Bowl full of food

Originally 皀, a *bowl* (豆 ≈ 皿 → 厶) with *white rice* (白) inside, a <u>bowl full of food</u>. The original glyph 皀 later simplified into the form 艮, where the left and lower strokes became united and the upper stroke disappeared.

爵 (爵) シャク 1321

Hand grabbing 爫 *a net* 罒 *that catches bowls full of food* 艮 *and the work* 寸 *of others*

peerage

即 (卽) ソク 1322 Ⓜ

Kneeling person in front of a bowl full of food

immediate

A *person kneeling* (卩) in front of a *bowl full of food* (艮), in the instant **immediately** before starting to eat.

節 節 セツ セチ ふし 1323

Part of a bamboo ⺮ that is immediate 即 to one another

node

既 既 キ すで.に 1324 Ⓢ

Person in front of a bowl who turns his head back

already

A person next to a *bowl full of food* (艮) who turns his head away and opens his mouth to exhale air (旡)—to burp—because he has eaten the food that **already** was inside. The element 旡 is the mirror version of the component 欠 (*person with an open mouth*), and consists of two legs (儿) and a head with an open mouth turned to the right (匚).

慨 慨 ガイ 1325

Heart-mind 忄 already 既(キ) set

repentance

概 概 ガイ 1326

Tree-wood 木 structure already 既(キ) erected

outline

食 食 飠 ショク ジキ く.う た.べる 1327 Ⓡ Ⓜ

Mouth over a bowl full of food

Food

to eat

Originally 㑒 [亼皀], a *mouth over* (亼 → 亽) a *bowl full of food* (皀 → 良 → 艮), a mouth **eat**ing the food inside.

When this component is placed to the left of the compounds it takes the simplified graph 飠.

飲 飲 イン の.む 1328

Eating 飠 with an open mouth 欠

to drink

餅 餅 ヘイ もち 1329

Food 飠 eaten by a row of people 并(ヘイ)

rice cake

1330

餌 ジ
餌 え
えさ

Food 飠 *that appeals to the ears* 耳 (ジ)

bait

1331

飼 シ
飼 か.う

Food 飠 *being deposited* 司 (シ)

to feed

1332

飽 ホウ
飽 あ.きる

Food 飠 *wrapping process* 包 (ホウ)

to get tired of

1333

飯 ハン
飯 めし

Food 飠 *upon which a hand arches* 反 (ハン)

meal

1334

養
養 ヨウ
やしな.う

Auspicious 羊 (ヨウ) *food* 食

to rear

1335

飾 ショク
飾 かざ.る

Bowl full of food 飠 *whereon a person* 人 → 𠂉 *puts a cloth* 巾

to decorate

1336

飢 キ
飢 う.える

Bowl full of uneaten food 飠 *on top of a stool* 几 (キ)

to starve

1337 Ⓜ

臼
臼 旧

キュウ
うす

Hollow vessel

mortar

A vessel or container that is kept empty inside, a <u>hollow vessel</u> that can refer more specifically to a **mortar**. The glyph 臼 is a modification of the element 日—graphically identical to the glyph for "sun" (日)—which can be ideographically related to the glyph 艮 (*bowl full of food*). Said element gets an opening in the middle (臼) to enhance the void in it, showing a hollow vessel that can be used as a 'mortar'.

In some compounds this component can take the form 旧, which is a phonetic association to the character 旧 (キュウ) (*old times*), which has a similar graphical structure.

児 児 ジ ニ 1338

Hollow 旧 person 儿

infant

毀 毀 キ 1339

Hollow cavity 臼 in the earth-soil 土 made with a mace 殳

destruction

陥 陥 ① カン ① おちい.る ② おとしい.れる 1340

Mountains 阝 making a leaning person 勹 → ⺈ fall into a hollow cavity 旧

① to collapse

② to make collapse

稲 稲 トウ いな- いね 1341

Plant producing "fruits" 禾 that can be grabbed ⺤ and put into a mortar 旧

rice plant

潟 潟 かた 1342

Water filling a hollow cavity from which birds drink

lagoon

Originally 舄 [臼㠯] and then 舄 [臼㒺], a *bird* (鳥 → 㠯 → 㒺) drinking *water* (水 → 氵) that fills a cavity (臼), a **lagoon** from which birds can drink water.

鼎 鼎 貝 テイ 1343 ㊔ 鼎 Ⓜ

cauldron

A <u>cauldron</u> with several sustaining legs. The central upper part 目 represents the container proper with some ornaments and the lower strokes 爿 represent the two handles on top and an indefinite number of legs below.

As a component this character adopts the simplified form 貝, which graphically matches the character 貝 (*seashell*) but has no etymological relation to it.

Legged ritual cauldron, called 'ding' (鼎)

貞
貞 テイ

Cauldron used in divination rituals

integrity

1344 Ⓢ

Originally 鼑 [⺊鼎], a ritual *cauldron* (鼎(テイ) → 貝) used in *divination* (卜 → ⺊ → ⺊), a cauldron of exclusively ritual use that, therefore, is not used in the kitchen, a cauldron that remains **integral** and pristine.

偵
偵 テイ

Person 亻 *of integrity* 貞(テイ)

investigator

1345

具
具 グ

Cauldron held by two hands

tool

1346 Ⓢ

Two hands (廾 → ハ) holding a *cauldron* (鼎 → 貝 → 目), in reference to the utility of said vessel as a **tool** for heating water.

惧
惧 グ

Heart-mind's 忄 *tool* 具(グ)

dread

1347

真
真 シン
ま

Person using a ritual cauldron as a tool

true

1348 Ⓢ

SPECIAL READING 真似 [まね]: *mimic*

Originally 眞 [匕具], a *person seen from the back* (匕 → 十) that is *holding a ritual cauldron with his two hands* in order to <u>use it as a *tool*</u> (具), a reference to the spiritual **truth** achieved through the use of different tools such as ritual cauldrons.

慎
慎 シン
つつし.む

Heart-mind 忄 *of a person using a ritual cauldron as a tool* 真(シン)

to be prudent

1349

填
填 テン

Earth 土 *used as a tool* 真(シン)

filling

1350

鬲 鬲

Three-legged cauldron 1351 Ⓜ

A <u>big cauldron</u> with a bowl (口) in the upper part and three bulky legs (冂) in the lower part.

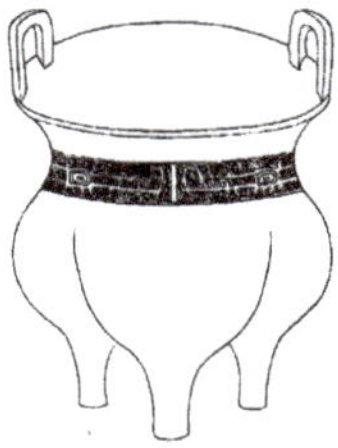

Three-legged ritual cauldron, called 'li' (鬲)

隔 隔 カク へだ.てる

Mountains 阝 hiding big cauldrons 鬲 1352

to isolate

融 融 ユウ

Big cauldron 鬲 containing burning insects 虫 1353

fusion

酉 酉 ユウ

Wine jar 1354 Ⓡ

Alcohol ㊔

rooster sign (Chinese zodiac) Ⓜ

A jar designed to store fermented alcoholic beverages for a long time. The strokes 兀 represent the mouth and neck of the jar, the lower strokes 囗 represent the outline of the body and the inner line 一 represents a decorative motive. The meaning of <u>wine jar</u> can be expanded into that of <u>alcohol</u> in some compounds.

Bronze ritual wine jar, called 'lei' (罍)

酵 1355
酵 コウ
Alcohol 酉 making process passed from parents to children 孝（コウ）
fermentation

酎 1356
酎 チュウ
Alcohol 酉 upon which work 寸 is done
rice wine

酸 1357
酸 サン
す.い
Alcohol 酉 that distributes energy to the feet 夋
acid

醜 1358
醜 シュウ
みにく.い
Alcohol 酉 that makes ghosts 鬼 appear
ugly

配 1359
配 ハイ
くば.る
Alcohol 酉 that is circulated 己（キ）
to distribute

酒 1360
酒 シュ
さけ
さか-
Fluid 氵 coming out of a wine jar 酉
sake (Japanese rice wine)

酬 1361
酬 シュウ
Alcohol 酉 and pieces of land 州（シュウ）
repay

酷 1362
酷 コク
Alcohol 酉 making words come out 告（コク）
cruel

醒 1363
醒 セイ
Alcohol intake 酉 and stargazing 星（セイ）
awake

酌 1364
酌 シャク
く.む
Alcohol 酉 poured with a ladle 勺（シャク）
to serve alcohol

醸 1365
醸 ジョウ
かも.す
Alcohol 酉 made thanks to work in the field 襄（ジョウ）
to brew

酔 醉 スイ よ.う 1366

Alcohol intake 酉 being finished 卆

to get drunk

酢 酢 サク す 1367

Alcohol 酉 covered with folded clothes 乍 during a fermentation process

vinegar

 酋 酋 1368 Ⓜ

Distributed alcohol

Libation

Wine jars' (酉) content being *distributed* (八 → ハ → ソ) as a libation—pouring alcohol for the gods—in religious rituals.

猶 猶 ユウ 1369

Libation 酋 made along an animal 犭 sacrifice

furthermore

 尊 尊 ソン たっと.い とうと.い 1370 Ⓢ

Hand working on a libation

precious

A *working hand* (寸) actively pouring alcohol in a *libation* (酋), an action that is considered as **precious**.

 畐 畐 ヒョク フク 1371 Ⓢ

Big wine vessel

A big wine vessel with a longer than normal neck, presumably with a capacity for a great alcohol content. The upper strokes 戸 represent the mouth and neck of the jar, whereas the lower strokes 田 represent the decorated body.

Bronze ritual wine jar with a long neck, called 'gu' (觚)

幅 幅 フク はば — *Cloth* 巾 *covering a big wine vessel* 畐 (フク) — **breadth** 1372

2. BAGS AND BOXES

A more modest type of container, or vessel, are those made of cloth or small filaments of wood or bamboo, such as 'bags' 西 that are closed at the top and good for storing and transporting objects, a function so convenient and necessary without which the small-scale serial 'production' and trade of commodities would not be possible, because serially produced goods have to be easily packed in 'several bags' 品.

Another type of basic container used to store other objects is the 'box' 匚 which, if it is made of bamboo and is flexible enough, can be 'bent' at will, reflecting in the box the folds of the material 曲.

西 西 襾 サイ セイ にし — *Bag* — **west** 1373 Ⓡ Ⓜ

Originally 卤, a bag (口)—decorated with some embroidery (メ)—that is closed on its upper part with a knot (⺊). The glyph suffered a gradual simplification in which the original form 卤 ended up becoming the current glyph 西 as the upper strokes ⺊ merged with the inner strokes メ. The meaning of **west** was probably taken through a phonetic loan, analogue to that of the character 東 (*backpack → east*), since it metaphorically evokes the image of a small bag hanging from a tree, a nest, awaiting for birds to come when the sun sets in the west.

When acting as a component the graph even takes a further simplification into the form 覀.

Small embroidered bag from Meiji period Japan

価 価 カ あたい *Person 亻 examining a bag's 覀 content* **price** 1374

煙 煙 エン けむ.る *Fire 火 burning a bag 覀 on top of earth-soil 土* **to smoke** 1375

覇 覇 ハ *Bag 覀 of leather 革 with meat 月 inside* **supremacy** 1376

要 要 ヨウ かなめ い.る *Bag of a woman* **to need** 1377 Ⓢ

Originally 𦥯 [臼囟女], *two hands* (臼) holding the figurative *bag* (囱 → 囟 ≈ 西) of a *woman* (女 ジョ), symbolizing the scene of a birth that indirectly refers to the female uterus and the primordial **need** of its existence and well-being for the survival and perpetuation of a certain social group. Over time the upper part of the character, 𦥑, ended up being simplified into 覀, erasing the element that represented two hands (臼).

腰 腰 ヨウ こし *Body part 月 where the women's uterine bag 要 ヨウ is placed* **hips** 1378

栗 栗 リ *Tree with bag-shaped fruits* chestnut (tree) 1379 ㊔ Ⓢ

A *tree* (木) that produces fruits with a spiked shell whose appearance resembles a *bag* (西 → 覀).

Chestnut fruit with its spiked shell

慄 1380

慄 リツ

Feeling 忄 *provoked by the sight of a spiky chestnut* 栗 (リ)

shudder

卑 1381 Ⓢ

卑 ヒ いや.しい

Hand holding a bag upside down

lowly

An *outstretched hand* (又 → ナ → 十) holding a *bag* upside down ((西 ← 卤) → 甶), signifying that the bag is empty and nothing comes out of it. An empty basket that, as such, figuratively represents scarcity and **low** social status.

碑 1382

碑 ヒ

Stone 石 *put in a low place* 卑 (ヒ)

tombstone

品 1383 Ⓡ Ⓢ

品 ヒン しな

Several small bags

product

Several small *bags* (西 ← 卤 → 囟 → 田 → 口×3), symbolizing a specific object or material that is constantly produced: a small-scale serial **product**ion.

臨 1384

臨 リン のぞ.む

Person looking down 𠂉 *into several products* 品 (ヒン)

to overlook

喿 1385 Ⓢ

喿 ソウ

Products of a tree

The *products* (品) that come from a *tree* (木), that is, fruits.

操 1386

操 ① ソウ ① あやつ.る ② みさお

Hand 扌 *taking the products of a tree* 喿 (ソウ)

① **to manipulate**

② fidelity

燥 1387

燥 ソウ

Fire 火 *burning the products of a tree* 喿 (ソウ)

dryness

藻 藻 ソウ も 1388

Plants 艹 *that are the product of trees* 喿(ソウ) *living under the water* 氵

seaweed

繰 繰 く.る 1389

Thread 糸 *that turns around an object shaped like the products of trees* 喿

to reel

 器 器 ① ② キ ② うつわ 1390

Several products acting as one

① **instrument**

② **vessel** (container)

Several small *products* (口×4 ≈ 品) interconnected, forming a *bigger* (大) product: A complex mechanism consisting of several parts, an **instrument.** The meaning of **vessel** is a semantic derivation resulting from the relationship between the general concept of 'instrument' with the particular concept of 'vessel shape' that characterized many of the ancient day-to-day instruments.

 匚 匚 乚 1391 Ⓡ Ⓜ

Open box

A box open at its top, presumably made of bamboo, turned vertically.

In some compounds this component gets simplified into 乚.

匿 匿 トク 1392

Hand hiding inside a box 匚 *the food to be eaten* 若(ジャク)

concealment

 匹 匹 ヒツ ひき 1393 Ⓜ

Energy inside a box

unit (of)

Energy *distributed* (八 → 儿) inside a *box* (匚), an ideographic representation of a box containing something inside: A packaged item, a **unit** of some object or article.

 甚 甚 ジン カン はなは.だ 1394 Ⓢ

Basket winnowing something into a box

exceedingly

A *basket winnowing* (𠀠 → 甘) by-products into a *box with content inside* (匹), **exceed**ing its capacity.

勘 1395
勘 カン
Exceedingly full box 甚 (カン) *touched by an outstretched arm* 力
perception

堪 1396
堪 カン
た.える
Earth 土 *filling an exceedingly full box* 甚 (カン)
to bear

区 1397 Ⓢ
区 ク
オウ
Box full of products
area

Originally 區 [匸品], several *products* (品 → メ) stored inside a *box* (匸), products delimited by the container's **area**.

欧 1398
欧 オウ
Area 区 (オウ) *where people exhale air* 欠
Europe

殴 1399
殴 オウ
なぐ.る
Area 区 (オウ) *that gets struck* 殳
to assault

枢 1400
枢 スウ
Tree-wood 木 *piece within a delimited area* 区 (オウ)
pivot

駆 1401
駆 ク
か.る
Horse 馬 *running into a delimited area* 区 (ク)
to spur

直 1402 Ⓢ
直
① ジキ
① チョク
①
ただち.に
② なお.す
Eye pointing straight ahead
① **straight**
② **to put straight**

The gaze of an *eye* (目) pointing **straight** towards a specific *thick rod* (十) kept inside a *box* (匸 → ㇗).

値 チ ね あたい 1403

値 *Person 亻 being straight 直（チョク）*

value

殖 ショク ふ.える 1404

殖 *Bone remains 歹 put straight 直（チョク） again*

to reproduce

植 ショク う.える 1405

植 *Tree 木 put straight 直（チョク）*

to plant

置 チ お.く 1406

置 *Net 罒 set straight 直（チョク）*

to put

悳 惪 1407 Ⓜ

Straight feeling

Originally 悳 [直心], a feeling that goes *straight* (直 → 𥄉 → 𠁥) to the *heart* (心).

聴 チョウ き.く 1408

聴 *Ear's 耳 straight feeling 惪*

to hear

𠃊米 1409 Ⓜ

Stored rice grains

Several grains of *rice* (米) stored in a *box* (匚 → 𠃊).

継 ケイ つ.ぐ 1410

継 *Thread 糸 tying together stored rice grains 𠃊米*

to take over

NOTE The meaning of this character is mainly related to the reception of inheritance, hence the representation of material provisions safely tied and stored.

曲 キョク ま.がる 1411

曲 *Bent bamboo box*

to bend

A box made of folded bamboo strips, which each fold visibly marked, a box that can be easily **bent**.

3. PLATES AND TRAYS

Complementing the vessels we have seen so far, there is a kind of food and drink container of more mundane appearance and greater availability, which makes it 'commonplace', but which is also suitable for use in religious rituals. That is the flat plate or tray 凡, which in turn can be used to contain minerals, such as cinnabar 丹, capable of creating a 'vermillion' pigment.

凡 凡 — ボン ハン — *Plate* **commonplace** — 1412 Ⓢ

A plate or tray with two legs and two handles and a flattened shape, a fairly **commonplace** object. The original form of the pictogram was something similar to the strokes 凡, which would later evolve into 冃 and finally, influenced by the flow of the strokes, into its current form 凡.

Bronze tray, called 'pan' (盤)

汎 汎 — ハン — *Water 氵 that is commonplace 凡 (ハン)* **all-inclusive** — 1413

帆 帆 — ハン ほ — *Cloth 巾 that is commonplace 凡 (ハン)* **sail** — 1414

同 同 — ドウ おな.じ — *Mouth eating from a plate* **same** — 1415 Ⓢ

A *mouth* (口) eating from a *plate* (凡 ← 冃), activity repeated throughout life in the **same** way by everybody.

1416

胴
胴 ドウ

Body part 月 with the same size 同 in most people

torso

1417

洞
洞 ドウ ほら

All water's 氵 same 同 container

cavity

1418

筒
筒 トウ つつ

All bamboo's 竹 same 同 form

cylinder

1419

興
興 キョウ コウ おこ.す

Two hands handing a plate to two other hands

to vitalize

Originally 舁 [臼同廾], *two hands* (廾 → 六) offering a *plate to be put in the mouth* (同) of a person who receives it with his or her *two hands* (臼 ≈ 廾): A plate of food offered to a person to give him energy and **vitalize** him.

1420 Ⓢ

斉
斉 セイ

Commonplace writings

even

Writings (文) that are *commonplace* ((冃 → 月) ≈ 凡), writings that have been regularized, matched so that it can be used **even**ly and understood by everyone.

1421

済
済 サイ す.む

Water 氵 that becomes an even 斉 course

to conclude

NOTE In reference to the end of a river at the river mouth.

1422

粛
粛 シュク

Hand stirring grain on a plate

quietly

A hand grasping the handle ((彐 + 丨) → 肀) of a *tray* ((凡 ≈ 月)→ ノ|) containing *rice grains* (米) while sieving the good grains from dust and other substances, an activity that must be done **quietly** and patiently.

風 風 フウ フ かぜ かざ-

Vessel of flying insects

wind 1423 Ⓜ

A metaphoric vessel—or *tray* (凡 → 几)—of flying insects (虫), the **wind** element that helps flying insects move.

嵐 嵐 あらし

Mountain 山 *with winds* 風

storm 1424

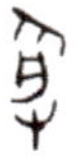

受 受 ジュ う.ける

Hand receiving a plate from another hand

to receive 1425 Ⓢ

An *outstretched hand* (又) **receiving** a *plate* (凡 → 冖) from a hand that was *grabbing* it (爪 → 爫).

授 授 ジュ さず.ける

Hand 扌 *giving something to a receiver* 受(ジュ)

to grant 1426

丹 丹 タン

Pigment on a plate

vermilion 1427

Originally 凡, a cinnabar stone (丶) deposited on a *plate* ((凡 ≈ 月) → 丹) to create a reddish pigment with it. It also alludes to the **vermilion** color of many lacquered containers—plates and trays among them—of ancient China.

青 青 セイ ショウ あお

Lush plant on a plate

blue

verdant

Clear 1428 Ⓢ

Originally 靑 [龶円], a *lush plant* (丰 → 龶) over a plate from which *pigment* (丹 → 円 → 月) is to be made. The pigment obtained from plants becomes **verdant** or **bluish**, taking into account that the Eastern notion for blue mingles with that of green. As a component, this character can also mean clear, as a reference to the bright and clean color of the pigment obtained from plants.

静 静 セイ ジョウ しず.か — *Cleared* 青 (セイ) *fight* 争 (ソウ) **calm** 1429

情 情 ジョウ セイ なさ.け — *Clear* 青 (ジョウ) *feelings* 忄 **emotion** 1430

請 請 セイ シン う.ける こ.う — *Speech* 言 *that is clear* 青 (セイ) **to request** 1431

晴 晴 セイ は.れる — *Sunlight* 日 *that is clear* 青 (セイ) **to be sunny** 1432

清 清 セイ ショウ きよ.い — *Water* 氵 *that is clear* 青 (セイ) **pure** 1433

精 精 セイ ショウ — *Rice* 米 *that is clear* 青 (セイ) **fine** 1434

 南 南 ナン ナ みなみ — *Wood generating fire* **south** 1435 Ⓜ

This is a character with a rather complex graphic evolution and semantic association. It represents, in origin, a *tree* (木) on top and a plate containing vermilion *pigment* (冃 ← 丹) at the bottom. The strokes of this sinogram, over time, got mixed and overlapped, and that is why the original compositional elements are no longer visible. The strokes of the "tree-wood" component (木) are attested in the elements 十, ヽ丿 and 丨 (木 → (十 + 个), 个 → (ヽ丿 + 丨)) of the contemporary graph. On the other hand, the strokes of the element "vermilion", are reflected in the lower element 冂 (冃 → 丹 → 冂 → 冂). The original ideographic composition of this graph refers to an association between wood and vermilion color, giving an association with fire and the red color in general, which, within the traditional East Asian conceptual framework of the five elements or five phases (*wu xing*, 五行), is directly associated with the **south** cardinal point. This conceptual framework, in turn, dictates that wood generates fire, thus reinforcing the relationship between the two compositional elements and meanings of the character.

献 献 ケン コン *Wood generating fire* 南 *used to heat or cook an animal* 犬 1436

contribution

 用 用 用 ヨウ もち.いる *Ritual plate* 1437 Ⓜ

to use

Originally 用, a vessel or *ritual plate* (凡 ← 月) **used** for *divinatory* (卜 → ト) or religious rites, the ultimate use of any vessel. Over time the upper stroke of the form 用 (一) became longer—joining the left and right ends of the character. In this way it is that the current form of the character 用 came to be.

When this character acts as a component it takes the following form: 用.

庸 庸 ヨウ *Two hands placing a lush plant* 庚 *on a ritual plate* 用 1438

ordinary

NOTE The ideographic composition of this character refers to the **ordinary** practice of using a ritual plate for mundane purposes such as the preparation of food.

 甬 甬 ヨウ *Divine message passing through a person* 1439 Ⓢ

A *mouth* (口 → マ) interpreting the messages obtained through the *ritual use of a plate* (用 → 用): the divine message that passes through a shaman.

踊 踊 ヨウ おど.る *Feet* 𧾷 *passing over* 甬(ヨウ) *a hole* 1440

to jig

NOTE Originally this character had the meaning of 'jumping'—meaning that is still maintained in Chinese. Ultimately the meaning of 'jumping' was associated with **jigging** to the rhythm of music.

痛 痛 ツウ いた.い *Illness* 疒 *going through* 甬(ヨウ) 1441

to hurt

勇 勇 ユウ いさ.む *Strength going through* 1442 Ⓢ

courage

Originally 勇 [甬力], with the variant 恿 [甬心] also attested, the [*emotional* = 心] *strength* (力)—**courage**—that a shaman goes *through* (甬 → 甬) while carrying a ritual.

湧 湧 ユウ わ.く *Water* 氵 *with courage* 勇 1443

to gush forth

甫 甫 ホ *Father handling a ritual plate* 1444 ㊔ Ⓢ

Beneficial

progenitor

A *father* (父 → 十 + 丶) handling a *ritual plate* (用 → 用), denoting the supposed <u>beneficial</u> way of conducting religious ceremonies as they are being guided by a figure with authority.

哺 哺 ホ *Mouth* 口 *performing a beneficial* 甫 *deed* 1445

suckling

捕 捕 ホ つか.まえる と.らえる *Hand* 扌 *becoming beneficial* 甫 1446

to catch

浦 浦 うら *Water* 氵 *that makes a place beneficial* 甫 1447

bay

補 補 ホ おぎな.う *Clothes* 衤 *that become beneficial* 甫 1448

to supplement

尃 尃 ハク *Beneficial work* 1449 Ⓢ

Work (寸) that is *beneficial* (甫).

縛 バク しばる 1450

Thread 糸 tying several beneficial works 尃 (ハク)

to bind

博 ハク バク 1451

Ten 十 beneficial works 尃 (ハク)

abounding

溥 ハク 1452 Ⓢ

Water's beneficial work

Water (水 → 氵) that does a beneficial work (尃 ハク).

薄 ハク うす.い 1453

Diet of plants 艹 *and water's beneficial work* 溥 (ハク)

thin

簿 ボ 1454

Bamboo book ⺮ *talking about water's beneficial work* 溥 (ハク)

bookkeeping

4. BOATS

The last kind of vessels to talk about are navigation vessels, 'boats' 舟, which are not a vessels understood as containers, but as means of transport. Although of a completely different typology to the other vessels seen so far, it is interesting to group boats within the semantic category of 'vessels' because the graphic composition of the component for "boat" (舟) is also quite similar to that of the "plate" component (凡) seen in the previous section.

舟 舟 月 シュウ ふね ふな- 1455 Ⓡ 舟 Ⓜ

boat

A small wooden **boat**, drawn vertically, with the contour and the central crossbar represented by the strokes 丹, two seats represented by the strokes 丶 and 丨, and the tip of the prow by the stroke ㇒.

In some components this graph takes the simplified form 月, which is graphically identical but etymologically unrelated to one of the simplified versions of the component for "meat" (肉 → 月).

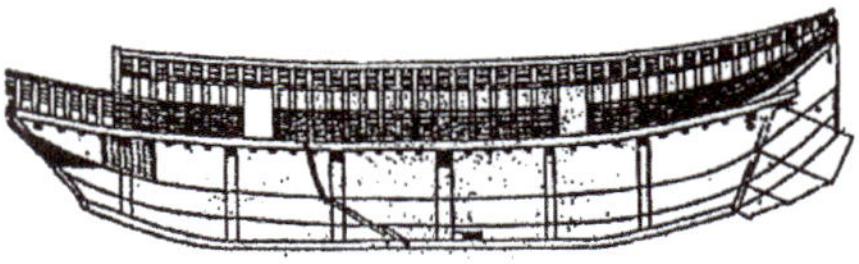

Small wooden boat from the Edo Japan

航 **航** コウ *Boat 舟 moving above and below the surface 亢 (コウ) of water* 1456
navigation

舶 **舶** ハク *Boat 舟 that is clearly 白 (ハク) seen* 1457
large ship

舷 **舷** ゲン *Boat's 舟 dim part 玄 (ゲン)* 1458
gunwale

艦 **艦** カン *Boat 舟 that is overseen 監 (カン)* 1459
warship

般 般 **般** ハン *Boat fixed with a mace* 1460 Ⓢ
generic

A *boat* (舟) being fixed or assembled by a *mace* (殳), a bad quality, **generic** boat.

搬 **搬** ハン *Hand 扌 putting goods on a generic boat 般 (ハン)* 1461
carrier

盤 **盤** バン *Generic 般 (ハン) food vessel 皿* 1462
plate

兪 兪 **兪** ユ *Mouth talking over a boat sailing in the water* 1463 Ⓢ
Accomplishment

Originally 兪 [亼⺝巛], a *mouth* metaphorically *talking* (亼) to a *boat* (舟 → ⺝) that sails on a *stream of water* (巛 → 巛 → 刂), implying the notion of the governance of a boat over the water, the <u>accomplishment</u> of being able to sail a boat.

愉 1464
愉 ユ
Feeling 忄 *of accomplishment* 俞(ユ)
pleasure

諭 1465
諭 ユ さと.す
Speech 訁 *that make accomplishments* 俞(ユ) *happen*
to admonish

喩 1466
喩 ユ
Words 口 *making understanding accomplished* 俞(ユ)
metaphor

癒 1467
癒 ユ い.える
Feeling 心 *of accomplished* 俞(ユ) *healing over an illness* 疒
to be cured

輸 1468
輸 ユ
Chariot 車 *accomplishing* 俞(ユ) *its purpose*
transport

前 1469 Ⓢ
前 ゼン まえ
Stopped boat
before
in front

Originally 歬 [止舟], and then 歬刂, a *stopped* (止 → 䒑) *boat* (舟 → 月). Later on the element 刂 (originally 巜 ← 巛: *stream of water*) was added to the composition, by analogy with the component 俞 (*mouth talking over a sailing boat*) and also to denote the idea that the boat remains stopped 'before' sailing in the water. The notion of **before** is given, therefore, by the understanding of the immobility of a ship, whose main function is to move, as an unnatural situation always prior to that movement. The meaning of **in front** is, on the other hand, a semantic association taken from the similarity between the concepts of 'before' and 'in front of', which is also given in English with expressions such as 'standing before you'.

煎 1470
煎 セン い.る
Heating done in front 前(ゼン) *of fire* 灬
to broil

 朕 朕 䑣 チン *Two hands handling the helm of a boat* **person in charge** 1471 Ⓜ

Two hands grabbing the rotating *knob* (关) of a *boat* (舟 → 月), or in other words, a person at the helm, a **person in charge**.

In the compounds this graph takes the peculiar arrangement 𦚏, which leaves space for the other components in the lower right corner.

謄 謄 トウ *People in charge* 𦚏 *repeating a speech* 言 **mimeograph** 1472

勝 勝 ①② ショウ ① まさ.る ② か.つ *Person in charge* 𦚏 *with strength* 力 ① **to surpass** ② **to win** 1473

 騰 騰 トウ *Person handling the reins of a horse* **pounce** 1474 Ⓢ

A *person in charge* (𦚏) handling the reins of a *horse* (馬) and making it gallop and **pounce**.

藤 藤 トウ ふじ *Plant* 艹 *that grows as fast as a pouncing horse* 騰(トウ) *goes* **wisteria** 1475

REVIEW ON VESSELS

皿益血衆監昜豆登壴豊皀即既食臼
鼎貞具真鬲酉酋尊畐

1 盜盟温塩猛覧濫藍賜頭痘澄喜鼓膨樹艶爵
節慨概飲餅餌飼飽飯養飾飢児毀陥稲潟偵
俱慎填隔融酵酎酸醜配酒酬醒酷酌醸酔酢
猶幅

西要票卑品栗器匚匹甚区直悳迷曲

2 価煙覇腰慓碑臨操燥藻繰匿勘堪欧殴枢駆
値殖植置聴継

凡同興斉粛風受丹青南用甬勇甫尃
溥

3

汎帆胴洞筒済嵐授静情請晴清精献庸踊痛
湧哺捕浦補縛博薄簿

舟般兪前朕騰

4

航舶舷艦搬盤愉諭喩癒輸煎謄勝藤

THE TERRITORIAL REALM

THE TERRITORIAL REALM

Territory is a broad concept that, however, takes a central stage in any settled society, since the identity of a society is almost always associated with the territory it is based on. The survival of a society is linked to the capacity of defending a territory, and for this defense it is necessary to use weapons. In ancient societies such as those of the time when Chinese characters were created, weapons were thus an essential element of communal life, and that is why they also play a major role within Chinese characters, as a symbol of the preservation of territory.

The concept of territory also gives rise to the concept of space. A territory can be interpreted in terms of several kinds of space: vertical space—which has to do with the relationship between heaven and earth—; horizontal space—which has to do with distances—; and circular space—which has to do with inhabited and controlled telluric territories. Within these spaces or territories, societies also build buildings that become part of the landscape, from four walls that form a hut, to palaces and watchtowers that end up conforming villages and cities interconnected by roads.

The different aspects of the territorial realm can be sorted out, then, through the following three groups: Characters used to represent *weapons*, characters used to represent *spaces*, and lastly, characters used to represent man-made *constructions*.

WEAPONS	SPACES	CONSTRUCTIONS
1. Daggers	1. The Vertical Plane	1. Walls and Roofs
2. Pole Weapons	2. The Horizontal Plane	2. Doors
3. Axes	3. The Circular Plane	3. Tall Buildings
4. Defensive Weapons		4. Roads
5. Bows and Arrows		

THE TERRITORIAL REALM AT A GLANCE

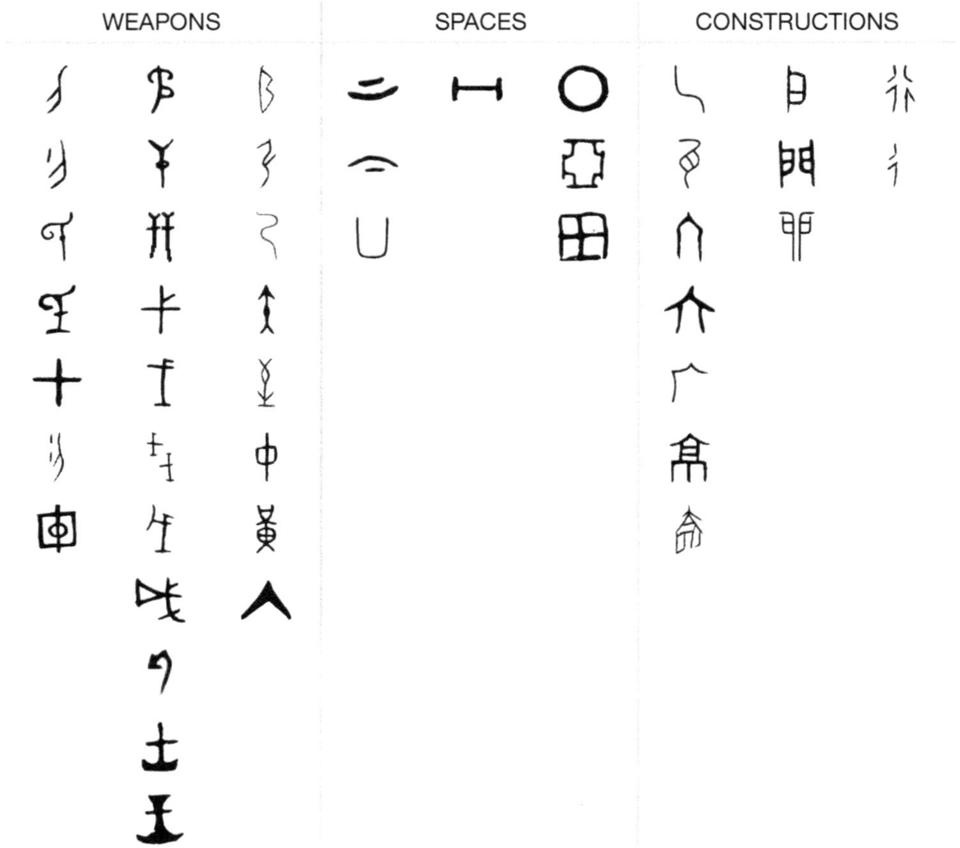

WEAPONS

1. DAGGERS

One of the most basic weapons is the knife or 'dagger' 刀, which is characterized by a sharp, cutting 'blade' 刃. To start with, daggers can be useful for cutting meat, plants or ropes, but also for killing prey. This function would soon also adopt a ritual aspect in religious sacrifices. In such sacrifices the weapon used would be a dagger with a thicker blade 氏, a ritual dagger that would ultimately also serve to denote clerical family clans and their 'surnames'.

刀 刀 刂 トウ かたな *Dagger* **saber** 1476 Ⓡ Ⓜ

A dagger with its blade slightly curved. The current glyph is visibly schematized, with a curved line ノ and another bent line 𠃌, representing the blade of a dagger or knife pointing downwards. Some graph examples of the bronze script like or more clearly show the pictographic origin of the character. The original meaning of 'dagger' gets expanded when the character acts as a standalone to that of **saber**.

In many compounds this sinogram adopts a simplified version: 刂, which is placed on the right side of the compounds.

Bronze dagger of the Shang dynasty

別 別 ベツ わか.れる *Pile of bones 另 cut with a dagger 刂* **to separate** 1477

剣 剣	ケン つるぎ	*Authority* 㑒(ケン) *shown in a dagger* 刂 **sword**	1478
帰 帰	キ かえ.る	*Leaving the dagger* 刂 → リ *and taking the broom* 帚 **to come home**	1479
削 削	サク けず.る	*Cereals and meat* 肖(ショウ) *cut with a dagger* 刂 **to pare**	1480
剰 剰	ジョウ	*Tops of trees* 乗(ジョウ) *cut with a dagger* 刂 **surplus**	1481
券 券	ケン	*Paper rolled up* 龹(カン) *and cut with a dagger* 刀 **ticket**	1482
刻 刻	コク きざ.む	*Framework* 亥(ガイ) *drawn with a dagger* 刂 **to carve**	1483
劇 劇	ゲキ	*Tiger* 虍 *and hog* 豕 *attacked by a dagger* 刂 **drama**	1484
解 解	カイ ゲ と.く	*Horns* 角 *of an ox* 牛 *cut with a dagger* 刀 **to loosen**	1485
判 判	ハン バン	*Something cut in half* 半(ハン) *with a dagger* 刂 **judgement**	1486
刷 刷	サツ す.る	*A mold sitting* 尸 *on a cloth* 巾 *cut with a dagger* 刂 **to print**	1487

初 初 シヨ はじ.め はつ そ.める うい- *Cloths* 衤 *cut with a dagger* 刀 *in order to make clothes* 1488

beginning

剥 剥 ハク は.ぐ *Rope of a pulley* 录（ロク） *cut off with a dagger* 刂 1489

to tear off

班 班 ハン *Several jewels* 玨（ハン） *cut by a dagger* 刂 → リ 1490

party (group)

罰 罰 バチ バツ *Net* 罒 *capturing a criminal that makes a confessional speech* 言 *whereupon a punishment through a dagger* 刂 *is made* 1491

punishment

剛 剛 ゴウ *Ridge* 岡（コウ） *of daggers* 刂 1492

sturdy

割 割 カツ わ.る さ.く *Harm* 害（ガイ） *caused with dagger* 刂 1493

to slash

副 副 フク *Big wine vessel* 畐（フク） *cut with a dagger* 刂 1494

supplemental

剤 剤 ザイ *Even* 斉（セイ） *cut made with a dagger* 刂 1495

dose

列 列 レツ *Cut bone remains* 1496 Ⓢ

array

Bone remains (歹) that are cut with a *dagger* (刀 → 刂) and orderly placed, **array**ed, for burials or sacrifices.

例
例 レイ たと.える
Person 亻 next to cut bone remains 列(レツ) 1497
to liken

烈
烈 レツ
Cut bone remains 列(レツ) *on fire 灬* 1498
ardent

裂
裂 レツ さ.く
Bone remains cut 列(レツ) *like clothes 衣* 1499
to tear apart

召
召 ショウ め.す
Words and a dagger 1500 Ⓢ
to summon

Words (口) pronounced while making a sacrifice with a *dagger* (刀) in order **summon** some deity or ancestor.

詔
詔 ショウ みことのり
Speech 訁 that summons 召(ショウ) 1501
imperial edict

招
招 ショウ まね.く
Hand 扌 holding a dagger while summoning words 召(ショウ) *are pronounced* 1502
to beckon

超
超 チョウ こ.える
Running 走 summoning 召(ショウ) 1503
to transcend

沼
沼 ショウ ぬま
Water 氵 that seems to summon 召(ショウ) *people or deities* 1504
marsh

紹
紹 ショウ
Thread 糸 linking the summoner 召(ショウ) *and the summoned* 1505
introduction

昭
昭 ショウ
Summoned sun 1506 Ⓢ
glittering

Sunlight (日) responding with its **glittering** to its allegorical *summoning* (召(ショウ)).

照 照 ショウ て.らす — *Glittering* 昭 (ショウ) *fire* 灬 — **to shine** 1507

分 分 ① ブ ① ブン ② フン ① わ.ける ③ わ.かる — *Dagger cutting and distributing* — ① **to divide** ② minute ③ **to understand** 1508 Ⓢ

A metaphorical *dagger* (刀) cutting and *distributing* (八 → ハ) something, a representation of the **division** of parts. The meaning of **understanding** derives from the notion of having to divide something into parts in order to analyze it in detail and thus comprehend the whole.

頒 頒 ハン — *Divided* 分 (フン) *heads* 頁 — **dissemination** 1509

NOTE 'Heads' understood here as 'people'.

雰 雰 フン — *Rain* 雨 *that gets divided* 分 (フン) — **atmosphere** 1510

NOTE Originally this character referred to 'mist'. Over time the sense of 'mist' got expanded into that of air or **atmosphere**.

粉 粉 フン こ こな — *Grains* 米 *that got divided* 分 (フン) — **powder** 1511

紛 紛 フン まぎ.れる — *Threads* 糸 *that get divided* 分 (フン) — **to be diverted** 1512

貧 貧 ビン ヒン まず.しい — *Division* 分 (フン) *of money* 貝 — **poor** 1513

盆 ボン *Divided 分(フン) food vessel 皿* 1514

tray

NOTE In the sense that a **tray** is a vessel without a lid: a divided vessel.

丯 *Lush plant cut by a dagger* 1515 Ⓜ

A *lush plant* (丰 → 丯) cut by a *dagger* (刀).

潔 ゲツ いさぎよ.い *Water 氵 and cut lush plants 丯 tied together with a thread 糸* 1516

unsullied

NOTE In reference to a sort of rudimentary broom made with a bunch of plants that cleans and purifies things or people with the help of water.

契 ケイ ちぎ.る *Person cutting a lush plant* 1517 Ⓢ

to pledge

A *person seen from the front* (大) *cutting some lush plants* (丯) that he will give as an offering when making an oath or **pledge**.

喫 キツ *Mouth 口 eating lush plants that have been cut by a person 契(ケイ)* 1518

consumption

制 セイ *Dagger cutting tree branches* 1519 Ⓢ

system

A *dagger* (刀 → 刂) *cutting tree branches* (朱 → 未), indicating the collection of materials used for building, which implies a sequential process based on an organized **system**.

製 セイ *System 制(セイ) of clothes 衣 production* 1520

manufacture

利 利 リ き.く

Fruits cut with a dagger 1521 Ⓢ

profit

Fruits (禾) of a fruit tree cut with a *dagger* (刀 → 刂), giving rise to a possible **profit**.

梨 梨 なし

Profitable 利 *tree* 木 1522

pear tree

痢 痢 リ

Illness 疒 *that becomes profitable* 利 (リ) 1523

diarrhea

NOTE It may refer to the fact that it is beneficial to be cured of a disease by expelling the bad things through **diarrhea.**

則 則 ソク

Money and daggers 1524 Ⓢ

rule

The implicit power derived from economy, *money* (貝), and the military, *daggers* (刀 → 刂). The legitimate and instigating power that establishes the **rules** and practices of a given society.

側 側 ソク がわ

Person 亻 *on the side of the rules* 則 (ソク) 1525

side

測 測 ソク はか.る

Water's 氵 *rules* 則 (ソク) 1526

to measure

刃 刃 ジン は

Edge of a dagger 1527 Ⓢ

blade

The edge of a *dagger* (刀), the **blade**, deliberately marked by an extra stroke (丶) that highlights it.

忍 忍 ニン しの.ぶ *Blade hurting feelings* **to put up with** 1528 Ⓢ

Ideographic compound that allegorically depicts a *heart* (心) that has been injured with the *blade* (刃[ジン]) of a dagger, feelings of emotional pain that one sometimes has to **put up with.**

認 認 ニン みと.める *Speech* 言 *that puts up with something* 忍[ニン] **to recognize** 1529

氏 氏 シ うじ *Dagger with a thick blade* **surname** 1530 Ⓢ

A dagger placed face down with a curved handle and a thick blade. The current glyph is a schematization of the curved handle of a dagger (厂) and the blade (乚), whose wider-than-normal thickness was originally indicated with a kind of thick mark that later became linearized by the stroke (一). The joint shape of the handle and the blade (氏) is similar to the reversed form of the character for "dagger" (刀 → 𠚣). The dagger represented by this character probably alludes to a type of ritual dagger used to carry out sacrifices, a task reserved for the shamanic or clerical class, which presumably liked or required to mark such an important object with distinguishing signs that would ultimately be associated with that particular clan or family from a high social stratum. In ancient times it was only these families of high social status that could be recognized by a specific symbol or name, something that would eventually lead to the concept of **surname.**

Ritual jade dagger with a slightly curved handle and a thick blade

婚 婚 コン *Woman* 女 *speaking* 曰 *of her new surname* 氏 **marriage** 1531

紙 紙 シ かみ — *Plant threads* 糸 *cut with a thick dagger* 氏(シ) *in order to produce paper* — **paper** 1532

 氏 氏 テイ — *Dagger stuck on the ground* — *Ground* 1533 Ⓢ

The ground (一) on which a *thick dagger* (氏) is stuck.

低 低 テイ ひく.い — *Person* 亻 *looking at the ground* 氐(テイ) — **low** 1534

抵 抵 テイ — *Hand* 扌 *leaning towards the ground* 氐(テイ) — **resistance** 1535

NOTE Ideogram that shows in a figurative way the action of the defense against a hit made by moving the arm down.

 民 民 ミン たみ — *Eye pierced by a dagger* — **common people** 1536 Ⓢ

A distorted eye—without the mark of the pupil (口)—pierced with a thick blade (弋)—like the one of the character 氏 (*thick dagger*). This character symbolizes a subject whose power of vision has been reduced so he can be easily controlled, becoming someone who "cannot see" what all is really about. The meaning of this glyph refers, in extension, to that of **common people**, subjects subordinated to a given authority.

眠 眠 ミン ねむ.る — *Eyes* 目 *of the common people* 民(ミン) — **to sleep** 1537

 七 七 乄 シチ なな.つ なの- — *Cut* — **seven** 1538 Ⓢ

This character originally represents a cross slice or cut (十), which later derived into the curved form 七 in order to be differentiated with the glyph 十 (*ten*). The borrowed meaning of 'seven' can be interpreted as a connection between the importance of "cut" bone marks in religious-divinatory rites (卜) and their close relationship with the **seven** great stars visible in the sky, also known as the seven luminaries (七曜): The sun, the moon, Mars, Mercury, Jupiter, Venus and Saturn.

As a component, this character can take the slanted form 乄.

叱 シツ *Words* 口 *that cut* 七(シチ) 1539
叱 しか.る
to scold

刈 *Criss-cross cuts* 乄 *made with a dagger* 刂 1540
刈 か.る
to mow

 切 セツ *Cut made with a dagger* 1541 Ⓢ
切 サイ
き.る
to cut

The action of *cutting* (七(シチ)) reinforced with the character for *dagger* (刀), a dagger making a **cut**.

杀 1542 Ⓢ
杀 サツ *Cut tree*

A *tree* (木) that is *cut* (七(シチ) → 乄).

サツ 1543
殺 サイ *Cut tree* 杀(サツ) *being struck* 殳
殺 セツ
ころ.す
to kill

刹 セツ *Tree cut* 杀(サツ) *with a dagger* 刂 *to make offerings* 1544
刹 サツ
shrine

 勿 1545 ㊔ Ⓢ
勿 モチ *Several cuts*
not

The blade of a *dagger* (刀 → 勹) making <u>several cuts</u> (ノ 丿).

1546

物 物 ブツ モツ もの

Cattle 牛 *killed by several cuts* 勿 (モチ)

thing

NOTE A dead ox or cow which is no longer a living being, but a still good: a **thing**.

2. POLE WEAPONS

In the battles of yesteryear, all kinds of melee weapons were used, among which, pole weapons, like 'spears' 矛 could give a great defensive advantage by allowing people to attack from a prudential distance. There was also a type of pole weapon that was even purely defensive, such as the *sasumata* or 'bident' 干, used in 'interventions' to trap criminals. Weapons more suited for attack were things such a simple 'stakes' 弋, their direct evolution, the 'dagger-axes' 戈, a further development, such as 'halberds' 戊 or even the more sophisticated 'thick-bladed halberd' 戌.

1547 Ⓡ Ⓜ

矛 矛 ム ほこ

spear

A **spear** with a pointed tip (マ), an elongated shaft (亅) and a rope (乛, ノ) serving as a grabber. The current glyph is quite different from the original pictograph, but resembles some other later versions of the glyph in which the rope grabber is more visible: .

Spear

1548

柔 柔 ジュウ ニュウ やわら.かい

Spear 矛 *made of wood* 木

pliant

1549 Ⓢ

務 務

ム
つと.める

Hand strongly wielding a weapon against a spear

to serve (in/as)

A *hand holding a mattock* (攵) that uses *strength* (力) against an enemy's spear (矛), in reference to the duty of the use of an armed force that people **serving** in the military have.

1550

霧 霧

ム
きり

Clouds serving 務(ム) *to form rain* ⻗

fog

1551 Ⓢ

干 干

①② カン
② ほ.す
② ひ.る

Bident

① **intervention**
② **to dry**

A spear with a thick shaft (十)—in which the horizontal line 一 acts as a linearized depiction of thickness—with a kind of hook with two prongs (一) that is used to immobilize the adversary. A weapon that is fairly commonly used in Asia even today, and which is called in Japan *sasumata* (刺股). In the West there is also a type of similar traditional weapon called <u>bident</u> (double-pointed spear). This weapon is used when one does not want to inflict serious harm on the opponent (for example, when the opponent is a petty criminal that has to be captured), a situation that arises in police interventions, hence the meaning of **intervention**. The meaning of **to dry** is due to the fact that the glyph 干 was used since ancient times as a folk alternative for the character 乾 (*to dry*), whose pronunciation is identical.

Head of a bident

1552

肝 肝

カン
きも

Body part 月 *that intervenes* 干(カン) *in digestion*

liver

1553
汗 汗 カン あせ
Water 氵 intervening 干 in cooling
sweat

1554
岸 岸 ガン きし
Mountains 山 and cliffs 厂 where water becomes dry 干
coast

1555
幹 幹 カン みき
Part of a tool held like a bident 干 that is straight like a person 𠆢 waking up with the early sun 𠦝
handle (of a tool)
trunk (of a tree)

1556
軒 軒 ケン のき
Parts of a chariot 車 shaped like bidents 干
eaves

1557
刊 刊 カン
Dry element 干 that can be cut with a dagger 刂
publication

1558 Ⓢ
幵 幵 開 ケイ
Two bidents
Flat

Two double-pointed spears or *bidents* (干×2 → 幵 → 开). This component adopts the meaning of flat or 'becoming flat', meaning which comes from the presumption that two bidents or *sasumatas* facing each other result in a draw, in a flat or equal outcome, because the *sasumata* acts as immobilizing defense weapon that prevents the performing of any attack.

1559
形 形 ギョウ ケイ かた かたち
Flat surface 开 a brush' hair 彡 draws on
shape

1560
研 研 ケン と.ぐ
Stone 石 becoming flat 开
to sharpen

刑 刑 ケイ *Flattening dagger* **penalty** 1561 Ⓢ

A *dagger* (刀 → 刂) that acts as an equalizer or *flattener* (开 ケイ) of society, as it is used to give **penalties**.

型 型 ケイ かた *Flattened 刑 (ケイ) earth-soil 土* **model** 1562

插 挿 ソウ さ.す *Hand introducing a bident in a hollow vessel* **to penetrate** 1563

Originally 插 [扌千臼], a *hand* (手 → 扌) grasping a *bident* (干 → 千) that is inserted into a *hollow container* (臼 → 臼), a depiction of a weapon able to **penetrate** objects. This ideogram is certainly understood as the representation of a culinary tool with two prongs (干), graph and meaning analogous to that of "pestle" (午).

弋 弋 *Stake* *Succession* 1564 Ⓡ Ⓜ

A stake (乀) traversing the ground (一), with a knob (丶) at the top, presumably made with a small branch. This component figuratively refers to the concept of succession or 'replacement', as stakes are tools that can be nailed in one place temporarily, then removed and nailed back to another place, successively.

弐 弐 ニ *One's 一 succession 弋 into two 二* **two** (in legal documents) 1565

代 代 ① ② タイ ① ② ダイ ① か.わる ② よ ③ しろ *People's succession* ① **to supersede** ② **era** ③ substitution 1566 Ⓢ

People's (人 → 亻) *succession* (弋), that is, people **superseding** each other, replacing themselves, also representing the concept of **eras** or superseding periods of time.

袋 **袋** タイ ふくろ — 1567

Superseding 代 (タイ) *clothes* 衣

sack

SPECIAL READING 足袋 [たび]: *Japanese socks with split toes*

貸 **貸** タイ か.す — 1568

Superseded 代 (タイ) *money* 貝

to lend

 式 **式** シキ — 1569 Ⓢ

Craft's succession

style

ceremony

The orderly *succession* (弋) of *crafts* (工) due to the existence of a predetermined **style.** The concept of "style" also derives into the notion of **ceremony**, as ceremonies are rituals that are subject to a particular predetermined style.

拭 **拭** ショク ぬぐ.う ふ.く — 1570

Hand 扌 *ceremonially* 式 (シキ) *moved*

to wipe

試 **試** シ こころ.みる ため.す — 1571

Speech 訁 *ceremonially* 式 (シキ) *made*

to test

 必 **必** 朩 ヒツ かなら.ず — 1572 Ⓢ

Distributed stakes

necessarily

Stakes (弋 → 乄 → 㔾) that are *distributed* (八 → ハ) on the ground, an action that is **necessary** in some important activities such as the establishment of military camps.

As a component the character can adopt the form 朩, which is somewhat more faithful to the original graphic composition.

泌 **泌** ヒツ ヒ — 1573

Fluid 氵 *that is necessarily* 必 (ヒツ) *expelled*

secretion

秘 秘 ヒ ひ.める

Fruits 禾 *that are ultimately necessary* 必(ヒツ) 1574

to conceal

 叔 叔 シュク

Necessary outstretched hand 1575 Ⓢ

uncle

SPECIAL READING 叔父 [おじ]: *uncle*

An *outstretched hand* (又) that is *necessary* (尗 ≈ 必), referring to a helping hand such as that of an **uncle** or someone close and familiar. The meaning of this character when acting as a component (*uncle*) is usually interpreted as someone who has an important social role.

督 督 トク

Uncle's 叔(シュク) *Eye* 目 1576

coach

淑 淑 シュク

Water 氵 *given by an uncle* 叔(シュク) 1577

graceful

 戈 戈

Dagger-axe 1578 Ⓡ Ⓜ

A weapon with an elongated blade shaped like a dagger (一), a rear spike (丶), a long shaft (乚) and a support foot (丿). A weapon known by the term dagger-axe.

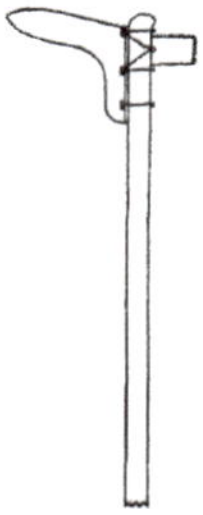

Head of a dagger-axe

戦 戦 ①②セン ①たたか.う ②いくさ

Capturing net 単(タン) *and dagger-axe* 戈 1579

① **to battle**
② **war**

NOTE Ideogram that associates weapons such as dagger-axes with the action or intention of capturing the enemy: a **battle**.

戯 戲 ギ たわむ.れる — *Dagger-axes 戈 brandished at the void 虚* — **spectacle** 1580

賊 賊 ゾク — *Money 貝 taken by cuts メ → 十 made with a dagger-axe 戈* — **rebel** 1581

伐 伐 バツ — *Dagger-axe through a person's body* — **felling** 1582 Ⓢ

A *person* (人 → 亻) that has been metaphorically **felled** off by a *dagger-axe* (戈) that has sliced his neck.

戒 戒 カイ いまし.める — *Two hands grabbing a dagger-axe* — **to warn against** 1583 Ⓢ

Two hands (廾) raising a *dagger-axe* (戈) in sign of threat or **warn**ing.

械 械 カイ — *Wooden 木 object used to warn people 戒 (カイ)* — **appliance** 1584

NOTE The original meaning of this compound was that of 'shackles' or 'fetter', but in modern Japanese the character is used almost exclusively in the word 機械 (きかい, *mechanism*).

戠 戠 ショク — *Dagger-axe producing sound* — *Contention* 1585 Ⓢ

The *sound* (音) produced by one *dagger-axe* (戈) colliding with another, an allegorical symbol of <u>contention</u> or discussion.

職 職 ショク — *Ear 耳 listening to contentions 戠 (ショク)* — **employment** 1586

識 識 シキ — *Speech* 言 *on contentions* 戠 (ショク) 1587

knowledge

織 織 シキ ショク — *Threads* 糸 *intertwining like clashing dagger-axes making sound* 戠 (ショク) 1588

weave

我 我 我 — ① ガ ① われ ② わ — *Hand grabbing a dagger-axe* 1589 Ⓢ

① **myself**

② **my**

A hand *grabbing* (手 ≈ 爪) a *dagger-axe* (戈), showing power or a certain status of nobility within a warrior stratum that infers a right to distinction and recognition of the person: an exaltation of the ego, which is represented with the personal pronoun **myself** or the possessive pronoun **my**.

餓 餓 ガ — *Food* 食 *approached by a hand grabbing a dagger-axe* 我 (ガ) 1590

hunger

義 義 義 ギ — *Auspicious myself* 1591 Ⓢ

righteousness

An *auspicious* (羊 → 𦍌) version of *myself* (我 (ガ)), the elevated or illuminated form of the ego, which is **righteous**.

儀 儀 ギ — *Person* 亻 *that is righteous* 義 (ギ) 1592

etiquette

議 議 ギ — *Speech* 言 *that is righteous* 義 (ギ) 1593

deliberation

犠 犠 ギ — *Cattle* 牛 *becoming righteous* 義 (ギ) 1594

sacrifice

 𢦏 サイ *Dagger-axe handled with talent* 1595 Ⓢ

Originally 𢦏 [才戈], and later 𢦏, the *talent* (才 → キ → 十) shown in the handling of a *dagger-axe* (戈) or, in other words: a weapon managed with talent.

戴 戴 タイ *Event that differentiates* 異 *someone with talent* 𢦏 (サイ) 1596

coronation

栽 栽 サイ *Tree-woods* 木 *distributed with talent* 𢦏 (サイ) 1597

plantation

裁 裁 ①②サイ ①た.つ ②さば.く *Clothes* 衣 *cut with talent* 𢦏 (サイ) 1598

① **to cut cloth**

② **to judge**

繊 纖 セン *Tiny* 糸 *threads* 絲 → 业 *cut with talent* 𢦏 (サイ) 1599

fiber

載 載 サイ の.せる *Chariot* 車 *driven with talent* 𢦏 (サイ) 1600

to get on

 幾 幾 キ *Person cutting small thicks of thread with a dagger-axe* 1601 Ⓢ

Commercial activity

how much

A *person* armed with a *dagger-axe* ((人 + 戈) → 戍) recounting several silk *cocoons* (幺幺), in reference to an authoritarian figure intervening as a moderator or accounting witness in a commercial activity thus determining **how much** something costs.

機 機 キ はた *Tree-wood* 木 *utensils useful for commercial activities* 幾 (キ) 1602

mechanism

 戔 戔 戋 セン *Dagger-axe fight* 1603 Ⓢ

Two *dagger-axes* (戈×2 → 戔) clashing with each other during a <u>fight</u>, representing a confrontation.

In most compounds this component takes the form 戋, which is a simplification where the strokes of the upper part of the original glyph got reduced to 彡 and 丶.

残 残 ザン のこ.る *Bone remains 歹 left after a dagger-axe fight 戋 (セン)* 1604

leftover

践 践 セン *Feet ⻊ leaving marks as a dagger-axe fight 戋 (セン)* 1605

tread

浅 浅 セン あさ.い *Water 氵 on top of which a dagger-axe fight 戋 (セン) can be made* 1606

shallow

桟 桟 サン *Piece of wood 木 that gets intersected like two clashing dagger-axes 戋 (セン)* 1607

cleat

箋 箋 セン *Slips of bamboo ⺮ where letters are written intertwined like two clashing dagger-axes 戔 (セン)* 1608

slip of paper

NOTE Originally referring to ancient books or notebooks written on bamboo strips that were used during the Shang dynasty.

 戊 戊 ボ *Halberd* fifth 1609 Ⓡ ㊔ Ⓜ

A pole weapon similar a dagger-axe (戈) but with its blade having a crescent curvature (丿) instead of the shape a dagger: a <u>halberd</u>.

Chinese halberd

越 越 エツ こ.える *Running 走 while holding a halberd 戊 → 戉* **to go across** 1610

茂 茂 モ しげ.る *Plants 艹 susceptible of being cut with a halberd 戊* **to overgrow** 1611

戚 戚 セキ *Necessary 尗 halberd 戊* (a) **relative** 1612

NOTE Ideogram understood as a reference to the defensive or military aid that a close a family or clan can provide.

蔵 蔵 ゾウ くら *Halberd being watched out behind some plants* **shed** 1613 Ⓢ

A place covered with *plants* (艹) where weapons such as *halberds* (戊) are kept and watched by *eyes looking down* (臣). An allegorical representation of a **shed** where valuable objects are stored.

臓 臓 ゾウ *Body part 月 acting as a shed 蔵 (ゾウ)* **viscera** 1614

 成 成 セイ ジョウ な.る *Halberd nailed somewhere* **to result in** 1615 Ⓢ

Originally 成 [戊丁 (テイ)], a *halberd* (戊) *nailed* (丁 → 𠃌) somewhere, symbolizing the conquest of a territory, a concrete **result**.

誠 **誠** セイ まこと 1616

Speech 言 *that gives results* 成 (セイ)

sincerity

城 **城** ジョウ しろ 1617

Earth-soil 土 *got as the result* 成 (セイ) *of a conquest*

castle

盛 **盛** ①②セイ ②ジウ ①も.る ②さか.る 1618

Results 成 (セイ) *manifested in food vessels* 皿

① to dish up

② to prosper

戊 戊 1619 Ⓜ

Big halberd

dog sign (Chinese zodiac)

A *halberd* (戊) with a big blade, which is marked by a horizontal stroke (一).

Head of a Chinese halberd with a broad blade

威 **威** イ 1620

Woman 女 *holding a big halberd* 戊

intimidation

滅 **滅** メツ ほろ.びる 1621

Water 氵 *floods, fire* 火 *and big halberds* 戊

to be ruined

NOTE Implying the destruction and **ruin** caused by a war.

歳 **歳** サイ セイ 1622

Time when one stops 止 *being small* 小 *and takes a big halberd* 戊

years old

SPECIAL READING 二十歳 [はたち]: *twenty years old*

 蔑 蔑 ベツ さげす.む — *Head crossed by a big halberd* — **to discard** 1623

The head of a person—represented by its *eyes* (罒) and eyelashes (艹)—pierced by a *big halberd* (戍). A **discard**ed enemy.

 武 武 ブ ム — *Marching with a thick blade dagger-axe* — **military** 1624 Ⓢ

Group in which *footsteps* (止) are made while carrying *big halberds* (戍 → 弋): the **military**.

賦 賦 フ — *Money* 貝 *collected by the military* 武(ブ) — **levy** 1625

3. AXES

Axes, like daggers, are objects that can be used both as work tools and weapons. That is why there are several types of axes, such as the primitive small 'axes'  斤 —used merely as tools—, or battle axes  士, which, when properly marked, served to tell apart different clans of noble 'gentlemen', within which, who carried the largest battle axe  王, was distinguished as the leader of the clan or, eventually, the 'king'.

 斤 斤 キン — *Axe* — **unit of weight** [*~0.6 kg*] 1626 Ⓡ Ⓜ

A rudimentary <u>axe</u> or hatchet, with its handle (丨) and a blade leaned to the left (⺁). As a standalone character this glyph is used to represent the **unit of weight** derived from the weight of a hatchet: approximately half a kilogram.

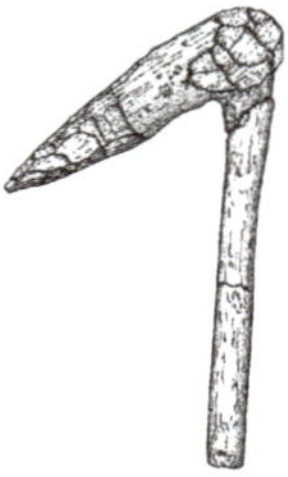

Primitive stone axe

析
析 セキ
Tree-wood 木 cut with an axe 斤 1627
chop

貭
質 シツ
シチ
チ
Axes 斤×2 that can be exchanged for money 貝 1628
quality

匠
匠 ショウ
Axes 斤 and boxes 匚 1629
artisan

断
断 ①②ダン
①た.つ
②ことわ.る
Stored rice grains 㡀 being cut off with an axe 斤 1630
① **to sever**
② **to dismiss**

折
折 セツ
お.る
Hand holding an axe 1631
Ⓢ
to break
to fold

A *hand* (手 → 扌) holding an *axe* (斤) to split—or **break**—some object or structure. The meaning of **fold**ing probably comes from the image of a tree trunk chopped with an axe that has fallen bent or 'folded'.

哲
哲 テツ
Folded 折 (セツ) words 口 1632
wisdom

NOTE A series of words that can be 'folded' in the sense that they can show various faces, deep words, full of **wisdom**.

誓 誓 セイ ちか.う — *Folded* セツ 折 *speech* 言 — **to vow** 1633

NOTE A speech or series of words that is embodied in a folded document and delivered to a religious institution.

 兵 兵 ヘイ ヒョウ — *Two hands grabbing an axe* — **soldier** 1634 Ⓢ

The person who, with his *two hands* (廾 → 六), grabs an *axe* (斤): a **soldier**.

浜 浜 ヒン はま — *Water* 氵 *whereby soldiers* ヘイ 兵 *camp* — **seashore** 1635

 斬 斬 ザン き.る — *Axe attack made while riding a chariot* — **to slice** (off) 1636 Ⓢ

An *axe* (斤) used while riding a *chariot* (車) that is, an axe that, thanks to its moving speed, can strike with such force that it **slices** what it encounters.

暫 暫 ザン — *Slice* ザン 斬 *of the sun* 日 — **temporarily** 1637

漸 漸 ゼン — *Water* 氵 *moving as the result of a slicing cut* ザン 斬 — **steadily** 1638

斥 斥 セキ — *Split axe* — **rejection** 1639 Ⓜ

An *axe* (斤) split or *cut* (乂 → ㇏) in the middle, a weapon or tool that is **reject**ed due to its lack of functionality.

訴 訴 ソ うった.える — *Speech* 言 *of rejection* 斥 — **to accuse** 1640

士 士 シ *Battle axe* knight **gentleman** 1641 Ⓡ Ⓢ

A large battle axe, with a big blade (一) and a handle (十) whose thickness is marked by a horizontal line (一). Battle axes were a characteristic object of knights—associated with **gentlemen** of the nobility—because their wide blades allowed to show a range of symbols characteristic of a certain clan. The upper horizontal line of this character appears longer than the lower one as a consensus to differentiate this graph from the character for "earth" (土).

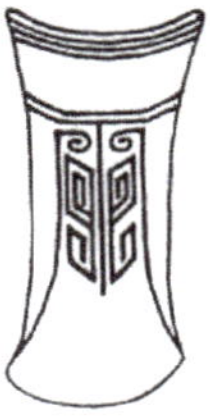

Blade of a bronze ceremonial axe from Shang dynasty China

仕 仕 シ ジ つか.える *Person* 亻 *next to a gentleman* 士(シ) **to work for** 1642

壮 壮 ソウ *Battle axe on a table* **robust** 1643 Ⓢ

A *battle axe* (士) on a *table* (丬(ショウ)), as a symbol of nobility and **robust**ness.

荘 荘 ソウ *Plants* 艹 *that are robust* 壮(ソウ) **solemn** 1644

装 装 ソウ ショウ よそお.う *Putting robust* 壮(ソウ) *clothes* 衣 *on* **to dress** 1645

吉 吉 キチ キツ *Words of a gentleman* **good luck** 1646 Ⓢ

Ceremonial *words* (口) pronounced by *gentlemen* (士) of the noble class in order to wish **good luck** and prosperity for the clan or nation.

詰 詰 キツ つ.める | *Speech* 言 *of good luck* 吉 (キツ) | 1647

to focus on

結 結 ケツ むす.ぶ ゆ.う | *Thread* 糸 *assuring good luck* 吉 (キツ) | 1648

to tie

NOTE Perhaps in relation to the complex Chinese decorative knots (中国結) used in the past as decorative elements of religious rituals.

Conceptualization of the 'endless knot' (盤長), considered as an auspicious symbol

---

 王 王 オウ | *Big battle axe* | 1649 Ⓡ Ⓢ

king

A *battle axe* (士 → 土) with a size that is larger than normal, riveted by the upper stroke (一) that suggests a hilt. While a standard battle axe is indicative of a noble class of knights, a greater axe is indicative of the leader of that class, which consequently derives into the concept of **king**.

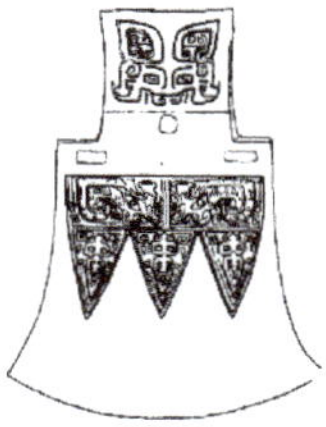

Blade of a big bronze axe from Shang dynasty China

弄
弄 ロウ もてあそ.ぶ

Big battle axe 王 (オウ) held by two hands 廾 1650

to fiddle with

旺
旺 オウ

Sun 日 and king 王 (オウ) 1651

vigorous

望
望 ボウ モウ のぞ.む

Perished 亡 (ボウ) body 月 of the king 王 (オウ) 1652

to wish for

SPECIAL READING 望月 [もちづき]: *full moon*

NOTE Understood as the wish for the return of a deceased king.

皇
皇 オウ コウ

Clearest 白 king 王 (オウ) 1653

emperor

SPECIAL READING 天皇 [てんのう]: *emperor of Japan*

狂
狂 キョウ くる.う

Animal 犭 acting like a king 王 (オウ) 1654

to rage

呈
呈 テイ

Words pronounced before the king 1655 Ⓢ

presentation

Words (口) pronounced before the *king* (王), a **presentation** or offering to the sovereign power.

聖
聖 セイ

Ear 耳 of the king who listens to a presentation made before him 呈 (テイ) 1656

holy

程
程 テイ ほど

Fruits 禾 presented before the king 呈 (テイ) 1657

extent

4. DEFENSIVE WEAPONS

After dealing with a series of attack weapons, it is only natural that the corpus of Chinese characters also depicts the defensive weapon par excellence: the shield 甲, which would later be associated with any kind of 'armor'.

甲 甲

カン
コウ

Shield
armor
first

1658 Ⓢ

Pictogram of a rudimentary circular shield with an opening in the middle (日), crossed by a handle (丨), an image taken later to indicate any type of protective armor. The main current meaning of this character is that of **first** in rank, meaning that originates from the Sinitic ordinal system known as Heavenly Stems (天干), in which ten concrete primitive characters are used to designate different ordinal positions, among which 甲 takes the first one, before 乙 (オツ). The adoption of this graph to mean 'first' may be due to the linkage of bone shells—associated with armors—with divination, being that material the first thing one needs to perform divination activities.

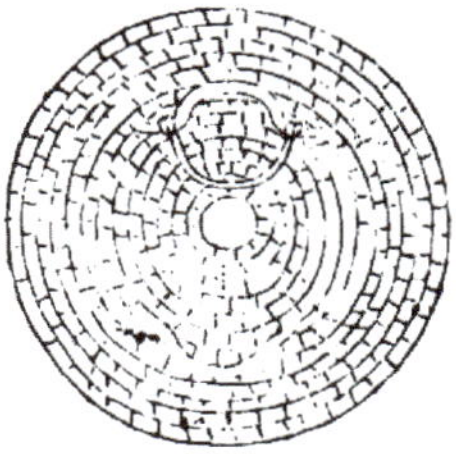

Rudimentary circular shield

押 押

オウ
お.す

Hand 扌 *holding a shield* 甲 (コウ)
to push

1659

岬 岬

みさき

Mountain 山 *acting as a shield* 甲
cape (of a coast)

1660

盾 盾

ジュン
たて

Person holding a shield
shield

1661 Ⓢ

A *person* (人 → 厂) holding a ***shield*** (甲 → 盾).

5. BOWS AND ARROWS

The last type of weapons appearing within the Chinese characters corpus are those that grant an advantage at a distance, projectile weapons: bows and arrows.

Most bows in Chinese antiquity had a serpentine shape, as they were composite 'bows': 弓. These bows were tied with thick strings 引 that, when they were 'pulled', could throw their projectile at a great distance. If, on the contrary, that string got detached from its bow, it became a loose 'rope' 弓 that could be used for other tasks.

Bows would be useless, however, if it were not for the 'arrows' 矢, capable of following a fixed path and passing through the 'middle' of a hoop 中 in shooting practice. In order for the flight of an arrow to be optimal and its impact to be striking, special attention had to be paid to the arrowheads 入, which should be made of a metal sharp enough for them to 'enter' the surface of what they hit.

弓
弓 キュウ ゆみ **bow** 1662 Ⓡ Ⓜ

A composite **bow**. In the modern form of the character the string is no longer visible, and only the limbs and handle (弓) are left.

Chinese composite bow

張
張 チョウ はる *Bow 弓 with an elongated 長 (チョウ) string* 1663

to extend

強 強 ①②キョウ ①②ゴウ ①つよ.い ②し.いる 1664

Bow 弓 (キュウ) string that makes energy flow ム and is thick as a serpent 虫

① **strong**

② **to coerce**

弧 弧 コ 1665

Bow 弓 shaped like a gourd plant's 瓜 (コ) hanging stem

arc

弥 弥 や 1666

Bow 弓 that is embroidered 尓

embroidered bow

TRIBE NAME USAGE 弥生 [やよい]: *Yayoi*

弦 弦 ゲン つる 1667

Bow's 弓 dim 玄 (ゲン) part

string

湾 湾 ワン 1668

Water's 氵 energy distributed 亦 along the coast in the form of a bow 弓

gulf

弾 弾 ①ダン ①たま ②はず.む ③ひ.く 1669

Bow 弓 that is simple 単 (タン)

① **bullet**

② **to be encouraged**

③ **to play** (an instrument)

NOTE 1. A bow-and–arrow-like weapon simplified to the simplest form: a **bullet**. 2. A bow that is simple to be handled: a bow whose use is **encouraged**. 3. A simple bow string: something that **plays music**.

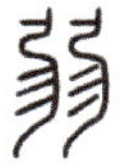

弱 弱 ジャク よわ.い 1670 Ⓢ

Bows with hairy strings

weak

Originally 弱, some *bows* (弓×2) whose strings are full of *hairs* (彡×2 → 冫×2), that is, bows with frayed strings, neglected bows whose functionality is **weak**ened.

溺 溺 デキ おぼ.れる — *Water 氵 that weakens people* 弱 (ジャク) → 弱 1671

to drown

発 発 ハツ ホツ — *Hand putting a bow string in motion* 1672 Ⓢ

launch

Two hands (廾 → 癶) grabbing the string of a bow (一), that gets propelled so that the projectile, the arrow, flies *upward* (癶). A scene that represents the throwing, or **launching** of an arrow.

引 引 イン ひ.く — *Tense string of a bow* 1673

to pull

The string (丨) of a *bow* (弓) being **pull**ed, tightened and stretched.

弓 弓 — *Loose string of a bow* 1674 Ⓜ

Rope

A string detached from its bow, loose, visibly curved, evoking the image of a rope. In modern writing this component takes a form that is virtually identical to the character for "bow" (弓), perhaps due to a semantic association.

弟 弟 ダイ デ テイ おとうと — *Stake being tied with a rope* 1675 Ⓢ

younger brother

A *rope* (弓) being tied to a *stake* nailed to the ground (弋 ≈ 丫). The action of nailing and tying stakes during the establishment of a military camp was a mechanic activity relegated to people with little or none authority. While the activity of distributing the stakes suggests the idea of a leader or family member with authority as an uncle (叔), the activity of tying the stakes firmly suggests the idea of a family member forced to follow orders, as is the **younger brother**.

第 第 ダイ — *Bamboo slips* ⺮ *sequentially ordered as older and younger brothers* 弟 (ダイ) → 弔 1676

ordinary number

弗
弗

Several stakes tied together with a rope
Annulment

1677
Ⓜ

Two *stakes* ((弋 ≈ 礻)×2 → ノ‖) tied together by a *rope* (弓), stakes that cancel out their stabilizing function to each other, because instead of being tied to a tent they happen to be tied among themselves. An image that serves to represent any kind of annulment.

沸
沸　フツ　わ.かす

Water 氵 *becoming annulled* 弗

to seethe

1678

費
費　ヒ　つい.やす

Annulment 弗 *of money* 貝

to spend

1679

弔
弔　チョウ　とむら.う

Person hanging from a rope

to mourn

1680

Originally 弔 [亻弓], a *person* (人 → 亻 → 丨) hanging from a *rope* (弓), dead due to suicide or execution. **Mourning** aroused by a violent death.

矢
矢　シ　や

arrow

1681
Ⓡ
Ⓜ

A big **arrow** with a pointed head (𠂉) on top, two vanes (人) at the bottom, and a shaft that has its thickness marked by a horizontal line (一).

Standard arrow

挨
挨　アイ

Hand 扌 *putting flowing energy* 厶 *in order to shoot an arrow* 矢

sequential

1682

族
族 ゾク
Flags 㫃 and arrows 矢 1683
tribe

NOTE Various people fighting or hunting under the same flag: a specific **tribe** or clan.

族
短 タン みじか.い
Arrow 矢 that fits in a lidded bowl 豆 1684
short

医
医 イ
Arrows 矢 being removed from wounded people and left in a box 匚 1685
doctor

知
知 チ し.る
Words penetrating like arrows 1686 Ⓢ
to know

The ability to pronounce a few *words* (口)—on a particular topic—with the speed and penetration of an *arrow* (矢). Perhaps this compound also referred, in origin, to discussions or conversations about bow hunting, an activity for which a certain **know**ledge is required.

痴
痴 チ
Ill 疒 knowledge 知(チ) 1687
foolishness

侯
侯 コウ
Person practicing archery on a cliff 1688 Ⓢ
governor

Originally 厌 [厂矢], an *arrow* (矢) being shot from a *cliff* (厂), referring to the activity of archery, firstly done by hunters that later would be transformed into noblemen or **governors**, as it is historically attested by the fact that archery practice was indeed done by noblemen in ancient Chinese dynasties. The component for "person" (人 → ⺈) was added later to the original glyph, forming the composition 矦, to put focus on the person doing the activity. Eventually, the element (⺈) was transformed into the composition 亻⺈, probably due to a graphic analogy with the most common form of the component for "person" (亻).

1689

候 候 コウ そうろう

Personal 亻 *activities' governor* 侯 (コウ) → 矦

climate

1690

喉 喉 コウ のど

Word's 口 *governor* 侯 (コウ)

throat

1691 Ⓢ

疾 疾 シツ

Illness caused by an arrow

disease

An *illness* (疒) or **disease** derived from infected wounds caused by *arrow* impacts (矢).

1692

嫉 嫉 シツ

Woman's 女 *disease* 疾 (シツ)

jealousy

1693 Ⓢ

至 至 シ いた.る

Arrow reaching its target

to arrive (at)

Pictographic and ideographic representation of an *arrow* facing downwards (矢 → 𠫔) reaching the *eaerth-soil* (土), **arriving** there.

1694 Ⓢ

屋 屋 オク や

Person sitting where he has arrived

salon

A *person sitting* (𠂆) in a place where he has just *arrived* (至), a place where people stay for a while, such as a hall, a house, a **salon** or any commercial establishment.

1695

握 握 アク にぎ.る

Hand 扌 *controlling a salon* 屋 (オク)

to take hold of

1696 Ⓢ

致 致 チ いた.す

Target being hit

to accomplish

A hand *hitting* (攵) on a specific place, foreseen as the target marked by an arrow that has *arrived* (至 (シ)) to the soil: A hit or impact given successfully, an

accomplishment.

緻
緻 チ
Thread 糸 weaving accomplished 致(チ) 1697
elaboration

備
備 ビ そな.える
Person next to two arrows and a ritual plate 1698
to have ready

Person (人 → 亻) **ready** with a *ritual plate* (用 → 用) and several arrows (矢×2 → 芖 → 严), the requirements needed for making an animal sacrifice.

到
到 トウ
Arrival point of an arrow marked with a dagger 1699 Ⓢ
arrival

A *dagger* (刀(ド) → 刂) marking on the ground the exact point at which an arrow has **arrived** (至).

倒
倒 トウ たお.れる
Person 亻 falling to the ground like a fallen arrow 到(トウ) 1700
to fall down

中
中 ジュウ チュウ なか
Arrow going through the middle of a hoop 1701 Ⓢ
middle

A throwing weapon—spear, arrow or dart (丨)—passing through a hoop (口) during a military practice session, an arrow passing through the **middle** of a hoop.

仲
仲 チュウ なか
Person 亻 in the middle 中(チュウ) 1702
in-between

忠
忠 チュウ
Feeling that goes through the middle 中(チュウ) *of the heart* 心 1703
loyalty

沖
沖 チュウ おき

Water 氵 of the middle 中(チュウ) of the sea 1704

open sea

衷
衷 チュウ

What is in the middle 中(チュウ) →𠁣 of clothes 衣 1705

inner

夬
夬

Hand throwing a dart through a hoop 1706 Ⓜ

Resolute

Originally 叏 [中又], then 叏, and later 夬, an *outstretched hand* (又 → メ → ㇇) throwing a dart (丨) through a hoop (囗 → ユ), a sign of decision and <u>resolution</u>.

快
快 カイ こころよ.い

Feeling 忄 that is resolute 夬 1707

pleasant

決
決 ケツ き.める

Waters' 氵 resolution 夬 1708

to decide upon

NOTE In reference to the need to make a **decision** when water has flooded a land.

黃
黄 オウ コウ き こ-

Arrow going towards a bullseye 1709 Ⓢ

yellow

A character with a rather complex and blurred graphical evolution, originally 黃 [廿更], it represents *two hands* holding an *arrow* ((廾 ≈ 臼 + 矢) → (日 + 夭) → 更) throwing it towards hoop (囗 → 廿 → 艹) representing a bullseye. This ideogram, which originally represents an archery scene, was eventually taken to designate the **yellow** color, by association, most probably, to the <u>bullseyes</u> that were allegedly marked with yellow paint. The idea of yellow color can be mnemonically associated with the component for "sun" (日) that can be imagined in the center of the compound.

1710
横 横 オウ よこ

Wood 木 part of an arrow that goes towards a bullseye 黄 (オウ)

sideways

NOTE Referring to the wooden part of the arrows—the shafts—which move horizontally towards the target.

1711 Ⓢ

𦰩 カン

Arrow missing its target

Originally 𦰩 [廿昊], an *arrow* (矢 → 天 → 夫) that has not passed yet through a hoop (囗), missing its target (囗 → 廿 → 艹).

1712
嘆 嘆 タン なげ.く

Words 口 referring to the missing of a target 𦰩 (カン)

to lament

1713
漢 漢 カン

Water 氵 missing its target 𦰩 (カン)

Chinese

NOTE This character actually refers to the Han (漢) ethnic group, a nomenclature that would later be used to describe everything that comes from the territories where the Han people inhabits, that is, China. The Han name comes from the era in which China was ruled by the Han Dynasty (201 BC - 210 AD), which in turn takes its name from the fief of origin of the dynasty's founder, located around the river Han. The name of this river derives, ultimately, from its association with the Milky Way, which was once called *Tianhan* (天漢), that is: *The celestial water that does not reach its target* (the sea in the Earth).

1714
難 難 ナン むずか.しい かた.い

Arrow missing 𦰩 (カン) *a flying bird 隹*

difficult

1715 Ⓢ

堇 堇 キン

Arrow lying on earth-soil

Unable to fight

Originally 堇 [𦰩土], an arrow that has *missed its target* (英 ← 𦰩) and lies flat on the *earth-soil* (土), scene that, by association, also refers to the inability to practice archery or any military activity. Over time, the strokes of the component for "arrow missing its target" (𦰩) lost its diagonal strokes and blended with the component for “earth” (土) forming the current form of the glyph: 堇.

僅 **僅** キン わず.か — 1716

Person 亻 unable to fight 堇 (キン)

trifle

勤 **勤** キン ゴン つと.める — 1717

Someone unable to fight 堇 (キン) *that is given another strength 力*

to be employed (at)

謹 **謹** キン つつし.む — 1718

Speech 言 unable to fight 堇 (キン)

discreet

入 **入** ニュウ い.れる はい.る — 1719 Ⓜ

Arrowhead

to enter

An arrowhead, something that **enters** through the surface of what is impacted by it.

Sample of an arrowhead

傷 **傷** ①②ショウ ①きず ②いた.む — 1720

Person 亻 with an arrowhead 入 → 𠂉 in his body that has made him a wound that shines like sun rays 昜 (ヨウ)

① **wound**
② **to be injured**

金 **金** ①②③キン ①コン ①③かね ①かな- — 1721 Ⓡ Ⓜ

Material used to make arrowheads and battle axes

① **metal**
② **gold**
③ **money**

Material of an indefinite form (丷) wherewith *arrowheads* (入 → 𠆢) and *big battle axes* (王) are manufactured: **metal** with which weapons are made. As a standalone, this character sometimes gets the original meaning of ‘metal’ expanded over time to the more specific meaning of **gold**, which, in turn, also leads to the meaning of **money**.

As a component, this character usually is placed to the right part of the compounds and adopts the abridged form 釒 .

銃
銃 ジュウ *Metal 釒 that should be set aside* 充 (ジュウ) 1722
gun

銀
銀 ギン *Metal 釒 that stays still* 艮 (コン) *over time* 1723
silver

鉄
鉄 テツ *Metal 釒 that can be easily be lost* 失 (シツ) 1724
iron

NOTE **Iron** is a type of metal that characteristically corrodes quite fast.

釜
釜 かま *Metal object* 金 → 㠯 *used by the father* 父 1725
iron pot

鍛
鍛 タン きた.える *Metal 釒 made step by step* 段 (ダン) 1726
to forge

鍋
鍋 なべ *Metal object 釒 where animal bones and backbones* 咼 *are boiled* 1727
cooking pot

鈴
鈴 リン レイ すず *Metal object 釒 used to give commands* 令 (レイ) 1728
small bell

鋭
鋭 エイ するど.い *Metal 釒 that is exposed* 兑 (エツ) 1729
sharp

銘
銘 メイ *Metal 釒 with names* 名 (メイ) *written on it* 1730
inscription

錯 **錯**	サク	*Metal objects* 金 *from older times* 昔 (シャク) **confusion**	1731
鋼 **鋼**	コウ はがね	*Metal* 金 *hard as a ridge* 岡 (コウ) **steel**	1732
鋳 **鋳**	チュウ い.る	*Making a metal* 金 *with longevity* 寿 (ジュ) **to cast**	1733
鎌 **鎌**	かま	*Metal object* 金 *with which work can be done simultaneously* 兼 *in the field* **sickle**	1734
鈍 **鈍**	ドン にぶ.い	*Metal* 金 *that is still growing* 屯 (トン) **to cast**	1735
鉢 **鉢**	ハチ ハツ	*Metal object* 金 *in which roots* 本 *of plants are buried* **plant pot**	1736
錬 **錬**	レン	*Metals* 金 *in a backpack* 東 **alchemy**	1737
録 **録**	ロク	*Metal* 金 *pulled from a well* 录 (ロク) **record**	1738

NOTE Probably referring to metal extractions that need to be **record**ed in mining actions.

釣 **釣**	チョウ つ.る	*Metal* 金 *taken with a ladle* 勺 (シャク) **to lure in**	1739
錦 **錦**	キン にしき	*Metal* 金 *decorating white cloth* 帛 **brocade**	1740

針 シン *Metal* 釒 *with the shape of a thick rod* 十 1741
針 はり **needle**

鎖 サ *Metal* 釒 *that is small* ⺌ *and goes through money* 貝 1742
鎖 くさり **chain**

NOTE In reference to the **chains** of coins that were used in antiquity, as it is explained in the description of the character 貫 (*to go through*).

鑑 カン *Metal* 釒 *being overseen* 監 (カン) 1743
鑑 かんが.みる **to heed**

鎮 チン *Metal* 釒 *used as a tool* 真 (シン) 1744
鎮 しず.まる **to appease**

銅 ドウ *Metal* 釒 *used to make plates from which one can eat* 同 (ドウ) 1745
銅 **copper**

銭 セン *Metal* 釒 *piece for which dagger-axe fights* 戔 (セン) *are made* 1746
銭 ぜに **coin**

朿 *Tree with arrowheads* 1747 Ⓜ
朿 *Thorns*

A *tree* (木) whose bark is full of spikes or <u>thorns</u> that look like arrowheads (入 → 冂).

策 サク *Bamboo* ⺮ *object with added thorns* 朿 1748
策 **stratagem**

刺 シ *Thorn* 朿 *penetrating like a dagger* 刂 1749
刺 さ.す **to pierce**

責 責 ① セキ ② せ.める *Money with thorns* 1750 Ⓢ

① **obligation**

② **to condemn**

Originally 賫 [朿貝], *money* (貝) that hurts like *thorns* (朿 → 龶), in presumable reference to monetary debt, an inherited **obligation** and threat of **condemn**ation in the case of non-payment.

債 債 サイ *Person* 亻 *tied to his obligations* 責(セキ) 1751

bond

漬 漬 つ.ける *Water's* 氵 *obligation* 責 1752

to soak

積 積 セキ つ.もる *Fruits'* 禾 *obligations* 責(セキ) 1753

to stack up

績 績 セキ *Threads'* 糸 *obligation* 責(セキ) 1754

spinning

REVIEW ON WEAPONS

刀列召昭分刧契制利則刃忍氏氐民
七切杀勿

1 別剣帰削剰券刻劇解判刷初剥班罰剛割副
剤例烈裂詔招超沼紹照頒雰粉紛貧盆潔喫
製梨痢側測認婚紙低抵眠叱刈殺刹物

矛務干开刑挿弋代式必叔戈伐戒戠
我義𢦏幾戔戊蔵成戌蔑武

2 柔霧肝汗幹岸軒刊形研型弐袋貸拭試泌秘
督淑戦戯賊械職識織餓儀議犠戴栽裁繊載
機残践浅桟箋越茂戚臓誠城盛威滅歳賦

斤折兵斬斥士壮吉王呈

3 析質匠断哲誓浜暫漸訴仕荘装詰結弄旺望
皇狂聖程

甲盾

4 押岬

弓弱発引弓弟弗弔矢知侯疾至屋致
備到中央黄𦰩堇入金束責

5 張強弧弥弦湾弾溺第沸費挨族短医痴候喉
嫉握緻倒仲忠沖衷快決横嘆漢難僅勤謹傷
銃銀鉄釜鍛鍋鈴鋭銘錯鋼鋳鎌鈍鉢錬録釣
錦針鎖鑑鎮銅銭策刺債漬積績

SPACES

1. THE VERTICAL PLANE

Within sinitic writing, there is a vertical cosmology that takes a primordial semantic part in the development of ideograms. That cosmology mainly addresses the Man-God vertical relation, within which the earthly being that is man is subordinated to the celestial dictation of God. This cosmological relation legitimized the ruling class of ancient China, because that class was understood as the intermediary between what is 'above'  上—heaven above earth—, and the people 'below'  下—or earth under heaven.

1755 Ⓜ

 上 二 上

① ジョウ
① ショウ
① うえ
① うわ-
① かみ
② あ.げる
③ のぼ.る

① **above**
② **to lift**
③ **to go up**
Heaven

A vertical space (一) above another vertical space (一), understood also as a simple conceptual and cosmological representation of <u>heaven</u> **above** earth, what is above superimposed on what is below. Over time the upper and lower line of the original glyph (⼆) got united by a vertical line (丨), probably due to a necessity of differentiating this character from the character for "two" (二). The original, simpler glyph, nevertheless, remains intact in many compounds.

1756 Ⓢ

 元 元

ガン
ゲン
もと

What is over people
origin

Heaven (⼆) <u>over</u> a *person* (人 → 儿). Heaven understood as the **origin** or originator of man, or, giving an oxymoron, the conscious man as the originator of heaven: The relationship between heaven and man as the conceptual origin of all things.

頑 1757

頑 ガン

Thoughts over 元 (ガン) *the head* 頁

obstinance

玩 1758

玩 ガン

Jewels 𤣩 *over people* 元 (ガン)

game

云 1759 ㊔ Ⓜ

云 ウン

Energy flowing in heaven

to express

Flowing energy (厶) above in *heaven* (二) or the sky.

伝 1760

伝 デン つた.える

Person 亻 *showing the flow of energy in heaven* 云

to transmit

魂 1761

魂 コン たましい

Energy from heaven's 云 *ghost* 鬼

spirit

陰 1762

陰 イン かげ

Mountains 阝 *reflecting a retained* 今 (キン) *flowing energy from the sky* 云

shade

yin (negative principle)

芸 1763

芸 ゲイ

Energy flowing in heaven 云 *directed towards plants* 艹

art

NOTE Most probably in reference to the transmission through generations of knowledge and arts related to the cultivation of plants, the backbone of any sedentary society.

転 1764

転 テン ころ.がる

Chariot 車 *moving like energy flowing in heaven* 云

to rotate

会 1765 Ⓢ

会 カイ エ あ.う

Person encountering energy flowing from heaven

to meet (with)

Ideogram that represents a *person* (人 → 𠆢) facing the *energy of heaven* (云) or divine energy: a transcendental **meet**ing.

絵 エ カイ *Threads* 糸 *meeting together* 会 (カイ) 1766

絵 カイ

painting
drawing

NOTE In clear reference to an embroidery or upholstery representing an image.

雲 雲 ウン くも *Flowing energy in the sky that generates rain* Ⓢ 1767

cloud

Energy flowing in heaven (云) capable of creating *rain* (雨 → 雨): the configuration of a **cloud**.

曇 ドン くも.る *Sun* 日 *turning into clouds* 雲 (ウン) 1768

曇

cloudy

亏 亏 于 *Energy unfolding in heaven* Ⓜ 1769

Energy from *heaven* (二) that gets *unfolded* (乙 → ㇉).

In some compounds the original form 亏 may appear simplified in the variant 于.

顎 ガク あご *Part of the head* 頁 *that allows the unfolding of energy into words* 口×2 1770

顎

jaw
chin

誇 コ ほこ.る *Speech* 言 *made by a big person* 大 *as if he was unfolding energy from heaven* 亏 1771

誇

to boast

汚 汚 ① オ ① きたな.い ② よご.す ② けが.す 1772

Water 氵 that gets unfolded 亏 → 丂

① **dirty**

② **to dirty**

芋 芋 いも 1773

Plant 艹 that unfolds energy 于

potato

示 示 示 ネ ジ シ しめ.す 1774 Ⓡ Ⓜ

Heaven communicating downwards

Divine power

display

to show

Heaven communicating with the earth (二 ← 上) by means of a conductive thread (亅) of energy that gets *distributed* (八 → ハ). An Ideographic representation of a <u>divine power</u> of communication understood as manifestations and revelations, what is taught by heaven, a **display** of the heavenly intangible realm in the earthly tangible world. A connotation that is ultimately expanded to the broad meaning of **to show**.

This character, when acting as a component, is placed to the left in the compounds and adopts the simplified form ネ.

奈 奈 ナ 1775

Big 大 display of divine power 示

where

PLACE NAME USAGE 奈良県 [ならけん]: *Nara Prefecture*

禍 禍 カ 1776

Divine power ネ upon bones and backbones 咼 (カ)

catastrophe

視 視 シ 1777

Divine power ネ getting seen 見

sight

祝 祝 シュク シュウ いわ.う 1778

Divine power ネ exercised through elder brothers 兄

to congratulate

祉 祉	シ	*Divine power's* ネ *footsteps* 止 (シ) **welfare**	1779
礼 礼	レイ ライ	*Divine power's* ネ *unfolded energy* 乚 **courtesy**	1780
神 神	シン ジン かみ かん- こう	*Divine power* ネ *expanding energy* 申 (シン) **god**	1781
社 社	シャ やしろ	*Divine power* ネ *represented on earth* 土 **society**	1782
祥 祥	ショウ	*Divine power* ネ *that is auspicious* 羊 (ヨウ) **auspiciousness**	1783
祖 祖	ソ	*Divine power* ネ *manifested in an altar of sacrifice* 且 (ソ) **ancestor**	1784
禅 禅	ゼン	*Divine power* ネ *that is simple* 単 (タン) **silent meditation** (Zen)	1785
福 福	フク	*Divine power* ネ *going through a big ritual vessel* 畐 (フク) **blessing**	1786
斎 斎	サイ	*Even* 斉 (セイ) → 齐 *divine power* 示 **purification**	1787
祈 祈	キ いの.う	*Divine power* ネ *invoked by an an axe* 斤 (キン) **to pray**	1788

祭 祭 サイ まつ.る *Hand giving meat to a divine power* 1789 Ⓢ

to worship

An *outstretched hand* (又 → ⺕) offering a piece of *meat* (月 → 夕), a scene depicting a sacrifice as a way of **worship**ing the numinous.

際 際 サイ きわ *Mountains* 阝 *that are worshiped* 祭(サイ) 1790

meeting point

尉 尉 イ *Sitting person working with divine power* 1791 Ⓢ

military officer

A *sitting person* (尸) who *works* (寸) with or through *divine power* (示), as a reference to the relation that the spiritual world had to the military power of ancient Chinese societies.

慰 慰 イ なぐさ.める *Feelings* 心 *of a person working with divine power* 尉(イ) 1792

to comfort

祟 祟 *Emerging divine power* 1793 Ⓜ

Divine power (示) *coming out and going forward* (出 → 士).

款 款 カン *Divine power emerging* 祟 *from a lack* 欠 1794

goodwill

隷 隷 レイ *Divine power emerging* 祟 *from a caught person* 隶 1795

subordinate

禁 禁 キン *Grove where divine power is shown* 1796 Ⓢ

prohibition

A *grove* (林) where *divine power* is *shown* (示), a sacred site reserved for secret rites which access is **prohibited** to the common people.

襟 **襟** キン えり *Part of clothes 衤 that is closed like a grove where divine power is shown* 禁(キン) 1797

collar

 票 **票** ヒョウ *Bag controlled by divine power* 1798 Ⓢ

ballot

A *bag* (襾 → 覀) with **ballots** inside whose result is decided by *divine power* (示).

漂 **漂** ヒョウ ただよ.う *Water 氵 carrying ballots* 票(ヒョウ) *away* 1799

to drift

標 **標** ヒョウ *Tree-wood 木 where ballots* 票(ヒョウ) *are hung* 1800

signpost

 平 **平** ビョウ ヘイ たい.ら ひら *Energy scattered through heaven and earth* 1801 Ⓢ

flat

Energy *distributed* (八 → ハ) between *heaven* and earth (二) through a conductive thread (丨) that unites them: Energy evenly distributed above and below. An ideographic representation of the equitable, or **flat** distribution of energy.

呼 **呼** コ よ.ぶ *Mouth 口 pronouncing a name clearly and flatly 平 → 乎* 1802

to call

評 **評** ヒョウ *Speech 言 flatly* 平(ビョウ) *inspected* 1803

evaluation

坪 **坪** つぼ *Earth-soil 土 flatly 平 extended* 1804

unit of land measurement [~3 m^2]

辛 シン *Person turned upside down under heaven* 1805
辛 立 から.い *Convict* M
spicy
eighth

A person turned upside down (⽺) under the mandate of *heaven* (二 → 亠), a person who is out of order and law, a criminal or a convict. The meaning of this character when it appears as a standalone is that of **spicy**, as a semantic association with the bitter—or spicy—situation of a condemned person.

In some compounds the original graph gets simplified into the form 立, graphically identical to the character for "standing person" (立).

辭 ①②ジ *Tongue 舌 of a convict 辛 speaking* 1806
辞 ①や.める
① **to resign**
② **terms**

接 セツ *Hand 扌 touching a convict 立 woman 女* 1807
接 つ.ぐ
to be in contact (with)

NOTE This compound is understood as a depiction of the contact with a woman who sells or who is forced to do sexual services. The compound 妾 (*convicted woman*) is, in fact, a character, albeit now in disuse, with the meaning of 'concubine' or 'mistress'.

辣 ラツ *Convicts 辛 → 𨐋 in a bundle 束* 1808
辣
harsh

竟 キョウ *Convict speaking* 1809
竟 *Suspect* S

Originally 竟 [立兄], a person speaking or *pronouncing words* (兄(キョウ) → 見) who becomes a *convict* (辛 → 立). A suspect who has to face or defend himself against the crime of which he is accused. Eventually the form 竟 derived into 竟, perhaps due to graphic confusion with the component 音 (*sound*).

境 キョウ ケイ さかい *Earth-soil 土 approached by suspects 竟(キョウ)* 1810
境
border

NOTE In reference to the everlasting threat of barbaric or rival peoples lurking at the **borders**, always suspected of being able to carry out an attack.

鏡 1811

鏡 キョウ かがみ

Metal 金 *that causes suspicion* 竟 (キョウ)

mirror

SPECIAL READING 眼鏡 [めがね]: *glasses*

NOTE In ancient times **mirrors** were made of polished bronze, and they were likely to cause suspicion among the uninitiated because of their ability to reflect images, something which makes them be easily associated with magic or sorcery.

Back of a Chinese bronze mirror

競 1812

競 キョウ ケイ きそ.う せ.る

Two suspects

to compete

Two *suspects* (竟 (キョウ) ← 竞×2) **competing** with each other to prove their innocence in a trial.

亲 1813 Ⓢ

亲 シン

Tree-wood being chopped down

Originally 亲 [辛木], a *tree* (木) *turned upside down under heaven* (辛 → 立), a tree that has suffered the allegorical condemnation of having been chopped down, as it if were the penalty of a convict of nature.

親 1814

親 ①②シン ①した.しい ②おや

Person looking 見 *at wood chopping* 亲 (シン)

① **to be familiar**

② **parent**

新 新 シン あたら.しい あら.た にい *Tree chopped with an axe* **new** 1815 Ⓢ

A tree *chopped* (亲) with an *axe* (斤), a tree felling optimally done: The obtention of **new** wood useful for the construction of new objects or sites.

薪 薪 シン たきぎ *Plants 艹 that can be chopped down with an axe 新 to make fire* **firewood** 1816

竜 龍 竜 リュウ たつ **dragon** 1817 Ⓢ

The original form of this character, still present in some compounds, shows a linearization of a pictogram representing a *snake*-like animal (㔾 ≈ 虫) with dorsal spikes (三) and a jagged open mouth (月) capable of condemning those that are *turned upside down below heaven* (辛 → 立). A majestic representation of a legendary animal commonly known as a **dragon** that in Chinese culture is normally associated with imperial sovereignty. The current version of this character when it appears as a standalone—and also as part of some compounds—is a simplification made in the form 竜, which is made with a variant of the component for "extended energy" (电 → 电) put below the component for "convict" (辛 → 立), suggesting that the dragon is a symbolic element of an energy capable of condemning or making convicts.

滝 滝 たき *Water 氵 with the strength of a dragon 竜* **waterfall** 1818

籠 籠 ①② ロウ ① かご ② こ.もる *Bamboo ⺮ with the strength of a dragon 龍* ① **basket** ② **to seclude** (oneself) 1819

襲 襲 シュウ おそ.う *Clothes 衣 with the strength of a dragon 龍* **succession** 1820

NOTE Originally this character had the meaning of 'several layers of clothing', a **succession** of clothes that makes a hard and strong dress.

 章 **章** シヨウ **badge** **chapter** 1821 Ⓢ

A round **badge** represented pictographically by the element 日—which can be associated with the component for "speaking" (曰), since a badge "speaks" about the rank or condition of the person wearing it. Over time the components 立 and 十 were added to the original pictogram. The component 十 (*thick rod*) was probably added to indicate the thickness of the badge, while the component 立, a simplification of the component for "convict" (辛) was probably added as a reference to the use of badges as identifiers, in this case in reference to a badge or insignia used to mark a convict. The meaning of 'badge' is expanded in Japanese also to the notion of 'section' or **chapter**.

彰 **彰** シヨウ *Badge* 章 (シヨウ) *shiny as hair* 彡 **distinct** 1822

障 **障** シヨウ さわ.る *Mountains* 阝 *blocking people with badges* 章 (シヨウ) **to interfere** (with) 1823

NOTE Referring to mountains as an impediment to military advance.

 童 **童** ドウ わらべ *Convict carrying a heavy load* **kid** 1824 Ⓢ

Originally 童 [立重], a *convict* (辛 → 立) carrying a *heavy load* (重 → 里), a convict doing forced labor: a person with no will. The idea of a person without free will was later associated with the idea of **kid**, meaning for which the character currently stands.

憧 **憧** シヨウ あこが.れる *Feelings* 忄 *of a kid* 童 (ドウ) **to long for** 1825

瞳 **瞳** ドウ ひとみ *Eye's* 目 *kid* 童 (ドウ) **pupil** (of eye) 1826

鐘 鐘 ショウ かね *Metal object* 金 *loud as a kid* 童(ドウ) 1827

bell

 業 業 業 ギョウ ゴウ ボク わざ *Person dealing with workers* 1828 Ⓢ

deal

A character with a rather complex graphic evolution, it represents a *person seen from the front* (大) dealing with two convicts working in the field (丵): A person dealing with workers. The upper part (丵) is a conjunction of two elements representing a *convict* working with *plants* ((辛 + 艹) → 莘×2 → 丵), to which the component for "person seen from the front" (大) is added, thus forming the composition 業. The general meaning of the character, being **deal**, is also related to that of 'work', 'business', or 'deeds'.

When this character acts as a standalone, it takes the form 業, where the component 大 (*person seen from the front*) has been transformed into 木 (*tree-wood*), perhaps due to a conceptual association between 'wood'—materials—and 'work'.

僕 僕 ボク *Person* 亻 *who deals with* 業(ボク) *things* 1829

I (male)

撲 撲 ボク *Hand* 扌 *dealing with* 業(ボク) *things* 1830

slap

SPECIAL READING 相撲 [すもう]: *sumo wrestling*

 亘 亘 コウ *Confined energy* 1831 ㊔ Ⓜ

span

Originally 亙, a stream of *rotating energy* (回 → 回 → 日) confined between *heaven* and earth (二).

恒 恒 コウ *Feelings* 忄 *that are confined* 亘 1832

permanent

垣 垣 かき *Earth-soil* 土 *confined* 亘 *to one particular space* 1833

hedge

 互 互 ゴ たが.い *Two confined intertwining energies* 1834

reciprocal

Two streams of unfolded energy currents *intertwining* (㐄 ≈ 丩(キュウ)) within a confined space between *heaven* and earth (二), trapped in a continuous cycle of **reciprocal** movement.

 五 五 ゴ いつ.つ *Crossing of the five elements* 1835 Ⓢ

five

The oldest recorded character referring to the number **five** is the glyph 〣, a reflection of the of the five counting rods used in the rod numeral system. Such a glyph, however, was soon replaced by the form 㐅, which is more legible and more distinct from other number characters such as 三 (*three*) or the old form for the number "four" (亖). The form 㐅 is most likely a variation of the character 互(ゴ) (*reciprocal*), adopted through a phonetic analogy. A possible subsequent interpretation is that the form 㐅 is an abstract representation of the crossing (㐅), within the boundaries marked by heaven and earth (二), of the five traditional elements (五行) associated with the five geographical points in the two-dimensional plane: north (water), south (fire), east (wood), west (metal) and center (earth). As time went by, the original graph 㐅 ended up becoming the current variant 五, wherein one of the diagonal lines is transformed into the stroke ㇕.

 吾 吾 ゴ *Crossing words* 1836 ㊔ Ⓢ

ego

Words (口) crossing at a central point like the *five* elements (五(ゴ)), the point of concentration of words, so to say, thoughts, conscience and, ultimately, the **ego**.

悟 悟 ゴ さと.る *Heart-mind* 忄 *of the ego* 吾(ゴ) 1837

to realize

語 語 ゴ かた.る 1838

Speech 言 *of the ego* 吾(ゴ)

to talk

下 下 1839 Ⓜ

① カ
① ゲ
① した
① しも
① もと
② お.りる
② さ.がる
③ くだ.さる

① **below**

② **to go down**

③ to confer

Originally 二, a vertical space (一) below another vertical space (一), understood also as a simple conceptual and cosmological representation of earth **bellow** heaven. Over time the upper and lower line of the original glyph (二) got united by a vertical line (丨), **going downwards**, probably due to the need of differentiating this character from the character for “two” (二), and also as an analogous reversion of the character for “above” (上).

峠 峠 とうげ 1840

Mountain part 山 *where one can go up* 上 *or down* 下

mountain pass

凵 凵 1841 Ⓡ Ⓜ

Pit

A pictographic representation of a hole or <u>pit</u> in the ground, with its walls (丨, 丨) and the bottom end (一).

去 去 1842 Ⓜ

キョ
コ
さ.る

Person in a pit

to go away

Originally 𠫓 [大凵], a *person seen from the front* (大 → 土) in a *pit* (凵 → 厶). Someone buried or hiding, someone who has **gone away**.

法 1843

法

ホウ
ハッ
ホッ

Water 氵 going away 去

law
method

NOTE This composition refers either to the laws established with respect to the distribution of water and irrigation, or to the observable **laws** of nature, wherein it is established that water is always in motion, always going away.

蓋 1844

蓋

ガイ
ふた

Plants 艹 covering a person that is in the pit 去 of a food vessel 皿

lid

 1845 Ⓢ

却

却

キャク

Person kneeling after going away

retreat

A *person kneeling* (卩) in the face of defeat after being allowed to *go away* (去) in **retreat.**

脚 1846

脚

キャク
キャ
あし

Body part 月 used in retreat 却

leg

 1847 Ⓢ

出

出

① シュツ
① スイ
① で.る
② だ.す

Footsteps coming out of a hole

① **to go out**
② **to get out**

Footsteps (屮 ≈ 止) **getting out** of a *pit* (凵).

拙 1848

拙

セツ
つたな.い

Hand 扌 going out 出 *of its intended way*

clumsy

 1849 Ⓢ

屈

屈

クツ

Person sitting on someone trying to get out

oppression

A *person sitting* (尸) on someone who tries to *get out* (出), preventing him to do so. A scene depicting a state of **oppression**.

掘 **掘** クツ ほ.る

Hand 扌 pressing things down 屈 (クツ) 1850

to dig

堀 **堀** ほり

Earth-soil 土 that has been pressed down 屈 1851

ditch

2. THE HORIZONTAL PLANE

In contrast to the vertical plane seen in the previous section, there is the horizontal or longitudinal plane, delimited by the existing distances from one point to another on a surface. The longitudinal distance that goes from one point to another establishes a 'delimited space' ⊢⊣冂 useful to distinguish a part from the whole wide horizontal space.

冂 冂 冖

Delimited space 1852 Ⓡ Ⓜ

A specific space that extends across (一) until it gets delimited between two ends (丨 亅): A horizontal delimited space.

壱 **壱** イチ

Person 匕 *coming out* 士 (シ) *of a delimited space* 冖 1853

one (in legal documents)

瞬 **瞬** シュン またた.く

Eye 目 *grabbed* 爫 *and delimited* 冖 *by an up-down movement* 舛 1854

to blink

塚 **塚** つか

Earth-soil 土 *serving as a delimiting space* 冖 *for hogs* 豕 1855

hillock

写 **写** シャ うつ.す

Delimited space 冖 *that is given* 与 1856

to transcribe

鬱 鬱 ウツ *A long-haired 彡 person 匕 of old age with an open skull 凶 ≈凶 inside a tin can 缶 buried under a space delimited 冖 by trees 木×2* 1857

depression

冠 冠 カン かんむり *Delimited space 冖 over people 元 (ゲン) who work 寸* 1858

crown

NOTE This ideographic compound alludes to the "**crown**" as the monarchical institution that reigns over the working people, however, today, this character refers rather to the object that is placed on the head.

 夢 夢 ム ゆめ *Eyes' vision under the space of an evening* 1859

dream

An *eye* (罒 ← 目) with its eye *leashes* (艹) under the figurative *delimited space* (冖) of an *evening* (夕), representing what the eyes "see" while sleeping at night.

 冘 冗 冘 ジョウ *Person within a delimited space* 1860 Ⓜ

superfluous

A *person* (人 → 儿 → 几) within a *delimited space* (冂 → 冖), without developing his full potential, leading a **superfluous** life.

When this character acts as a component it can take the slightly varied form 冘.

沈 沈 チン しず.む *Water 氵 becoming the delimiting space of a person 冘* 1861

to submerge

枕 枕 まくら *Wooden 木 piece delimiting the space where a person 冘 rests* 1862

pillow

NOTE **Pillows** in ancient China were made of wood.

 売 売 バイ う.る *Person emerging from his delimited space* 1863 Ⓜ

to sell

Although this character was originally 賣 [士罒貝], a *net* (罓 ← 网 → 罒 → 冖) of *money* (貝 → 儿) that *comes out* (出 → 士), emerging thanks to some sale, it later took the simplified version 売, which was a primitive component of its own representing the idea of a *person delimited by a space* (冗 → 冗) who emerges *out* of it (出 → 士) thanks to **sell**ing products.

1864

読 読 トウ トク ドク よ.む

Speech 言 emerging from a delimited space 売

to read

1865

続 続 ゾク つづ.く

Thread 糸 emerging from a delimited space 売

to continue

1866 Ⓢ

殻 殻 カク から

Mace striking something that emerges from a delimited space

husk

A mace *striking* (殳) fruit or grain to make its inner part emerge from the *space delimited* (売 ≈ 売) by its **husk**.

1867

穀 穀 コク

Fruitful 禾 husks 殻 → 殸

cereals

1868 Ⓢ

愛 愛 アイ

Hand grabbing a still feeling

love

A hand metaphorically *grabbing* (爪 → 爫) the *space delimited* (冂 → 冖) by a *feeling* (心) that is kept *still* (夂): The captured instant of a deep **love**.

1869

曖 曖 アイ

Days 日 of love 愛

not clear

1870 Ⓢ

憂 憂 ユウ うれ.える う.い

Head delimited by a still feeling

to grieve

A *head* (頁 → 百) acting as the *delimited space* (冂 → 冖) of a *feeling* (心) that is kept *still* (夂): The head trying to rationalize a deep feeling, an action that leads to a state of anguish and **grief**.

優 優 — ①② ユウ / ① やさ.しい / ② すぐ.れる — *Person 亻 next to another person who is grieving* 憂 (ユウ) — 1871

① **tender**
② **to outstrip**

 隺 隺 — *Bird flying within a delimited space* — 1872 Ⓜ

A *bird* (隹) flying within a *delimited space* (冂 → 冖), a bird whose flight is limited.

確 確 — カク / たし.か — *Stone 石 hitting a bird whose flight is limited 隺* — 1873

assurance

鶴 鶴 — つる — *Poultry bird 鳥 whose flight is limited 隺* — 1874

crane

 軍 軍 — グン (キ) — *War chariots delimiting a space* — 1875 Ⓢ

army

A *delimited space* (冖) protected or conquered by a series of war *chariots* (車). A group of war chariots forming an **army** capable of covering a large territory.

揮 揮 — キ — *Hand 扌 in the army* 軍 (キ) — 1876

mandate

輝 輝 — キ / かがや.く — *Light 光 in the army* 軍 (キ) — 1877

to sparkle

 帯 帯 — タイ / お.びる — 1878 Ⓢ

belt
to carry

The upper part of the compound, 卌, is a pictographic representation of an ornamented **belt**. The lower part is a later addition made to ideographically specify the meaning of the character, since a belt is a *cloth* (巾) that acts as a *delimiting space* (冖) of the upper and lower part of a garment. This character also takes the meaning of to **carry** by a semantic association with the fact that belts are also occasionally used to carry things.

滞 滞 タイ とどこお.る

Water 氵 *becoming a figurative belt* 帯(タイ) 1879

to stagnate

円 円 エン まる.い

Delimited space with a center 1880

roundness

monetary unit [*yen*]

A *space delimited* (冂) by two ends that extend horizontally (一) and vertically (丨): a **round** space. The meaning of 'roundness' was expanded over time to refer to coins and, more specifically, the Japanese national currency: the **yen**.

 方 方 ホウ かた

Dagger pointing towards a delimited space 1881 Ⓢ

direction

A *dagger* (刀 → 力) pointing towards a *delimited space* (冂 → 冖 → 亠), pointing towards a specific **direction**.

妨 妨 ボウ さまた.げる

Woman 女 *in one's direction* 方(ホウ) 1882

to disturb

肪 肪 ボウ

Part of meat 月 *pointed with a dagger* 方(ホウ) 1883

fatness

訪 訪 ホウ たず.ねる おとず.れる

Speech 訁 *pointing towards* 方(ホウ) *someone* 1884

to call on

to visit

倣 倣 ホウ なら.う

Person 亻 *directed* 方(ホウ) *by hits* 攵 1885

to emulate

坊 坊 ボウ ボッ

Earth-soil 土 *where a monk is directed to* 方(ホウ) 1886

monk's dwelling

boy

1887

防 防 ボウ ふせ.ぐ

Mountains ⻖ *preventing a dagger that is pointing towards it* 方(ホウ)

to defend

1888

芳 芳 ホウ かんば.しい

Plants 艹 *that point to the nose like a dagger* 方(ホウ)

fragrant

1889

紡 紡 ボウ つむ.ぐ

Thread 糸 *pointing towards* 方(ホウ) *the spinner*

to spin

1890 Ⓢ

放 放 ホウ はな.す

Hand holding a mattock hitting a dagger that is pointing towards it

to release

A *hand holding a mattock that hits* (攵) a *dagger that was pointing towards it* (方(ホウ)), someone **releasing** himself from the menace of a weapon, someone being released from an external power.

1891

激 激 ゲキ はげ.しい

Water 氵 *that gets clearly* 白 *released* 放 *from a fountain*

violent

1892

敷 敷 フ し.く

Beneficial things 甫 → 㫪 *being released* 放(ホウ)

to lay out

1893

傲 傲 ゴウ

Person 亻 *coming out* 士 → 土 *after being released* 放(ホウ)

pride

1894 Ⓢ

央 央 オウ

Person in the middle of a delimited space

center

A *person seen from the front* (大) in the middle of a *delimited space* (冂 → 冂), in the **center**.

1895

映
映 エイ / うつ.す / は.える

Sunlight 日 *in the center* 央(オウ)

to reflect

1896

英
英 エイ

Plants' 艹 *center* 央(オウ)

mighty

England

1897 Ⓢ

市
市 ①② シ / ② いち

Delimited space from which a foot emerges

① **market**

② **city**

Originally 市, a *delimited space* (冂) from which a foot *comes out* ((亠 + 丨) ← 十 ← 土 ← 㞢(シ)). A foot coming out of a delimited space, in reference to a person who leaves home and interacts with the outside world—the **market** or the **city**—where social and mercantile relations are carried out.

1898

姉
姉 シ / あね

Woman 女 *that goes out to the market* 市(シ)

elder sister

SPECIAL READING 姉さん [ねえさん]: *elder sister*

1899

肺
肺 ハイ

Body part 月 *from which air comes out as a foot coming out from a delimited space* 巿

lungs

1900

柿
柿 かき

Tree 木 *fruit popular in the market* 市

persimmon (*Diospyros kaki*)

1901 Ⓜ

Divine power distributed in a delimited space

Divine power distributed (((二 → 亠) + (八 → ソ) ≈ 示) within a *delimited space* (冂), the space where the divine power is manifest, a religious space.

傍 ボウ 1902
傍 かたわ.ら

Person 亻 *going towards* 方 (ホウ) *the space where divine power is distributed* 㐫

nearby

帝 テイ 1903
帝

Distributed divine power that makes people go back Ⓢ

empire

Divine power distributed in a delimited space (冂 → 亠) that makes people always go *back* (帀 → 巾) to it, in reference to an **empire**.

諦 テイ 1904
諦 あきら.める

Speech 訁 *towards the empire* 帝 (テイ)

to resign oneself (to)

締 テイ 1905
締 し.まる

Threads 糸 *of the empire* 帝 (テイ)

to tighten

啇 テキ 1906
啇

Old space where divine power is distributed Ⓢ

Custom

An *old* (古) *space where divine power is distributed* (冂), a religious domain that comes from yesteryear: a custom.

嫡 チャク 1907
嫡

Woman 女 *married by custom* 啇 (テキ)

legitimate wife

摘 テキ 1908
摘 つ.む

Hand 扌 *taking something by custom* 啇 (テキ)

to pluck

敵 テキ 1909
敵 かたき

Customary 啇 (テキ) *target of hits* 攵

enemy

滴 テキ 1910
滴 しずく
したた.る

Fluid 氵 *showing customary habits* 啇 (テキ)

drop (of fluid)

3. THE CIRCULAR PLANE

The enlargement of the longitudinal horizontal space made simultaneously in several directions creates a new type of space: the circular or 'encircled space' ○ 口, which is not delimited by two points but by a number of infinite points that end up forming a circle.

If the perimeter of a circular space is modified, areas of several forms, or polyhedra, arise. One the most basic areas is the square, that can be used to represent various functional surfaces such as an underground crypt 亜 where the deceased were buried in preparation for a trip to the afterlife or 'secondary' life, or rice 'fields' 田, which are represented as a square divided into several parts.

○ 口   *Encircled space*   1911 Ⓡ Ⓜ

A space that is perimetrically delimited, an <u>encircled space</u>, originally circular in form (○ → 口).

囚 シュウ   *Person 人 enclosed in an encircled space 口*   1912

captured

団 ダン トン   *Work 寸 within an encircled space 口*   1913

group

困 コン こま.る   *Tree 木 enclosed in an encircled space 口*   1914

to be bothered

菌 キン   *Plant 艹 that is fruitful 禾 inside an encircled space 口*   1915

fungus

germ

圏 ケン   *Rolled 巻 (カン) encircled space 口*   1916

circle

国 **国** コク くに 1917

Jewel 玉 (ギョク) *conforming an encircled space* 口

country

囲 **囲** イ かこ.む 1918

Well 井 *surrounded by an encircled space* 口

to surround

邑 **邑** 阝 乡 ユウ 1919 Ⓡ ㊔ 邑 Ⓜ

Skillful people within an encircled space

town

People with *big hands* (巴), referring to skilled or hardworking people, within an *encircled space* (口). A delimited broad space where hard-working people live: a town.

This component is most often placed to the right of the compounds and takes the abbreviated form 阝, graphically identical to the abbreviated form of the component with the meaning of "mountains" (阜 → 阝), which, on the other hand, is always located to the left. In the rare occasion when the component 邑 has to be placed on the left side of the compounds, it takes the form 乡, thus avoiding any confusion.

郊 **郊** コウ 1920

Part of town 阝 *were land interchanges* 交 (コウ) *are made*

outskirts

郡 **郡** グン 1921

Part of town 阝 *ruled by a mister* 君 (クン)

district

邪 **邪** ジャ 1922

Town 阝 *attacked by fangs* 牙 (ガ)

injustice

SPECIAL READING 風邪 [かぜ]: *common cold*

邦 **邦** ホウ 1923

Lush 丰 → 扌 *town* 阝

homeland

都 シ ト みやこ 1924

都

Town 阝 *where people do actions* 者 (シャ)

metropolis

郵 ユウ 1925

郵

Part of town 阝 *where messages droop* 垂

mail post

邸 テイ 1926

邸

The ground 氏 (テイ) *of a town* 阝

estate

舎 シャ 1927 Ⓡ Ⓢ

舎

Remaining encircled space

cottage

An *encircled space* (囗) that *remains* (余 → 余 → 余 → 亼) despite the passing of time, a family house or **cottage**.

捨 シャ す.てる 1928

捨

Hand 扌 *leaving things inside a cottage* 舎 (シャ)

to dump

舗 ホ 1929

舗

Cottage 舎 *that is beneficial* 甫 (ホ)

store

那 ナ 1930

那

Bamboo in a town

alluring

Originally 䢷 [冄邑], a *town* (邑 → 阝) full of *bamboo* (竹 ≈ 林 → 冄 → 冄), an **alluring** town.

擁 ヨウ 1931

擁

Hand taking possession of a town with water and birds

embracement

Originally 攡 [扌邕隹], a *hand* (手 → 扌) figuratively taking possession of a *town* (邑 → 乡) surrounded by a *river* (巛 → 亠) and *birds* (隹). A town or settlement that is easy to **embrace**.

郎
郎
ロウ
Good town 1932
offspring Ⓢ

A *good* (良 → 良) *town* (邑 → 阝), a town with **offspring** that guarantees its survival.

郷
郷
キョウ
ゴウ
Towns sharing a bowl full of food 1933
hometown Ⓢ

Several *towns* ((邑×2) → (乡 + 阝)) around a *bowl full of food* (皀) that is shared among them. An ideographic representation of the economic and social interaction among several communal entities which eventually become the **hometown** of all the people participating in them.

響
響
キョウ
ひび.く
Hometown's 郷(ギョウ) *sounds* 音 1934
echo

因
因
イン
よ.る
Person inside an encircled space 1935
to be caused by Ⓢ

A *person seen from the front* (大) within an *encircled space* (囗). A figurative representation of an idealist or determinist understanding of **cause**-effect relationships, since the content—a person—is delimited by the continent—an encircled space. To put it differently: A person's circumstances caused by his environment (the encircled space).

姻
姻
イン
What a woman 女 *causes* 因(イン) 1936
matrimony

恩
恩
オン
Cause 因(イン) *of the heart-mind* 心 1937
grace

咽
咽
イン
Words 口 *causing* 因(イン) *thing* 1938
larynx

音 音 バイ *Person standing outside of an encircled space* *Surpassing the limits* 1939 Ⓢ

A person *standing* (立) outside an *encircled space* (口), a person who has gone outside the boundaries, someone who has <u>surpassed</u> his limits.

倍 倍 バイ *Person* 亻 *surpassing his limits* 音(バイ) 1940

double

培 培 バイ つちか.う *Earth-soil* 土 *surpassing its limits* 音(バイ) 1941

to cultivate

陪 陪 バイ *Mountains* 阝 *surpassing their limits* 音(バイ) 1942

obeisance

賠 賠 バイ *Money's* 貝(バイ) *limits being surpassed* 音(バイ) 1943

compensation

剖 剖 ボウ *Surpassed limits* 音(バイ) *being cut with a dagger* 刂 1944

dissection

部 部 ブ *Surpassed limits* 音(バイ) *in a town* 阝 1945

section

SPECIAL READING 部屋 [へや]: *room*

正 正 𤴓 ショウ セイ ただ.しい まさ *Footstep entering an encircled space* 1946 Ⓢ

correct

Originally 足, A *footstep* (止) taken towards the interior of an *encircled space* (口 → 一), a person <u>entering</u> the established limits, a person who follows the social precepts in a **correct** way.

In some components this character takes the variant 𤴓.

婿 婿 セイ むこ — *Woman's 女 entering 疋 (セイ) body 月* — **bridegroom** 1947

証 証 ショウ — *Speech 言 that is correct 正 (ショウ)* — **proof** 1948

政 政 セイ ショウ まつりごと — *Correct 正 (セイ) use of hits 攵* — **government** 1949

礎 礎 ソ いしずえ — *Stone 石 sustaining tall structures like trees 林 correctly 疋 (ショウ)* — **foundation stone** 1950

疎 疎 ソ うと.い — *Correctness 疋 (ショウ) → ⻊ in a bundle 束* — **sparse** 1951

整 整 セイ ととの.う — *Bundle 束 of hits 攵 that sustain correctness 正 (セイ)* — **to be in order** 1952

旋 旋 セン — *Flag 方 correctly 疋 (セイ) handled* — **rotation** 1953

NOTE A flag that after a victory, since it was not captured by the enemy, is able to turn around—**rotate**—and return to the base: the correct path of a flag.

症 症 ショウ — *Illness 疒 entering 正 (ショウ) signals* — **symptoms** 1954

是 是 是 ゼ — *Entering sun* — **being** 1955 Ⓢ

The *sun* (日 → 日) entering the day as a *foot entering an encircled space* (正 (セイ) → 疋), the Sun beginning the cycle of the day as a figurative representation of the state of **being**, what *is* it is because it has been born, it has started like the sun starts the day.

題
題 ダイ
What is 是 *the head* 頁 *of an argument* 1956
topic

提
提 テイ さ.げる
Hand 扌 *being* 是 *itself* 1957
to take along

堤
堤 テイ つつみ
Earth-soil 土 *being itself* 是 1958
dike

疑
疑 ギ うたが.う
Person asking where the arrow that struck him comes from 1959 Ⓢ
to question

A character with a rather complex graphic evolution, originally 矢, it represented a man with an *open mouth* (欠 → 𠂉 → マ) who holds an *arrow* (矢), suggesting a scene in which said man is **questioning** the origin of the arrow he is holding. Over time two elements were added to the original character to reinforce the intended meaning. The first of these elements is 疋, a *foot entering a space* (正 → 疋), which adds the implication that the found arrow has entered the body of the questioner. The second element added is 匕 (*person from behind*), which adds the representation of the person asked. The current version of the character reflects, then, someone hurt by an arrow, asking another person who is the one that shot at him.

擬
擬 ギ
Hand 扌 *questioning* 疑 *movements* 1960
imitation

凝
凝 ギョウ こ.る
Ice-like 冫 *question* 疑 1961
to stiffen

各
各 カク おのおの
Still foot in an encircled space 1962 Ⓢ
Stationary
each

A *still foot* (夂), stationary, limited by an *encircled space* (口), representing the state of immobility of **each** person, at least in ancient societies.

落 落 ラク お.ちる — *Plants 艹 and water 氵 becoming stationary* 各 [ラク] — 1963
to fall off

格 格 カク コウ — *Tree-wood 木 being stationary* 各 [カク] — 1964
form

絡 絡 ラク から.む — *Thread 糸 making things stationary* 各 [ラク] — 1965
to entangle

賂 賂 ロ — *Money 貝 becoming stationary* 各 [ラク] — 1966
bribe

酪 酪 ラク — *Jars 酉 that become stationary* 各 [ラク] — 1967
dairy products

路 路 ロ -じ — *Foot and leg moving in an encircled space* — 1968 Ⓢ
path

Stationary encircled space (各 [ラク]) on which *feet and legs* (足 → ⻊) go through: a **path.**

露 露 ロ ロウ つゆ — *Rain's 雨 path* 路 [ロ] — 1969
dew

韋 韋 イ — *Feet moving around an encircled space* — 1970 Ⓢ

Two footsteps ((㞢, 㐄) ≈ 止×2) moving around a circular enclosure, someone encircling an encircled space (囗).

偉 偉 イ えら.い — *Person 亻 moving around an encircled space* 韋 [イ] — 1971
superb

韓 **韓** カン — *Sunshine* 卓(カン) *around which people move* 韋 — **Korea** 1972

NOTE This character originally referred to a tribe of ancient China called *Han* (different to the current Han people, written as 漢), whose name was similar to the Han tribes of the Korean peninsula to which the same character was assigned. Eventually South **Korea** took the name of those tribes, and also its character, for the vernacular name of their country.

緯 **緯** イ — *Thread* 糸 *moving around* 韋(イ) — weft **latitude** 1973

㕣 **㕣** エン — *Energy distributed and moving in an encircled space* 1974 Ⓢ

Energy *distributed* (八 → ハ) in an *encircled space* (口), moving inside.

沿 **沿** エン そ.う — *Water* 氵 *moving in an encircled space* 㕣(エン) — **to run along** 1975

船 **船** セン ふね ふな- — *Boat* 舟 *moving in an encircled space* 㕣(エン) — **ship** 1976

鉛 **鉛** エン なまり — *Metal* 金 *moving in an encircled space* 㕣(エン) — **lead** (metal) 1977

四 **四** シ よ.つ — *Encircled space being distributed* — **four** 1978

An *encircled space* (口) whose area has been *distributed* (八 → 儿), a space divided in implicit **four** parts.

谷 **谷** コク たに — *Water current flowing through an encircled space* — **valley** 1979 Ⓢ

Originally 㕣 [𠆢口], *streams of water* (𠆢 ≈ (㕣 ← 川) → 八) that pass through a *space encircled* (囗) by implicit mountains: a **valley**.

俗 俗 ゾク — *People* 亻 *in a valley* 谷 (コク) — **folk** — 1980

欲 欲 ヨク / ほ.しい / ほっ.する — *Valley* 谷 (ヨク) *leaving one's mouth open* 欠 — **wanted** — 1981

SPECIAL READING 浴衣 [ゆかた]: *yukata (Japanese light robe)*

浴 浴 ヨク / あ.びる — *Water* 氵 *in a valley* 谷 (ヨク) — **to bathe in** — 1982

裕 裕 ユウ — *Clothes* 衤 *filling a valley* 谷 (ヨク) — **plentiful** — 1983

固 固 コ / かた.い — *Old encircled space* — **solid** — 1984 Ⓢ

An *old* (古 (コ)) *encircled space* (囗), limits or limitations that have been there for ages, something **solid** and difficult to change.

個 個 コ — *Person* 亻 *that is solid* 固 (コ) — **individual** — 1985

箇 箇 カ — *Bamboo object* ⺮ *that is solid* 固 (コ) — **article** (of) — 1986

錮 錮 コ — *Restraining metal* 釒 *that is solid* 固 (コ) — **imprisonment** — 1987

哀 哀 アイ あわ.れむ *Clothes acting as a limiting space* 1988 Ⓜ

to pity

Clothes (衣 → 𠆢) forming an *encircled space* (口), clothing becoming the essence of its wearer, a person conditioned to his clothes, a figurative image that represents the spiritual subjugated by the delimitation of matter: something unfortunate and **pitiable**.

睘 睘 *Eye looking at a material that delimits a space* 1989 Ⓢ

An *eye* (目 → 罒) looking at *delimiting matter* (哀 → 𧘇 → 𧘇), an eye looking and desiring the matter.

環 環 カン *Jade disk* 王 *materialistically looked after* 睘 1990

ring

袁 袁袁 *Foot coming out of the limitations of material things* 1991 Ⓢ

A foot *coming out* (出 → 土 → 十) of what is *delimited by matter* (哀 → 𧘇).

This character usually takes the modified form 袁.

猿 猿 エン さる *Animal* 犭 *out of the limitations of material things* 袁 1992

monkey

園 園 エン その *Encircled space* 口 *where the limitations of material things are trespassed* 袁 1993

park

員 員 イン *Money in an encircled space* 1994 Ⓢ

employee

A person who earns *money* (貝) in a limited quantity that is figuratively represented by an *encircled space* (口): an **employee**.

損 損 ソン そこ.なう — *Hand* 扌 *interfering in the salary of an employee* 員(イン) 1995

to damage

韻 韻 イン — *Sounds* 音(オン) *made by an employee* 員(イン) 1996

rhyme

 周 周 シュウ まわ.り — *Encircled space of a ritual plate* 1997 Ⓢ

circumference

An *encircled space* (囗) conforming the the shape of a *ritual plate* (用 → 円): a **circumference.**

彫 彫 チョウ ほ.る — *Space of a plate* 周(シュウ) *wherein hair-shaped* 彡 *marks are made* 1998

to engrave

調 調 チョウ しら.べる — *Speech* 言 *structured as a circumference* 周(シュウ) 1999

to tune

 或 或 ワク — *Encircled space defended by dagger-axes* 2000 ㊔ Ⓢ

or

A *dagger-axe* (戈) figuratively creating a barrier (㇒) around an encircled space (囗): a territory defended by weapons.

惑 惑 ウク まど.う — *Defended* 或(ワク) *heart-mind* 心 2001

infatuation

域 域 イキ — *Earth-soil* 土 *liable to be defended* 或(ワク) 2002

region

 咸 咸 カン — *Territory protected by big halberds* 2003 Ⓢ

An *encircled space* (囗) protected by *big halberds* (戌): a heavily defended territory.

減 減 ゲン へ.る — *Water* 氵 *flooding over a heavily defended territory* 咸 (カン) — 2004

to diminish

 感 感 カン — *Protected feeling* — 2005 Ⓢ

sensation

A *feeling* (心) heavily protected, understood as a **sensation** that lasts over time as a *territory that is heavily defended* (咸 カン).

憾 憾 カン — *Feeling* 忄 *that remains a lasting sensation* 感 (カン) — 2006

regret

 辟 辟 ヘキ — *Imprisioned convict* — 2007 Ⓢ

A *convict* (辛) *sitting* (尸) in an *encircled space* (口): an imprisoned convict.

壁 壁 ヘキ かべ — *Earth* 土 *encircling an imprisoned convict* 辟 (ヘキ) — 2008

wall

癖 癖 ヘキ くせ — *Illness* 疒 *in an imprisoned convict* 辟 (ヘキ) — 2009

tendency

璧 璧 ヘキ — *Jewel* 玉 *buried next to sacrificed imprisoned convicts* 辟 (ヘキ) — 2010

ritual jade disc (*bi*)

 極 極 ① キョウ ② ゴク ② きわ.まる — *Person stretching between two extremes* — 2011

① to reach an extreme

② pole

Originally 亟 [二口勹又], an *outstretched hand* (又) placing a person who is *leaning* (勹) constricted by a *space delimited* (口) by two ends (二), one lower end and one upper end: A person that stretches between two **extremes**. Over time the component 木 (*tree-wood*) was added to the compound in order to reinforce the secondary meaning of **pole** that the character eventually adopted, depicting the 'pole' as a wooden element (木) that reaches two extremes (亟), the lower floor and the upper roof.

 図 **図** ①②ズ ①②ト ②はか.る *Drawing within an encircled space* ① **diagram** ② **to plan** 2012

Originally 圖 [口啚(口+亩)], an *encircled space* (口) in which a *person* (人 → 亠) moves from one space to another ((口×3) → (口 + 回)). In short, a representation within a two-dimensional plane of a route or path: a drawn **diagram**. Over time the inner strokes (啚) were simplified into the form 义.

凸 **凸** トツ *Convex space* **convex** 2013

A space coming out of an encircled space: a **convex** space.

凹 **凹** オウ *Concave space* **concave** 2014

A space subtracted from an encircled space: a **concave** space.

 亜 **亜** ア *Plant of a crypt for burials* **secondary** 2015 Ⓢ

Originally 亞, a crypt or underground burial chamber where deceased people of great importance like kings or aristocrats were buried together with precious belongings, sacrificed animals, and servants that were intended to accompany them in the afterlife, or so to say, the **secondary** life. The ground plants of ancient Chinese crypts were in the shape of a cross because of the symbolic implication that comes with adding an entrance door to each of the sides, highlighting the interconnection between the divine and the terrestrial. It is also said that this shape is due to an old belief saying that evil spirits hide in the corners, so eliminating the corners guaranteed a safe journey towards the other world.

Early examples of pictographic representations of crypts with objects and living beings

悪 アク 2016
悪 オ
わる.い

Feeling 心 arising from the sight of a crypt 亜(ア)

bad

田 田 デン 2017
た

rice field Ⓡ
Field Ⓜ

SPECIAL READING 田舎 [いなか]: *countryside*

A cultivated **rice field** or paddy seen from above, with visible separations (十) within an *encircled space* (囗).

界 カイ 2018
界

Jam 介(カイ) of fields 田

boundary

雷 ライ 2019
雷 かみなり

Phenomenon produced in a field 田 of rain 雨

thunder

畑 はた 2020
畑 はたけ

Fields 田 that can be burnt with fire 火

field

NOTE Alluding to **fields** that can be burned for regeneration, unlike rice fields that cannot be burned due to their watery condition.

奮 フン 2021
奮 ふる.う

Bird unfolding its wings 奞 over a field 田

to rouse

畔 ハン 2022
畔

Fields 田 divided in halves 半(ハン)

paddy ridge

累 ルイ 2023
累

Fields 田 tyed by a thread 糸

accumulation

町 チョウ 2024
町 まち

Fields 田 around which buildings are nailed 丁(チョウ)

neighborhood

畿 畿 キ

Fields 田 *where commercial activity is done* 幾(キ) → 戋 2025

suburbs of the capital city

略 略 リャク

Field 田 *becoming stationary* 各(ラク) 2026

abbreviation

 胃 胃 イ

Body part that digests products from the field 2027 Ⓜ

stomach

Part of the body (肉 → 月) in charge of digesting products from the *field* (田): the **stomach.**

膚 膚 フ

Something that ends up in the stomach 胃 *of a tiger* 虍 2028

epidermis

 曽 曽 ゾ ソウ

Field products distributed in a tasting mouth 2029 Ⓢ

former

Rice field (田) thanks to which food has been *distributed* (八 → ハ → ソ) towards a *mouth capable of tasting* it (甘 → 曰), a reference to the source of things, something that **former**ly took place.

僧 僧 ソウ

Person 亻 *next to former things* 曽(ソウ) 2030

monk

層 層 ソウ

Person 亻 *sitting on former things* 曽(ソウ) 2031

(social) **stratum**

憎 憎 ゾウ にく.む

Heart-mind 忄 *focusing on former things* 曽(ソウ) 2032

to hate

増 増 ゾウ ふ.える ま.す

Earth-soil 土 *with a former* 曽(ソウ) *history* 2033

to increase

贈
贈 ソウ ゾウ おく.る 2034

Money 貝 becoming a former thing 曽[ソウ]

to give as a gift

男
男 ダン ナン おとこ 2035 Ⓜ

Strength of the field

man

The working *strength* (力) in the *field* (田): the **man**.

虜
虜 リョ 2036

Man 男 under the jaws of a tiger 虍

captive

里
里 ② リ ① さと 2037 Ⓡ Ⓢ

Earth-soil next to fields

① hamlet

② **unit of land measurement** [*~0.5 km²*]

Earth-soil (土) surrounded by *fields* (田) where people reside: a **hamlet**. This character takes as its main meaning that of a **unit of land** measurement equivalent to half a square kilometer, a semantic association probably originating from the approximate size of a typical hamlet.

野
野 ヤ の 2038

What is before 予[ヨ] *hamlets 里*

plains

埋
埋 マイ う.める 2039

Earth-soil 土 filled with a hamlet 里

to fill up

厘
厘 リン 2040

Hamlet 里[リ] *limited by a cliff 厂*

unit of length [*0.3 mm*]

裏
裏 リ うら 2041

Hamlet 里[リ] *covered by clothes 衣*

undersurface

理
理 リ 2042

Jewels 王 around which a hamlet 里[リ] *forms*

reason

2043

塁 **塁** ルイ

Earth-soil surrounded by several fields
(military) **base**

Originally 壘 [畾土], *earth-soil* (土) encompassing several *fields* (田×3 → 畾 → (田 + 㐅). An extensive and well-stocked territory, capable of housing a military **base.**

2044 Ⓢ

苗 **苗** ビョウ なえ なわ-

Plants growing in a field
seedling

Plants (艹) growing in a *field* (田) thanks to a **seedling.**

2045

描 **描** ビョウ え.がく か.く

Hand 扌 *making seedlings* 苗 (ビョウ) *on a paper*
to paint
to draw

2046

猫 **猫** ビョウ ねこ

Animal 犭 *eating seedlings* 苗 (ビョウ)
cat

2047 Ⓢ

農 **農** ノウ

Person working with a tool over seedlings
agriculture

The activity professed by people that handle *agricultural tools* (辰) in order to work with *seedlings* (苗 → 曲): **agriculture.**

2048

濃 **濃** ノウ こ.い

Water 氵 *used in agriculture* 農 (ノウ)
dense

2049 Ⓢ

果 **果** ①② カ ② は.たす

Products coming from fields and trees
① **fruit**
② **to do completely**

SPECIAL READING 果物 [くだもの]: *fruit*

Field (田) and *tree* (木) represented as the elements capable of bearing **fruit.** The secondary meaning of **to do completely** derives from the analogy made between fruits and results coming out of doing something completely.

課 課 カ — *Speech* 訁 *with fruits* 果(カ) 2050

lesson

菓 菓 カ — *Plants* 艹 *and fruits* 果(カ) 2051

candy

裸 裸 ラ はだか — *Clothes* 衤 *peeled like a fruit* 果(カ) 2052

naked

SPECIAL READING 裸足 [はだし]: *barefoot*

 番 番 バン — *Isolated grains from a field* 2053 Ⓢ

number in a series

Each *isolated grain* (釆) of a *rice field* (田), a metaphorical representation of a particular number extracted from a larger **series of numbers.**

藩 藩 ハン — *Series* 番(バン) *of owned lands conformed by plants* 艹 *and water* 氵 2054

fiefdom

翻 翻 ホン ひるがえ.す — *Series* 番(バン) *of wing* 羽 *movements* 2055

to turn over

 彙 彙 イ — *Animals, fields and trees* 2056

same kind

Ideographic composition that reflects a figurative space that *delimits* (冖) the elements “animal” (彑), “*field*” (田) and “*tree*” (木): A group of elements that are capable of producing food, a group of elements of the **same kind.** The element 彑 is a reduction of the pictogram 象, similar to the component 豕 (*hog*), which indicates an animal with a large head, four legs and a tail, probably depicting a wild boar.

 畜 畜 チク — *Dim thing in the field* 2055 Ⓢ

livestock

Something that is *dim* (玄) within a wide *field* (田), but that is part of it. Ideographic composition referring to **livestock** understood as a complementary element to agriculture.

2058

蓄 チク
蓄 たくわ.える

Plants 艹 *and livestock* 畜 (チク)
to amass

2059

畝
畝 うね

Long mark in the field
furrow

Originally 畞 [田十久], a *thick mark* (十 → 亠) *longitudinally* (久) made in a *field* (田): a **furrow**.

2060

画
画 ① カク ② ガ

Hand making furrows in the field
① **brush-stroke**
② **picture**

Originally 畫 [聿田一], a hand holding a *brush* (聿 → 𦘒 → 丅) that draws, on a surface, some **strokes** (一 → 凵) like furrows on a field (田). This composition also represents the product produced by that brush: a **picture**.

REVIEW ON SPACES

上元云会雲亏示祭尉赤禁票平辛竟
競亲新竜章童業亘互五吾下凵去却
出屈

1 頑玩伝魂陰芸転絵曇顎誇汚芋奈禍視祝祉
礼神社祥祖禅福斎祈際慰款隷襟漂標呼評
坪辞接辣境鏡親薪滝籠襲彰障憧瞳鐘僕撲
恒垣悟語峠法蓋脚拙掘

冂夢冗壳殻愛憂隺軍帯円方放央市
⿱亠冂帝商

2 壱瞬塚写鬱冠沈枕堀読続穀曖優確鶴揮輝
滞妨肪訪倣坊防芳紡激敷傲映英姉肺柿傍
諦締嫡摘敵滴

口邑舎那擁郎郷因咅正是疑各路韋
合四谷固哀睘袁員周或成感辟極図
凸凹亜田胃曽男里塁苗農果番彙畜
畝画

3 囚団困菌圏国囲郊郡邪邦都郵邸捨舗響姻
恩咽倍培陪賠剖部婿証政礎疎整旋症題提
堤擬凝落格絡賂酪露偉韓緯沿船鉛俗欲浴
裕個箇錮環猿園損韻彫調惑域減憾壁癖璧
悪界雷畑奮畔累町畿略膚僧層憎増贈虜埋
厘裏野理描猫濃課菓裸藩翻蓄

CONSTRUCTIONS

1. WALLS AND ROOFS

The primordial part of any type of construction or building is the 'wall' 廴, which offers protection to the outside world. On top of the wall, made with a specific material such as 'tiles' 瓦, the 'roof' 宀 is placed, thus making a 'building' conformed by a 'wall and a roof' 广 that will be used to shelter people and things.

廴 廴

Wall 2061 Ⓡ Ⓜ

A schematic and distorted representation of a <u>wall</u> (ㇵ) placed perpendicularly to the ground (㇏).

建 建 ケン コン た.てる

Hand painting a wall with a brush 2062 Ⓢ

to build

A hand holding a *brush* (聿) used to paint a *wall and the ground* (廴), as an allegorical allusion to creation and, consequently, construction and **build**ing.

健 健 ケン すこ.やか

Person 亻 *able to build* 建 (ケン) 2063

healthy

鍵 鍵 ケン かぎ

Metal object 金 *made for buildings* 建 (ケン) 2064

key

廷 廷 テイ

People guarding the earth-soil behind a wall 2065 Ⓢ

court

A *person* (人 → 𠂉) managing the *earth-soil* (土 → 士) behind a *wall* (廴). The walls behind which those who manage the land are housed: A government palace or a **court**.

艇
艇 テイ

Boats 舟 used around the court 廷 (テイ) 2066

small boat

 延 **延** エン の.ばす

Foot crossing a wall 2067 Ⓢ

to stretch

A *foot entering* (正 → 疋) or crossing through a *wall* (廴), representing someone who **stretch**es his way beyond physical limits.

誕
誕 タン

Speech 言 commemorating the crossing of a wall 延 (エン) 2068

nativity

 瓦 **瓦** ガ かわら

ceramic tile 2069 Ⓡ Ⓜ

Schematic representation of a ceramic roof **tile**. The outer strokes (瓦) represent the edge of the tile, and the inner dot (丶) represents some kind of decoration or engraving.

瓶
瓶 ビン

Ceramic tiles 瓦 placed side by side 并 2070

jar

 宀 **宀** 宀

Roof 2071 Ⓡ Ⓜ

Under a roof

Two walls and a two-winged roof of a building. This pictograph is used semantically to reflect the idea of a place <u>under a roof</u>. The stroke at the top (丶) represents the top edge of the roof and the lower strokes (冖) represent the wings of the roof and two walls.

In some compounds this component takes the flattened form 宀, which is placed at the top of the compounds.

字
字 ジ あざ

What a child 子 (シ) *learns under a roof 宀* 2072

letter

SPECIAL READING 文字 [もじ]: *letter*

宮 宮 キュウ グウ ク みや 2073

Backbone 呂 of a kingdom protected under a roof 宀

royal residence

宴 宴 エン 2074

Women 女 speaking 日 under a roof 宀

banquet

宙 宙 チュウ 2075

Figurative roof 宀 that causes things 由

universe

宣 宣 セン 2076

Confined energy 亘 under the roof 宀 of a court

proclamation

寛 寛 カン 2077

Person looking 見 how plants 艹 grow under a roof 宀

leniency

宅 宅 タク 2078

Roof 宀 under which the sprout 乇 of a family can be conceived

residence

宵 宵 ショウ よい 2079

Time when grains and meat 肖 are stored under the roof 宀

early night

寮 寮 リョウ 2080

Place under a roof 宀 where bonfires 尞 are made

dormitory

蛇 蛇 ジャ ダ へび 2081

Serpent 虫 from which a person 匕 hides under the roof 宀

snake

寄 寄 キ よ.る 2082

Something unusual 奇 under a roof 宀

to draw near

寝 寝	シン ね.る	*Broom* 𠬶 (シン) *left on a table* 丬 *under a roof* 宀 **to lie down**	2083
宝 宝	ホウ たから	*Jewels* 玉 (ギョク) *kept under a roof* 宀 **treasure**	2084
賓 賓	ヒン	*Steps* 歩 → 𡳾 *of a person going towards a roofed* 宀 *place where he leaves money* 貝 **visitor**	2085
貯 貯	チョ	*Money* 貝 *nailed* 丁 (チョウ) *under a roof* 宀 **savings**	2086
寧 寧	ネイ	*Net* 罒 *of feelings* 心 *nailed* 丁 *under a roof* 宀 **composure**	2087
富 富	フ フウ とみ	*Big wine vessels* 畐 (フク) *kept under a roof* 宀 **to be rich**	2088
寡 寡	カ	*Head* 頁 → 頁 *under a roof* 宀 *that has been divided* 分 **widow** **scanty**	2089
室 室	シツ むろ	*Roofed place* 宀 *where one arrives* 至 (シ) *and stays* **room**	2090
寂 寂	ジャク セキ さび.しい	*Uncle* 叔 (シュク) *under a roof* 宀 **lonesome**	2091
宇 宇	ウ	*Roof* 宀 *from which energy in heaven unfolds* 于 **cosmos**	2092

宰
宰 サイ

Convicts 辛 under a roof 宀 2093

supervision

審
審 シン

Rice grains singled out from a field 番 inspected under a roof 宀 2094

scrutiny

内
内 ナイ ダイ うち

Person inside a roofed place 2095 Ⓢ

inside

A *person* (人) **inside** a place covered by a *roof* (冂 → 冂).

納
納 ノウ トウ ナッ ナ ナン おさ.まる

Threads 糸 going inside 内(ナイ) 2096

to fit into

安
安 ① アン ① ② やす.い

Woman under a roof 2097 Ⓢ

① **safe**

② cheap

A *woman* (女) *under a roof* (冂 → 宀), **safe** from external dangers. The meaning of **cheap** comes from a phonetic borrowing.

案
案 アン

Safe 安(アン) tree-woods 木 2098

proposal

守
守 シュ ス まも.る も.る

Work under a roof 2099 Ⓢ

to guard

Work (寸(スン)) done *under a roof* (冂 → 宀), **guard**ing the household and the family economy.

狩 狩 シュ か.り

Animal 犭 *brought under a roof by a working hand* 守 (シュ) 2100

hunting

 官 官 カン

Someone leaving traces under the roofs 2101 Ⓢ

bureaucrat

Someone who leaves *traces* (𠂤 → 㠯) *under the roofs* (冂 → 宀), either of the homes of people or government institutions: a **bureaucrat**.

棺 棺 カン

Wooden 木 *case used for dead bureaucrats* 官 (カン) 2102

coffin

管 管 カン くだ

Bamboo stalk ⺮ *used as a brush by bureaucrats* 官 (カン) 2103

tube

館 館 カン やかた

Place where bureaucrats 官 (カン) *eat* 𩙿 2104

building

 穴 穴 穴 ケツ あな

Roof through which energy is distributed 2105 Ⓡ Ⓜ

hole

A *roof* (冂 → 宀) through which energy can be *distributed* (八), a roof that allows matter to pass through it, a roof with a **hole**.

When this character appears as a component it adopts the slightly modified form 穴 and is placed at the top of the compounds.

突 突 トツ つ.く

Big person 大 *passing through a hole* 穴 2106

to poke

窓 窓 ソウ まど

Hole 穴 *through which the public heart-mind* 悤 (ソウ) → 忩 *can be seen* 2107

window

2108
究 究 キュウ きわ.める
Arm 九 (キュウ) rummaging through a hole 穴
to research

2109
窯 窯 ヨウ かま
Hole 穴 with fire 灬 where auspicious 羊 (ヨウ) things are burnt
kiln

2110
搾 搾 サク しぼ.る
Hand 扌 passing folded clothes 乍 (サク) through a hole 穴
to wring

2111
窃 窃 セツ
Cut 切 (セツ) made through a hole 穴
stealth

2112
窮 窮 キュウ きわ.まる
Body 身 bent like a bow 弓 (キョウ) stuck in a hole 穴
to take to the extreme

2113
窒 窒 チツ
Arrow arriving 至 (シ) at a hole 穴 and being stuck in there
blockage

2114
窟 窟 クツ
Hole 穴 in which people sit down and come out 屈 (クツ)
cavern

2115

商 商 ショウ あきな.う
Convict introduced through a hole into an encircled space
to trade

A *convict* (辛 → 立) introduced through a *hole* (穴 → 冗 → 冂) into an encircled space (囗), in reference to slave confinement and **trade**.

2116 Ⓢ

奐 奐 カン
Two hands taking a person out of a hole

Two *outstretched hands* (廾 → 大) taking out a *leaning person* (勹 → ⺈) who was stuck in a *hole* (穴 → 冗 → 冂).

喚 喚 カン — *Shouting mouth* 口 *of a person who is taken out of a hole* 奐 (カン) 2117

scream

換 換 カン か.える — *Hand* 扌 *taking someone out of a hole* 奐 (カン) 2118

to substitute

NOTE This character can be interpreted as a representation of assisted childbirth, understood as the **substitution** of a generation for another.

罙 罙 — *Wooden stick being introduced into a hole* 2119 Ⓜ

Originally 宷 [穴木], a *wooden* (木) stick being <u>introduced</u> into a *hole* (穴 → 穴).

探 探 タン さが.す さぐ.る — *Hand* 扌 *introducing a wooden stick into a hole* 罙 2120

to look for

深 深 シン ふか.い — *Water-filled* 氵 *hole into which one can introduce a stick* 罙 2121

deep

空 空 ①②クウ ①あ.ける ①から ②そら — *Hole made with a hoe* 2122 Ⓢ

① **to empty**

② **sky**

A *hoe* (工) making a *hole* (穴 → 穴), creating an **empty** space. The notion of ‘empty space’ was later taken in Japanese also to designate the concept of **sky**.

控 控 コウ ひか.える — *Hand* 扌 *that is empty* 空 (クウ) 2123

to not do too much

宛 宛 エン あ.てる — *Huddled person at night under a roof* 2124 Ⓢ

to address

Someone who returns to a place *under a roof* (冂 → 宀) in which he can *huddle in the evening* (宛 エン) to sleep, somewhere considered as one's home, where his **address** is situated at.

腕 腕 ワン うで 2125

Body part 月 able to address 宛 (エン) something

arm

奥 奥 オウ おく 2126

Two hands placing rice under a roof

interior

Two hands (廾 → 大) depositing grains of *rice* (米) inside a place protected by a *roof* (冖 → 宀), referring to the action of keeping something inside, in the **interior**.

家 家 カ ケ いえ や 2127 Ⓢ

Hogs under a roof

house

A *roof* (冖 → 宀) under which *hogs* (豕) are raised, in reference to a household capable of sustaining itself through food production: a **house**.

嫁 嫁 カ とつ.ぐ よめ 2128

Woman 女 brought to a house 家 (カ)

wedding

稼 稼 カ かせ.ぐ 2129

Fruitful 禾 house 家 (カ)

to earn

宜 宜 ギ 2130 Ⓜ

Altar of sacrifice placed under a roof

appropriate

An *altar of sacrifice* (且) placed *under a roof* (冖 → 宀) to be protected from the elements, something more **appropriate** or suitable than placing it outside.

畳 畳 ジョウ たたみ 2131

Figurative field 田 in which it is appropriate 宜 → 冝 to sit on

tatami

2132 Ⓜ

𡨄

Two hands storing hoes under a roof

Shelter

Two hands (廾 → ハ) putting several tools like *hoes* (工×4 → 㠭 → 井) in a place protected by a *roof* (冂 → 宀), a <u>shelter</u> that serves as a warehouse.

2133

寒 寒 カン さむ.い

Ice 冫 *making people seek a shelter* 𡨄

cold

2134

塞 塞 サイ ソク ふさ.ぐ

Earth 土 *mounds before a shelter* 𡨄

to stand in the way

2135 Ⓢ

宿 宿 シュク やど

Roof under which one hundred people can sleep

lodging

A *roof* (冂 → 宀) under which *one hundred* (百) *people* (人 → イ) can sleep: a **lodging** or an inn.

2136

縮 縮 シュク ちぢ.む

Tiny 糸 *lodging* 宿 (シュク)

to shrink

2137 Ⓢ

宓 宓 ミツ

Necessity under a roof

Concealing

Something *necessary* (必 (ひつ)) *under a roof* (冂 → 宀), alluding to the necessities of a household, something that usually is <u>conceal</u>ed to people outside the family.

2138

密 密 ミツ

Something concealed 宓 (ミツ) *behind a mountain* 山

secrecy

2139

蜜 蜜 ミツ

Something produced by concealed 宓 (ミツ) *insects* 虫

honey

寅 寅 イン

Archery under a roof

tiger sign (Chinese zodiac)

2140 ㊔ Ⓢ

Two hands holding an *arrow* ((廾 ≈ 臼 + 矢) → (日 + 夫) → 寅) *under a roof* (宀), implying the practice of indoors archery, reinforcing the idea of archery practiced for training or fun, as opposed to archery done in hunting or warfare.

演 演 エン

Archery 寅 (イン) *made in a place surrounded by water* 氵

performance

2141

完 完 カン

Roof over a person

completion

2142 Ⓢ

A *roof* (冂 → 宀) *over a person* (元 (ゲン)), an image of a building **completed** with a roof under which people can stay.

院 院 イン

Building completed 完 (カン) *next to the mountains* 阝

institutional building

institution

2143

NOTE Probably originally referring to religious temples, which used to be built near mountains.

宗 宗 シュウ ソウ

Divine power under a roof

religion

2144 Ⓢ

Divine power (示) appearing or being interpreted *under a roof* (冂 → 宀), in reference to a building where a connection with the divine is established: a temple dedicated to **religion**.

踪 踪 ソウ

Feet 𧾷 *around a religious* 宗 (ソウ) *building*

whereabouts

2145

崇 崇 スウ

Sacred mountain 山 *important for religion* 宗 (ソウ)

adoration

2146

寮 察 サツ

Worshipping made under a roof

observation

2147 (S)

A *worshipping* (祭 [サイ]) or offering of sacrifices made *under a roof* (冂 → 宀), a religious activity that can be done in more detail and attentive **observation** than if it were performed outdoors.

擦 擦 サツ す.る

Hand 扌 *movement made with deep observation* 察 [サツ]

to rub

2148

向 向 コウ む.かう

Roof over an encircled space

to face towards

2149 (M)

A *roof* (冂) **facing towards** the ground formed by an *encircled space* (口).

尚 尚 龸 ショウ

Open space

yet

2150 (S)

A roof and an encircled space (向) through which energy can be *distributed* (八 → ハ → ソ), implicitly representing a building with some kind of <u>opening</u> whereby energy or air can pass: A place that is **yet** to be finished.

When acting as a component, this graph takes the modified form 龸, which is placed on top of the compounds.

党 党 トウ

Place open 龸 [ショウ] *for a person* 儿

political faction

2151

掌 掌 ショウ

Open 龸 [ショウ] *hand* 手

handling

2152

堂 堂 ドウ

Open 龸 [ショウ] *earth-soil* 土

hall

2153

常 常	ジョウ つね とこ		*Open* 尚(ショウ) *cloth* 巾 **usual**	2154
	賞 賞	ショウ	*Open money* **reward**	2155 Ⓢ

Money (貝) that is distributed in an *open space* (尚(ショウ) → 龸), or that is figuratively open for any participant: a prize or **reward**.

償 償	ショウ つぐな.う	*Person* 亻 *giving a reward* 賞(ショウ) **to compensate** (for)	2156

	定 定	ジョウ テイ さだ.める	*Roof under which a foot enters* **to settle**	2157 Ⓢ

A *roof* (宀 → 宀) under which there is a space in which a *foot enters* (正(セイ) → 疋), **settling** inside.

綻 綻	タン ほころ.びる	*Plant threadx* 糸 *settled* 定 *to grow* **to begin to open**	2158
錠 錠	ジョウ	*Metal* 金 *that is settled* 定(ジョウ) **lock**	2159

	客 客	キャク カク	*Stationary person under a roof* **guest**	2160 Ⓢ

Person being *stationary* (各(カク)) *under a roof* (宀 → 宀), hosted as a **guest**.

2161

額

額

① ガク

② ひたい

Part of the head 頁 that stands still under the figurative roof that is the crown 客 (キャク)

① ② **forehead**

① picture frame

2162

容

容

ヨウ

Valley under a roof

container [*fig.*]

Ⓢ

A *roof* (冂 → 宀) covering a *valley* (谷 (ヨク)), image understood allegorically as a cavity in which there may be some content, a valley covered with a roof conceived as a figurative **container**.

2163

溶

溶

ヨウ

と.ける

Water 氵 *poured into a container* 容 (ヨウ)

to dissolve

2164

実

実

① ジツ

② み

③ みの.る

Fruits kept under the roof

① **reality**

② **substance**

③ **to bear fruit**

Originally 實 [宀貫], everything that *passes through* (貫) the *roof* (冂 → 宀), interpreted as the celestial roof, the sky, or the universe as it is also reflected in the characters 宙 (*universe*) and 宇 (*cosmos*). Everything that happens under the sky: **reality**. Over time the component 貫 was abbreviated into the form 夫, thus creating the current simplified version 実. The meaning of 'reality' also derives in the notion of 'what is real', which in turn derives into the concept of **substance**, and that of 'making reality' or **to bear fruit**.

2165

𤇾 龸

エイ

Roof covered with flames

Ⓢ

Originally 𤇾, a *roof* (冂 → 宀 → 冖) covered with *fire* flames (火×2 → 炏). The meaning of this component may have a figurative sense, which lets interpret the notion of <u>covered with flames</u> as something that instigates energy or vigor. Currently this component always appears in its simplified version 龸.

営 **営** エイ いとな.む — *Backbones 呂 covered with flames ⺍* — **to conduct** — 2166

労 **労** ロウ — *Arm 力 covered with flames ⺍* — **labor** — 2167

栄 **栄** エイ さか.える は.える — *Tree-wood 木 covered with flames ⺍* — **to flourish** — 2168

蛍 **蛍** ケイ はたる — *An insect 虫 covered with flames ⺍* — **firefly** — 2169

 𦥯 ⺍ カク — *Building of a roof* — 2170 Ⓢ

Originally 𦥯 [臼爻冖], *two hands* (臼) laying wooden bars (爻) in order to build a *roof* (冂 → 宀 → 冖), sense that is used mainly in a figurative way to imply some sort of acquired knowledge. Currently this component always appears in its simplified version ⺍, which looks graphically identical to the also simplified version of the component 𤇾 (*roof covered with flames*).

学 **学** ガク まな.ぶ — *Child's 子 roof being built ⺍* — **to learn** — 2171

覚 **覚** カク おぼ.える さ.める — *Person looking 見 how his roof is being built ⺍* — **to become aware** — 2172

 六 **六** ロク むっ.つ — *Hut* — **six** — 2173 Ⓜ

SPECIAL READING 六日 [むいか]: *sixth day of the month*

A pictographic representation of a hut with a roof with two protruding wings (亠) and two walls (八), leading to a graphic composition quite similar to the component 冂 (*roof*). This character was chosen in ancient times to denote the meaning **six** for its phonetic value, the pictograph of a hut, nevertheless, can be figuratively understood as a place that has six directions: four walls (south, north, east, west), the roof (top), and the floor (bottom).

冥 冥 メイ ミョウ *Sunlight 日 delimited 冖 by a hut 六* 2174

gloom

广 广 ゲン *Wall and roof* 2175 Ⓡ

Building Ⓜ

A roof (亠) and a wall (丿), simultaneously representing the exterior and the interior part of a building.

応 応 オウ こた.える *Building 广 for the heart-mind 心* 2176

to respond

序 序 ジョ *What is built before 予 (ヨ) the walls and roof 广* 2177

preface

庁 庁 チョウ *Building 广 that is nailed 丁 (チョウ)* 2178

government office

座 座 ザ すわ.る *People working in pottery wheels 坐 (ザ) inside a building 广* 2179

to sit

店 店 テン みせ *Building 广 where things are taken up 占 (セン)* 2180

shop

床 床 ショウ ① とこ ② ゆか *Wooden 木 object inside a building 广* 2181

① **bed**

① **floor**

NOTE The second meaning of **floor** was taken as a derivation of the original meaning of **bed**, since ancient Chinese people used to sleep—have beds—on the floor.

廉 2182
廉 レン
People working simultaneously 兼 inside a building 广
respectable

粧 2183
粧 ショウ
Grains 米 and earth 土 decorating the walls and roof of a building 广
cosmetics

庫 2184
庫 コ ク
Building 广 where chariots 車 are kept
warehouse

底 2185
底 テイ そこ
Building's 广 ground 氏(テイ)
bottom

廃 2186
廃 ハイ すた.れる
Something launched 発(ハツ) inside a building 广
to go out of use

廊 2187
廊 ロウ
Building's 广 offspring 郎(ロウ)
outside corridor

庭 2188
庭 テイ にわ
Part of a building 广 where the court 廷(テイ) plays
garden

府 2189 Ⓢ
府 フ
Building to which people are attached
bureaucratic office
borough

A governmental *building* (广) or **borough** to which people are *attached* (付(フ)) since certain important bureaucratic procedures are carried out there.

腐 2190
腐 フ くさ.る
Meat 肉 left in a bureaucratic office 府(フ)
to rot

広 2191 Ⓢ
広 コウ ひろ.い
Building with flowing energy inside
wide

A *building* (广) with a **wide** space in its interior through which energy can *flow* (ム).

拡 2192
拡 カク
Hand 扌 *widening* 広 (コウ)
extension

鉱 2193
鉱 コウ
Metal 釒 *that is wide* 広 (コウ)
mineral

庶 2194 Ⓢ
庶 庶 广 ショ
Words beside a fireplace inside a building
multitude

Mouths (廿 ← 口) talking around the *fire* (火 → 灬) of a fireplace inside a *building* (广): An activity carried out by a **multitude** of people.

When this character acts as a component it takes the abbreviated form 广, which is placed at the top of the compounds.

席 2195
席 セキ
Multitude 广 (ショ) *of cloths* 巾
seat

SPECIAL READING 寄席 [よせ]: *entertainment hall*

NOTE In clear reference to the floor seats that were used by the ancient Chinese and that is still used in Japan.

度 2196 Ⓢ
度 度
① ド
① ト
② タク
② たび
Multitude of outstretched hands
① **degree** (of)
② **occasion**

A *multitude* (庶 → 广) of outstretched *hands* (又) having the **occasion** of measuring something comparatively, checking the **degree** of its extension.

渡 2197
渡 ト
わた.る
Water 氵 *whose degree* 度 (ト) *of depth has been checked*
to cross over

2198 Ⓢ

麻 麻 マ あさ

Trees inside a building

hemp

A *grove* (林) of plants that can be seen inside *buildings* (广), as **hemp** was formerly widely used for the manufacture of simple and comfortable clothing that can be worn at home.

2199

摩 摩 マ

Hand 手 *touching hemp* 麻 (マ)

friction

2200

魔 魔 マ

Ghosts 鬼 *emerging from the intake of hemp* 麻 (マ)

demon

NOTE Hemp can be associated with hallucinations—and visions of **demons**—due to the psychoactive effects appearing when the plant is smoked.

2201

磨 磨 マ みが.く

Stone 石 *smoothing hemp* 麻 (マ)

to polish

2202

厳 厳 ゲン ゴン きび.しい おごそ.か

Words bravely pronounced inside a building

severe

Originally 嚴 [吅广敢], several *words* (口×2 → 吅 → 䒑) pronounced *bravely* (敢 (カン)) inside a *building* (广), referring to a **severe** behavior either at home or within governmental institutions.

2. DOORS

While the essential structural elements of a building are the walls and roofs, it is equally certain that for a building to be truly functional it must have a 'door' 戸 that serves as an entrance and exit. If the building is large enough, it will have a matching door, with two panels, a big door or 'gate' 門, that can be wide open, thus becoming an 'open door' 卯 useful to allow the flow of people.

 戸 戸 コ と **door** 2203 Ⓡ Ⓜ

Originally 戶, a pictograph of a **door**, with a jamb (丿) and a single panel (日 → 可).

肩 肩 ケン かた *Body part 月 that moves like a door panel 戸* 2204

shoulder

炉 炉 ロ *Fire 火 behind a door 戸* 2205

hearth

扇 扇 セン おうぎ *Wing-shaped 羽 object that moves like a door 戸* 2206

fan

扉 扉 ヒ とびら *Door 戸 that has panels flapping against each other like two opposed wings 非 (ヒ)* 2207

front door

所 所 ショ ところ *Door 戸 defended by an axe 斤* 2208

place

SPECIAL READING 所為 [せい]: *consequence*

房 房 ボウ ふさ *Something pointing towards 方 (ホウ) the threshold of a door 戸* 2209

tuft

啓 啓 ケイ *Hand hitting 攵 a door 戸 off making an encircled open space 口* 2210

disclosure

 戻 戻 レイ もど.る *Person walking through a door* 2211 Ⓢ

to turn back

A *person seen from the front* (大) coming in through a *door* (戸), as he **turns back** home.

涙 2212

涙 ルイ なみだ

Water drops 氵 emerging when someone turns back 戻 (ルイ) after a long trip

tears

2213 Ⓢ

雇 雇 コ やと.う

Bird returning through a door

to employ

A messenger *bird* (隹) that, after being thrown into the air, returns home and passes through the *door* (戸) of the house: An animal that can be **employed** to perform a certain function.

顧 2214

顧 コ かえり.みる

Returning bird's 雇 (コ) head 頁

to look back

2215 Ⓢ

扁 扁 ヘン

Book beneath a door

A *book* (卌 → 冊) introduced beneath the threshold of a *door* (戸).

偏 2216

偏 ヘン かたよ.る

Person 亻 picking up a book left beneath a door 扁 (ヘン)

to incline

編 2217

編 ヘン あ.む

Thread 糸 tying books that are left beneath a door 扁 (ヘン)

to compile

2218 Ⓢ

倉 倉 ソウ くら

Place behind a door where objects come together

storehouse

A place behind a *door* (戸 ← 戸) where several objects *come together* (合 (ゴウ) → (亼 + 口)): a **storehouse.**

創 2219

創 ソウ つく.る

Storehouse 倉 (ソウ) wherein material is cut with a dagger 刂

to prepare

門 門 | モン かど | *Two doors* **gate** | 2220 Ⓡ Ⓜ

Two *door* panels ((戸 ← 戸)×2 → (門 ≈ 門) forming a two-panel door: a big door or a **gate**. As a component this character takes the plural meaning of doors.

關 関 | カン かか.わる せき | *Knobs 关 and their doors 門* **to be related** | 2221

聞 聞 | ブン モン き.く | *Ear 耳 attached to doors 門(モン)* **to listen** | 2222

問 問 | モン と.う とん | *Words 口 opening doors 門(モン)* **to ask** | 2223

閱 閲 | エツ | *Exposure 兑(エツ) of what is behind the doors 門* **inspection** | 2224

闇 闇 | やみ | *Sounds 音 heard behind the doors 門 as a clue of what is behind them and cannot be seen* **darkness** | 2225

閑 閑 | カン | *Wooden 木 bar placed against the doors 門 in order to avoid disturbance* **quiet** | 2226

欄 欄 | ラン | *Tree-wood 木 element sustaining doors 門 that stand like a backpack 柬 stuck in the ground* **column** | 2227

閉 閉 | ヘイ し.める と.じる | *Several lifted sticks 才(サイ) placed against the doors 門 as a lock* **to close** | 2228

鬪 鬪 トウ たたか.う — *Doors* 門 *behind which there are lidded bowls* 豆 (トウ) *and work* 寸 — **to contend** 2229

NOTE This character can be understood as a depiction of a rudimentary manufacturing group making products that have to compete and **contend** in the market.

開 開 カイ あ.ける ひら.く — *Two bidents* 开 (ケイ) *pushed against doors* 門 — **to open** 2230

閥 閥 バツ — *Craft link between people felling trees* 伐 (バツ) *and people making doors* 門 — **lineage** 2231

閣 閣 カク — *Stationary place* 各 (カク) *behind doors* 門 — **chamber** 2232

間 間 間 カン ケン あいだ ま — *Sunlight passing through the threshold of a door* — **interval** 2233 Ⓢ

Sunlight (日) passing through the spatial **interval** left by the threshold of a *door* (門).

簡 簡 カン — *Bamboo strips'* ⺮ *intervals* 間 (カン) — **brief** 2234

閏 閏 閏 ジュン — *King passing through doors* — intercalation 2235 ㊔ Ⓢ

A *king* (王) passing through the *doors* (門) of a palace upon being crowned, succeeding a previous king and preceding a later king, forming part of an intercalation of royal successors.

潤 潤 ジュン うるお.う — *Water* 氵 *intercalations* 閏 (ジュン) — **to be moist** 2236

卯 卯 卯 リュウ — *Open door* — rabbit sign (Chinese zodiac) 2237 ㊔ Ⓢ

The two panels of an open door, turned outwards. The graph 卯 is a simplification of the original form 丣, which is a modification of the component 門 (門, *door*), thus graphically suggesting the opening of the panels through the inversion of the elements.

柳 柳 リュウ やなぎ — *Tree* 木 *whose branches open outwards like an open door* 卯 (リュウ) — **willow tree** (*Salix alba*) 2238

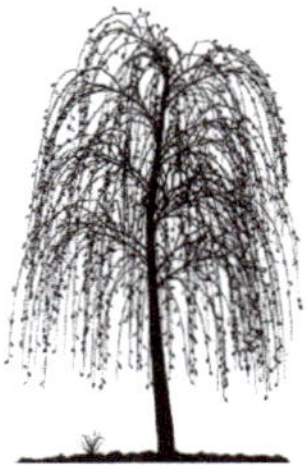

A willow tree

貿 貿 ボウ — *Door open* 卯 → 卯 *to money* 貝 — **commerce** 2239

留 留 留 リュウ ル と.める — *Door open to a field* — **to stay put** 2240 Ⓢ

A *door open* (卯 (リュウ) → 卯) to a *field* (田), where the peasants had to **stay put** working.

瑠 瑠 ル — *Jewel* 王 *that stays put* 留 (ル) — **lapis lazuli** 2241

3. TALL BUILDINGS

When construction techniques reach a certain level in a society, tall buildings begin to appear. One of the early tall buildings were the watchtowers 帛 京, which were used to defend the population of big cities or the 'capital cities' of kingdoms. The watchtower functions, within Chinese characters, as the main element from which several characters related to large-scale constructions derive.

帛	京 京	キョウ ケイ	*Watchtower* **capital city**	2242 Ⓢ

A watchtower, placed somewhere to defend a town or a population of significant size where important people live. The upper strokes 亠 reflect the two winged roof of the tower, the central strokes 口 show the upper part of the tower, that seems to have a window to facilitate surveillance, and the lower strokes 小 are a depiction of the base of the tower that elevates the structure as a whole. When this glyph appears on its own, it takes the associated meaning of **capital city**, related to the notion of a big city protected by watchtowers.

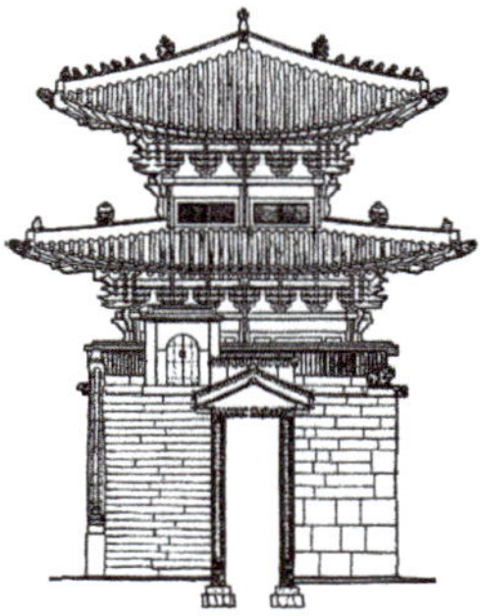

Model of a Chinese watchtower

涼 涼	リョウ すず.しい	*Water flow* 氵 *surrounding a watchtower* 京 **refreshing**	2243
鯨 鯨	ゲイ くじら	*Fish* 魚 *visible from a watchtower* 京 (ケイ) **whale**	2244

2245 Ⓢ

就 **就** シュウ ジュ つ.く

Arm reaching a watchtower

to attain

A person *raising his arm* (尤) to reach a *watchtower* (京), conquering it: someone **attain**ing an intended goal.

2246

蹴 **蹴** シュウ け.る

Foot ⻊ *on an attained watchtower* 就 [シュウ]

to kick

2247 Ⓢ

景 **景** ケイ

Sun illuminating the views from a watchtower

scenery

SPECIAL READING 景色 [けしき]: *scenery*

The *sun* (日 → 日) illuminating a **scenery** seen from the top of a *watchtower* (京 [ケイ]).

2248

憬 **憬** ケイ

Heart-mind 忄 *aroused from the view of a scenery* 景 [ケイ]

aspiration

2249

影 **影** エイ かげ

Scenery 景 [ケイ] *covered by hair* 彡

shadow

2250 Ⓢ

享 **享** キョウ

Child in a watchtawer

enjoyment

Ideographic representation of a *child* (子) inside a *watchtower* (京 [キョウ] → 古), bringing **enjoyment** to the otherwise rather dull place.

2251

郭 **郭** カク

Enjoyment 享 [キョウ] *of a town* 阝

fortification

2252 Ⓢ

孰 **孰** ジュク

Person working with enjoyment

A person *working with his hands* (丮 → 丸) while he is *enjoying* (享) himself.

熟 熟 ジュク う.れる — *Working with enjoyment* 孰 (ジュク) *burnt with fire* 灬 — **mature** 2253

塾 塾 ジュク — *Earth-soil* 土 *where people work with enjoyment* 孰 (ジュク) — **cram school** 2254

 高 高 コウ たか.い — *Tall tower* — **high** 2255 Ⓢ

A *watchtower* (京 (キョウ) → 亠) with a large *encircled space* (囗) at its base, denoting a large size and, consequently, also a great **height**.

稿 稿 コウ — *Fruitful* 禾 *tall tower* 高 (コウ) — **draft** 2256

NOTE It represents, figuratively, the idea of having to draw a plan or write a **draft** before building any edification such as a tall tower that is stable and serves its purpose.

豪 豪 ゴウ — *Hog* 豕 *inside a tall tower* 高 → 亠 — **extraordinary** 2257

 喬 喬 キョウ — *Person on top of a tall tower* — tall 2258 ㊔ Ⓢ

A person *wiggling* (夭) as he waves his hands or moves on top of a *tall tower* (高 (コウ) → 冋).

橋 橋 キョウ はし — *Tree-wood* 木 *tall structure on top of which a person can pass through* 喬 (キョウ) — **bridge** 2259

矯 矯 キョウ た.める — *Arrow* 矢 *thrown by a person from the top of a tower* 喬 (キョウ) — **to straighten** 2260

亭
亭 テイ — *Nailed tower* — **pavilion** 2261 Ⓢ

A building with a structure similar to that of a *tall tower* (高 → 亠), rising above the ground by means of a series of columns with the appearance of large *nails* (丁 テイ) instead of a stone or earth base that forms an encircled space or enclosure as it is depicted in the character 高 (*big tower*): a Chinese **pavilion.**

Model of an ancient Chinese pavilion

停
停 テイ — *Person 亻 stopping by a pavilion 亭 (テイ)* — **halt** 2262

复
复 フク — *Foot getting in and coming out of a tower* 2263 Ⓢ

Originally 复 [亯夂], and then 复, a *foot pointing downwards* (夂), coming out of a *tower* (高 → 亯 → 亩 → 白) from which it has previously entered. Ideogram suggesting the getting in and coming out of a place.

腹
腹 フク はら — *Body part 月 that goes in and out 复 (フク)* — **abdomen** 2264

SPECIAL READING お腹 [おなか]: *belly*

複
複 フク — *Clothes 衤 going in and out 复 (フク)* — **double fold** 2265

2266

厚 **厚** コウ あつ.い

Tall tower that has fallen off a cliff

thick

This character in its current version masks its etymological graphic origin due to the confusion and modification of the strokes through analogies. When looking at its original graphic form, however, its ideographic sense becomes fairly clear. This character represents a high tower turned upside down (高 → 亯 → 㫗 → 𣆪) under a *cliff* (厂). The part 子, now graphically identical to the component for "child", arises from the confusion of the strokes of the lower part of the tower turned upside down (𠂢) with the primitive form of the "child" character (𠂢 ≈ 孚 ← 子), most probably also due to the influence of the graphic analogy with the character 享 (*child in a watchtower*). Be it as it may, the original image therefore reflects the idea of a tall tower that has overturned and fallen over a cliff due to its **thick**ness and weight.

2267

壇 **壇** タン ダン

Earth-soil over which a tower is built

platform

This character is a derivation of the primitive pictogram 亩, which schematically represents a raised rudimentary construction, probably a barn, with a pointed roof (亠) and a middle structure with some type of opening (回). Over time, the component 旦 (タン) (*sun rising over the ground*) was added to the pictogram for its phonetic and semantic value, suggesting the notion of height. Eventually another component was added, 土 (*earth-soil*), in order to specify that the composition refers to a structure placed on the ground. The meaning of this compound finally becomes that of **plat**form, associated with the notion of a raised building or place.

4. ROADS

After having traveled all over the World of Kanji, we come across an allegorical element that sums up very well the entire journey undertaken so far: the road, since roads 行 on which people 'go' are used as figurative or physical guide to a safe journey for both the student and the traveler.

2268 Ⓡ Ⓜ

行 行 行

① ギョウ
① コウ
① アン
① い.く
① ゆ.く
② おこな.う

Roads
① to go
② to carry out

SPECIAL READING 流行る [はやる]: *to be popular*

Pictogram that represents an intersection between four roads, denoting physical or figurative ways to **go**. The original pictogram represented said roads with a quadrangular shape: , but later strokes began to be distorted, turning into the more slanted form  (行).

When the character acts as a component its compositional elements may become more spaced to make room for other components in the middle: 彳亍.

2269
街 街
ガイ
カイ
まち
Roads 彳亍 paved with earth 土
street

2270
桁 桁
けた
Tree-wood 木 pieces seen on roads 行
beam

2271
衝 衝
ショウ
Roads 彳亍 getting piled up with earth 重 (ジュウ)
collision

2272
術 術
ジュツ
Roads 彳亍 separated from the rest 朮 ジュツ
technique

2273
衡 衡
コウ
Roads 彳亍 with big 大 corners 角 → 𩵋
balance

2274
衛 衛
エイ
Roads 彳亍 on top of which feet can move around 韋 (イ)
protection

彳	⺅ 彳	*Road*	2275 Ⓡ Ⓜ

One of the <u>roads</u> that intersect at a crossroad (行 → 彳).

律 律	リツ リチ	*Road 彳 drawn with a brush 聿* **arrangement**	2276
役 役	ヤク エキ	*Road 彳 defended with maces 殳* **duty**	2277
徹 徹	テツ	*Figurative road 彳 helping a child being brought up by hitting* 敵テツ **thoroughness**	2278
得 得	トク え.る う.る	*Road 彳 on which people work 寸 since the daybreak 旦* **to gain**	2279
径 径	ケイ	*Figurative road 彳 going through a potter's wheel on which a hand is working* 圣ケイ **diameter**	2280
徒 徒	ト	*Road 彳 used as the path on top of which feet run 走* **on foot**	2281
待 待	タイ ま.つ	*Road 彳 towards a temple 寺* **to wait**	2282
微 微	ビ	*Person kneeling 儿 → 兀 as he goes through a road 彳 in the mountain 山 while being hit 攵* **faint**	2283

SPECIAL READING 微笑む [ほほえむ]: *to smile*

徐 徐 ジョ | *Road 彳 becoming remains 余* (ヨ) | **gradually** 2284

彼 彼 ① ヒ ① かの ② かれ | *Road's 彳 skin 皮* (ヒ) | ① **that** ② **he** 2285

NOTE The skin of a street serves as a reference to the visible face of things, on the street or not, something—**that**—which can be easily seen and pointed out. The meaning of **he** is a clear semantic association with the meaning of 'that'.

後 後 ①② ゴ ①② コウ ①② あと ① うし.ろ ② のち ③ おく.れる | *Still foot 夂 figuratively hanging like a cocoon 幺 on a road 彳* | ① **behind** ② **later** ③ **to be late** 2286

SPECIAL READING 明後日 [あさって]: *day after tomorrow*

NOTE Understood as a metaphorical reference to the slow movement of someone who falls **behind**.

往 往 オウ | *Road's 彳 main 主 course* | **journey** 2287

御 御 ギョ ゴ おん- | *Road 彳 where people work using mortars and pestles 卸* | **honorable** 2288

徳 徳 トク | *Road 彳 leading to straight feelings 恵* | **virtue** 2289

循 循 ジュン | *Road 彳 round like a shield 盾* (ジュン) | **circulation** 2290

征 征 セイ 2291

Road 彳 towards which one enters 正(セイ)

conquest

従 従 ジュウ ジュ ショウ したが.う 2292 Ⓢ

People's footsteps on a road

to follow

Originally 從, several *people* (人×2 → 从 → 䒑) **following** each other's *footsteps* (止 → 龰) on a *road* (彳).

縦 縦 ジュウ たて 2293

Threads 糸 *following* 従(ジュウ) *each other in a loom*

vertical height

徴 徴 チョウ 2294 Ⓢ

Road leading to a mountain of jewels that can be mined

indication

A *road* (彳) leading to a *mountain* (山) with *jewels* (玉 → 王) inside that can be mined with a *mattock* (攵), an **indication** guiding someone to some valuable place.

懲 懲 チョウ こ.りる 2295

Indications 徴(チョウ) *of the heart-mind* 心

to learn by experience

復 復 フク 2296 Ⓢ

Road where people goes in and out

time and again

A foot that goes *in and out* (复(フク)) on a *road* (彳), a road that is walked **time and again**.

履 履 リ は.く 2297

Sitting 尸 *time and again* 復

to put on (lower-body clothing)

覆 フク おお.う くつがえ.す — *Something that is done to a bag 襾 time and again 復 (フク)* 2298
to cover

辵 辶 — *Foot on a road* 2299
Movement Ⓡ Ⓜ

Originally 辵 [彡⺊], and later 辶, *footsteps* (止 → ⺊ → ⻌) on a *road* (彳 → 彡 → 氵 → 丶), indicating movement.

迅 ジン — *Movement* 辶 *of a working person* 丸 → 卂 2300
rapid

迎 ゲイ むか.える — *Person moving* 辶 *to kneel before another person* 卬 2301
to go out to meet

逆 ギャク さか.らう — *Movement* 辶 *going upside down* 屰 2302
to go against

遇 グウ — *Movement* 辶 *incited by a masked dancer* 禺 (グ) 2303
encounter

退 タイ しりぞ.く — *Movement* 辶 *becoming still* 艮 2304
to step aside

過 ① カ ① す.ぎる ② あやま.ち — *Movement* 辶 *of a pile of bones and backbones* 咼 (カ) 2305
① **to go beyond**
② fault

NOTE A pile of bones that indicates the sense of dying, and a movement that connotes the sense of the afterlife. A pile of bones moving as an allegory of the soul **going beyond**.

送 ソウ おく.る — *Movement* 辶 *instigated by an opening* 关 2306
to send (off)

選 選 セン えら.ぶ — *Movement ⻌ of two circulating energies 已×2 acting together 共* 2307

to choose

遡 遡 ソ さかのぼ.る — *Movement ⻌ of a new moon* 朔 ソ 2308

to go back

巡 巡 ジュン めぐ.る — *Movement ⻌ of a stream of water* 巛 2309

to go around

返 返 ヘン かえ.す — *Movement ⻌ reversing* 反 ハン 2310

to return (something)

逃 逃 トウ に.げる のが.れる — *Movement ⻌ incited by a bad omen* 兆 チョウ 2311

to escape

途 途 ト — *Movement ⻌ that remains* 余 2312

route

速 速 ソク はや.い すみ.やか — *Movement ⻌ in a bundle* 束 ソク 2313

quick

遭 遭 ソウ あ.う — *Movement ⻌ of sergeants and soldiers* 曹 ソウ 2314

to come across

透 透 トウ す.ける — *Movement ⻌ that is excelling* 秀 シュウ 2315

to show through

述 述 ジュツ の.べる — *Movement ⻌ of a hand separating a grain of rice from the rest* 朮 ジュツ 2316

to recount

迫 迫	ハク せま.る	*Movement ⻌ that is clear* 白（ハク） **to be imminent**	2317
進 進	シン すす.む	*Moving ⻌ bird* 隹 **to advance**	2318
逐 逐	チク	*Moving ⻌ hog* 豕 **chase**	2319
遂 遂	スイ と.げる	*Movement ⻌ of distributed hogs* 㒸 **to consummate**	2320
造 造	ゾウ つく.る	*Movement ⻌ announced* 告（コク） **to create**	2321
逸 逸	イツ	*Movement ⻌ made by a person that is about to avoid* 免 *something* **deviation**	2322
達 達	タツ	*Movement ⻌ that is big* 大 → 土 *and auspicious* 羊 **achievement**	2323
遅 遅	チ おく.れる おそ.い	*Movement ⻌ made while sitting* 尸 *on a sheep* 羊 **slow**	2324
逮 逮	タイ	*Movement ⻌ caught* 隶 **apprehension**	2325
縫 縫	ホウ ぬ.う	*Threads* 糸 *moving ⻌ and forming something like lush plants* 夆（ホウ） **to sew**	2326

遜 **遜** ソン — 2327

Movement ⻌ of the descendants 孫 (ソン)

humility

遊 **遊** ユウ / ユ / あそ.ぶ — 2328

Children 子 *moving* ⻌ *flags* 㫃

to play

遺 **遺** イ / ユイ — 2329

Movement ⻌ that is valuable 貴 (キ)

bequest

連 **連** ①② レン / ① つら.なる / ② つ.れる — 2330

Moving ⻌ chariots 車

① to stand in a row
② to take along with

遷 **遷** セン — 2331

Someone moving ⻌ and circulating 㔾 *with a big* 大 *bag* 覀

relocation

遵 **遵** ジュン — 2332

Movement ⻌ that is precious 尊 (ソン)

obedience

通 **通** ツウ / ツ / かよ.う / とお.る — 2333

Movement ⻌ done while passing through 甬

to pass through

SPECIAL READING 融通 [つゆずう]: *loan*

辺 **辺** ヘン / あた.り / -べ — 2334

Moving ⻌ dagger 刀

proximity

NOTE Analogy made taking into consideration the dagger as a short-range weapon, which must be close to the target, in **proximity**, in order to reach it.

近 **近** キン / ちか.い — 2335

Moving ⻌ axe 斤 (キン)

near

NOTE In a similar fashion to the character 辺 (*proximity*), the axe in this character denotes a short-range non shootable weapon, which is associated with the concept of closeness or vicinity.

逝 逝	セイ いく ゆく	*Person moving* 辶 *after having grabbed an axe* 折 (セツ) **to depart**	2336
迭 迭	テツ	*Movement* 辶 *that is dropped* 失 (シツ) **dismissal**	2337
込 込	こ.む	*Movement* 辶 *that enters* 入 **to go into**	2338
運 運	ウン はこ.ぶ	*Moving* 辶 *army* 軍 (グン) **to go ahead**	2339
適 適	テキ	*Movement* 辶 *that is customary* 啇 (テキ) **aptness**	2340
違 違	イ ちが.う	*Movement* 辶 *of two feet encircling a space* 韋 (イ) **to differ**	2341
還 還	カン	*Movement* 辶 *made by a person looking back at a material thing* 睘 (カン) **comeback**	2342
遠 遠	エン オン とお.い	*Movement* 辶 *of a person that comes out of the limitations of material things* 袁 (エン) **far**	2343
週 週	シュウ	*Movement* 辶 *like a circumference* 周 (シュウ) **week**	2344

NOTE In clear reference to the circular nature of measured time.

避 避 ヒ さ.ける 2345

Movement ⻍ *of an imprisoned convict* 辟(ヘキ)

to avert

遮 遮 シャ さえぎ.る 2346

Movement ⻍ *among a multitude* 庶(ショ)

to obstruct

遍 遍 ヘン 2347

People moving ⻍ *towards books left beneath a door* 扁(ヘン)

throughout

道 道 ドウ トウ みち 2348 Ⓢ

Head guiding movement

road-way

The *head* (首) that guides the *movement* (⻍) in a road, an idea prosaically interpreted as a path with a head, a **road-way** with a beginning and an end.

導 導 ドウ みちび.く 2349

Road-way 道(ドウ) *for work* 寸

to guide

迶 迶 ズイ 2350 Ⓢ

Having movement

An ideographical compound expressing the concept of *having* (有) *movement* (⻍).

髄 髄 ズイ 2351

Bone 骨 *that has movement* 迶(ズイ)

marrow

随 随 ズイ 2352 Ⓜ

Mountains that have movement

consecutive

Mountains (阜 → 阝) that *have movement* (迶(ズイ)), a place of **consecutive** traffic.

墮
堕 ダ

Earth-soil 土 *on mountains with movement* 随 → 陏 2353

degeneration

追
追 ツイ お.う

Movement following traces 2354 Ⓜ

to run after

Movement (辶) **running after** *traces* (𠂤 [スイ]) left by someone.

遣
遣 ケン つか.う

Someone grabbing a person 虫 *and making him run after* 追 → 追 *something* 2355

to make use of

迷
迷 メイ まよ.う

Movement tiny as rice 2356

to lose one's way

SPECIAL READING 迷子 [まいご]: *lost child*

Movement (辶) that is undertaken on a road that becomes tiny and indistinguishable like *rice grains* (米 [ベイ]) as the intended path becomes blurry and one **gets lost.**

謎
謎 なぞ

Speech 訁 *that makes people get lost* 迷 2357

riddle

遞
逓 テイ

Tiger moving on a cliff to capture a person 2358

relay

Originally 遞 [厂虎辶], a *cliff* (厂) on top of which there is a *tiger* (虎 → 虍 → 乕) moving (辶) in order to catch a person, suggesting a **relay** in the food chain, the completion of one's life cycle and continuinsg of another, thus complying with the unity of the universe through the eternal cycle. All that has a beginning has and end, and the end is also the beginning.

Congratulations for completing the journey through the World of Kanji

REVIEW ON CONSTRUCTIONS

廴建廷延瓦宀内安守官穴商奐罙空
宛奥家宜𡨄宿宓寅完宗察向尚賞定
客容実𤇾𦥯六广府広庶度麻厳
1 健鍵艇誕瓶字宮宴宙窓宣寛宅宵寮蛇寄寝
宝賓貯寧富寡室寂宇宰審納案狩棺管館突
究窯搾窃窮窒窟喚換探深控腕嫁稼畳寒塞
縮密蜜演院踪崇擦党掌堂常償綻錠額溶営
労栄蛍学覚冥応序庁座店床廉粧庫底廃廊
庭腐拡鉱席渡摩魔磨

戸戻雇扁倉門間閏卯留
2 肩炉扇扉所房啓涙顧偏編創関聞問閲闇閑
欄閉闘開閥閣簡潤柳貿瑠

京就景享孰高喬亭复厚壇
3 涼鯨蹴憬影郭熟塾稿豪橋矯停腹複

行彳従徴復辶道遀随追迷逓
街桁衝術衡衛律役徹得径徒待微徐彼後往
御徳循征縦懲履覆迅迎逆遇退過送選遡巡
4 返逃途速遭透述迫進逐遂造逸達遅逮縫遜
遊遺連遷導通辺近逝迭込運適違還遠週避
遮遍導髄堕遣謎

APPENDICES & INDICES

SEMANTIC COMPONENTS

Humans

人	1
欠	2
匕	4
北	7
尸	10
丮	12
勹	14
匃	15
卩	16
卬	17
色	22
女	23
母	27
乃	30
身	31
𠫓	33
子	35
大	37
天	39
立	40
夭	47
𢆉	49
幸	50
執	51
老	55
而	57
文	58
久	59
冎	61
肉	62
育	65
骨	67
歺	68
死	69
囟	70
異	71
心	81
思	87
目	88
見	90
臣	97
臥	99
首	100
頁	101
自	106
耳	108
彡	110
口	115
舌	126
言	128
曰	136
替	143
音	144
亼	153
手	164
又	184
右	185
𠬝	190
有	196
丈	200
吏	201
聿	206
殳	211
攴	215
敏	217
寸	226
廾	235
虫	236
关	240
爪	244
孚	246
力	254
尢	265
止	266
走	271
足	273
夊	276
舛	278
癶	279
巿	291

Nature

厶	291
鬼	298
乙	303
八	309
亦	310
夋	318
乞	325
回	338
日	345
晶	365
夕	368
多	369
夜	373
月	374
水	377
㳄	409
沃	410
𠂢	416
氷	422
川	428
雨	442
火	451
灰	458
光	460
赤	461
土	466
圭	477
丘	487
山	488
阜	493
厂	502
厄	505
产	507
石	518
万	536
厉	537
屮	539
卌	560
卉	579
丰	588
麦	590
坴	604
埶	607
世	618
竹	619
木	631
林	654
桼	671
耒	684
本	687
頼	702
禾	717
歩	755
米	759
娄	766
鹵	769
采	776
虫	793
蜀	798
魚	802
再	804
隹	810
集	826
奞	827
鳥	837
羽	841
犬	855
臭	863
豸	869
豕	876
彖	878
馬	890
能	897
虎	900
虚	903
兔	905
角	906
牛	908
羊	915
鹿	930
隶	935
革	941
幺	943
𢆶	948
糸	956
維	983
显	991
甶	994
恵	996

Matter

㫃	1018
片	1032
疒	1038
斗	1045
串	1057
缶	1061
卸	1066
巾	1083
帛	1090
帚	1092
衣	1102
冃	1123
一	1131
一	1132
十	1136
居	1149
貝	1158
玉	1183
巩	1208
両	1240
車	1242
井	1253
网	1258
卓	1271
皿	1293
血	1300
易	1306
壴	1313
豊	1318
皀	1320
即	1322

PHONOSEMANTIC COMPONENTS

Humans

次	3
比	5
化	6
介	8
亡	9
尼	11
[illegible]	13
免	19
[illegible]	20
[illegible]	21
毎	28
充	34
[illegible]	38
並	42
亢	44
太	45
交	46
夫	53
長	54
孝	56
尺	60
[illegible]	72
凶	75
[illegible]	434
呂	77
[illegible]	79
予	80
[illegible]	92
面	96
毛	112
[illegible]	114
司	119
兄	122
呉	124
旨	137
[illegible]	140
意	145
甘	149
由	150
牙	152
令	154
合	157
今	158
念	161
[illegible]	162
失	183
及	186
奴	193
妻	195
[illegible]	197
取	199
君	201
父	205
[illegible]	209
[illegible]	218
友	221
[illegible]	225
付	232
射	233
共	237
保	242
[illegible]	247
[illegible]	250
[illegible]	251
争	253
加	258
[illegible]	259
九	262
[illegible]	269
先	270
[illegible]	280
志	281
寺	283
[illegible]	289

Nature

以	296
台	299
[illegible]	307
[illegible]	314
公	321
[illegible]	323
气	324
己	326
包	332
申	336
[illegible]	339
句	342
昆	351
普	352
旦	355
[illegible]	360
旬	363
参	366
[illegible]	370
名	372
[illegible]	375
明	376
永	413
[illegible]	419
冬	427
[illegible]	432
州	437
昔	438
需	449
炎	455
黒	459
[illegible]	464
[illegible]	480
[illegible]	482
[illegible]	485
反	509
[illegible]	513
段	516
卜	525
占	530
兆	532
余	541
早	545
[illegible]	546
朝	548
生	551
告	556
星	557
不	558
[illegible]	571
若	574
荒	576
[illegible]	581
[illegible]	592
寿	595
奉	597
[illegible]	601
唐	603
舞	611
[illegible]	613
屯	615
瓜	629
[illegible]	655
乗	659
采	660
相	664
某	668
者	674
[illegible]	680
朱	689
末	692
未	694
束	700
東	704
曹	708
重	710
動	713
量	716
秀	728
委	730
兼	732
秋	735
垂	737
小	741
肖	742
少	747
巻	771
暴	773
[illegible]	778
白	779
皆	783
泉	787
原	789
属	800
[illegible]	805
焦	824
[illegible]	829
[illegible]	834
[illegible]	846
非	851
然	865
[illegible]	871
求	874
隊	879
[illegible]	881
象	886
為	888
半	913
善	925
敬	927
皮	936
波	939
楽	950
玄	945
[illegible]	952
系	985
孫	987
県	988

Matter

[illegible]	998
考	1001
可	1003
何	1007
奇	1009
才	1014
主	1021
几	1026

Territory

SAME GRAPH COMPONENTS

Definition	Main	Variant	Variant	Main	Definition
person	人	儿	儿	卩	*kneeling person*
person seen from the front | big	大	土	土		earth-soil
person working with his hands	丮	丸	丸		round
meat | *body part*	肉	月	月		moon
		月	月	舟	boat
skull	囟	田	田		field
eye	目	罒	罒	罓	*net*
mouth		口	囗		*encircled space*
spoken words		曰	曰	甘	*mouth with food inside* | sweet
			曰	日	*sunlight* | sun | day
two hands	廾	八	八	八	*distributed energy* | eight
foot coming out	㞢	士	士		big battle axe | knight
two counting rods | two		二	二	上	above | *heaven*
mountains	阜	◐ 阝	◑ 阝	邑	*town*
small plant	屮	十	十		*thick rod* | ten
seashell | *money*		貝	貝	鼎	*cauldron*
bow		弓	丂		*lose string of a bow* | *rope*
roof covered with flames	𤇾	龸	龸	𤇾	*building of a roof*

ENGLISH DEFINITIONS

A

abandonment	棄	1284
abbreviation	略	2026
abdomen	腹	2264
abduction	拉	170
ability	技	1155
able	可	1003
abounding	博	1451
above	上	1755
accept	承	243
accompany	伴	914
accomplish	致	1696
accordance	諾	575
accumulation	累	2023
accurate	詳	918
accuse	訴	1640
achievement	達	2323
acid	酸	1357
act violently	暴	773
actor	俳	852
add	加	238
add up	足	273
address	宛	2124
adhere	貼	1168
admonish	諭	1465
admonition	警	928
adoration	崇	2146
advance	進	2318
affair	事	208
affectionate	慈	953
affixed	附	497
aforementioned	該	883
after	狙	1073
again	又	184
age	齢	770
agriculture	農	2047
aid	扶	173
aim	的	1050
air	気	775
alchemy	錬	1737
all-inclusive	汎	1413
alliance	盟	1295
allow	譲	1218
alluring	那	1930
alone	独	859
already	既	1324
also	亦	310
amass	蓄	2058
amusement	娯	125
ancestor	祖	1784
and	而	57
angle	角	906
announce	告	556
answer	答	622
anxiety	虞	901
apellation	称	1100
apologize	謝	234
appearance	相	664
appease	鎮	1744
appliance	械	1584
apprehension	逮	2325
approach	拶	431
appropriate	宜	2130
approval	賛	1161
approximately	約	1051
aptness	適	2340
arbitrary	恣	84
arc	弧	1665
arch	反	509
ardent	烈	1498
area	区	1397
argument	論	1080
arm	腕	2125
armor	甲	1658
army	軍	1875
aroma	香	720
around	頃	102
arrangement	律	2276

C

child	子	35
chin	顎	1770
Chinese	漢	1713
chinquapin	椎	821
chirp	鳴	838
choose	選	2307
chop	析	1627
chopsticks	箸	679
chronicle	紀	971
chrysanthemum	菊	763
circle	圏	1916
circular design	巴	21
circulation	循	2290
circumference	周	1997
city	市	1897
clap	拍	781
clean	浄	400
cleanse	汰	383
clear	明	376
clear away	払	294
cleared land	拓	521
clearness	瞭	682
cleat	桟	1607
clerk	係	986
climate	候	1689
close	閉	2228
cloth	巾	1083
clothes	衣	1102
clothing	服	192
cloud	雲	1767
cloudy	曇	1768
clumsy	拙	1848
coach	督	1576
coal	炭	491
coarse	粗	1072
coast	岸	1554
coat of arms	紋	960
cocoon	繭	1101
code	典	1081
coerce	強	1664
coffin	棺	2102
coin	銭	1746
cold	寒	2133
collapse	陥	1340
collar	襟	1797
colleague	僚	681
collision	衝	2271
color	色	22
color	彩	661
column	欄	2227
come	来	699
come across	遭	2314
come home	帰	1479
come together	合	157
comeback	還	2342
comfort	慰	1792
command	令	154
commander	帥	1085
commerce	貿	2239
commitment	託	614
common people	民	1536
commonplace	凡	1412
companion	侶	78
compare	比	5
compensate	償	2156
compensation	賠	1943
compete	競	1812
compile	編	2217
completely	全	1192
completion	完	2142
composure	悠	420
composure	寧	2087
comrade	輩	1251
concave	凹	2014
conceal	秘	1574
concealment	匿	1392
conclude	済	1421
condemn	責	1750
condition	態	898
conduct	営	2166
confer	下	1839

D

E

elephant	象	836
elevate	挙	1056
embarrassment	羞	920
embrace	抱	334
embracement	擁	1931
emit	射	233
emotion	情	1430
emperor	皇	1653
empire	帝	1903
employ	雇	2213
employed (at)	勤	1717
employee	員	1994
employment	職	1586
empress	后	121
empty	空	2122
emulate	倣	1885
enclosure	封	479
encompassing	羅	1264
encounter	遇	2303
encourage	薦	933
encouraged	弾	1669
encouragement	奨	1037
end	終	975
endearment	恋	311
endeavor	励	538
ending	末	692
endure	被	1107
enemy	敵	1909
England	英	1896
engrave	彫	1998
enjoyable	楽	950
enjoyment	享	2250
enraged	憤	1178
entangle	絡	1965
enter	入	1719
entrust	預	105
entrustment	嘱	801
envy	羨	922
epidemic	疫	1040
epidermis	膚	2028
equivalent (to)	等	626
era	代	1566
erasure	抹	693
erection	勃	594
escape	逃	2311
establish	設	213
estate	邸	1926
ethics	倫	1079
etiquette	儀	1592
Europe	欧	1398
evaluation	評	1803
even	斉	1420
even more	更	1236
evening	夕	368
every	毎	28
everyone	皆	783
exalt	褒	1104
examination	検	637
exceedingly	甚	1394
excel	秀	730
excellent	佳	478
exceptional	希	1089
excerpt	抄	750
exchange	替	143
exclamation	喝	141
exclusive	専	995
exemplary	範	1250
exhibit	陳	706
exhibition	展	1215
existence	存	1015
expand	伸	337
explain	説	317
explosion	爆	774
exposure	披	937
expound	申	336
express	云	1759
expulsion	排	854
exquisite	妙	748
extend	張	1663
extension	拡	2192
extent	程	1657
extraction	抽	180
extraordinary	豪	2257
exuberant	滋	954

folk	俗	1980
follow	従	2292
follower	供	238
following	翌	842
fontain	泉	787
food	糧	765
foodstuff	料	1046
foolish	愚	86
foolishness	痴	1687
foot and leg	足	273
foot of a mountain	麓	931
force	勢	608
ford	渉	758
forehead	額	2161
forest	森	658
forge	鍛	1726
forget	忘	82
form	格	1964
former	曽	2029
fortification	郭	2251
fortune	幸	50
foundation	本	687
foundation stone	礎	1950
fountainhead	源	791
four	四	1978
fourth	丁	1228
fragrant	芳	1888
frame	枠	1116
freeze	凍	705
freight	搭	572
fresh	鮮	924
fret	焦	824
friction	摩	2199
friend	友	221
friendly	懇	872
frightening	怖	1088
from	乃	30
front door	扉	2207
frost	霜	666
fruit	果	2049
fruit [*fig.*]	禾	717
fulfill	満	1241
full	満	1241
fungus	菌	1915
fur	毛	112
furrow	畝	2059
furthermore	猶	1369
fusion	融	1353

G

gain	得	2279
gallbladder	胆	358
game	玩	1758
game-hunting	猟	862
gap	隙	743
garden	庭	2188
garment	衣	1102
gate	門	2220
gather	集	826
gaze	眺	533
gem	珠	1186
gender	性	553
general	将	1036
generation	世	618
generic	般	1460
gentle	妥	245
gentleman	士	1641
germ	菌	1915
get angry	怒	194
get dark	暮	584
get drunk	酔	1366
get dry	乾	547
get fat	肥	64
get fired up	燃	866
get late	更	1236
get on	載	1600
get out	出	1847
get rid of	脱	315
get thin	痩	1041
get tired	疲	1044
get tired of	飽	1332
get together	併	43

H

hang	掛	529
happenstance	故	1145
harass	虐	904
harbor	港	397
hard	硬	1238
harm	害	1286
harmonious	睦	605
harsh	辣	1808
harvest	穫	836
hate	憎	2032
have	有	196
have ready	備	1698
hawser	綱	1267
he	彼	2285
head	頭	1309
head [fig.]	首	100
headgear	帽	1125
headland	崎	1011
heal	治	403
healthy	健	2063
heap	堆	819
hear	聴	1408
heart	心	81
hearth	炉	2205
heat	焼	484
heaven	天	39
heavy	重	710
hedge	垣	1833
heed	鑑	1743
heirdom	嗣	1076
hem	裾	1151
hemp	麻	2198
hermit	仙	489
hide	隠	498
high	高	2255
high building	楼	768
highness	陛	500
hill	丘	487
hillock	塚	1855
hillside	阪	512
hinder	阻	1069
hips	腰	1378
history	史	204
hit	当	745
hold	持	286
hold in arms	抱	334
hole	穴	2105
holy	聖	1656
homeland	邦	1923
hometown	郷	1933
honey	蜜	2139
honorable	御	2288
hoop	輪	1252
horizon	涯	514
horn	角	906
horse	馬	890
horse chestnut	栃	649
horse sign	午	1059
horseman	騎	1013
hot (thing)	熱	609
hot (weather)	暑	675
hot water	湯	407
house	家	2127
how much	幾	1601
huge	巨	1225
human skin	肌	1027
humanity	仁	1134
humble	謙	734
humility	遜	2327
hundred	百	1132
hundred million	億	146
hunger	餓	1590
hunting	狩	2100
hurt	痛	1441
husband	夫	53
husk	殻	1866
hustle	奔	580

I

I	私	724
I (male)	僕	1829
ice	氷	422

J

juice	汁	1139
jump	跳	535
jurisdiction	轄	1287

K

kernel	核	885
key	鍵	2064
kick	蹴	2246
kid	童	1824
kidnapping	拐	175
kidney	腎	198
kill	殺	1543
kiln	窯	2109
kind	種	727
king	王	1649
knee	膝	672
knight	士	1641
know	知	1686
knowledge	識	1587
Korea	韓	1972
kudzu	葛	564

L

labor	労	2167
lack	欠	2
lacquer	漆	673
ladle	斗	1045
lady	婦	1093
lagoon	潟	1342
lake	湖	1146
lament	悼	1272
lamp	灯	1232
land	陸	606
land lot	壌	1219
lapis lazuli	瑠	2241
large ship	舶	1457
larynx	咽	1938
late	後	2286
later	後	2286
latitude	緯	1973
laugh	笑	620
launch	発	1672
law	法	1843
lawn	芝	567
lay out	敷	1892
laziness	惰	1213
lead	率	946
lead (metal)	鉛	1977
leaf	葉	653
leak out	漏	448
lean	傾	103
leap	躍	847
learn	学	2171
learn by experience	懲	2295
learn from	習	845
leather	革	941
leave	離	1274
leave out	省	749
lecture	講	806
left hand side	左	1211
leftover	残	1604
leg	脚	1846
legitimate wife	嫡	1907
lend	貸	1568
length	丈	200
leniency	寛	2077
lesson	課	2050
letter	字	2072
level	準	1140
leveling	均	475
levy	賦	1625
lewd	淫	1222
lid	蓋	1844
lie down	寝	2083
lift	上	1755
light	光	460
light (weight)	軽	1248
like	好	36
liken	例	1497
likeness	如	118
limb	肢	1154
limit	限	495

meal	飯	1333
means	措	441
measure	測	1525
meat	肉	62
mechanism	機	1602
medicine	薬	951
meet (with)	会	1765
meeting point	際	1790
melting	冶	425
membrane	膜	582
menacing	嚇	462
mend	繕	981
merit	勲	715
metal	金	1721
metaphor	喩	1465
method	法	1843
metropolis	都	1924
middle	中	1701
mighty	英	1896
military	武	1624
military camp	屯	615
military officer	尉	1791
milk	乳	306
mimeograph	謄	1472
mind	心	81
mineral	鉱	2193
mingle	交	46

ministry	省	749
minute	分	1508
mirror	鏡	1811
miscellaneous	雑	1118
misfortune	厄	505
mister	君	203
mixed	混	391
model	型	1562
modification	革	941
moist	潤	2236
mold	模	651
moldable	塑	469
money	金	1721
monitary unit [yen]	円	1880
monk	僧	2030
monkey	猿	1992
month	月	374
mood	気	775
moon	月	374
moreover	且	1067
morning	朝	548
mortar	臼	1337
mosquito	蚊	796
mother	母	27
mottled	斑	1190
mountain	山	488
mountain pass	峠	1840

mountain range	阜	493
mourn	弔	1680
mourning	喪	264
mouth	口	115
move	動	713
mow	刈	1540
Mr.	様	923
mulberry tree	桑	683
multitude	庶	2194
music	楽	950
mutual	相	664
my	我	1589
mysself	我	1589

N

nail	爪	244
naked	裸	2052
name	名	372
narrow	狭	858
nativity	誕	2068
navigation	航	1456
near	近	2335
nearby	傍	1902
necessarily	必	1572
neck	首	100
need	要	1377
needle	針	1741

rub	擦	2143
ruined	滅	1621
rule	則	1524
ruler	司	119
run	走	271
run after	追	2354
run along	沿	1975
run out	尽	423

S

saber	刀	1473
sack	袋	1567
sacrifice	犠	1594
sacrificial animal	牲	912
sad	悲	853
safe	安	2097
sail	帆	1414
sake	酒	1360
sake cup	杯	650
salary	俸	593
sale	販	1169
saliva	唾	733
salon	屋	1694
salt	塩	1297
saltpeter	硝	744
same	同	1415
same kind	彙	2055
samurai	侍	284
sand	砂	753
sand [fig.]	沙	752
satisfy	添	411
save	救	875
savings	貯	2086
say	言	128
scanty	寡	2089
scar	痕	1039
scarlet	朱	689
scatter	散	628
scenery	景	2247
scheme	謀	670
school	校	633
science	科	1047
scold	叱	1539
scream	喚	2117
scroll	巻	771
scrutiny	審	2094
sea	海	381
search	索	990
seashell	貝	1158
seashore	浜	1635
season	季	718
seat	席	2195
seaweed	藻	1388
seclude (oneself)	籠	1819
second (2nd)	乙	303
second (time unit)	秒	754
secondary	亜	2015
secrecy	密	2138
secretion	泌	1573
section	部	1945
see	見	90
seed	種	727
seedling	苗	2044
seek	捜	465
seethe	沸	1678
selection	択	174
self	己	326
sell	売	1863
semantic reading	訓	430
semi-	准	818
send (off)	送	2306
sensation	感	2005
sense	念	161
sensibility	敏	217
sentence	句	342
separate	別	1477
sequential	挨	1682
sergeant	曹	708
serious	篤	895
servant	奴	193
serve	務	1549

slice (off)	斬	1636
slide	滑	385
slip of paper	箋	1608
slope	坂	511
slow	遅	2324
small	小	741
small bell	鈴	1728
small boat	艇	2066
smash	砕	1115
smear	塗	543
smell	臭	863
smell good	匂	15
smile	笑	620
smoke	煙	1375
smoky scent	薫	712
smooth	滑	385
snake	蛇	2081
snatch	奪	828
sneer	嘲	549
sniff	嗅	864
snow	雪	446
soak	漬	1752
society	社	1782
soft	軟	1243
soil	土	466
soldier	兵	1634
solemn	荘	1644
solid	固	1984
solitary	孤	630
someone	誰	813
soul	霊	444
sound	音	144
soup	汁	1139
source	原	789
south	南	1435
span	亘	1831
spare time	暇	517
sparkle	輝	1877
sparse	疎	1951
speak	話	135
spear	矛	1547
special	特	911
speciality	専	995
spectacle	戯	1580
speech	言	128
spend	費	1679
sphere	玉	1183
spicy	辛	1805
spin	紡	1889
spine	脊	66
spinning	績	1754
spirit	魂	1761
splendor	華	740
spot	点	531
spout	噴	1179
sprain	挫	481
springtime	春	617
spur	駆	1401
squat	坐	480
squeeze	絞	959
stack up	積	1753
stagnate	滞	1879
stalk	茎	568
stand (up)	立	40
stand in a row	連	2330
stand in the way	塞	2134
star	星	557
start	始	300
starve	飢	1336
state of things	状	1035
station	駅	892
stay	居	1149
stay put	留	2240
steadily	漸	1638
steal	盗	1294
stealth	窃	2111
steam	蒸	578
steel	鋼	1732
step aside	退	2304
step on	踏	402
steps	段	516
stick	棒	651
sticky	粘	762

T

take	取	199
take (time or money)	掛	529
take along	提	1957
take along with	連	2330
take command	執	51
take hold of	握	1695
take off	外	528
take over	継	1410
take part in	携	811
take pictures	撮	1130
take the extreme	窮	2112
take up	占	530
talent	才	1014
talk	語	1838
tall	喬	2258
Tang dynasty	唐	603
tariff	租	1071
taste	味	696
tatami	畳	2131
taught	教	216
tax	税	725
tea	茶	570
teach	教	216
teacher	師	290
tear apart	裂	1499
tear off	剥	1489
tears	涙	2212
technique	術	2272
teeth	歯	769
tell	言	128
temple	寺	283
temporarily	暫	1637
ten	十	1136
ten thousand	万	536
ten-day period	旬	363
tendency	癖	2009
tender	優	1871
tense	緊	966
termination	罷	1262
terrific	凄	425
test	試	1571
that	彼	2285
thick	厚	2266
thigh	股	212
thin	薄	1453
thing	物	1546
think	思	87
third	丙	1233
thirsty	渇	389
this	此	269
thoroughness	徹	2278
thou	爾	1099
thought	想	665
thousand	千	1141
thread	糸	956
threaten	脅	260
three	三	1135
thrifty	倹	163
throat	喉	1690
throughout	遍	2347
throw	投	214
thunder	雷	2019
thus	然	865
ticket	券	1482
tide	潮	550
tie	結	1648
tiger	虎	900
tiger sign	寅	2140
tighten	締	1905
till	耕	1254
timber	材	1017
time	時	350
time and again	復	2296
times	回	338
timidity	臆	147
tin can	缶	1061
together	共	237
token	符	623
tolament	嘆	1712
tombstone	碑	1382
tongue	舌	126

V

valley	谷	1979
valuable	貴	1174
value	値	1403
vapor	汽	405
various	諸	675
vassal	臣	97
vegetables	菜	663
vein	脈	417
venerable old man	翁	844
verdant	青	1423
verge	縁	984
verification	験	894
vermilion	丹	1427
vertical height	縦	2293
vessel (container)	器	1390
vessel (vehicle)	隻	815
vicarious	摂	224
view	観	831
vigorous	旺	1651
village	村	639
vinegar	酢	1367
violate	犯	857
violent	激	1891
virtue	徳	2289
viscera	臓	1614
visit	訪	1884
visitor	賓	2085
vitalize	興	1419
voice	声	524
void	虚	903
volume	量	716
volume of a book	冊	1075
vomit	吐	471
vow	誓	1633

W

wait	待	2282
walk	歩	755
wall	壁	2008
wanted	欲	1981
war	戦	1579
warehouse	庫	2184
warm (air temperature)	暖	349
warm (thing)	温	1296
warn against	戒	1583
warrior	侍	284
warship	艦	1459
wash	洗	401
watching	看	176
water	水	377
water well	井	1253
waterfall	滝	1818
watery	津	393
watery way	河	1005
wave	波	939
waver	揺	1065
weak	弱	1670
weaken	衰	1113
wealth	財	1172
wear	着	917
wear (an object)	脇	261
weave	織	1588
wedding	嫁	2128
wedft	緯	1973
week	週	2344
weekday	曜	848
weigh	量	716
weird	怪	486
welfare	祉	1779
west	西	1373
western	洋	921
wet	湿	993
whale	鯨	2244
what	何	1007
wheat	麦	590
wheel	輪	1252
where	奈	1775
whereabouts	踪	2145
whirlpool	渦	386

Y

Z

STRONG PHONETIC COMPONENTS

A

AI

愛 曖

AN

安 案

B

BA

馬 罵

BAI

貝 買

咅 倍

培 賠

陪

BAKU

暴 爆

BATSU

伐 閥

BO

莫 慕

募 暮

墓

baku

漠 幕

BŌ

亡 忘

忙 望

mō

妄 盲

冒 帽

某 謀

BOKU

菐 僕

撲

BU

無 舞

無

BYŌ

苗 描

猫

C

CHI

知 痴

致 緻

CHIKU

畜 蓄

CHŌ

長 帳

張

兆 挑

跳 眺

tō

桃 逃

朝 嘲

潮

丁 頂

町 庁

徴 懲

CHOKU

直

shoku

殖 植

chi

値 置

CHŪ

中 仲

忠 沖

D

DO

奴 怒

努

DŌ

動 働

同 胴

洞 銅

童 瞳

shō

憧 鐘

道 導

E

EI

永 詠

泳

EN

袁 猿

園 遠

㕣 沿

鉛

ETSU

兑 悦

閲

F

FU

夫 扶

付 符

附

府 腐

普 譜

卜 訃

赴

布 怖

FUKU

畐 幅

副 福

复 腹

複

復 覆

FUN

賁 憤

噴 墳

分 雰

粉 紛

G

GA

牙 芽

雅

我 餓

GAI

圭 街

厓 涯

崖

亥 骸

該 劾

害

katsu

轄 割

GEN

原 源

玄 舷

弦

元

gan

頑 玩

GI

義 儀

議 犠

疑 擬

GO

呉 娯

誤

五

吾 悟

語

GŪ

禺 偶

隅 遇

具 惧

GUN

軍

gi

揮 輝

GYO

魚 漁

H

HA

波 破

HAKU

白 伯

拍 泊

舶 迫

HAN

㔾 氾

犯 範

反 坂
阪 板
版 販
飯

半 伴
判 畔

凡 汎
帆

般 搬

班 斑
班

HEI

并 併
塀 餅

丙 柄
病

敝 弊
蔽 幣

HEKI

辟 壁
癖 璧

HEN

扁 偏
編 遍

HI

比 批

卑 碑

非 悲
扉

hai
俳 排
輩

皮 披
疲 被
彼

HITSU

必 泌

HO

甫 捕
哺 浦
博 補
舗

HŌ

包 抱
泡 砲
胞 飽

夆 峰
蜂 縫

奉 俸

方 訪
芳

放 倣
bō
妨 肪
訪 坊
防 紡
房 傍

HYŌ

表 俵

票 漂
標

I

I

委 萎

意
oku
億 臆
憶

衣 依

尉 慰

韋 偉
緯 違

IN

員 韻

因 姻
咽

J

JI

耳 餌

寺 侍
持 時

茲 慈
滋 磁

JIN

甚
kan
勘 堪

JO

女 如

JŌ

乗 剰

襄 嬢
譲 壌
醸

定 錠

JU

需 儒

受 授

JŪ

充 銃

十 汁

重
shu
腫 種

従 従

JUKU

孰 塾
熟

JUN

旬 殉

盾 循

JUTSU

朮 術
述

K

KA

化 貨
花 靴

咼 渦
禍 過

加 架

可 河
苛 歌

何 荷

果 課
菓

家 嫁
稼

KAI

介 界

皆 諧
陛 楷

褱 懐
懐

戒 械

会 絵

KAKU

蒦 穫
獲

各 格
閣
raku
落 絡
酪

KAN

𠦝 乾
韓

雚 歓
観 勧

貫 慣

睘 環
還

監 艦
鑑
ran
覧 濫
藍

干 肝
汗 幹
刊

感 憾

奐 換
喚

完 冠

官 棺
管 館

間 簡

KATSU

曷 喝
渇 葛
褐

KEI

頃 傾

奚 渓
鶏

敬 警

圣 茎
経 軽
径

系 係

开 形
刑 型

景 憬

KEN

>
>

剣 (see below)

義 儀
議 儀

奇 騎
寄

几 机
飢

其 期
基 棋
旗 机
飢

既
gai
慨 概

幾 機
畿

KIN

堇 僅
謹 勤

斤 近

禁 襟

KITSU

吉 詰

KO

瓜 孤
弧

古 故
枯 湖

固 個
錮

雇 顧

KŌ

交 効
校 絞
郊

亢 抗
坑 航

孝 酵

口 后

更 梗
硬

ム 勾

広 鉱

公
shō
訟 松

丂 巧
考

荒 慌

冓 講
溝 構
購

侯 候
喉

岡 綱
鋼

工 項
攻 功
江 虹
紅 貢

広 鉱

高 稿

KOKU

告 酷

谷
yoku
欲 浴

KON

艮 恨
根 痕

貇 懇
墾

昆 混

KOTSU

骨 滑

KU

区 駆
ō
欧 殴

KUN

君
gun
群 郡

熏 勲
薫

KUTSU

屈 掘
堀 窟

KYAKU

却 脚

KYO

巨 拒
距

KYŌ

夾 挟
狭 峡

共 供
恭

劦 脅
協

竟 境
鏡

郷 響

喬 嬌
橋 矯

凶 胸

KYŪ

九 究

及 吸
扱 級

求 救
球

M

MA

麻 摩
魔 磨

MAI

毎
kai
悔 海

MAN

曼 慢
漫

MATSU

末 抹

MEI

名 銘

明 盟

MEN

面 麺

MI

民 眠

未 味
魅
mai
妹 昧

MIN

民 眠

MITSU

宓 密
蜜

MŌ

毛 耗

MON
文 紋
MU
矛
務 霧

N

NEN
念 捻
然 燃
NI
二 仁
弐
NIN
忍 認
壬 妊
任
NŌ
㐫 脳
悩
農 濃

O

Ō
央
ei
映 英
黄 横
王 旺

R

REI
令 冷
零 齢
鈴
REKI
厤 歴
暦
RETSU
列 烈
裂
RI
利 梨
痢
离 離
璃
里 裏
理
RIN
侖 倫
輪
RO
路 露
ROKU
录 緑
録
RYO
虍 慮
虜
RYŌ
尞 僚
瞭 療
寮
良
rō
朗 浪
郎 廊
量 糧
RYŪ
㐬 流
硫

S

SA
左 佐
SAI
采 彩
採 菜
才
zai
在 材
財
𢦏 栽
裁 載
祭 際
SAKU
乍 作
搾 昨
酢
SAN
参 惨
SATSU
察 擦
SEI
生 姓
性 牲
星 醒
青 静
情 請
晴 清
精
成 誠
盛
制 製
正 政
整 征
shō
正 証
政 症
so
疎 礎
SEKI
昔 惜
籍
責 積
績
SEN
占
ten
点 店
泉 腺
線
戔 践
浅 箋
銭
SETSU
切 窃
SHA
射 謝
者 煮
sho
諸 署
暑 緒
舎 捨
SHAKU
尺 釈
taku
択 沢
SHI
次 姿
恣 諮
資
司 伺
詞 嗣
飼
旨 指
脂
支 肢
枝
ki
伎 岐
止 歯
祉
此 雌
紫
氏 紙
士 仕
志 誌
市 姉
SHIN
辰 娠
唇 振
震
心 芯
𠬶 侵
浸 寝
申 伸
紳 神
真 慎
亲 親
新 薪
SHITSU
失
tetsu
鉄 迭
疾 嫉

SHŌ
升 昇
焦 礁
章 鄣
障
小
少 省
抄
肖 消
硝 宵
将 奨
尚 掌
賞 償
召 招
詔 沼
紹
昭 照

SHOKU
戠 職
織

SHU
取 趣
朱 殊
株 珠
主
chū
注 柱
駐
守 狩

SHŪ
州 酬
秋 愁
周 週
chō
彫 調
就 蹴

SHUKU
叔 淑
宿 縮

SO
朔 塑
遡
且 阻
租 粗
狙 組
祖

SŌ
争
shō
浄 静
忩 総
窓
叟
捜 痩
早 草
相 想
霜
喿 操
燥 藻
壮 荘
装
倉 創
曽 僧
層
zō
憎 増
贈

SOKU
足 促
捉
束 速
則 側
測

SON
孫 遜

SOTSU
卒 率

SUI
垂 睡
卆 粋
酔

T

TAI
代 貸
袋
帯 滞
台 怠
胎

TAKU
乇 託
宅

TAN
旦 胆
担 壇

TEI
氐 低
抵 邸
底
貞 偵
呈 程
帝 諦
締
廷 艇
庭
亭 停

TEKI
啇 嫡
摘 敵
滴 適

TETSU
㪿 撤
徹

TŌ
荅 搭
搭
唐 糖
東 凍
棟
朕 謄
騰 藤
豆 頭
痘 闘
到 倒

TON
屯 頓

TSŪ
甬 痛
通

U

U
于 芋
宇
羽
yoku
翌 翼

Y

YO
予 預
余
jo
叙 除
徐
to
塗 途

YŌ
昜 揚
陽 瘍
羊 洋
様 養
shō
詳 祥
要 腰
䍃 揺
謡
用 庸
容 溶

YU
由 油
chū
抽 宙
兪 愉
喩 諭
輸 癒

YŪ
勇 湧
憂 優

Z

ZA
坐 挫
座

ZAN
斬 暫

ZE

是

tei

提 堤

ZEN

善 膳

繕

全

sen

詮 栓

ZETSU

舌

katsu

括 活

ZŌ

象 像

蔵 臓

ZUI

随 髄

随

ONYOMI READINGS INDEX

KUNYOMI READINGS INDEX

A

N

O

S

U

W

Y

RADICALS' MAIN MEANINGS

1	一		line	1131
2	丨	丿 亅	column	-
3	ノ		slash	-
4	丶		dot	-
5	㇕	㇆ ㇖	upper corner	-
6	㇄	く	lower corner	-
7	𠂉		slash & line	-
8	亠		dot & line	-
9	乂		cross	-
10	人	亻 儿	person	1
11	欠		open mouth	2
12	匕		reverse person	4
13	尸		sitting person	10
14	勹		leaning person	14
15	卩	儿	kneeling person	16
16	女		woman	23
17	子		child	35
18	大		big person	37
19	立		standing person	40
20	幸		fortune	50
21	老	耂	old person	55
22	文		tattooed person	58
23	尺		calf	60
24	肉	月 ⺝	meat	62
25	骨		bones	67
26	歹		remaining bones	68
27	異		masked person	71
28	心	忄 ⺗	heart	81
29	目	罒	eye	88
30	見		looking person	90
31	頁		head	101
32	耳		ear	108
33	彡		hair	110
34	口		mouth	115
35	舌		tongue	126
36	言		words	128
37	音		sound	144
38	亼		talking mouth	153
39	手	扌	hand	164
40	又	𠂇 彐	outstretched hand	184
41	殳		hand & mace	211
42	攵		hand & mattock	215
43	寸		working hand	226
44	廾		two hands	235
45	爪	爫	grabbing hand	244
46	争		fighting hand	253
47	力		arm	254
48	尢		outstretched arm	265
49	止	龰	footstep	266
50	走		walking foot	271
51	足	⻊	foot & leg	273
52	夊		still foot	276
53	舛		moving feet	278
54	癶		feet going upward	279
55	卝		footprint	289
56	鬼		ghost	298

57	乙	乚	*unfolded energy*	303
58	八	ハ丷	*distributed energy*	309
59	日	曰	*sun*	345
60	夕		*crescent moon*	368
61	月		*full moon*	374
62	水	氵氺	*water*	377
63	氷	冫	*ice*	422
64	雨	⻗	*rain*	442
65	火	灬	*fire*	451
66	光		*light*	460
67	土		*earth*	466
68	山		*mountain*	488
69	阜	◐ 阝	*mountains*	493
70	厂		*cliff*	502
71	石		*stone*	518
72	𠦝		*sunshine*	546
73	艹		*plants*	560
74	丰	龶	*lush plant*	588
75	麦		*barley*	590
76	奉	𡗗	*two hands & plant*	597
77	竹	⺮	*bamboo*	619
78	木		*tree*	631
79	耒		*branched tree*	684
80	東		*bundle*	700
81	禾		*fruit tree*	717
82	米		*rice*	759
83	歯		*teeth*	769
84	白		*white rice*	779
85	虫		*serpent*	793
86	魚		*fish*	802
87	隹		*bird*	810
88	鳥		*poultry*	837
89	羽		*wings*	841
90	犬	犭	*dog*	855
91	豸		*fierce animal*	869
92	馬		*horse*	890
93	虎	虍	*tiger*	900
94	角		*horn*	906
95	牛	牜	*cattle*	908
96	羊	⺶	*sheep*	915
97	鹿		*deer*	930
98	隶		*caught animal*	935
99	革		*leather*	941
100	幺		*coccon*	943
101	糸		*thread*	956
102	丂		*stick*	998
103	㫃		*flaming flag*	1018
104	片		*table*	1032
105	疒		*bed*	1038
106	斗		*ladle*	1045
107	巾		*cloth*	1083
108	衣	衤	*clothes*	1102
109	十		*thick rod*	1136
110	貝		*money*	1158
111	玉		*jewel*	1183
112	車		*chariot*	1242
113	皿		*vessel*	1293
114	豊		*bounty vessel*	1318
115	艮		*food vessel*	1320
116	食	飠	*mouth & vessel*	1327
117	酉		*jar*	1354
118	西	覀	*bag*	1373
119	品		*products*	1383
120	匚		*box*	1391
121	舟		*boat*	1455
122	刀	刂	*dagger*	1476
123	矛		*spear*	1547
124	弋		*stake*	1564

125	戈		*halberd*	1578
126	戊		*big halberd*	1609
127	斤		*axe*	1626
128	士		*big axe*	1641
129	王		*battle axe*	1649
130	弓		*bow*	1662
131	矢		*arrow*	1681
132	金	釒	*metal*	1721
133	示	礻	*divine power*	1774
134	凵		*pit*	1841
135	冂	冖	*delimited space*	1852
136	囗		*encircled space*	1911
137	邑	◐阝	*town*	1919
138	舍		*cottage*	1927
139	田		*field*	2017
140	里		*hamlet*	2037
141	廴		*wall & floor*	2061
142	瓦		*roof tile*	2069
143	宀		*roof*	2071
144	穴	宂	*open roof*	2105
145	广		*wall & roof*	2175
146	戸		*door*	2203
147	門		*gates*	2220
148	行		*roads*	2268
149	彳		*way*	2275
150	辶		*movement*	2299

RADICALS INDEX

2136 CHARACTERS INDEX

RESOURCES

Etymological Data and Images

Xiaoxue Sinica - 漢字古今字資料庫. Accessed January, 2020.
http://xiaoxue.iis.sinica.edu.tw/

Vividict.com - 象形字典 (n.d.). Accessed September, 2017.
http://www.vividict.com/

Multi-fuction Chinse Character Database - 漢語多功能字庫. Accessed September 2017.
http://humanum.arts.cuhk.edu.hk/Lexis/lexi-mf/

Shirakawa, S. (2003). *Jōyō jikai* (常用字解). Tōkyō.

Liao, W. (2014). *Han zi shu* (漢字樹). Beijing.

Japanese Dictionaries

Kanji Jitennon Online - 漢字辞典オンライン. Accessed September, 2017.
http://kanji.jitenon.jp/

Jisho.org: Japanese Dictionary. Accessed January, 2020.
http://jisho.org/

Wiktionary. Accessed January, 2020.
https://www.wiktionary.org

Glyph Supplements

GlyphWiki - メインページ. Accessed January, 2020.
http://www.glyphwiki.org/

Lightning Source UK Ltd.
Milton Keynes UK
UKHW022353230720
367034UK00006B/21

9 788409 004218